Classics

in Policing

Steven G. Brandl

University of Wisconsin-Milwaukee

David E. Barlow

University of Wisconsin-Milwaukee

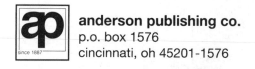

anderson publishing co.
p.o. box 1576
cincinnati, oh 45201-1576

Classics in Policing

ISBN 0-87084-234-X
Library of Congress Catalog Number 96-83681

 The text of this book is printed on recycled paper.

Gail Eccleston *Editor*   *Editor in Chief* Kelly Grondin

Preface

At the core of the police literature there exists a collection of major theoretical and empirical works that represent significant contributions to knowledge in the field of policing. Traditional textbooks, however, can only provide an interpretation of these readings. *Classics in Policing* is designed to provide students with easy access to the actual words and ideas offered by scholars in their classic contributions to police theory and research.

We believe that it is important for students to read firsthand these important and influential works on policing. In this way, students can evaluate the work directly and be challenged to construct their own interpretations regarding the significance and meaning of the work, rather than relying on others to assess and interpret the works for them. A major difficulty of such an endeavor, however, is that exploring all these works in their entirety is much more than what can be reasonably expected from a student upon the completion of a single course in policing. Therefore, an important contribution to learning provided by this text is that it reproduces the essence of these critical readings in a condensed and manageable format, which makes it possible for students to be exposed to these classic works in a single semester course without being overwhelmed by them.

There are potential problems in assembling such a collection of readings. First, there are articles and book excerpts that constitute major contributions to the policing literature that are not included in *Classics*. Some readings could not be included simply because of space constraints and costly permission fees. Second, the selection of works that are widely recognized as "classics" inherently results in a conservative bias in that it reinforces and perpetuates a traditional mainstream perspective that has been taught down through the major institutions of higher learning. Almost by definition the selections represent mainstream thought and marginalize nontraditional voices; however, even nontraditional and multicultural perspectives would do well to launch their analysis from these classics, if only as a point of departure or critique. As such, it is important to realize that the readings contained here represent a scholarly foundation of policing, not *the* scholarly foundation of policing.

This book divides the classic literature in policing into three primary sections. Section I, "Police History and Role," contains writings that describe and explain the nature of the police function in U.S. society from an historical perspective. Section II, "Police Discretion," includes major works that have examined the causes and consequences of police discretionary decisions. Section III, "Police Strategies," consists of writings on the effectiveness of the most influential police operational strategies. We believe that this collection of writings provides students with a substantial and necessary foundation on which to base an understanding of the police.

Steven G. Brandl
David E. Barlow

Contents

Section I
POLICE HISTORY AND ROLE

Introduction

Social institutions, such as the police, are human constructions that form and develop in relation to various political, economic, and social forces. Modern-day police did not simply arrive on the social scene abstracted from their past; the role of the police in United States has been forged over a long period of time. Therefore, any attempt to describe the police and their function must begin with an analysis of their historical development. This section of *Classics in Policing* includes readings that place the police in historical perspective.

The first reading, "Historical Roots of Police Behavior: Chicago, 1890-1925" by Mark Haller (1976), uses the Chicago Police Department to provide an illustration of nineteenth-century policing in the United States. Haller identifies four interrelated orientations to explain police behavior during this time period. First, the police and the courts were highly decentralized. Therefore, their approach to law enforcement largely reflected the values of the communities in which they operated. Second, the police were a significant resource at the control of local political organizations. They were manipulated by powerful local political machines in ways that served to preserve and strengthen these organizations. Third, similar to all criminal justice institutions of the time, the police operated as rackets; their day-to-day operations functioned as income-producing activities for the people who worked in the system. Fourth, the police and other criminal justice personnel developed informal systems of operation that facilitated the use of police justices, interwoven relationships between detectives and professional criminals, various forms of corruption, the use of vague laws to control dangerous classes, and the widespread use of curbside justice and police violence.

The significance of this article is two-fold. First, the description of this early period of policing provides critical information about what is traditionally defined as the first stage of public policing in the United States. Second, this article identifies certain characteristics of policing that formulated during this embryonic phase and that continue to impact modern policing. A fascinating way of analyzing Mark Haller's

1

article is to apply these characteristics to modern U.S. police agencies. In doing so, we see how specific reforms were introduced to change certain characteristics, how some of these characteristics are still fundamental to any description of police in U.S. society, and how various current reforms attempt to re-establish certain apparently lost characteristics. In various ways and with diverse outcomes, each of the other selected readings in this section follow this course of investigation.

The second reading, Samuel Walker's (1977) "Introduction" to *A Critical History of Police Reform: The Emergence of Professionalism*, describes the era of policing in the United States that is traditionally identified as the second stage. Walker presents the history of policing as progress along a scale of professionalism. Professionalism was an important outgrowth of the turn-of-the-century reform movement designed to radically alter the negative characteristics of policing that existed in the first stage. The crusade to create a professional police organization through the establishment of professional knowledge, professional autonomy, and the service ideal, reflects an aggressive assault on police corruption and political control. The resultant police institution became much more bureaucratic, formal, centralized, and scientifically managed. Walker refutes the myth of an unchanging police department by providing evidence of police institutions as dynamic agencies of change vis-à-vis the nature of work performed, the character of police officers, and the structure of police organization.

The "Summary" of *The 1968 Report of the National Advisory Commission on Civil Disorders* describes possibly the most critical moment in modern policing, as it signaled the demise of the second stage of policing. The rebellions of the 1960s, particularly the African-American struggle for Civil Rights, created a serious crisis of legitimacy for the state. This crisis was especially intense for the state's institutions of social control because, as significant segments of the population sought to transform U.S. social and power relations, they came to envision the police as the primary obstacle to justice. Many of the characteristics of the police which this report openly criticizes were essential elements of the professional model of policing. In addition, several of the recommendations for change are contrary to the nature of professionalism. Specifically, the police are described as being too autonomous and separated from the people in the community that they served. The report further recommends that the police be more accountable and less independent from local community control. This report is possibly the most thorough examination of civil disorder in America and its recommendations have been repeated in nearly every police commission report that has since been produced.

The fourth reading in this section of *Classics in Policing*, George L. Kelling and Mark H. Moore's "The Evolving Strategy of Policing," describes the two eras of policing discussed above in order to identify and shape the third and most recent stage of policing which they call the "Community Problem-Solving Era." This article incorporates the ideas of many of their previous writings that, in combination, establish an important contribution to traditional interpretations of the historical development and future direction of policing in America. Based on the concept of a "corporate strategy," Kelling and Moore divide the history of police in the U.S. into three eras (Political, Reform, and Community Problem-Solving), and describe each era in terms of legitimacy and authorization, the police function, organizational design, external relationships, demand management, principal programs and technologies, and measured outcomes. The Political Era roughly reflects the period described in Haller's (1976) article, while the depiction of the Reform Era is an attempt to capture many of the developments in policing that Walker's (1977) article addressed. The descriptions of the weaknesses in the Reform Era policing strategy reflect many of the concerns that were identified in the "Summary" of *The 1968 Report of the National Advisory Commission on Civil Disorders* (i.e., a defensive strategy and an inability to adjust to the changing social circumstances of the 1960s and 1970s). The most immediate concern of Kelling and Moore, however, is the need to guide the next stage in policing, the Community Problem-Solving Era, which is a new approach designed to overcome the weaknesses of the Reform Era. Their concern is that the old strategies, administrative procedures, and operational theories do not fit this new way of policing and must be transformed as well. For example, the trend by police to preserve their independent professional autonomy operates against the grain of Community Problem-Solving Policing and actually hinders their ability to achieve their full potential to effectively fight crime. Kelling and Moore suggest that police executives should rely on this interpretation of history to guide their construction of a new management philosophy.

In the fifth selected reading, "'Broken Windows' and Fractured History: The Use and Misuse of History in Recent Police Patrol Analysis," Samuel Walker (1984) challenges the interpretation of history upon which Kelling and Moore's article is originally based. The primary critique by Walker is that the work of Kelling, Wilson, and Moore relies on a historical interpretation that suggests that during the Political Era, the police enjoyed a high degree of legitimacy among the various communities' residents that was largely eroded by the Reform Era's dependence on technology (most specifically the patrol car) and various operational strategies that de-personalized the police and disconnected them from the communities' average residents. First, Walker suggests that the combination of the telephone and the patrol car may have actually increased the intimacy of police-citizen contacts. Second, the idea that the Reform Era police were fundamentally engaged in crime-fighting rather than order-maintenance is more rhetoric than reality. Walker's third point is that the political legitimacy of the police in the nineteenth century was in constant dispute and often violently challenged. Fourth, with their customary practices of graft, political corruption, brutal curbside justice, inefficiency, and inaction, the Political Era police are a poor model for guiding the future of policing in the United States. Finally, Walker suggests that Kelling, Wilson, and Moore participate in an historical analysis that is a nostalgic misreading of history that romanticizes the "cop-on-the-beat" and nineteenth-century urban life in a way that fails to recognize that reforming the Reform Era will involve much more than a return to some mythical period in history.

The final reading in this section, an excerpt from Egon Bittner's (1967) book *The Functions of the Police in Modern Society*, further demonstrates the dilemma of police reform when Bittner suggests that the fundamental problem with police legitimacy is structural. Egon Bittner describes the discriminating quality that characterizes the social role of police in modern society as the ability and authority to use essentially unrestricted coercive force. According to Bittner, force is the one element of policing that unifies all types of police activity. This structural component of policing produces three basic structural determinants that are fundamental to the police function. First, police work is a tainted occupation. Because of the police officer's power to use force, and because the nature of police work is inherently dirty and dangerous and involves interacting with violent and devious people, the popular perception of the police is that they are to be both feared and admired, and they are observed with both fascination and contempt. Second, police work is inherently crude. The police regularly must address serious moral ambiguities, as they are required to settle disputes between human beings by initiating force that opposes some human interest. The use of force to resolve complex human problems requires the police to handle subtle human conflicts and address profound legal and moral questions, without the benefit of time and careful reflection. The police must act in a relatively crude manner in order to resolve these conflicts. Third, the ecological distribution and development of police reflects a whole range of public prejudices. Whether the distribution is based on department organization or individual officer decision-making, the dominant public prejudice that ethnic and racial minorities, the poor, and the young are more likely to be criminal than other citizens generates a situation where some people will receive more extensive police scrutiny simply because of their status characteristics. This structural determinate of policing does not create social cleavages, especially since it is produced by these cleavages, but it does have a socially divisive effect in that it magnifies them. For example, the selective deployment of officers that focuses police attention on young urban African-American males is caused by entrenched social inequalities and prejudices; and, although police discrimination is not the cause of racism, this differential treatment intensifies the divisions between African-Americans and whites in American society.

The fact that Bittner defines these traits of the social reality of police work as structural demonstrates the limitations of police reform in that simply altering policing strategies, improving management techniques, and/or upgrading the quality of police personnel will not resolve these conflicts in the police function. They existed in the Political Era and Reform Era of policing, and they are likely to persist in the Community Problem-Solving Era.

Mark H. Haller

Historical Roots of Police Behavior: Chicago, 1890-1925[*]

In order to understand patterns of police behavior in American cities at the turn of the century, it is important to grasp a crucial fact: the police, although they were formally engaged in *law* enforcement, were little oriented toward legal norms.[1] As late as 1900, when Chicago's police department numbered 3,225 men, there was no organized training. New policemen heard a brief speech from a high-ranking officer, received a hickory club, a whistle, and a key to the call box, and were sent out on the street to work with an experienced officer.[2] Not only were policemen untrained in law, but they operated within a criminal justice system that generally placed little emphasis upon legal procedure. Most of those arrested by the police were tried before local police justices, who rarely had legal training. Those arrested seldom had attorneys, so that no legal defense was made. Thus, there were few mechanisms for introducing legal norms into the street experiences and crime control activities of policemen.

If patterns of police behavior cannot be understood in terms of an orientation toward law, how can they be understood? Four interrelated orientations explain much of the day-to-day behavior of the police, as well as other criminal institutions, in their order maintenance functions during the late nineteenth and early twentieth centuries. First of all, police and courts were highly decentralized and often reflected, in important ways, the values of local communities. Democratic sensitivi-

Source: Mark H. Haller (1976). "Historical Roots of Police Behavior: Chicago, 1890-1925." *Law and Society Review*, 10:303-323. Reprinted by permission of the Law and Society Association.

[*]I wish to thank the Center for Studies in Criminal Justice in the Law School of the University of Chicago for support that has made possible my research into the history of crime and criminal justice and to thank especially Norval Morris, Hans Mattick, and Franklin E. Zimring for their assistance and encouragement. A number of scholars, particularly Perry Duis, David R. Johnson, and Wilbur R. Miller, strengthened this article by their comments and criticisms.

[1] See, for instance, Mark H. Haller, "Urban Crime and Criminal Justice: The Chicago Case," 57 *J. Am. Hist.* 619-635 (1970).

[2] For size, see *Report of the General Superintendent of Police . . . for the Fiscal Year Ending December 31, 1900* (1901). Newspaper reports on induction of new policemen in Chicago *Daily News*, May 4, 1905; Chicago *Record-Herald*, March 20, 1906; and Chicago *Tribune*, November 3, 1906. Most newspaper stories in the period 1904 to 1908 are taken from the Herman F. Schuettler Scrapbooks (2 Vols.), Chicago Historical Society.

ties rather than legal norms were expected to guide police behavior and check abuses.[3] Secondly, the police, part of a larger political system, were a significant resource at the command of local political organizations. Police, courts, and prosecutor provided political leaders with patronage jobs, were a source of favors for constituents, and were important agencies for collecting the money that lubricated political campaigns. Thirdly, criminal justice institutions operated as rackets— providing the means by which policemen and other officials earned extra income. Finally, policemen and other criminal justice personnel developed informal systems of operation that reflected their own subculture and organizational needs. These informal methods of operation bore, at best, only an indirect relationship to the formal legal system.

In short, the police perceived their responsibilities from a number of overlapping orientations. The purpose of this paper is to examine several aspects of police organization and behavior in Chicago from 1890 to 1925 in order to explore the ways in which various orientations shaped day-to-day police behavior.

Recruitment and Control

America's major cities developed modern, unified police departments in the 1840's and 1850's. Chicago, a burgeoning rail center and Great Lakes port, established its department in 1855. By the post-Civil War period, in Chicago as in other cities, the department had two major branches. Most policemen were in the patrol service. They wore uniforms and badges, carried handguns and hickory sticks, and patrolled assigned beats. Other policemen served as detectives. They often wore plain clothes and were responsible primarily for criminal investigations. A military model determined the department's organization, symbolized by the fact that supervisory officers had military titles of sergeant, lieutenant, and captain.[4] In more than a century from the Civil War to the present, city police have undergone little change in organization or function. Those changes that occurred have resulted primarily from technology. Most important were communications and transportation advances: the call box, telephone, motorcycle, automobile, and radio. Of much less importance were new investigative techniques such as photography, fingerprinting, chemical analysis of evidence, and, eventually, computer storage and retrieval of information.

---

[3] This has been argued by Wilbur R. Miller in an important article, "Police Authority in London and New York City, 1830-1870," 8 *J. Soc. Hist.* 81-95 (1975).

[4] For founding of Chicago police, see John J. Flinn, *History of the Chicago Police* (1887; republ. Montclair, N.J., 1973), hereinafter Flinn, *Chicago Police;* also an excellent unpublished study by David R. Johnson, "Policing the Underworld, 1800-1885: An Experiment in Democratic Crime Control" (1975).

Despite technological change, policing has remained labor intensive, so that the basic orientations of patrolmen and detectives have continued to determine police activities.

Chicago policemen came to their jobs from a skilled or semi-skilled blue collar experience and from an ethnic, disproportionately Irish, background. In 1887, in a city that was 40 percent foreign born, some 54 percent of the force was foreign born. In a city in which the Irish-born and their children were less than 20 percent of the population, about half the force was Irish—fully 35 percent Irish-born and another 13 percent, at least, of Irish parentage. Only the German-born, with 10 percent of the force, constituted a rival ethnic group within the department.[5] Ethnic diversity continued into the twentieth century, as a 1908 news story made clear:

> Assistant Chief of Police [Herman] Schuettler's ambition to have every nationality represented on the Chicago Police force came one step nearer realization yesterday when Frank Z. Khubier . . . was sworn in as one of seventy-four probationary patrolmen. Khubier is a Persian, having been born at Teheran. . . . A Chinese patrolman is all that is lacking now, according to the assistant chief.

In 1913, at a time when the department numbered slightly more than 4,000, there were 83 black policemen.[6]

Biographical sketches of policemen in an 1887 history of the department listed such previous occupations as machinists and other skilled factory operatives, teamsters, construction workers, railroad men, and craftsmen of various sorts. Commenting on 84 new recruits in 1906, a newspaper noted: "Street car motormen, press feeders, teamsters, city firemen, clerks and patrol wagon drivers were the principal occupations." Police work, then, ranked as a high status blue collar occupation.[7]

The background of the force was intimately tied to its methods of operation. Because new recruits, many of whom were born abroad and most of whom had left school by the age of 13 or 14, were put on the streets without training, it is clear that no legal expertise was expected of them. Instead, it was through ethnic diversity that the department related to an ethnically diverse city in which substantial proportions of the population spoke no English and distrusted authority. Black detectives were assigned to pursue black felons hiding in black neighbor-

---

[5] These are my computations based on nearly 1,100 biographical sketches in Flinn, Chicago Police at chs. 19 & 23-28. Ethnic figures for Chicago from U.S. Bureau of the Census, *Compendium of the Eleventh Census: 1890* Part III, 75, 83 (1897).

[6] *Record-Herald,* April 3, 1908; Juvenile Protection Association, *The Colored People of Chicago* (1913).

[7] Flinn, Chicago Police; *Record-Herald,* Oct. 27, 1906.

hoods; Italian policemen before World War I were given special responsibility to control the "black hand" gangs that preyed on the city's Italians through extortion. When policemen were protectors or coordina-
tors of crime, Jewish policemen were often the primary protectors of
Jewish pickpockets and other Jewish thieves, while black patrolmen
were assigned to the precincts of politically powerful black gamblers to
help operate their gambling enterprises.[8]

During these years, little attention was given to formal training;
when such training did appear, it had low priority and reflected the
department's military conception of organization. Apparently beginning
in the fall of 1910, a one-month school for recruits operated sporadical-
ly until it was abolished in 1919. Re-established in the 1920's, the
school became institutionalized, and all recruits were required to
attend. In the month of training about one-quarter of the time was
devoted to close-order drill, another quarter to revolver and other
weapons training, another to departmental rules and to laws and ordinances (learned in alphabetical order), and a final quarter to tours of
courts and specialized divisions of the department. A 1929 study of the
recruit school found not only that the instruction was inadequate but,
as has generally been the case with police training, no recruit had ever
failed the course.[9]

The police department operated under the pervasive influence of
local ward organizations and the mayor's office. Until 1895 the Chicago police were not under civil service. Yet the introduction of civil service at that time, although altering the formal rules for recruitment and
promotion, probably had little significant impact upon police behavior.
Before civil service, a tradition had already grown up that, in general, a
policeman had job security, so that little turnover occurred with a
change in administration. But local ward leaders, both before and after
the introduction of civil service, often influenced assignments and promotions. The police superintendent was generally chosen from among
the captains and inspectors on the basis of his known loyalty to the
party organization that won the last election; and, until the 1960's, his

---

[8] Humbert S. Nelli, *Italians in Chicago, 1880-1930: A Study in Ethnic Mobility* ch. 5 (1970) and
Chicago Daily News, Nov. 21, 1907. For Jewish detectives working with Jewish criminals, see various investigative reports in Charles E. Merriam papers, Univ. of Chicago Library, including
Report of Investigator Friedner, Nov. 20, 1914, and Report of No. 100, Nov. 12, 1914, and other
reports in Box 88, folder 6. During a city council committee investigation of corruption, headed by
Merriam, investigators were hired to hang out in the underworld and prepare daily reports. These
reports are invaluable in providing a picture of police/criminal interaction.

[9] For discussion of training, see Alexander R. Piper, *Report on Police Discipline and Administra-
tion* 13 (City Club of Chicago, Publ. No. 1, 1904); *Record-Herald,* March 20, 1906; Chicago Civil
Service Commission, *Final Report: Police Investigation* 50 (1912); Police Department, City of
Chicago, *Annual Report* 55 (1916); *id.* (1921-22), at 76; *id.* (1923) at 51; *id.* (1925) at 62; Citi-
zens' Police Committee, *Chicago Police Problems* 79-84 (1931); and Mark H. Haller "Civic
Reformers and Police Leadership: Chicago, 1905-1935," in Harlan Hahn, ed., *Police in Urban
Society* esp. 49-50 (1971).

office was in city hall rather than police headquarters. Captains and inspectors were assigned to districts and precincts to work with locally powerful ward political leaders. Patrolmen and detectives, in turn, often linked themselves to political factions and, in any event carried out the political policies of local police captains. Those wishing to avoid punitive assignments far from home or ambitious to rise in the department had to be skillful in finding their way through the complicated maze of urban politics.[10]

As important cogs in political machines, policemen were expected to contribute a portion of their salaries to the dominant party. (Before the 1904 election, Mayor Carter H. Harrison had the police payday moved forward, so that the police would have an opportunity to make an extra contribution to the fund being raised for the mayor's supporters.) The police, in addition, sold tickets to party picnics, distributed campaign posters, and in some cases worked the precincts in the days before the election. Furthermore, powerful local politicians, especially in ethnic and slum neighborhoods, financed their organizations through levies upon businesses, and the police often assessed and collected such payments. This was true not only of illegal activities such as houses of prostitution and gambling dens but also of legal activities: saloons, pool halls, dance halls, and numerous retail stores. Finally, of course, police aided local politicians by ignoring or protecting those illegal activities carried on by local politicians and, sometimes, by harassing illegal activities of political rivals.[11] In many ways, then, police behavior was shaped by the organizational needs of political factions; control of the police department, because of its size and crucial role in the city, was a major prize that went with political success.

If police were tied to politics, they were also tied in important respects to the neighborhood. Patrolmen, because they walked their beats with only minimal supervision, spent much of their time in saloons, barbershops, and other neighborhood centers. In 1880, when the department proposed to install call boxes so that a policeman would have to report periodically to the station, the patrolmen resisted the innovation out of an unrealistic fear that they might have to patrol their beats. When an investigator studied the city's police for several months in 1903-1904, however, he found only one patrolman in the

---

[10] On job security before civil service, see David R. Johnson, "Law Enforcement in Chicago, 1875-1885," at 16 (unpublished research paper 1968). On introduction of Civil Service, Joseph Bush Kingsbury, Municipal Personnel Policy in Chicago 1895-1915 (Ph.D. dissertation in Political Science, Univ. of Chicago, 1923). On political influence in the department, see Lloyd Wendt and Herman Kogan, *Lords of the Levee: The Story of Bathhouse John and Hinky Dink* 165, 175, 181-182, & *passim* (1943); also *Senate Report* on the Chicago Police System (1898); and numerous stories in Chicago newspapers.

[11] On 1904 election, see *Inter-Ocean,* April 30, 1904. For other accounts of political activities, see Report of Investigator Thompson, Dec. 22, 1914, and many other reports by investigators in Merriam papers, Box 88, folder 5; *Record-Herald,* March 26, 1905 & April 29, 1907; Chicago *Tribune,* June 21, 1905 & April 18, 1907.

city who walked his beat for as long as thirty minutes. Lax central supervision and police socializing on the job make it likely that policemen came to reflect the values of those members of the neighborhood with whom they had ongoing social contacts.[12]

In these formative years, then, the police had strong ties to local politics, neighborhood institutions, and ethnic communities. Neither their training nor the civil service system provided an alternative orientation toward a formal system of rules or laws.

Police and Courts

Police behavior was also shaped in part by the criminal court system. (Unfortunately, the criminal courts and prosecutor are the legal institutions that have probably received the least study by legal historians.) Until 1906 police justices handled the bulk of routine criminal cases in Chicago. This included ordinance violations, misdemeanors, and preliminary hearings in felony cases. Although justices in Cook County outside the city received fees according to the fines that they levied, police justices in Chicago received a salary from the city and remitted the fines to the city treasury. (If a police justice held court at night, however, he could retain a portion of the fees as a form of overtime payment.) Police justices were selected locally and were active in local politics—thus reinforcing neighborhood and political dominance of the criminal justice system. In police districts with high arrest rates, the police courts of Chicago operated like lower courts elsewhere: through the mass processing of persons arrested for minor offenses. Because few defendants had a specific charge made against them and few had defense attorneys, it seems clear that, when there was any hearing at all, inquiry was generally made not into legal guilt or innocence but rather into the status of the defendant in the community. Year after year, most defendants brought before the courts were discharged, so that the courts served as a clearing house where, following a lecture of warning, defendants were turned loose after several hours or several days in the police lockup.[13]

In 1906, after a reform crusade led by élite members of the local bar, Chicago became one of the first cities to replace the justice courts with a Municipal Court system for both criminal and civil matters. The

---

[12] On call boxes, see Flinn, *Chicago Police* ch. 20. Police behavior on the beat is discussed in Piper, *supra,* note 9, esp. at 6-10, 44, and Appendix A and E. For follow-up news stories, see Chicago *Tribune,* March 21 & 22, 1904.

[13] Sigmund Zeisler, "Report of the Committee on the Expediency of Calling a Constitutional Convention," in Illinois State Bar Association, *Proceedings of the Twenty-Sixth Annual Meeting,* Part II, 145-146, (1902); Robert McCurdy, "The Law Providing for a Municipal Court in Chicago," Illinois State Bar *Proceedings . . . of the Thirtieth Annual Meeting* Part II, 82-84 (1906); Albert Lepawsky, *The Judicial System of Metropolitan Chicago* 99-101, 144-155 (1932).

municipal Court was a unified court, with a chief justice and associate justices who were required to be lawyers and were elected for terms of six years. Immediately after establishment of the Municipal Court, police arrests fell by one-third (from 91,554 in 1906 to 63,132 in 1907). According to the Chief Justice, the decline resulted because the new court imposed higher legal standards upon the police. But given the continuation of mass processing of most suspects, and the absence of defense attorneys for most defendants, the change in the lower courts did not result in more than a marginal introduction of legal standards into criminal justice.[14]

The new court, despite the optimistic hopes of its supporters, increasingly fell under the influence of local ward politicians. Judgeships were a reward for service to political factions, judges generally continued to serve as ward leaders after election to the bench, and political considerations and political favors often shaped judicial decisions. In the 1920's, in fact, judges often did not hold court on election day, for the entire staff—bailiffs, clerks, and the judges themselves—were busy working their precincts. Furthermore, assistant corporation counsels and assistant state's attorneys were often assigned to local courts at the behest of local political leaders.[15]

---

[14] For founding of the Municipal Court , see Herman Kogan, *The First Century: The Chicago Bar Association 1874-1974,* 110-116(1974); McCurdy, *supra,* note 13, at 81-99; Municipal Court of Chicago, *First Annual Report . . .* Dec. 3, 1906, to Nov. 30, 1907 (1907). Arrest statistics from *Report* of the General Superintendent of Police for the years 1906 and 1907; analysis of the statistics in the correspondence of Chief Justice Harry Olson in Municipal Court papers, Chicago Historical Society.

On mass processing and non-legal orientation, see Raymond Moley, "The Municipal Court of Chicago," *Illinois Crime Survey* esp. 404-410 (1929); Paul Livingstone Warnshuis, Crime and Criminal Justice among the Mexicans of Illinois, esp. ch. 4 (M.A. thesis Univ. of Chicago, 1930); Herbert S. Futran, The Morals Court of Chicago (typewritten research paper dtd. March 1928), Burgess papers. Nels Anderson in 1922 described a visit to the Municipal Court presided over by Judge Joseph S. LaBuy. The judge ordered that the bull pen be emptied, and some 50 defendants crowded in front of the bench. After making a few jokes, the judge asked how many were working men. Nearly all hands were raised. So the judge asked, "Is there anybody here that is not a working man?" One Polish defendant, who had not understood the question, raised his hand. His case was dismissed for being an honest man. The clerk began to call the names that the defendants had given when arrested but got no answers. When one man finally responded, he was complimented by the judge for remembering his name and his case was dismissed. The judge asked anyone with a dollar to raise his hand—the implication being that they would be fined a dollar. About half of the hands went up. The judge then tried one man and fined him $5.00 after which he asked: "How many of you men will go to work?" Every hand was raised. The judge warned, "If I catch any of you back here again I'll give you $200 and costs," and dismissed them. More than 50 cases were thus disposed of in less than 30 minutes. See Document 80, Report of Visit to Police Court, Aug. 28, 1922, in Burgess papers.

[15] On the background of judges, see Lepawsky, *supra,* note 13, at ch. 7; also Edward M. Martin, *The Role of the Bar in Electing the Bench in Chicago, passim* (1936); Judge M.L. McKinley, "Crime and the Civic Cancer—Graft" 6 Chicago *Daily News* Reprints, 4, 22-23 (1923). For general insight into management of the Municipal Court until 1930, see the extensive Municipal Court papers. On election day activity, see "Reports Concerning the Criminal Court," *Criminal Justice* 11 (1930); on assignment of prosecutors, see Samuel E. Pincus to Mayor William E. Dever, Nov. 18, 1924, in William E. Dever papers, Chicago Historical Society, folder 13.

Both policemen and court officials often used the criminal justice system to supplement their incomes. Before 1906, in police districts adjoining the skidrows and redlight areas, the police sometimes made night raids for profit. One hundred or more persons would be rounded up. The bailbondsman charged $1.00 to $5.00 for a bond and the police justice received a fee of $1.00 from the defendant for agreeing to the bond. The money was, of course, shared with the arresting officers. After establishments of the Municipal Court, this particular racket ceased, but mutually beneficial relations continued between judges, bailiffs, bondsmen, police, and members of the underworld.[16]

Police and Crime Control

In order to understand the interrelationships of police and professional thieves, it is necessary to keep in mind a number of factors. To begin with, the main expertise of a detective was his knowledge of the underworld—his ability to recognize criminals and to keep informed concerning when and how they operated. For these purposes, detectives developed informers and maintained extensive informal relationships with the underworld. Often they exchanged freedom from arrest for information. Even conscientious detectives were so involved with the underworld that there was only a thin line between being guardians against crime and partners with criminals. In addition, relationships between detectives and thieves were often influenced by the fact that some thieves had ties with politicians made by performing services on election day or by hanging out in saloons operated by persons with political influence. As a result, there was often an uneasy alliance of professional thieves, police, and politicians.[17]

Pickpocket gangs, for instance, sometimes divided territories under the guidance of the police. Then, if an individual citizen lost his wallet and made a complaint, detectives would know which gang was working the area and could recover the stolen property. On other occasions, pickpocket gangs would take a patrolman into partnership. When a victim discovered a hand in his pocket, an obliging policeman would be at hand to hustle the pickpocket away (and later set him free). In the coordination of con games in 1914, the bunco squad insisted that a con man, newly arrived in the city, would be subject to arrest unless he sought out a member of the squad and made a payment of $20.00. This gave the con man the privilege of operating; but, if a victim made a complaint to the police, then the con man involved was expected to

---

[16] *Senate Report, supra,* note 10 at 21; Franklin Matthews, "Wide-Open Chicago," 42 *Harper's Weekly* 90 (1898); William Stead, *If Christ Came to Chicago* 19-20 (1894).
[17] See references in footnote 18.

share ten percent of the take with the police—apparently as a penalty for operating so ineffectively that a complaint resulted. The system even allowed for credit arrangements. A down-and-out con man could request permission to work until he had earned his $20.00 fee.[18]

Close relationships between detectives and criminals could also be a basis for harassment. One of the standard crime control measures used by detectives was to "vag" known criminals until they left town. That is, known criminals were arrested for vagrancy (having no visible means of support) and taken to court to be fined. Faced with repeated arrests, thieves, might well seek a more congenial city in which to practice their professions.[19]

Members of the professional underworld, because of their knowledge of the realities of the system, did not approach the police and courts as legal institutions but as rackets to be manipulated. If possible, of course, underworld figures established mutually profitable relationships with policemen or politicians to protect themselves against arrest. If arrested, their first move was to attempt to bribe the arresting officer or the police sergeant. If that failed, a number of strategies remained: pay a political fixer to bring pressure upon the police or court; visit the complaining witness and offer full or partial restitution in return for an agreement to drop charges; or jump bail until witnesses were no longer interested. Only as a last resort did a criminal turn to a legal defense. Even then, he would feel that conviction resulted from his failure to find the proper strings for manipulating the outcome rather than from a triumph of legal norms.[20]

Another common police tactic, used when a particularly notorious crime occurred or when newspapers complained of a crime wave, was for police officials to order dragnet arrests. In the early 1890's, for instance, when the police were attempting to reduce crime on the near South Side, a newspaper reported:

---

[18] On con men, see Informant B, Special Report, July 28, 1914, Merriam papers, Box 87, folder 4; Informant C, Special Report, Aug. 1, 1914, Merriam papers, Box 87, folder 5. On pickpockets, see Chicago *Journal*, Oct. 30, 1907; Memorandum from Fletcher Dobyns, Oct. 2, 1914, in Merriam papers, Box 86, folder 2; John Landesco, "The Criminal Underworld of Chicago in the '80's and '90's," 25 *J. Crim. L. & Criminology* 341-357 (1934), and "Chicago's Criminal Underworld of the '80's and '90's," 25 *J. Crim. L. & Criminology* 928-940 (1935).

[19] Langdon W. Moore, *His Own Story of His Eventful Life* 466 (1893); printed Report of Activities from January 29, 1918, to June 24, 1918, of Vagrancy Court in Chicago Municipal Court papers, folder 35. In Chicago *Post*, Nov. 1, 1907, Chief George M. Shippy was quoted: "Recently we have arrested every known pickpocket and had them arraigned in the Municipal Court. The judges have made records of their names, and each has been given a certain number of days in which to find respectable employment or get out of town." Also *Daily News*, April 19, 1907.

[20] The court game is described in Clifton R. Wooldridge, *Hands Up! In the World of Crime, Or 12 Years a Detective* 471-476, & *passim* (1901); also Special Report by Informant B, Aug. 31, 1914, Merriam papers, Box 87, folder 4; Landesco, *supra*, note 18, "Criminal Underworld of Chicago," 341-346.

> All Thursday afternoon and evening the Harrison Street wagon was kept busy rattling over the pavements bringing in colored and white men and women of evil reputation. Some were arrested in the streets and alleys, and others were taken from the most notorious brothels on Plymouth and Custom House places. About 200 men and women of vile character were captured.
>
> Last night the raiding was kept up with unabated vigor and at least 200 or more prisoners were landed at the station.

In the event of a "crime wave," the purpose was to drive the "lawless elements" underground and, no doubt, to present the appearance of police vigor. After a notorious crime, those arrested in dragnet raids were searched and interrogated. This standard police technique was so firmly entrenched that in 1906 the police chief explained:

> We can't do away with [the dragnet]. The detectives and patrol-men get their order to bring them all in. . . . And the chances are that nine times out of ten the persons picked up are not guilty of the crime. But if the tenth time we should get the guilty man we are all repaid, as is society.[21]

Finally, the police believed that, in the prevention of crime, the control of tramps and other rootless men was a central responsibility. As the major rail center and crossroads of the Midwest, as well as the most rapidly growing city in the nation, Chicago had a constant stream of persons flowing into and through the city. Skidrow areas west and south of the Loop housed thousands of men (and boys) who sought occasional work and often lived in the interstices of industrial society. In part, the police exercised control by their standard system of harassment through vagrancy and disorderly conduct laws. In 1876, the police Superintendent argued for a stronger vagrancy law "so that [strangers] could be sent out of the way of doing harm, without waiting until they commit some crime." For, he warned, "in the absence of any crime committed by them a good vagrancy law is the only safeguard, and the only way by which they can effectually be disposed of." Until at least the 1930's, vagrancy and disorderly conduct constituted between 40 and 66 percent of all arrests each year; those arrested were

---

[21] Quotations from 1892 newspaper clipping in Burgess papers and from Chicago *Tribune*, Feb. 18, 1906. In August 1905, Chief John M. Collins ordered a squad of 54 detectives: "You are the men who are to catch the thieves and hold-up men. I am going to send you into each quarter of the city after suspicious characters. There must be no partiality. Arrest every man you see loafing around with the look of a criminal. The streets will be safer with those fellows at Harrison street [station]. Pickpockets and confidence men are included in my orders." *Inter-Ocean*, Aug. 1, 1905; for follow-up, see *Inter-Ocean*, Aug. 3, 1905, and Chicago *Chronicle*, Aug. 6, 1905. See also Wooldrige, *supra*, note 20, at 440; Frances Opal Brooks, "Crime in 1908," at 6, 11, 24 (typewrit-ten term paper dtd. Winter 1928), Burgess papers; stories in Chicago *Tribune*, Sept. 9, 1904; *Record-Herald*, July 23, 1905; and in Chicago newspapers for March 4, 1908.

disproportionately young men, out of work, and often from out of town. Yet such statistics do not capture the complexity of police interreaction with the homeless. Police stations, until the opening of a municipal lodging house in the early twentieth century, were regularly thrown open in the winter as sleeping quarters for the homeless. Indeed, arrests often functioned partly as a disguised room-for-the-night, since most of those arrested for vagrancy and disorderly conduct were released after a warning by the judge. In a variety of ways, then, the police managed and serviced a rootless population that they, and others, defined to be particularly prone to crime and disorder.[22]

Police and Public Morals

Throughout the nineteenth and early twentieth centuries, urban moralistic reformers were shocked by the drunkenness, gambling, and open prostitution that, from their point of view, corrupted the morals of youth and made cities dangerous and unpleasant places to live. They brought pressure upon politicians and criminal justice officials to secure enforcement of saloon closing laws and of laws forbidding gambling and prostitution. The policies of the police not only highlighted the distance that separated police values from those of moralistic reformers but also revealed much about the attitudes and forces that shaped police behavior.

In Chicago, although state law required that saloons be closed on Sundays and at a set hour each night, actual enforcement policies were mediated through the local political system. Despite their dedication and fervor, those citizens who favored temperance and strict enforcement of liquor laws were a hopeless minority in the face of strong support for "personal liberty." From 1873 until the coming of prohibition, no mayoral candidate stood a chance if he was suspected of favoring enforcement of saloon closing laws. Carter H. Harrison, III, the popular and respected mayor from 1897 to 1905, was clear in his statement of policy:

> I don't believe in closing saloons on Sunday. I do believe in lowering the blinds and closing the front doors. . . . I don't believe in closing saloons at midnight. . . . Public sentiment is against enforcing them [saloon laws]. The man doesn't live who could shut up Chicago saloons on Sunday. I shall not try to do it.

[22] Quotation from *Report of the General Superintendent . . . 1876* 12 (1877). Statistics on arrests are my calculations from figures in the annual police reports; see also Johnson, *supra,* note 10, at 10-12. On the role of police among tramps, see annual police reports; Nels Anderson, *The Hobo: The Sociology of the Homeless Man* (1923); and early chapters of Ben L. Reitman, "Following the Monkey," (unpublished autobiography in Library of the Univ. of Illinois at Chicago Circle).

Politicians, reacting to dominant opinion, determined that, behind the occasional semblance of a closed saloon, men might drink as they wished. The policy reflected police values as well; for the police were recruited from among the Irish, Germans, and other groups that were the strongest friends of personal liberty.[23]

Within the context of an open city, there existed, nevertheless, considerable neighborhood diversity. Many neighborhoods, in fact, had prohibition ordinances or local option—either because they retained their local saloon laws when annexed to the city in the late 1880's or because of a state local option law passed in the early twentieth century. The densely populated inner city had a high concentration of saloons, while the peripheral regions of the city, containing most of the land area but a minority of the population, excluded or restricted saloon operations. In some peripheral areas, neighborhood associations, spurred on by Protestant religious leaders, were able to shape their neighborhoods to their own values. But, despite vigorous legal and political campaigns, they were unable, except in tangential and temporary ways, to secure strict and uniform law enforcement applicable to the entire city. State law yielded to political pressures representing neighborhood customs.[24]

The coming of prohibition in 1920 created a new legal situation, but not a new political situation. Chicago politicians vied with each other in condemning the new laws, Chicago citizens expressed their opposition through several referenda, and the police chiefs in the 1920's—with one possible exception—kept liquor in their offices to serve visitors. Against a background in which federal enforcement was at first minimal and corrupt and in which bootleggers enjoyed local political protection, the city's police quickly established friendly relationships with bootleggers, gladly accepted favors that ranged from money to free booze, escorted beer trucks through the city's streets, and peddled confiscated liquor in station houses. Then from 1923 until 1927 Mayor William E. Dever, despite his personal opposition to prohibition, insisted that police enforce the law; and a reluctant police force closed many breweries and distilleries and raided speakeasies. But the established relationships of police and bootleggers, combined with police opposition to prohibition enforcement, were too tenacious for the mayor to break. When Dever failed to win re-election in 1927

---

[23] Quotation from Matthews, *supra*, note 16, at 90. On the history of the saloon issue, see Arthur Burrage Farwell, "Sunday closing in Chicago," printed history in Julius Rosenwald papers, Univ. of Chicago Library, Vol. 12; John E. George, "The Saloon Question in Chicago," 2 *Econ. Studies* 96-100 (1897); Victor S. Yarros, "The Sunday Question in Chicago," *Nat. Munic. Rev.* 75-80 (1910). For the general political background, see Alex Gottfried, *Boss Cermak of Chicago* (1962); Joel A. Tarr, *A Study in Boss Politics: William Lorrimer of Chicago* 18-23, 192 *& passim* (1971).

[24] Chicago Commission on the Liquor Problem, *Preliminary Report* (December 1916); Hyde Park Protective Association papers, Chicago Historical Society; Tarr, *supra*, note 23, at 184; Michael Perman, "Towards a Dry Chicago," undated, unpublished seminar paper.

because of his attempts to enforce the law, the police rapidly and openly resumed the patterns of cooperation with bootleggers that had been disrupted but not destroyed during his administration. Once more, the political system shielded the police from pressures to treat the liquor problem as one of law enforcement.[25]

Police displayed a variety of attitudes toward gambling and prostitution. Policemen, themselves sports fans and bettors, attended the races at the tracks around the city and hung out at gambling houses, where they might play a friendly game of poker or place bets on their favorite nags. They had little more inclination to enforce gambling laws than they had to enforce saloon closing laws. As for prostitution, the police thought that such activity was inevitable and could not be prevented; hence, the best policy was to permit redlight entertainment districts rather than pursue a policy of enforcement that would drive prostitutes into respectable residential neighborhoods. When the redlight districts flourished in the years before 1913 or 1914, serious police efforts were aimed primarily at regulation rather than strict law enforcement. The police sometimes arrested streetwalkers; periodically they raided sporting houses that robbed customers or held young girls against their wills; and, to avoid upsetting respectable citizens, they removed houses from streetcar lines and tried to prevent naked girls from leaning out of windows to advertise their charms. But the police seldom bothered well-run brothels or interfered with soliciting in bars or second-class hotels. In short, until pressured to change their policies in the period of 1912 to 1914, the police acted to provide a minimal regulation of illegal activity.[26]

Police policies toward prostitution and gambling reflected local opinion as well as the values of the police themselves. In neighborhoods where the men were interested in sports and gambling, gambling rooms, local bookmakers, and the policy wheels were accepted recre-

---

[25] Chicago bootlegging has been dealt with in numerous books and articles; for instance, John Kobler, *Capone: The Life and World of Al Capone* (1971). On drinking by police chiefs, Fred D. Palsey, *Al Capone: The Biography of a Self-Made Man* 163 (1931). On enforcement under Dever, see the extensive Dever papers. Much about local enforcement can be learned through Justice Department records; see Central Files of the Department of Justice, No. 23-23-0 through 626, in Washington National Records Center, Suitland, Md. For newspaper clippings and other records, see Chicago Crime Commission, Files No. 600-609, 3485, and others. On the prohibition referenda, see John M. Allswang, *A House for All Peoples: Ethnic Politics in Chicago*, 1890-1936, 119-121 (1971).

[26] The structure of Chicago prostitution has been extensively dealt with: Walter C. Reckless, *Vice in Chicago* (1933); The Vice Commission of Chicago, *The Social Evil in Chicago* (1911); Charles Washburn, *Come into My Parlor: A Biography of the Aristocratic Everleigh Sisters of Chicago* (1936); Herbert Asbury, *Gem of the Prairie: An Informal History of the Chicago Underworld*, chs. 4, 8, 9 (1940). Relations of the police to the vice districts are revealed in the investigative reports, Merriam papers, boxes 87 & 88. With regard to gambling, see Mark H. Haller, "The Rise of Gambling Syndicates," unpublished chapter for a book on the history of Chicago crime; also John Landesco, *Organized Crime in Chicago* chap. 3 (new ed. 1968); *Senate Report, supra*, note 10, at 13-14, 18-20.

ation activities. Within the segregated entertainment districts, customers and entrepreneurs wished the saloons, dancehalls, burlesque shows, and parlor houses to operate with minimal interference. Moreover, in tolerating gambling and prostitution, police acted in the service of powerful local politicians, some of whom collected substantial funds from entrepreneurs in the entertainment districts and many of whom were partners in gambling syndicates. Indeed, in some wards the political organization and gambling syndicates were so intertwined that they were virtually one and the same. In such wards local political leaders selected the police captain for the precinct chiefly on the basis of his sympathy with local gamblers, and some patrolmen in the neighborhood served virtually as employees of local gamblers.[27]

Finally, the tolerant attitude of policemen toward gambling and vice arose from a desire to supplement their incomes. Gamblers, despite their political influence, usually made goodwill contributions to the police, and assignment to the entertainment districts constituted a lucrative and interesting challenge for patrolmen and detectives. Toleration of neighborhood gambling and segregated red light districts, however, did not exist because of payoffs to police. Rather, the corrupt relationships institutionalized a policy of tolerance and regulation that the police would have followed anyway.[28]

Police Violence

The basic theme thus far has been that the police were not oriented primarily toward legality in their law enforcement activities. No such discussion would be complete without considering the patterns of police use of illegal violence. Leaving aside the police use of violence in controlling riots,[29] there were essentially three circumstances under which violence, *as an accepted norm,* became part of police procedure.

First of all, many policemen believed that they should themselves, at times, mete out punishment to wrongdoers. Policemen on patrol, particularly in high-crime areas, were often expected to be able to physical-

---

[27] See references in footnote 24. For the general impact of prostitution and gambling on politics, see Wendt and Kogan, *supra,* note 10; for the specific impact of gamblers, see Harold F. Gosnell, *Negro Politicians: The Rise of Negro Politics in Chicago* 122-135 (Phoenix ed. 1966); and Chicago Crime Commission, File No. 65.

[28] See references in footnotes 24 & 25. For additional information about relations between police and prostitutes, see extensive investigative reports in Committee of Fifteen Files, University of Chicago Library; also Investigator's Report, "Law Enforcement and Police," Nov. 29, 1922, in Juvenile Protective Association papers, Library of the University of Illinois at Chicago Circle, folder 94, and other investigative reports in the J.P.A. papers.

[29] For extensive discussion of police use of violence during riots, see Flinn, *Chicago Police;* Howard B. Myers, "The Policing of Labor Disputes in Chicago, A Case Study" (Ph.D. Dissertation, Univ. of Chicago, 1929); William M. Tuttle, Jr., *Race Riot: Chicago in the Red Summer of 1919* (1920); and news clippings in Schuettler scrapbooks.

ly dominate their beats and to handle suspicious persons or minor crimes without resort to arrest. This was particularly true before the installation of call boxes in 1880. Arrests were difficult to make. A patrolman, unable to summon assistance, had to walk his prisoner as much as a mile to the station house. Drunks might be taken in a wheelbarrow. Reminiscing about his early days on the force in the 1880's, a Deputy Superintendent stated in 1906: "It was not customary for a policeman to arrest anyone for a small matter, then. The hickory had to be used pretty freely."[30]

Furthermore, in many neighborhood it was understood that adults might punish rowdy teenagers. Policemen, as adult authority figures, sometimes whipped delinquent boys, believing that this was a more effective deterrent than an arrest and incarceration among adult criminals. One day, for instance, the parents of a Polish teenager told Gus, a Polish cop, that their son was at the station on a charge of theft. Gus explained in an interview:

> I went down and said, "Mike, did you take those things from that garage?" And he knew I had the goods on him, so he admitted it. Then, bang, I socked him with my fist behind the ear. I just kept beating the stuffins out of him, then I said "Mike, you know better than that. You got a good father and mother; good Polish people. Don't let me catch you taking anything again; if you do, what you got now will be nothing to what you'll get then." Then I took him to the captain and said, "This boy has learned a good lesson." The captain let him go. The boy is a good boy now, and every time he sees me, he says, "Gus, I want to thank you for that trimming you gave me. It made a man out of me." That's my motto, scare 'em to death and knock the hell out of them, and then let them go."

While summary punishment by the police sometimes aroused public outcry, it was sanctioned by the police subculture and was often supported by local opinion.[31]

A second type of police violence occurred as a tactic to persuade a recalcitrant defendant to confess his guilt or to reveal the names of accomplices. Indeed, standard interrogation in important cases, and many less important cases, was to place a suspect in the "sweat box," as it was called, for hours or days, until he broke down under continu-

---

[30] Chicago *American*, June 17, 1906.

[31] Quotation from Everett C. Hughes, "The Policeman as a Person," (typewritten research paper dtd. 1925), Burgess papers; there are other similar stories in this paper. See also H. Lowenthal, "Juvenile Officer Kasarewyski," (handwritten term paper [1920's]), Burgess papers. An interesting discussion concerning a more recent period can be found in Gerald D. Suttles, *The Social Order of the Slum: Ethnicity and Territory in the Inner City* 204 (1968).

ous questioning. Newspapers often reported such events without comment, as the following example from 1906 demonstrates:

> John L. Voss, accused by the police of the murder of his wife and the burning of his home to destroy the evidence of his crime, yesterday admitted to Assistant Chief of Police Schuettler and Inspector George M. Shippy that he had purchased a revolver and a box of cartridges some time prior to the crime on Sunday morning.
>
> The admission, wrung from the prisoner after three days of cross examination, is regarded as important.

Such interrogations were publicly justified by police spokesmen and were regularly conducted by detectives and by high officials in the department. For, as the Chicago *Tribune* pointed out: "Every police department in this country has its 'sweaters' or inquisitors, and long practice has made them adepts at the art, if so it may be called."[32]

The detention of suspects for hours or days without charges or legal safeguards was the context within which physical violence—the third degree—was often practiced to speed up the process of interrogation. The point is not that one can easily collect numerous harrowing stories of beatings used to secure confessions. (After the murder of Bobbie Franks, for instance, the Chicago police forced a confession from an innocent school teacher before the evidence finally pointed to Nathan Leopold and Richard Loeb.) The point rather is that, although police officials did not publicly admit the use of violence, the third degree was an accepted part of investigative work. Representatives of the State's Attorney, to say nothing of the police chief or other high officers, were sometimes present while the third degree was being administered. It was employed against juvenile as well as adult suspects; and elite reformers often gained knowledge of the system through their work with youthful offenders. By the 1920's, police terminology was that suspects were taken to the "gold fish room"—the "gold fish" being a length of cable or rubber hose used to strike the suspect without leaving marks. When a court in the early 1920's excluded the confession of a defendant who had made a statement after being sweated (and beaten), one police official claimed that, if the decision was allowed to stand, ninety-five percent of the work of the department would be nullified.

---

[32] Quotations from *Inter-Ocean*, Aug. 1, 1906; Chicago *Tribune*, Feb. 18, 1906. For a long feature story describing Assistant Superintendent Schuettler's methods of sweating, see Chicago *American*, March 25, 1906. Other stories in *Inter-Ocean*, Aug. 1 & Nov. 6, 1906; Chicago *American*, Nov. 24, 1933.

Another complained: "We are permitted to do less every day. Pretty soon there won't be a police department."[33]

Finally, the police subculture often sanctioned violence to uphold the personal dignity of the policeman. Such violence, given the absence of civil liberties organizations to monitor police violations of individual rights, was seldom recorded; and, when reported in newspapers, was difficult to distinguish from the random violence that some policemen occasionally visited upon citizens.[34]

In the case of police use of violence, as in other violations of law by policemen, there was little recourse for an aggrieved citizen. Very early, the police developed a group loyalty that required policemen to rally to the defense of an officer in trouble. Top officials of the department told new recruits that, if they could not say something good about fellow officers, they should remain silent. In 1906 a recruit showed that he had correctly learned the lesson when he told a reporter: "I will not report any police officer for neglect of duty, because I have been told not to. . . . If I reported some policeman I would likely be transferred to any outlying station." When charges were brought against a policeman, conviction was difficult for a number of reasons. As one city hall official told a reporter in 1905, "It is well nigh impossible to convict a favored policeman of any offense. . . . If ten witnesses testify to a certain set of facts, and their testimony is unshaken, the defendant puts twenty police witnesses on the stand to testify to an entirely different set of facts." There were other strategies, as well. Witnesses against policemen would be told the wrong date for a hearing so that they would not appear. In many cases, other policemen harassed, arrested or even drove out of town unfriendly witnesses. Already, the police saw themselves as a beleaguered and misunderstood group, dependent upon each other for support, and fiercely loyal to a cop in need.[35]

* * * * *

---

[33] Quotation from news story cited in typewritten "Extract from Decision of Illinois Supreme Court, 1922," in John Howard Association papers, Chicago Historical Society, Box 4. For information about beatings of juveniles, see "The Gold Fish or Third Degree" [undated], a typewritten paper of a neighborhood boy; and "The Squealer" [undated], a statement by a delinquent, both in Burgess papers; also "The Treatment of the Juvenile Offender" (a handwritten speech in Evelina Belden Paulson papers dtd. March 1914) in Library of the University of Illinois at Chicago Circle. For adults, see Zechariah Chafee, Jr., et. al., The Third Degree: Report to the National Commission on Law Observance and Enforcement 123-137 (republished 1969); George Murray, The Madhouse on Madison Street 259 (1965); and copy of letter of John B. Skinner to Morgan Collins, Sept. 16, 1925, in Chicago Crime Commission, File No. 600-9.

[34] During late 1906, Chicago papers reported a number of cases of police brutality; see, for instance, Record-Herald and Examiner, Dec. 14, 1906, Chicago Tribune, Dec. 14 & 15, 1906.

[35] Quotations from Chicago Chronicle, Dec. 21, 1906, and Chicago Record-Herald, March 26, 1905. See also Record-Herald, Sept. 24, 1907; Chicago Tribune, Jan. 3, 1907; and Citizens' Association of Chicago, Bulletin No. 12 (Jan. 20, 1904).

It is important, in conclusion, to place these remarks in perspective. Obviously, policemen did not spend their whole time taking bribes, soliciting votes, harassing tramps, beating suspects, and assisting gamblers. Policemen on patrol, indeed, spent most of their time doing nothing at all—or in such routine activities as learning the beat or socializing with local people. Those assigned to outlying residential neighborhoods might go for days or weeks without making an arrest or engaging in law enforcement activities. Even when the police were active, they were often involved in functions only indirectly related to crime control. Police took injured persons to hospitals, mediated family quarrels, rounded up stray dogs for the city pound, returned lost children to parents, directed traffic on the downtown streets and at bridge crossings, removed dead horses from city streets, reported broken gas lamps, and performed the innumerable services that have always constituted most police work.

Furthermore, police orientation toward values other than legal norms developed within a context in which the police mirrored what other groups within the society often defined as proper police behavior. The legislative intent in passing broad and vague statutes governing disorderly conduct and vagrancy was to provide tools by which local authorities could control those classes of the population that were, or seemed to be, threats to local social order. The use that police made of such statutes conformed to legislative intent. Although courts sometimes found that police acted illegally and the prosecutor sometimes criticized the police for inefficient handling of evidence, courts and prosecutors generally supported the non-legal orientations of the police. According to the value system accepted by most elected officials, politics was a matter of deals and favors; and most city agencies were as corrupt or as politically manipulated as the police. Hence, the orientation of the police was in keeping with the expectations of the officials elected to make policy and did not differ in kind from other municipal departments. Finally, although groups of élite reformers often attacked the police for corruption and sometimes insisted that certain laws—laws dealing with alcohol or prostitution, for instance— be more vigorously enforced, the same groups often approved of dragnet raids and other harassing tactics. The non-legal orientation of the police, in short, reflected not only the beliefs and background of the police but the expectations of the wider society relevant in defining the role of the police.

Besides, state laws and municipal ordinances directly and indirectly influenced the police in a number of ways. The laws against gambling and prostitution, for instance, were the basis for the police definition of such activities as their particular responsibility. The police became, therefore, the major regulating agency; and the laws provided the leverage used by the police to enforce the regulations. Furthermore, when reformers launched campaigns against gambling or prostitution, the police bore the brunt of the attack. Likewise, the laws against burglary and larceny conditioned the complex ways that police and thieves adapted to each other through systems of informers, bribes, regulation, and harassment. The legal system, too, determined that prosecutors and judges would review certain police decisions on an ongoing basis. To some extent, the prosecutors and courts were a channel for political influence; to some extent the mass processing of less serious crimes and plea bargaining of felonies muted the degree to which prosecutors and courts could convey legal values; but, especially after creation of the municipal court in 1906, the courts and defense attorneys sometimes introduced legal values into the criminal justice process. In a variety of ways, the police made use of or took account of the law and legal institutions in carrying out their crime control functions.

During the twentieth century, in fact, a variety of factors have brought legal norms to bear upon police behavior at a gradually accelerating pace. There has been a growing requirement that judges, even in the lowest criminal courts, be lawyers and that such courts be courts of record. Concurrently, through expanding systems of public defenders and other means, defendants even in the lower courts increasingly have had counsel. Appellate courts have not only extended the right to counsel and imposed exclusionary rules concerning confessions and other types of evidence, but have also declared unconstitutional many of the vague laws, including disorderly conduct and vagrancy laws, which once constituted the majority of arrests and were the means by which police detained and regulated those whom they regarded as suspicious, deviant, or disturbing to the community. Finally, a number of civic organizations (often lawyer-dominated, like the American Civil Liberties Union) have been founded and, in recent years, have more or less systematically monitored police behavior in large cities. As a result of a variety of pressures, police during the twentieth century, especially in major cities, have gradually, often grudgingly, brought their behavior more in keeping with legal norms. The trend has run counter to the historically entrenched police orientations and has been accompanied by bitterness on the part of both police and police critics.

Samuel Walker

A Critical History of Police Reform: The Emergence of Professionalism— Introduction

The myth of the unchanging police dominates much of our thinking about the American police. In both popular discourse and academic scholarship one continually encounters references to the "tradition-bound" police who are resistant to change. Nothing could be further from the truth. The history of the American police over the past one hundred years is the story of drastic, if not radical change. Neither the citizen nor the police officer of one hundred years ago would recognize contemporary police service. The most obvious changes are technological: the adoption of the patrol car and the other paraphernalia of crime fighting. Even more important are the less obvious changes in the idea of police service. Not only are public expectations of the police vastly different, but the attitudes of police officers themselves about their work have undergone dramatic change.[1]

This book is a study of the changes that have overtaken police service in America during the past century. It is an examination of police reform from the middle of the nineteenth century through the end of the 1930s. At the turn of the century, reform ideas coalesced around the idea of professionalization. The goal of achieving professional status for the police became the dominant rationale for a wide variety of reform strategies. This book examines the origins, development, and fruition of the idea of police professionalization.

By the end of the 1930s the dominant features of modern American police administration has [sic] taken shape. Police organizations conformed to a single model: large bureaucratic structures organized along hierarchical, semi-military lines. For the rank and file, police work was a life-long career and the officers themselves were increasingly drawn into a tight-knit subculture. Almost no new ideas or techniques were

Source: Samuel Walker (1977). "Introduction." *A Critical History of Police Reform: The Emergence of Professionalization,* pp. ix-xv. Lexington, MA: Lexington Books. Reprinted courtesy of Samuel Walker, University of Nebraska at Omaha.

[1] Samuel Walker, "The Urban Police in American History: A Review of the Literature," *Journal of Police Science and Administration* IV (September 1976):252-260.

introduced in police administration from the 1940s- through the mid-1960s. The national crisis over the role of the police that erupted in the 1960s, then, was a direct consequence of several decades of police reform. The history of the police professionalization movement sheds new light on the origins of our contemporary police problems.

The concept of professionalism provides a framework for the various reform ideas that were proposed for the police as well as the actual changes that were effected. This history of the police, then, draws upon the theoretical literature of the sociology of the professions. According to the dominant school of thought, professional status consists of three basic dimensions: professional knowledge, professional autonomy, and the service ideal. A profession is characterized by a complex and esoteric body of knowledge, capable of being codified and applied to social problems. Professionals are the experts who have mastered that body of knowledge through intensive training. Professionals also hold a monopoly on the right to use their expertise and to exclude others from dealing with their area of interest. Professional autonomy comes with monopoly status: they assume the responsibility for recruiting, training, and supervising new practitioners. They are responsible not only for maintaining standards of performance, but also for generating new knowledge in the field. In return for their monopoly power, professionals commit themselves to a service ideal. Their activities are directed not toward self-gain but toward the interests of their clients and the general public.

No single occupation, of course, fully achieves the professional ideal. These attributes of professionalism form a continuum which makes it possible to compare different occupations and changes within particular occupations. The history of the police, for example, becomes intelligible when we think of it in terms of its halting progress along the scale of professionalism. The idea that policing was a calling, a life-long career, did not begin to emerge until very late in the nineteenth century. By the same token, the idea of a police science, an abstract body of knowledge related to police work, was also extremely slow in developing. The outward forms of professional autonomy—professional associations, journals, etc.—did not fully appear until the twentieth century. Finally, the notion that the police should be committed to an abstract ideal of public service, rather than narrow parochial or political service, has also been slow in developing. Change with respect to all of the various attributes of professionalism help to illuminate the evolution of the police in the United States.[2]

A rigorous definition of professionalism serves to clarify how far short of the goal of full professional status the police now stand. It also helps to expose the emptiness of much of the rhetoric concerning police professionalism. For much of the public the term professionalism is a

---

[2] For the best summary of the literature, see W. E. Moore, *The Professions. Rules and Roles* (New York: Russell Sage, 1970).

vague and ill-defined synonym for something better than what presently exists. Frequently, the demand for professionalism translates into little more than calls for improved training and more education for police officers. The writings of liberal critics of the police are filled with simplistic ideas of this sort. At the same time, police officials frequently define professionalism in terms of technology. Sophisticated equipment is often taken as evidence of professional status. Police officials have also used the rhetoric of professionalism quite selectively to deflect criticism. The idea of professional autonomy is used to argue that outsiders (that is, liberal critics, the courts, militant blacks) are incapable of understanding the realities) of police work and, thus, should have no voice in police affairs.[3]

Equally important, a rigorous definition of professionalism helps to clarify the distinction between professionalism and bureaucracy. The distinction is crucial to understanding the nature of the contemporary police. Despite the rhetoric of professionalism, the American police have not developed along lines similar to the acknowledged professions of law, medicine, and education. Rather, police service has evolved along bureaucratic lines. The most "professional" departments have been those in which the rank-and-file officer is subject to the tightest internal supervision. The trend has been to limit rather than enhance the autonomy of the front-line practitioner. Moreover, police careers are largely restricted to closed bureaucratic structures, with little or no opportunity for advancement by way of moving laterally from one agency to another. The closed structure of police organizations has become one of the prime points of attack for police reformers in the 1970s.[4]

The emergence of nearly autonomous police bureaucracies is one of the main themes of modern police history. A major part of that theme is the growing self-consciousness and assertiveness of the rank and file. That self-consciousness finally found an institutional framework with the dramatic upsurge in police unionism in the late 1960s. Today, the rank and file, through their unions, are major actors in determining the future of policing in America. Although the reformers around the turn of the century failed to recognize it, the eventual autonomy of the rank and file was an inevitable consequence of the reforms they sought.[5]

Police unions serve as the focal point of much of the contemporary concern about the police. To some, the possibility of police strikes represents the spectre of lawlessness and anarchy. The record suggests that these fears are grossly exaggerated. More seriously, however, the power of police unions on a day-to-day basis raises fundamental questions

---

[3] Samuel Walker, "Police Professionalism: Another Look at the Issues," *Journal of Sociology and Social Welfare* 111 (July 1976): 701-710.
[4] See Jerome Skolnick, *Justice Without Trial* (New York: John Wiley, 1966), pp. 230-245.
[5] See Wallace S. Sayre and Herbert Kaufman, *Governing New York City. Politics in the Metropolis* (New York: Russell Sage, 1960).

about the responsiveness of the police to the public. Without indulging in fantasies of incipient fascism, it is appropriate to ask whether independent and aggressive police unions pose a threat to the idea of a democratic police, one that is responsive to the public at large.[6]

These concerns connect with issues that are the proper subject of any history of the police. The most fundamental issue is simply the question of what role the police have played in American society. A brief review of the slim body of literature on police history reveals three distinct schools of thought. The first school of thought might be called the "heroic" view of the police. As the agents of law and authority, the argument runs, the police contribute to the progress of civilization. This view is most popular among historians of the English police. Charles Reith introduced his account with a chapter on "The Overlooked Dependence of Authority, in History, on Means of Securing Observance of Laws." In short, the police have made a notable contribution to the growing civility of English society. This view has not received a forceful statement with respect to the American police, however.[7]

An alternative to the heroic view, and the dominant school of thought on the police, is the urbanization-social control thesis. The police as a formal social agency, this argument holds, emerged in response to the growing urbanization and resulting social disorder of Anglo-American society in the early nineteenth century. Roger Lane and James Richardson, in their histories of the Boston and New York City police departments, emphasize the impact of urban growth, immigration, and a wave of riots in stimulating the establishment of the first police departments. Perhaps the most sophisticated version of this argument is to be found in Allan Silver's seminal essay on "The Demand for Order in Civil Society: A Review of Some Themes in the History of Urban Crime, Police and Riot." Like the schools and numerous other social agencies, the modern police penetrated the daily lives of citizens as never before and were designed to create, maintain, and extend order in an increasingly complex urban-industrial society.[8]

Although it remains the dominant view of the police, the urbanization-social control thesis is not without problems. First, it tends to overestimate the degree of social order prior to the modern police era. Abundant evidence, however, suggests that violence and lawlessness did

---

[6] For a suggestive discussion of the role of police unions, see George L. Kelling and Robert B. Kliesmet, "Resistance to the Professionalization of the Police," *The Law Officer* V (September 1972): 16-22.

[7] Charles Reith, *The Blind Eye of History* (Montclair, New Jersey: Patterson Smith, 1975), pp. 13-21.

[8] Allan Silver, "The Demand for Order in Civil Society: A Review of Some Themes in the History of Urban Crime, Police, and Riot." In *The Police. Six Sociological Essays* David J. Bordua, ed. (New York: John Wiley, 1967), pp. 1-24; Roger Lane, *Policing the City. Boston 1822-1885* (Cambridge: Harvard University Press, 1967); James Richardson, *The New York Police: Colonial Times to 1901* (New York: Oxford University Press, 1970).

not necessarily increase in the early nineteenth century. Second, and perhaps more important, the social control view assumes a neutral role for the police. It is based on the assumption, implicit or explicit; that there is a shared definition of "public order," and that all groups in society share the benefits of the order that the police maintain. Such a view, however, ignores some of the most obvious conflicts in American history. The fierce struggle over the control of the police developed precisely because the police could be and were in fact used to benefit different groups in different ways.

The major alternative to the urbanization-social control view is a Marxist interpretation of American police history. There is as yet no fully developed Marxist history of the American police. Nonetheless, one finds the outlines of such an interpretation in the writings of an emerging school of radical criminology. The Marxist interpretation is rather straightforward: American society is based on a capitalist economy; the institutions of society reflect the interests of the dominant economic groups; the police play their assigned role by repressing those groups and individuals who threaten the elite.[9]

The Marxist view offers a challenging argument. It is difficult to deny, for example, that the police have actively harassed dissident political movements and played a major role in preserving white supremacy both north and south. Furthermore, the history of American labor relations is punctuated with numerous incidents of police attacks on labor unions and their leaders. Finally, much police reform has been motivated by a desire to enhance the legitimacy of the police by eliminating the more blatant abuses. This certainly explains the periodic campaigns against the third degree and other forms of police misconduct.

In the end, however, the Marxist interpretation fails to account for some of the more important aspects of police history. The main failure lies in the confusion of intent with result. There can be no doubt that members of an American elite sought to control the police for their own ends. Yet it is equally clear that they failed to achieve this goal. Throughout the nineteenth century and into the twentieth, the police remained firmly in the grip of political machines that were not controlled by any elite. The police were hardly the passive tools of industrialists. Indeed, most police reform efforts sprang from an attempt to break the control of immigrant and working class-based political machines. The heart of much of the controversy around the police was that the police openly subverted the intent of the laws, particularly those concerned with drinking.

---

[9] Sidney L. Harring and Lorraine M. McMullin, "The Buffalo Police 1872-1900: Labor Unrest, Political Power and the Creation of the Police Institution," *Crime and Social Justice* IV (Fall-Winter 1975): 5-14; *The Iron Fist and the Velvet Glove* (Berkeley: Center for Research on Criminal Justice, 1975).

The history of police reform that follows opts for a view that falls somewhere in between the urbanization-social control and the Marxist views. It attempts to take into account the complexities and ambiguities of the American social structure. American society has been divided not just along economic lines, but along racial, ethnic, and religious lines as well. The result has been that both middle and lower classes have been deeply divided internally. In many respects, divisions of race and ethnicity have overshadowed those of economic class. Unable or unwilling to challenge the economic elite working class groups have often directed much of their hostility toward rival working class groups. Often, these divisions have been consciously manipulated by the economic elite.[10]

The social structure of American society is further complicated by its relative political openness. It has been possible for groups with little economic power to gain a modicum of political power and social status through electoral politics. The urban political machine became one of the principal means by which various groups could gain some control over their lives. The police were perhaps the most important part of the political machines, because of the patronage jobs they offered, the status of being the official agents of the established order and because of the very real power to enforce or subvert the law.

Finally, this history of the police attempts to take into account another aspect of modern society: the steadily growing autonomy of organized interest groups. The most powerful of these groups represent some common economic or occupational interest. The history of the police in the twentieth century is the story of the growing occupational identity and search for autonomy by local police bureaucracies. This development was one of the unintended consequences of the professionalization movement. The occupational identity of the police further complicates the class and ethnic divisions of society. Consider the predicament of the white police officer, perhaps a second generation American of eastern European stock. Is he a "worker" in the traditional blue collar sense of the word, or is he a "new professional"? Consider, for that matter, the even more complex situation of the black police officer. Does he identify primarily as a black person, with deep-seated grievances against the established order? Or does he identify as a police officer, the agent of that established order? Or do both white and black police officers identify primarily as policemen and think of themselves as a completely distinct and isolated group in society? There are no easy answers to these questions. They are raised primarily to suggest the hazards of making facile generalizations about the American police.

---

[10] This view builds upon the work of Samuel Hays, "The Politics of Municipal Reform in the Progressive Era," *Pacific Northwest Quarterly* LV (October 1965): 157-169, Robert Wiebe, *The Search for Order* (New York: Hill & Wang, 1967); and, Herbert G. Gutman, *Work, Culture and Society in Industrializing America* (New York: Knopf, 1975).

It is appropriate at this point to indicate the scope and methodology of this history of police reform. It seeks to trace the development of reform, of the professionalization movement, on the national level, indicating the general periods of change. Any national history of the American police confronts certain inescapable problems. The historic localism of American policing, the existence of an estimated 25,000 different law enforcement agencies, makes generalization difficult. The police in various cities are subject to unique factors. Moreover, the process of reform has been extremely uneven. Some departments reformed long before others; some reformed only to quickly slide back into older patterns; some police departments, it has been suggested, have never reformed at all.

Despite these problems, it is possible to ascertain general patterns of development common to the police as a whole. One of the central arguments of this book is that around the turn of the century the *idea* of professionalization gained hegemony in police circles. Moreover, there developed a rough consensus about the specific items on the reform agenda. The techniques of managerial efficiency became the dominant motif of police professionalism. A subtheme, and often a conflicting one, was the definition of professionalism in terms of social reform: the idea that the police should be an instrument in the general betterment of society. One can trace these different ideas throughout the history of police reform.

To identify general patterns of development, this study of police reform is an exercise in historical sociology. That is to say, the insights of contemporary sociologists (and social scientists in other disciplines) are used to illuminate the history of the police, to bring order out of a chaotic mass of detail. The concept of professionalization, as an analytical framework, is drawn from the work of the sociology of the professions. Also, the literature on the sociology of the police is used to identify the central elements of policing in America. In a recent review of the literature, Lawrence W. Sherman identifies ten principal findings about the police. These, in turn, can be usefully arranged into three general categories: the nature of police work, the character of police officers, and the structure of police organizations.[11]

Police work in America is characterized by three distinct phenomena. First, the police officer exercises an enormous degree of discretion and, as a consequence, has an enormous impact on the overall operations of the criminal justice system. Second, Sherman points out that there is some evidence to suggest that police actions "amplify" deviant or criminal behavior. While this view remains arguable, the basic phenomenon remains: that police actions have an enormous impact on the behavior of the citizenry. Finally, social scientists have persuasively doc-

---

[11] Lawrence W. Sherman, "The Sociology and the Social Reform of the American Police: 1950-1973," *Journal of Police Science and Administration* II, no. 2 (1974): 255-262.

umented the fact that the bulk of police work is devoted to noncriminal "service" duties, and that most actions are *re*active—a response to a citizen request for service. These insights offer suggestive leads for historical investigation. Clearly, technological developments in the area of communications have wrought a revolution in the nature of police work and the pattern of police-community relations.

The characteristics of police officers is a second major area of investigation. Sherman identifies three major findings. First, "The police occupation is isolated from the general community, with great internal solidarity and secrecy." Second, it is generally argued that the attitudes of police officers are shaped less by their background characteristics and more by a process of occupational socialization. Finally, this socialization process has resulted in the emergence of a distinct police subculture that often contains "general values and practices which deviate widely from legal and organizational rules." The police subculture is an historical phenomenon. This history of the police argues that its development has been one of the profound indirect and unanticipated consequences of professionalization.

The nature of police organizations forms the third major area of concern. Sherman points out that "Policemen work within a nondemocratic organizational context which is antithetical to the democratic values they are supposed to protect in society." This fact has had profound implications for police behavior which is subject to a wide variety of influences. Sherman points out that the "Varieties of police behavior depend upon specific situational, organizational and community factors." His final conclusion is that organizational change offers perhaps the best prospect for changing police behavior. He notes the wide interest in administrative decentralization and debureaucratization as reform strategies. The centralized and authoritarian nature of contemporary police organizations is also an historical phenomenon. This history of the police argues that militarization was a consequence of professionalization, often seized upon as a reform strategy. The story of the shift from decentralized, nonmilitaristic police organizations to centralized and militaristic ones can hopefully provide insight into both the promise and the pitfalls of contemporary decentralization strategies.

As a history of police reform on the national level an effort has been made to present as representative a picture as possible. The existing literature on the history of the police concentrates heavily on New York City, Boston, Chicago, and Los Angeles. This account attempts to balance that material by exploring the police experience in such midwestern industrial cities as Cleveland, Cincinnati, Detroit, Milwaukee, Kansas City, and St. Louis. The research is based on an extensive survey of annual reports, other municipal documents, and investigations of the police by public and private agencies. National developments have been traced through the work and publications of professional associations in the fields of law enforcement, social work, and public administration. The International Association of Chiefs of Police, the National Conference of Charities and Corrections, National Institute of Public Administration, and the International City Management Association have provided valuable insights into developments in policing.

Finally, this account could not have been written without the previous work done by a number of historians. The published work of Roger Lane, Mark Haller, Wilbur Miller and James Richardson yield invaluable insights. At the same time, much has been learned from the work of social scientists in other disciplines. The work of Jerome Skolnick, James Q. Wilson, William A. Westley, and David Bayley deserves particular mention. The author hopes this account will contribute to the ongoing study of the American police begun by these scholars.

The 1968 Report
of the National Advisory Commission
on Civil Disorders—Summary

Introduction

The summer of 1967 again brought racial disorders to American cities, and with them shock, fear, and bewilderment to the Nation.

The worst came during a 2-week period in July, first in Newark and then in Detroit. Each set off a chain reaction in neighboring communities.

Only July 28, 1967, the President of the United States established this Commission and directed us to answer three basic questions:

> What happened?
> Why did it happen?
> What can be done to prevent it from happening again?

To respond to these questions, we have undertaken a broad range of studies and investigations. We have visited the riot cities; we have heard many witnesses; we have sought the counsel of experts across the country.

This is our basic conclusion: Our Nation is moving toward two societies, one black, one white—separate and unequal.

Reaction to last summer's disorders has quickened the movement and deepened the division. Discrimination and segregation have long permeated much of American life; they now threaten the future of every American.

This deepening racial division is not inevitable. The movement apart can be reversed. Choice is still possible. Our principal task is to define that choice and to press for a national resolution.

To pursue our present course will involve the continuing polarization of the American community and, ultimately, the destruction of basic democratic values.

The alternative is not blind repression or capitulation to lawlessness. It is the realization of common opportunities for all within a single society.

This alternative will require a commitment to national action—compassionate, massive, and sustained, backed by the resources of the

Source: Report of the National Advisory Commission on Civil Disorders—Summary, pp. 1-13 (1968). Washington, DC: U.S. Government Printing Office.

most powerful and the richest nation on this earth. From every American it will require new attitudes, new understanding, and, above all, new will.

The vital needs of the Nation must be met; hard choices must be made, and, if necessary, new taxes enacted.

Violence cannot build a better society. Disruption and disorder nourish repression, not justice. They strike at the freedom of every citizen. The community cannot—it will not—tolerate coercion and mob rule.

Violence and destruction must be ended—in the streets of the ghetto and in the lives of people.

Segregation and poverty have created in the racial ghetto a destructive environment totally unknown to most white Americans.

What white Americans have never fully understood—but what the Negro can never forget—is that white society is deeply implicated in the ghetto. White institutions created it, white institutions maintain it, and white society condones it.

It is time now to turn with all the purpose at our command to the major unfinished business of this Nation. It is time to adopt strategies for action that will produce quick and visible progress. It is time to make good the promises of American democracy to all citizens—urban and rural, white and black, Spanish-surname, American Indian, and every minority group.

Our recommendations embrace three basic principles:

- To mount programs on a scale equal to the dimension of the problems;

- To aim these programs for high impact in the immediate future in order to close the gap between promise and performance;

- To undertake new initiatives and experiments that can change the system of failure and frustration that now dominates the ghetto and weakens our society.

These programs will require unprecedented levels of funding and performance, but they neither probe deeper nor demand more than the problems which called them forth. There can be no higher priority for national action and no higher claim on the Nation's conscience.

We issue this report now, 5 months before the date called for by the President. Much remains that can be learned. Continued study is essential.

As Commissioners we have worked together with a sense of the greatest urgency and have sought to compose whatever differences exist among us. Some differences remain. But the gravity of the problem and the pressing need for action are too clear to allow further delay in the issuance of this report.

I. WHAT HAPPENED?

Chapter 1.—Profiles of Disorder

The report contains profiles of a selection of the disorders that took place during the summer of 1967. These profiles are designed to indicate how the disorders happened, who participated in them, and how local officials, police forces, and the National Guard responded. Illustrative excerpts follow:

Newark

* * * It was decided to attempt to channel the energies of the people into a nonviolent protest. While Lofton promised the crowd that a full investigation would be made of the Smith incident, the other Negro leaders began urging those on the scene to form a line and march toward the city hall.

Some persons joined the line of march. Others milled about in the narrow street. From the dark grounds at the housing project came a barrage of rocks. Some of them fell among the crowd. Others hit persons in the line of march. Many smashed the windows of the police station. The rock throwing, it was believed, was the work of youngsters; approximately 2,500 children lived in the housing project.

Almost at the same time, an old car was set afire in a parking lot. The line of march began to disintegrate. The police, their heads protected by World War I-type helmets, sallied forth to disperse the crowd. A fire engine, arriving on the scene, was pelted with rocks. As police drove people away from the station, they scattered in all directions.

A few minutes later a nearby liquor store was broken into. Some persons, seeing a caravan of cabs appear at city hall to protest Smith's arrest, interpreted this evidence that the disturbance had been organized, and generated rumors to that effect.

However, only a few stores were looted. Within a short period of time, the disorder appeared to have run its course.

* * * * *

* * * On Saturday, July 15 [Director of Police Dominick Spina received a report of snipers in a housing project. When he arrived he saw approximately 100 National Guardsmen and police officers crouching behind vehicles, hiding in corners, and lying on the ground around the edge of the courtyard.

Since everything appeared quiet and it was broad day-light, Spina walked directly down the middle of the street. Nothing happened. As he came to the last building of the complex, he heard a shot. All around him the troopers jumped, believing themselves to be under sniper fire. A moment later a young Guardsman ran from behind a building.

The director of police went over and asked him if he had fired the shot. The soldier said "Yes," he had fired to scare a man away from a window; that his orders were to keep every-one away from windows.

Spina said he told the soldier: "Do you know what you just did? You have now created a state of hysteria. Every Guardsman up and down this street and every state policeman and every city policeman that is present thinks that somebody just fired a shot and that it is probably a sniper."

A short time later more "gunshots" were heard. Investigating, Spina came upon a Puerto Rican sitting on a wall. In reply to a question as to whether he knew "where the firing is coming from?" the man said:

"That's no firing. That's fireworks. If you look up to the fourth floor, you will see the people who are throwing down these cherry bombs."

By this time four truckloads of National Guardsmen had arrived and troopers and policemen were again crouched everywhere looking for a sniper. The director of police remained at the scene for 3 hours, and the only shot fired was the one by the Guardsman.

Nevertheless, at 6 o'clock that evening two columns of National Guardsmen and State troopers were directing mass fire at the Hayes housing project in response to what they believed were snipers.***

Detroit

* * * A spirit of carefree nihilism was taking hold. To riot and destroy appeared more and more to become ends in them-selves. Late Sunday afternoon it appeared to one observer that the young people were "dancing amidst the flames."

A Negro plainclothes officer was standing at an intersection when a man threw a Molotov cocktail into a business establishment at the corner. In the heat of the afternoon, fanned by the 20 to 25 miles per hour winds of both Sunday and Monday, the fire reached the home next door within minutes. As residents uselessly sprayed the flames with garden hoses, the fire jumped from roof to roof of adjacent two- and three-story buildings. Within the hour the entire block was in flames. The ninth house in the burning row belonged to the arsonist who had thrown the Molotov cocktail.***

* * * * *

Employed as a private guard, 55-year-old Julius L. Dorsey, a Negro, was standing in front of a market when accosted by two Negro men and a woman. They demanded he permit them to loot the market. He ignored their demands. They began to berate him. He asked a neighbor to call the police. As the argument grew more heated, Dorsey fired three shots from his pistol into the air.

The police radio reported: "Looters—they have rifles." A patrol car driven by a police officer and carrying three National Guardsmen arrived. As the looters fled, the law-enforcement personnel opened fire. When the firing ceased, one person lay dead.

He was Julius L. Dorsey. * * *

* * * * *

* * * As the riot alternately waxed and waned, one area of the ghetto remained insulated. On the northeast side the residents of some 150 square blocks inhabited by 21,000 persons had, in 1966, banded together in the Positive Neighborhood Action Committee (PNAC). With professional help from the Institute of Urban Dynamics, they had organized block clubs and made plans for the improvement of the neighborhood.***

When the riot broke out, the residents, through the block clubs, were able to organize quickly. Youngsters, agreeing to stay in the neighborhood, participated in detouring traffic. While many persons reported sympathized with the idea of a rebellion against the "system" only two small fires were set— one in an empty building.

* * * * *

* * * According to Lieutenant General Throckmorton and Colonel Bolling, the city, at this time, was saturated with fear. The National Guardsmen were afraid, the citizens were afraid, and the police were afraid. Numerous persons, the majority of them Negroes, were being injured by gunshots of undetermined origin. The general and his staff felt that the major task of the troops was to reduce the fear and restore an air of normalcy.

In order to accomplish this, every effort was made to establish contact and rapport between the troops and the residents. The soldiers—20 percent of whom were Negro—began helping to clean up the streets, collect garbage, and trace persons who had disappeared in the confusion. Residents in the neighborhoods responded with soup and sandwiches for the troops. In areas where the National Guard tried to establish rapport with the citizens, there was a similar response.

New Brunswick

* * *A short time later, elements of the crowd—an older and rougher one than the night before—appeared in front of the police station. The participants wanted to see the mayor.

Mayor [Patricia] Sheehan went out onto the steps of the station. Using a bull horn, she talked to the people and asked that she be given an opportunity to correct conditions. The crowd was boisterous. Some persons challenged the mayor. But, finally, the opinion, "She's new! Give her a chance!" prevailed.

A demand was issued by people in the crowd that all persons arrested the previous night be released. Told that this already had been done, the people were suspicious. They asked to be allowed to inspect the jail cells.

It was agreed to permit representatives of the people to look into the cells to satisfy themselves that everyone had been released.

The crowd dispersed. The New Brunswick riot had failed to materialize.

Chapter 2.—Patterns of Disorder

The "typical" riot did not take place. The disorders of 1967 were unusual, irregular, complex, and unpredictable social processes. Like most human events, they did not unfold in an orderly sequence. However, an analysis of our survey information leads to some conclusions about the riot process.

In general:

- The civil disorders of 1967 involved Negroes acting against local symbols of white American society, authority, and property in Negro neighborhoods—rather than against white persons.

- Of 164 disorders reported during the first nine months of 1967, eight (5 percent) were major in terms of violence and damage; 33 (20 percent) were serious but not major; 123 (75 percent) were minor and undoubtedly would not have received national attention as riots had the Nation not been sensitized by the more serious outbreaks.

- In the 75 disorders studied by a Senate subcommittee, 83 deaths were reported. Eighty-two percent of the deaths and more than half the injuries occurred in Newark and Detroit. About 10 percent of the dead and 36 percent of the injured were public employees, primarily law officers and firemen. The overwhelming majority of the persons killed or injured in all the disorders were Negro civilians.

- Initial damage estimates were greatly exaggerated. In Detroit, newspaper damage estimates at first ranged from $200 to $500 million; the highest recent estimate is $45 million. In Newark, early estimates ranged from $15 to $25 million. A month later the damage was estimated at $10.2 million, 80 percent in inventory losses.

In the 24 disorders in 23 cities which we surveyed:

- The final incident before the outbreak of disorder, and the initial violence itself, generally took place in the evening or at night at a place in which it was normal for many people to be on the streets.

- Violence usually occurred almost immediately following the occurrence of the final precipitating incident, and then escalated rapidly. With but few exceptions, violence subsided during the day, and flared rapidly again at night. The night-day cycles continued through the early period of the major disorders.

- Disorder generally began with rock and bottle throwing and window breaking. Once store windows were broken, looting usually followed.

- Disorder did not erupt as a result of single "triggering" or "precipitating" incident. Instead, it was generated out of an increasingly disturbed social atmosphere, in which typically a series of tensions-heightening incidents over a period of weeks or months became linked in the minds of many in the Negro community with a reservoir of underlying grievances. At some point in the mounting tension, a further incident—in itself often routine or trivial—became the breaking point and tension spilled over into violence.

- "Prior" incidents, which increased tensions and ultimately led to violence, were police actions in almost half the cases; police actions were "final" incidents before the outbreak of violence in 12 of the 24 surveyed disorders.

- No particular control tactic was successful in every situation. The varied effectiveness of control techniques emphasizes the need for advance training, planning, adequate intelligence systems, and knowledge of the ghetto community.

- Negotiations between Negroes—including young militants as well as older Negro leaders—and white officials concerning "terms of peace" occurred during virtually all the disorders surveyed. In many cases, these negotiations involved discussion of underlying grievances as well as the handling of the disorder by control authorities.

- The typical rioter was a teenager or young adult, a life-long resident of the city in which he rioted, a high school dropout; he was, nevertheless, somewhat better educated than his nonrioting Negro neighbor, and was usually underemployed or employed in a menial job. He was proud of his race, extremely hostile to both whites and middle-class Negroes and, although informed about politics, highly distrustful of the political system.

A Detroit survey revealed that approximately 11 percent of the total residents of two riot areas admitted participation in the rioting, 20 to 25 percent identified themselves as "bystanders," over 16 percent identified themselves as "counterrioters" who urged rioters to "cool it," and the remaining 48 to 53 percent said they were at home or elsewhere and did not participate. In a survey of Negro males between the ages of 15 and 35 residing in the disturbance area in Newark, about 45 percent identified themselves as rioters, and about 55 percent as "noninvolved."

- Many rioters were young Negro males. Nearly 53 percent of arrestees were between 15 and 24 years of age; nearly 81 percent between 15 and 35.

- In Detroit and Newark about 74 percent of the rioters were brought up in the North. In contrast, of the noninvolved, 36 percent in Detroit and 52 percent in Newark were brought up in the North.

- What the rioters appeared to be seeking was fuller participation in the social order and the material benefits enjoyed by the majority of American citizens. Rather than rejecting the American system, they were anxious to obtain a place for themselves in it.

- Numerous Negro counterrioters walked the streets urging rioters to "cool it." The typical counterrioter was better educated and had higher income than either the rioter or the noninvolved.

- The proportion of Negroes in local government was substantially smaller than the Negro proportion of population. Only three of the 20 cities studied had more than one Negro legislator; none ever had a Negro mayor or city manager. In only four cities did Negroes hold other important policymaking decisions or serve as heads of municipal departments.

- Although almost all cities had some sort of formal grievance mechanism for handling citizen complaints, this typically was regarded by Negroes as ineffective and was generally ignored.

- Although specific grievances varied from city to city, at least 12 deeply held grievances can be identified and ranked into three levels of relative intensity:

First level of intensity
  1. Police practices.
  2. Unemployment and underemployment.
  3. Inadequate housing.

Second level of intensity:
  4. Inadequate education.
  5. Poor recreation facilities and programs.
  6. Ineffectiveness of the political structure and grievance mechanisms.

Third level of intensity:
  7. Disrespectful white attitudes.
  8. Discriminatory administration of justice.
  9. Inadequacy of Federal programs.
  10. Inadequacy of municipal services.
  11. Discriminatory consumer and credit practices.
  12. Inadequate welfare programs.

- The results of a three-city survey of various Federal programs—manpower, education, housing, welfare and community action—indicate that, despite substantial expenditures, the number of persons assisted constituted only a fraction of those in need.

The background of disorder is often as complex and difficult to analyze as the disorder itself. But we find that certain general conclusions can be drawn:

- Social and economic conditions in the riot cities constituted a clear pattern of severe disadvantage for Negroes
compared with whites, whether the Negroes lived in the
area where the riot took place or outside it. Negroes had
completed fewer years of education and fewer had attended high school. Negroes were twice as likely to be unemployed and three times as likely to be in unskilled and service jobs. Negroes averaged 70 percent of the income
earned by whites and were more than twice as likely to be
living in poverty. Although housing cost Negroes relatively more, they had worse housing—three times as likely to
be overcrowded and substandard. When compared to
white suburbs, the relative disadvantages was even more
pronounced.

A study of the aftermath of disorder leads to disturbing conclusions.
We find that, despite the institution of some postriot programs:

- Little basic change in the conditions underlying the outbreak of disorder has taken place. Actions to ameliorate
Negro grievances have been limited and sporadic; with
but few exceptions, they have not significantly reduced
tensions.

- In several cities, the principal office response has been to
train and equip the police with more sophisticated
weapons.

- In several cities, increasing polarization is evident, with
continuing breakdown of interracial communication, and
growth of white segregationist or black separatist groups.

Chapter 3.—Organized Activity

The President directed the Commission to investigate "to what
extent, if any, there has been planning or organization in any of the
riots."

To carry out this part of the President's charge, the Commission
established a special investigative staff supplementing the field teams
that made the general examination of the riots in 23 cities. The unit
examined data collected by Federal agencies and congressional committees, including thousands of documents supplied by the Federal Bureau
of Investigation, gathered and evaluated information from local and
state law enforcement agencies and officials, and conducted its own
field investigation in selected cities.

On the basis of all the information collected, the Commission concludes that:

> The urban disorders of the summer of 1967 were not caused
> by, nor were they the consequence of, any organized plan or
> "conspiracy."

Specifically, the Commission has found no evidence that all or any of the disorders or the incidents that led to them were planned or directed by any organization or group, international, national, or local.

Militant organizations, local and national, and individual agitators, who repeatedly forecast and called for violence, were active in the spring and summer of 1967. We believe that they sought to encourage violence, and that they helped to create at atmosphere that contributed to the outbreak of disorder.

We recognize that the continuation of disorders and the polarization of the races would provide fertile ground for organized exploitation in the future.

Investigations of organized activity are continuing at all levels of government, including committees of Congress. These investigations relate not only to the disorders of 1967 but also to the actions of groups and individuals, particularly in schools and colleges, during this last fall and winter. The Commission has cooperated in these investigations. They should continue.

II. Why Did It Happen?

Chapter 4.—The Basic Causes

In addressing the question "Why did it happen?" we shift our focus from the local to the national scene, from the particular events of the summer of 1967 to the factors within the society at large that created a mood of violence among many urban Negroes.

These factors are complex and interacting; they vary significantly in their effect from city to city and from year to year; and the consequences of one disorder, generating new grievances and new demands, become the causes of the next. Thus was created the "thicket of tension, conflicting evidence, and extreme opinions" cited by the President.

Despite these complexities, certain fundamental matters are clear. Of these, the most fundamental is the racial attitude and behavior of white Americans toward black Americans.

Race prejudice has shaped our history decisively; it now threatens to affect our future.

White racism is essentially responsible for the explosive mixture which has been accumulating in our cities since the end of World War II. Among the ingredients of this mixture are:

- *Pervasive discrimination and segregation* in employment, education, and housing, which have resulted in the continuing exclusion of great numbers of Negroes from the benefits of economic progress.

- *Black in-migration and white exodus,* which have produced the massive and growing concentrations of impoverished Negroes in our major cities, creating a growing crisis of deteriorating facilities and unmet human needs.

- *The black ghettos,* where segregation and poverty converge on the young to destroy opportunity and enforce failure. Crime, drug addiction, dependency on welfare, and bitterness and resentment against society in general and white society in particular are the result.

At the same time, most whites and some Negroes outside the ghetto have prospered to a degree unparalleled in the history of civilization. Through television and other media, this affluence has been flaunted before the eyes of the Negro poor and the jobless ghetto youth.

Yet these facts alone cannot be said to have caused the disorders. Recently, other powerful ingredients have begun to catalyze the mixture:

- *Frustrated hopes* are the residue of the unfulfilled expectations aroused by the great judicial and legislative victories of the civil rights movement and the dramatic struggle for equal rights in the South.

- *A climate that tends towards approval and encouragement of violence* as a form of protest has been created by white terrorism directed against nonviolent protest; by the open defiance of law and Federal authority by state and local officials resisting desegregation; and by some protest groups engaging in civil disobedience who turn their backs on nonviolence, go beyond the constitutionally protected rights of petition and free assembly, and resort to violence to attempt to compel alteration of laws and policies with which they disagree.

- *The frustrations of powerlessness* have led some Negroes to the conviction that there is no effective alternative to violence as a means of achieving redress of grievances, and of "moving the system." These frustrations are reflected in alienation and hostility toward the institutions

of law and government and the white society which controls them, and in the reach toward racial consciousness
and solidarity reflected in the slogan "Black Power."

• *A new mood* has sprung up among Negroes, particularly
among the young, in which self-esteem and enhanced
racial pride are replacing apathy and submission to "the
system."

• *The police are not merely a "spark" factor.* To some
Negroes police have come to symbolize white power,
white racism and white repression. And the fact is that
many police do reflect and express these white attitudes.
The atmosphere of hostility and cynicism is reinforced by
a widespread belief among Negroes in the existence of
police brutality and in a "double standard" of justice and
protection—one for Negroes and one for whites.

* * * * *

To this point, we have attempted only to identify the prime components of the "explosive mixture." In the chapters that follow we seek
to analyze them in the perspective of history. Their meaning, however,
is clear:

In the summer of 1967, we have seen in our cities a chain reaction of racial violence. If we are heedless, none of us shall escape the
consequences.

Chapter 5.—Rejection and Protest: A Historical Sketch

The causes of recent racial disorders are embedded in a tangle of
issues of circumstances—social, economic, political, and psychological—which arise out of the historic pattern of Negro-white relations in
America.

In this chapter we trace the pattern, identify the recurrent themes of
Negro protest and, most importantly, provide a perspective on the
protest activities of the present era.

We describe the Negro's experience in America and the development
of slavery as an institution. We show his persistent striving for equality
in the face of rigidly maintained social, economic, and education barriers, and repeated mob violence. We portray the ebb and flow of the
doctrinal tides—accommodation, separation, and self-help—and their
relationship to the current theme of Black Power. We conclude:

The Black Power advocates of today consciously feel that they
are the most militant group in the Negro protest movement.
Yet they have retreated from a direct confrontation with
American society on the issue of integration and, by preaching

separatism, unconsciously function as an accommodation to white racism. Much of their economic program, as well as their interest in Negro history, self-help, racial solidarity and separation, is reminiscent of Booker T. Washington. The rhetoric is different, but the ideas are remarkably similar.

Chapter 6.—The Formation of the Racial Ghettoes[1]

Throughout the 20th century the Negro population of the United States has been moving steadily from rural areas to urban and from South to North and West. In 1910, 91 percent of the Nation's 9.8 million Negroes lived in the South and only 27 percent of American Negroes lived in cities of 2,500 persons or more. Between 1910 and 1966 the total Negro population more than doubled, reaching 21.5 million, and the number living in metropolitan areas rose more than fivefold (from 2.6 million to 14.8 million). The number outside the South rose elevenfold (from 885,000 to 9.7 million).

Negro migration from the South has resulted from the expectation of thousands of new and highly paid jobs for unskilled workers in the North and the shift to mechanized farming in the South. However, the Negro migration is small when compared to earlier waves of European immigrants. Even between 1960 and 1966, there were 1.8 million immigrants from abroad compared to the 613,000 Negroes who arrived in the North and West from the South.

As a result of the growing number of Negroes in urban areas, natural increase has replaced migration as the primary source of Negro population increase in the cities. Nevertheless, Negro migration from the South will continue unless economic conditions there change dramatically.

Basic data concerning Negro urbanization trends indicate that:

- Almost all Negro population growth (98 percent from 1950 to 1966), is occurring within metropolitan areas, primarily within central cities.[2]

- The vast majority of white population growth (78 percent from 1960 to 1966) is occurring in suburban portions of metropolitan areas. Since 1960, white central-city populations has declined by 1.3 million.

---

[1] The term "ghetto" as used in this Report refers to an area within a city characterized by poverty and acute social disorganization and inhabited by members of a racial or ethnic group under conditions of involuntary segregation.

[2] A "central city" is the largest city of a standard metropolitan statistical area, that is, a metropolitan area containing at least one city of 50,000 or more inhabitants.

- As a result, central cities are becoming more heavily Negro while the suburban fringes around them remain almost entirely white.

- The 12 largest central cities now contain over two-thirds of the Negro populations outside the South, and almost one-third of the Negro total in the United States.

Within the cities, Negroes have been excluded from white residential areas through discriminatory practices. Just as significant is the withdrawal of white families from, or their refusal to enter, neighborhoods where Negroes are moving or already residing. About 20 percent of the urban population of the United States changes residence every year. The refusal of whites to move into "changing" areas when vacancies occur means that most vacancies eventually are occupied by Negroes.

The result, according to a recent study, is that in 1960 the average segregation index for 207 of the largest U.S. cities was 86.2. In other words, to create an unsegregated population distribution, an average of over 86 percent of all Negroes would have to change their place of residence within the city.

Chapter 7.—Unemployment, Family Structure, and Social Disorganization

Although there have been gains in Negro income nationally, and a decline in the number of Negroes below the "poverty level," the condition of Negroes in the central city remains in a state of crisis. Between 2 and 2.5 million Negroes—16 to 20 percent of the total Negro population of all central cities—live in squalor and deprivation in ghetto neighborhoods.

Employment is a key problem. It not only controls the present for the Negro Americans, but, in a most profound way, it is creating the future as well. Yet, despite continuing economic growth and declining national unemployment rates, the unemployment rate for Negroes in 1967 was more than double that for whites.

Equally important is the undesirable nature of many jobs open to Negroes and other minorities. Negro men are more than three times as likely as white men to be in low-paying, unskilled, or service jobs. This concentration of male Negro employment at the lowest end of the occupational scale is the single most important cause of poverty among Negroes.

In one study of low-income neighborhoods, the "sub-employment rate," including both unemployment and underemployment, was about 33 percent, or 8.8 times greater than the overall unemployment rate for all U.S. workers.

Employment problems, aggravated by the constant arrival of new unemployed migrants, many of them from depressed rural areas, create persistent poverty in the ghetto. In 1966, about 11.9 percent of the Nation's whites and 40.6 percent of its nonwhites were below the poverty level defined by the Society Security Administration (in 1966, $3,335 per year for an urban family of four). Over 40 percent of the nonwhites below the poverty level live in the central cities.

Employment problems have drastic social impact in the ghetto. Men who are chronically unemployed or employed in the lowest status jobs are often unable or unwilling to remain with their families. The handicap imposed on children growing up without fathers in an atmosphere of deprivation is increased as mothers are forced to work to provide support.

The culture of poverty that results from unemployment and family breakup generates a system of ruthless, exploitative relationships with the ghetto. Prostitution, dope addiction, and crime create an environmental "jungle" characterized by personal insecurity and tension. Children growing up under such conditions are likely participants in civil disorder.

Chapter 8.—Conditions of Life in the Racial Ghetto

A striking difference in environment from that of white, middle-class Americans profoundly influences the lives of residents of the ghetto.

Crime rates, consistently higher than in other areas, create a pronounced sense of insecurity. For example, in one city one low-income Negro district had 35 times as many serious crimes against persons as a high-income white district. Unless drastic steps are taken, the crime problems in poverty areas are likely to continue to multiply as the growing youth and rapid urbanization of the population outstrip police resources.

Poor health and sanitation conditions in the ghetto result in higher mortality rates, a higher incidence of major diseases, and lower availability and utilization of medical services. The infant mortality rate for non-white babies under the age of 1 month is 58 percent higher than for whites; for 1 to 12 months it is almost three times as high. The level of sanitation in the ghetto is far below that in high-income areas. Garbage collection is often inadequate. Of an estimated 14,000 cases of rat bite in the United States in 1965, most were in ghetto neighborhoods.

Ghetto residents believe they are exploited by local merchants; and evidence substantiates some of these beliefs. A study conducted in one city by the Federal Trade Commission showed that higher prices were charged for goods sold in ghetto stores than in other areas.

Lack of knowledge regarding credit purchasing creates special pitfalls for the disadvantaged. In many states, garnishment practices compound these difficulties by allowing creditors to deprive individuals of their wages without hearing or trial.

Chapter 9.—Comparing the Immigrant and Negro Experience

In this chapter, we address ourselves to a fundamental question that many white Americans are asking: Why have so many Negroes, unlike the European immigrants, been unable to escape from the ghetto and from poverty?

We believe the following factors play a part:

- *The maturing economy.*—When the European immigrants arrived, they gained an economic foothold by providing the unskilled labor needed by industry. Unlike the immigrant, the Negro migrant found little opportunity in the city. The economy, by then matured, had little use for the unskilled labor he had to offer.

- *The disability of race.*—The structure of discrimination has stringently narrowed opportunities for the Negro and restricted his prospects. European immigrants suffered from discrimination, but never so pervasively.

- *Entry into the political system.*—The immigrants usually settled in rapidly growing cities with powerful and expanding political machines, which traded economic advantages for political support. Ward-level grievance machinery, as well as personal representation, enabled the immigrant to make his voice heard and his power felt.

  By the time the Negro arrived, these political machines were no longer so powerful or so well equipped to provide jobs or other favors, and in many cases were unwilling to share their remaining influence with Negroes.

- *Cultural factors.*—Coming from societies with a low standard of living and at a time when job aspirations were low, the immigrants sensed little deprivation in being forced to take the less desirable and poorer paying jobs. Their large and cohesive families contributed to total income. Their vision of the future—one that led to a life outside of the ghetto—provided the incentive necessary to endure the present.

> Although Negro men worked as hard as the immi-
> grants, they were unable to support their families. The
> entrepreneurial opportunities had vanished. As a result of
> slavery and long periods of unemployment, the Negro
> family structure had become matriarchal; the males
> played a secondary and marginal family role—one which
> offered little compensation for their hard and unreward-
> ing labor. Above all, segregation denied Negroes access to
> good jobs and the opportunity to leave the ghetto. For
> them, the future seemed to lead only to a dead end.

Today, whites tend to exaggerate how well and quickly they escaped from poverty. The fact is that immigrants who came from rural back-grounds, as many Negroes do, are only now, after three generations, finally beginning to move into the middle class.

By contrast, Negroes began concentrating in the city less than two generations ago, and under much less favorable conditions. Although some Negroes have escaped poverty, few have been able to escape the urban ghetto.

III.   What Can Be Done?

Chapter 10.—The Community Response

Our investigation of the 1967 riot cities establishes that virtually every major episode of violence was foreshadowed by an accumulation of unresolved grievances and by widespread dissatisfaction among Negroes with the unwillingness or inability of local government to respond.

Overcoming these conditions is essential for community support of law enforcement and civil order. City governments need new and more vital channels of communication to the residents of the ghetto; they need to improve their capacity to respond effectively to community needs before they become community grievances; and they need to pro-vide opportunity for meaningful involvement of ghetto residents in shaping policies and programs which affect the community.

The Commission recommends that local governments:

- Develop Neighborhood Action Task Forces as joint com-munity-government efforts through which more effective communication can be achieved, and the delivery of city services to ghetto residents improved.

- Establish comprehensive grievance-response mechanisms in order to bring all public agencies under public scrutiny.

- Bring the institutions of local government closer to the people they serve by establishing neighborhood outlets for local, state, and Federal administrative and public service agencies.

- Expand opportunities for ghetto residents to participate in the formulation of public policy and the implementation of programs affecting them through improved political representation, creation of institutional channels for community action, expansion of legal services, and legislative hearings on ghetto problems.

In this effort, city governments will require State and Federal support. The Commission recommends:

- State and Federal financial assistance for mayors and city councils to support the research, consultants, staff, and other resources needed to respond effectively to Federal Program initiatives.

- State cooperation in providing municipalities with the jurisdictional tools needed to deal with their problems; a fuller measure of financial aid to urban areas; and the focusing of the interests of suburban communities on the physical, social, and cultural environment of the central city.

Chapter 11.—Police and the Community

The abrasive relationship between the police and minority communities has been a major—and explosive—source of grievance, tension, and disorder. The blame must be shared by the total society.

The police are faced with demands for increased protection and service in the ghetto. Yet the aggressive patrol practices thought necessary to meet these demands themselves create tension and hostility. The resulting grievances have been further aggravated by the lack of effective mechanisms for handling complaints against the police. Special programs for bettering police-community relations have been instituted, but these alone are not enough. Police administrators, with the guidance of public officials, and the support of the entire community, must take vigorous action to improve law enforcement and to decrease the potential for disorder.

The Commission recommends that city government and police authorities:

- Review police operations in the ghetto to ensure proper conduct by police officers, and eliminate abrasive practices.

- Provide more adequate police protection to ghetto residents to eliminate their high sense of insecurity and the belief in the existence of a dual standard of law enforcement.

- Establish fair and effective mechanisms for the redress of grievances against the police and other municipal employees.

- Develop and adopt policy guidelines to assist officers in making critical decisions in areas where police conduct can create tension.

- Develop and use innovative programs to insure wide-spread community support for law enforcement.

- Recruit more Negroes into the regular police force, and review promotion policies to insure fair promotion for Negro officers.

- Establish a "Community Service Officer" program to attract ghetto youths between the ages of 17 and 21 to police work. These junior officers would perform duties in ghetto neighborhoods, but would not have full police authority. The Federal Government should provide support equal to 90 percent of the costs of employing CSO's on the basis of one for every 10 regular officers.

Chapter 12.—Control of Disorder

Preserving civil peace is the first responsibility of government. Unless the rule of law prevails, our society will lack not only order but also the environment essential to social and economic progress.

The maintenance of civil order cannot be left to the police alone. The police need guidance, as well as support, from mayors and other public officials. It is the responsibility of public officials to determine proper police policies, support adequate police standards for personnel and performance, and participate in planning for the control of disorders.

To maintain control of incidents which could lead to disorders, the Commission recommends that local officials:

- Assign seasoned, well-trained policemen and supervisory officers to patrol ghetto areas, and to respond to disturbances.

- Develop plans which will quickly muster maximum police manpower and highly qualified senior commanders at the outbreak of disorders.

- Provide special training in the prevention of disorders, and prepare police for riot control and for operation in units, with adequate command and control and field communication for proper discipline and effectiveness.

- Develop guidelines governing the use of control equipment and provide alternatives to the use of lethal weapons. Federal support for research in this area is needed.

- Establish an intelligence system to provide police and other public officials with reliable information that may help to prevent the outbreak of a disorder and to institute effective control measures in the event a riot erupts.

- Develop continuing contacts with ghetto residents to make use of the forces for order which exist within the community.

- Establish machinery for neutralizing rumors, and enabling Negro leaders and residents to obtain the facts. Create special rumor details to collect, evaluate, and dispel rumors that may lead to a civil disorder.

The Commission believes there is a grave danger that some communities may resort to the indiscriminate and excessive use of force. The harmful effects of overreaction are incalculable. The Commission condemns moves to equip police departments with mass destructive weapons, such as automatic rifles, machine guns, and tanks. Weapons which are designed to destroy, not to control, have no place in densely populated urban communities.

The Commission recommends that the Federal Government share in the financing of programs for improvement of police forces, both in their normal law enforcement activities as well as in their response to civil disorders.

To assist government authorities in planning their response to civil disorder, this report contains a Supplement on Control of Disorder. It deals with specific problems encountered during riot control operations, and includes:

- Assessment of the present capabilities of police, National Guard and Army forces to control major riots, and recommendations for improvement.

- Recommended means by which the control operations of those forces may be coordinated with the response of other agencies, such as fire departments, and with the community at large.

- Recommendations for review and revision of Federal,
  state and local laws needed to provide the framework for
  control effort and for the callup and interrelated of public
  safety forces.

Chapter 13.—The Administration of Justice Under Emergency Conditions

In many of the cities which experienced disorders last summer, there were recurring breakdowns in the mechanisms for processing, prosecuting, and protecting arrested persons. These resulted mainly from long-standing structural deficiencies in criminal court systems, and from the failure of communities to anticipate and plan for the emergency demands of civil disorders.

In part, because of this, there were few successful prosecutions for serious crimes committed during the riots. In those cities where mass arrests occurred, many arrestees were deprived of basic legal rights.

The Commission recommends that the cities and the states:

- Undertake reform of the lower courts so as to improve the
  quality of justice rendered under normal conditions.

- Plan comprehensive measures by which the criminal justice system may be supplemented during civil disorders so
  that its deliberate functions are protected, and the quality
  of justice is maintained.

Such emergency plans require broad community participation and dedicated leadership by the bench and bar. They should include:

- Laws sufficient to deter and punish riot conduct.

- Additional judges, bail and probation officers, and clerical staff.

- Arrangements for volunteer lawyers to help prosecutors and
  to represent riot defendants at every stage of proceedings.

- Policies to insure proper and individual bail, arraignment,
  pretrial, trial, and sentencing proceedings.

- Adequate emergency processing and detention facilities.

Chapter 14.—Damages: Repair and Compensation

The Commission recommends that the Federal Government:

- Amend the Federal Disaster Act—which now applies only to natural disasters—to permit Federal emergency food and medical assistance to cities during major civil disorders, and provide long-term economic assistance afterwards.

- With the cooperation of the states, create incentives for the private insurance industry to provide more adequate property insurance coverage in inner-city areas.

The Commission endorses the report of the National Advisory Panel on Insurance in Riot-Affected Areas: "Meeting the Insurance Crisis of our Cities."

Chapter 15.—The News Media and the Disorders

In his charge to the Commission, the President asked: "What effect do the mass media have on the riots?"

The Commission determined that the answer to the President's question did not lie solely in the performance of the press and broadcasters in reporting the riots. Our analysis had to consider also the overall treatment by the media of the Negro ghettos, community relations, racial attitudes, and poverty—day by day and month by month, year in and year out.

A wide range of interviews with Government officials, law enforcement authorities, media personnel and other citizens, including ghetto residents, as well as a quantitative analysis of riot coverage and a special conference with industry representatives, leads us to conclude that:

- Despite instances of sensationalism, inaccuracy and distortion, newspapers, radio and television tried on the whole to give a balanced, factual account of the 1967 disorders.

- Elements of the news media failed to portray accurately the scale and character of the violence that occurred last summer. The overall effect was, we believe, an exaggeration of both mood and event.

- Important segments of the media failed to report adequately on the causes and consequences of civil disorders and on the underlying problem of race relations. They have not communicated to the majority of their audience—which is white—a sense of the degradation, misery, and hopelessness of life in the ghetto.

These failings must be corrected, and the improvement must come from within the industry. Freedom of press is not the issue. Any effort to impose governmental restrictions would be inconsistent with fundamental constitutional precepts.

We have seen evidence that the news media are becoming aware of and concerned about their performance in this field. As that concern grows, coverage will improve. But much more must be done, and it must be done soon.

The Commission recommends that the media:

- Expand coverage of the Negro community and of race problems through permanent assignment of reporters familiar with urban and racial affairs, and through establishment of more and better links with the Negro community.

- Integrate Negroes and Negro activities into all aspects of coverage and content, including newspaper articles and television programming. The news media must publish newspapers and produce programs that recognize the existence and activities of Negroes as a group within the community and as a part of the larger community.

- Recruit more Negroes into journalism and broadcasting and promote those who are qualified to positions of significant responsibility. Recruitment should begin in high schools and continue through college; where necessary, aid for training should be provided.

- Improve coordination with police in reporting riot news through advance planning, and cooperate with the police in the designation of police information officers, establishment of information centers, and development of mutually acceptable guidelines for riot reporting and the conduct of media personnel.

- Accelerate efforts to insure accurate and responsible reporting of riot and racial news, through adoption by all news-gathering organizations of stringent internal staff guidelines.

- Cooperate in the establishment of a privately organized and funded Institute of Urban Communications to train and educate journalists in urban affairs, recruit and train more Negro journalists, develop methods for improving police-press relations, review coverage of riots and racial issues, and support continuing research in the urban field.

Chapter 16.—The Future of the Cities

By 1985, the Negro population in central cities is expected to increase by 68 percent to approximately 20.3 million. Coupled with the continued exodus of white families to the suburbs, this growth will produce majority Negro populations in many of the Nation's largest cities.

The future of these cities, and of their burgeoning Negro populations, is grim. Most new employment opportunities are being created in suburbs and outlying areas. This trend will continue unless important changes in public policy are made.

In prospect, therefore, is further deterioration of already inadequate municipal tax bases in the face of increasing demands for public services, and continuing unemployment and poverty among the urban Negro population:

Three choices are open to the Nation:

- We can maintain present policies, continuing both the proportion of the Nation's resources now allocated to programs for the unemployment and the disadvantaged, and the inadequate and failing effort to achieve an integrated society.

- We can adopt a policy of "enrichment" aimed at improving dramatically the quality of ghetto life while abandoning integration as a goal.

- We can pursue integration by combining ghetto "enrichment" with policies which will encourage Negro movement out of central city areas.

The first choice, continuance of present policies, has ominous consequences for our society. The share of the Nation's resources now allocated to programs for the disadvantaged is insufficient to arrest the deterioration of life in central-city ghettos. Under such conditions, a rising proportion of Negroes may come to see in the deprivation and segregation they experience, a justification for violent protest, or for extending support to now isolated extremists who advocate civil disruption. Large-scale and continuing violence could result, followed by white retaliation, and, ultimately, the separation of the two communities in a garrison state.

Even if violence does not occur, the consequences are unacceptable. Development of a racially integrated society, extraordinarily difficult today, will be virtually impossible with the present black central-city population of 12.1 million has grown to almost 21 million.

To continue present policies is to make permanent the division of our country into two societies: one, largely Negro and poor, located in the central cities; the other, predominantly white and affluent, located in the suburbs and in outlying areas.

The second choice, ghetto enrichment coupled with abandonment of integration, is also unacceptable. It is another way of choosing a permanently divided country. Moreover, equality cannot be achieved under conditions of nearly complete separation. In a country where the economy, and particularly the resources of employment, are predominantly white, a policy of separation can only relegate Negroes to a permanently inferior economic status.

We believe that the only possible choice for America is the third—a policy which combines ghetto enrichment with programs designed to encourage integration of substantial numbers of Negroes into the society outside the ghetto.

Enrichment must be an important adjunct to integration, for no matter how ambitious or energetic the program, few Negroes now living in central cities can be quickly integrated. In the meantime, large-scale improvement in the quality of ghetto life is essential.

But this can be no more than an interim strategy. Programs must be developed which will permit substantial Negro movement out of the ghettos. The primary goal must be a single society, in which every citizen will be free to live and work according to his capabilities and desires, not his color.

Chapter 17.—Recommendations for National Action

Introduction

No American—white or black—can escape the consequences of the continuing social and economic decay of our major cities.

Only a commitment to national action on an unprecedented scale can shape a future compatible with the historic ideals of American society.

The great productivity of our economy, and a Federal revenue system which is highly responsive to economic growth, can provide the resources.

The major need is to generate new will—the will to tax ourselves to the extent necessary to meet the vital needs of the Nation.

We have set forth goals and proposed strategies to reach those goals. We discuss and recommend programs not to commit each of us to specific parts of such programs, but to illustrate the type and dimension of action needed.

The major goal is the creation of a true union—a single society and a single American identify. Toward that goal, we propose the following objectives for national action:

- Opening up opportunities to those who are restricted by racial segregation and discrimination, and eliminating all barriers to their choice of jobs, education, and housing.

- Removing the frustration of powerlessness among the disadvantaged by providing the means for them to deal with the problems that affect their own lives and by increasing the capacity of our public and private institutions to respond to these problems.

- Increasing communication across racial lines to destroy stereotypes, halt polarization, end distrust and hostility, and create common ground for efforts toward public order and social justice.

We proposed these aims to fulfill our pledge of equality and to meet the fundamental needs of a democratic and civilized society—domestic peace and social justice.

Employment

Pervasive unemployment and underemployment are the most persistent and serious grievances in minority areas. They are inextricably linked to the problem of civil disorder.

Despite growing Federal expenditures for manpower development and training programs, and sustained general economic prosperity and increasing demands for skilled workers, about 2 million—white and non-white—are permanently unemployed. About 10 million are underemployed, of whom 6.5 million work full time for wages below the poverty line.

The 500,000 "hard-core" unemployed in the central cities who lack a basic education and are unable to hold a steady job are made up in large part of Negro males between the ages of 18 and 25. In the riot cities which we surveyed, Negroes were three times as likely as whites to hold unskilled jobs, which are often part time, seasonal, low paying and "dead end."

Negro males between the ages of 15 and 25 predominated among the rioters. More than 20 percent of the rioters were unemployed, and many who were employed held intermittent, low status, unskilled jobs which they regarded as below their education and ability.

The Commission recommends that the Federal Government:

- Undertake joint efforts with cities and states to consolidate existing manpower programs to avoid fragmentation and duplication.

- Take immediate action to create 2 million new jobs over the next 3 years—1 million in the public sector and 1 million in the private sector—to absorb the hard-core unemployed and materially reduce the level of underemployment for all workers, black and white. We proposed 250,000 public sector and 300,000 private sector jobs in the first year.

- Provide on-the-job training by both public and private employers with reimbursement to private employers for the extra costs of training the hard-core unemployed, by contract or by tax credits.

- Provide tax and other incentives to investment in rural as well as urban poverty areas in order to offer the rural poor an alternative to migration to urban centers.

- Take new and vigorous action to remove artificial barriers to employment and promotion, including not only racial discrimination, but, in certain cases, arrest records or lack of a high school diploma. Strengthen those agencies such as the Equal Employment Opportunity Commission, charged with eliminating discriminatory practices, and provide full support for Title VI of the 1964 Civil Rights Act allowing Federal grant-in-aid funds to be withheld from activities which discriminate on grounds of color or race.

The Commission commends the recent public commitment of the National Trades Council of the Building and Construction Trades Union, AFL-CIO, to encourage and recruit Negro membership in apprenticeship programs. This commitment should be intensified and implemented.

Education

Education in a democratic society must equip children to develop their potential and to participate fully in American life. For the community at large, the schools have discharged this responsibility well. But for many minorities, and particularly for the children of the ghetto, the schools have failed to provide the educational experience which could overcome the effects of discrimination and deprivation.

This failure is one of the persistent sources of grievance and resentment within the Negro community. The hostility of Negro parents and students toward the school system is generating increasing conflict and causing disruption within many city school districts. But the most dramatic evidence of the relationship between education practices and civil disorders lies in the high incidence of riot participation by ghetto youth who have not completed high school.

The bleak record of public education for ghetto children is growing worse. In the critical skills—verbal and reading ability—Negro students are falling further behind whites with each year of school completed. The high unemployment and underemployment rate for Negro youth is evidence, in part, of the growing educational crisis.

We support integration as the priority education strategy; it is essential to the future of American society. In this last summer's disorders we have seen the consequences of racial isolation at all levels, and of attitudes toward race, on both sides, produced by three centuries of myth, ignorance, and bias. It is indispensable that opportunities for interaction between the races be expanded.

We recognize that the growing dominance of pupils from disadvantaged minorities in city school population will not soon be reversed. No matter how great the effort toward desegregation, many children of the ghetto will not, within their school careers, attend integrated schools.

If existing disadvantages are not to be perpetuated, we must drastically improve the quality of ghetto education. Equality of results with all-white schools must be the goal.

To implement these strategies, the Commission recommends:

- Sharply increased efforts to eliminate de facto segregation in our schools through substantial federal aid to school systems seeking to desegregate either within the system or in cooperating with neighboring school systems.

- Elimination of racial discrimination in Northern as well as Southern schools by vigorous application of Title VI of the Civil Rights Act of 1964.

- Extension of quality early childhood education to every disadvantaged child in the country.

- Efforts to improve dramatically schools serving disadvantaged children through substantial federal funding of year-round quality compensatory education programs, improved teaching, and expanded experimentation and research.

- Elimination of illiteracy through greater Federal support for adult basic education.

- Enlarged opportunities for parent and community participation in the public schools.

- Reoriented vocational education emphasizing work-experience training and the involvement of business and industry.

- Expanded opportunities for higher education through increased federal assistance to disadvantaged students.

- Revision of state aid formulas to assure more per student aid to districts having a high proportion of disadvantaged school age children.

The Welfare System

Our present system of public welfare is designed to save money instead of people, and tragically ends up doing neither. This system has two critical deficiencies:

First, it excludes large numbers of persons who are in great need, and who, if provided a decent level of support, might be able to become more productive and self-sufficient. No Federal funds are available for millions of unemployed and underemployed men and women who are needy but either aged, handicapped nor the parents of minor children.

Second, for those included, the system provides assistance well below the minimum necessary for a decent level of existence, and imposes restrictions that encourage continued dependency on welfare and undermine self-respect.

A welter of statutory requirements and administrative practices and regulations operate to remind recipients that they are considered untrustworthy, promiscuous, and lazy. Residence requirements prevent assistance to people in need who are newly arrived in the state. Searches of recipients' homes violate privacy. Inadequate social services compound the problems.

The Commission recommends that the Federal Government, acting with state and local governments where necessary, reform the existing welfare system to:

- Establish for recipients in existing welfare categories, uniform national standards of assistance at least as high as the annual "poverty level" of income, now set by the Social Security Administration at $3,335 per year for an urban family of four.

- Require that all states receiving Federal welfare contributions participate in the Aid to Families with Dependent Children-Unemployment Parents Program (AFDC-UP) that permits assistance to families with both father and mother in the home, thus aiding the family while it is still intact.

- Bear a substantially greater portion of all welfare costs—at least 90 percent of total payments.

- Increase incentives for seeking employment and job training, but remove restrictions recently enacted by the Congress that would compel mothers of young children to work.

- Provide more adequate social services through neighborhood centers and family-planning programs.

- Remove the freeze placed by the 1967 welfare amendments on the percentage of children in a State that can be covered by Federal assistance.

- Eliminate residence requirements.

As a long-range goal, the Commission recommends that the Federal Government seek to develop a national system of income supplementation based strictly on need with two broad and basic purposes:

- To provide, for those who can work or who do work, any necessary supplements in such a way as to develop incentives for fuller employment.

- To provide, for those who cannot work and for mothers who decide to remain with their children, a minimum standard of decent living, and to aid in saving children from the prison of poverty that has held their parents.

A broad system of supplementation would involve substantially greater Federal expenditures than anything now contemplated. The cost will range widely depending on the standard of need accepted as the "basic allowance" to individuals and families, and on the rate at which additional income above the level is taxed. Yet if the deepening cycle of poverty and dependence on welfare can be broken, if the children of the poor can be given the opportunity to scale the wall that now separates them from the rest of society, the return on this investment will be great indeed.

Housing

After more than three decades of fragmented and grossly underfunded Federal housing programs, nearly 6 million substandard housing units remain occupied in the United States.

The housing problem is particularly acute in the minority ghettos. Nearly two-thirds of all nonwhite families living in the central cities today live in neighborhoods marked by substandard housing and general urban blight. Two major factors are responsible:

First: Many ghetto residents simply cannot pay the rent necessary to support decent housing. In Detroit, for example, over 40 percent of the non-white occupied units in 1960 required rent of over 35 percent of the tenants' income.

Second: Discrimination prevents access to many nonslum areas, particularly the suburbs, where good housing exists. In addition, by creating a "back pressure" in the racial ghettos, it makes possible for landlords to break up apartments for denser occupancy, and keeps prices and rents of deteriorated ghetto housing higher than they would be in a truly free market.

To date, Federal programs have been able to do comparatively little to provide housing for the disadvantaged. In the 31-year history of subsidized Federal housing, only about 800,000 units have been constructed, with recent production averaging about 50,000 units a year. By comparison, over a period only 3 years longer, FHA insurance guarantees have made possible the construction of over 10 million middle and upper income units.

Two points are fundamental to the Commission's recommendations:

First: Federal housing programs must be given a new thrust aimed at overcoming the prevailing patterns of racial segregation. If this is not done, those programs will continue to concentrate the most impoverished and dependent segments of the population into the central-city ghettos where there is already a critical gap between the needs of the population and the public resources to deal with them.

Second: The private sector must be brought into the production and financing of low and moderate-rental housing to supply the capabilities and capital necessary to meet the housing needs of the Nation.

The Commission recommends that the Federal Government:

- Enact a comprehensive and enforceable Federal open-housing law to cover the sale or rental of all housing, including single-family homes.

- Reorient Federal housing programs to place more low- and moderate-income housing outside of ghetto areas.

- Bring within the reach of low- and moderate-income families within the next 5 years 6 million new and existing units of decent housing, beginning with 600,000 units in the next year.

To reach this goal we recommended:

- Expansion and modification of the rent supplement program to permit use of supplements for existing housing, thus greatly increasing the reach of the program.

- Expansion and modification of the below-market rate program to enlarge the interest subsidy to all sponsors, provide interest-free loans to nonprofit sponsors to cover preconstruction costs, and permit sale of projects to non-profit corporations, co-operatives, or condominiums.

- Creation of an ownership supplement program similar to present rent supplements, to make home ownership possible for low-income families.

- Federal writedown of interest rates on loans to private builders constructing moderate-rent housing.

- Expansion of the public housing program, with emphasis on small units on scattered sites, and leasing and "turnkey" programs.

- Expansion of the Model Cities program.

- Expansion and reorientation of the urban renewal program to give priority to projects directly assisting low-income households to obtain adequate housing.

Conclusion

One of the first witnesses to be invited to appear before this Commission was Dr. Kenneth B. Clark, a distinguished and perceptive scholar. Referring to the reports of earlier riot commissions, he said:

> I read that report * * * of the 1919 riot in Chicago, and it is as if I were reading the report of the investigating committee on the Harlem riot of '35, the report of the investigating committee on the Harlem riot of '43, the report of the McCone Commission on the Watts riot.
>
> I must again in candor say to you members of this Commission—it is a kind of Alice in Wonderland—with the same moving picture reshown over and over again, the same analysis, the same recommendations, and the same inaction.

These words come to our minds as we conclude this report.

We have provided an honest beginning. We have learned much. But we have uncovered no startling truths, no unique insights, no simple solutions. The destruction and the bitterness of racial disorder, the harsh polemics of black revolt and white repression have been seen and heard before in this country.

It is time now to end the destruction and the violence, not only in the streets of the ghetto but in the lives of people.

George L. Kelling & Mark H. Moore

The Evolving Strategy
of Policing

Policing, like all professions, learns from experience. It follows, then, that as modern police executives search for more effective strategies of policing, they will be guided by the lessons of police history. The difficulty is that police history is incoherent, its lessons hard to read. After all, that history was produced by thousands of local departments pursuing their own visions and responding to local conditions. Although that varied experience is potentially a rich source of lessons, departments have left few records that reveal the trends shaping modern policing. Interpretation is necessary.

Methodology

This essay presents an interpretation of police history that may help police executives considering alternative future strategies of policing. Our reading of police history has led us to adopt a particular point of view. We find that a dominant trend guiding today's police executives— a trend that encourages the pursuit of independent, professional autonomy for police departments—is carrying the police away from achieving their maximum potential, especially in effective crime fighting. We are also convinced that this trend in policing is weakening *public* policing relative to *private* security as the primary institution providing security to society. We believe that this has dangerous long-term implications not only for police departments but also for society. We think that this trend is shrinking rather than enlarging police capacity to help create civil communities. Our judgment is that this trend can be reversed only by refocusing police attention from the pursuit of professional autonomy to the establishment of effective problem-solving partnerships with the communities they police.

Delving into police history made it apparent that some assumptions that now operate as axioms in the field of policing (for example that effectiveness in policing depends on distancing police departments from

Source: George L. Kelling and Mark H. Moore (1988). "The Evolving Strategy of Policing." *Perspectives on Policing,* Number 4:1-15. Washington, DC: National Institute of Justice.

politics; or that the highest priority of police departments is to deal with serious street crime; or that the best way to deal with street crime is through directed patrol, rapid response to calls for service, and skilled retrospective investigations) are not timeless truths, but rather choices made by former police leaders and strategists. To be sure, the choices were often wise and far-seeing as well as appropriate to their times. But the historical perspective shows them to be choices nonetheless, and therefore open to reconsideration in the light of later professional experience and changing environmental circumstances.

We are interpreting the results of our historical study through a framework based on the concept of "corporate strategy."[1] Using this framework, we can describe police organizations in terms of seven interrelated categories:

- The sources from which the police construct the legitimacy and continuing power to act on society.

- The definition of the police function or role in society.

- The organizational design of police departments.

- The relationships the police create with the external environment.

- The nature of police efforts to market or manage the demand for their services.

- The principal activities, programs, and tactics on which police agencies rely to fulfill their mission or achieve operational success.

- The concrete measures the police use to define operational success or failure.

Using this analytic framework, we have found it useful to divide the history of policing into three different areas. These eras are distinguished from one another by the apparent dominance of a particular strategy of policing. The political era, so named because of the close ties between police and politics, dated from the introduction of police into municipalities during the 1840's, continued through the Progressive period, and ended during the early 1900's. The reform era developed in reaction to the political. It took hold during the 1930's, thrived during the 1950's and 1960's, began to erode in the 1970's. The reform era now seems to be giving way to an era emphasizing community problem solving.

By dividing policing into these three eras dominated by a particular strategy of policing, we do not mean to imply that there were clear boundaries between the eras. Nor do we mean that in those eras everyone policed in the same way. Obviously, the real history is far more complex than that. Nonetheless, we believe that there is a certain professional ethos that defines standards of competence, professionalism, and excellence in policing; that at any given time, one set of concepts is more powerful, more widely shared, and better understood than others; and that this ethos changes over time. Sometimes, this professional ethos has been explicitly articulated, and those who have articulated the concepts have been recognized as the leaders of their profession. O.W. Wilson, for example, was a brilliant expositor of the central elements of the reform strategy of policing. Other times, the ethos is implicit—accepted by all as the tacit assumptions that define the business of policing and the proper form for a police department to take. Our task is to help the profession look to the future by representing its past in these terms and trying to understand what the past portends for the future.

The Political Era

Historians have described the characteristics of early policing in the United States, especially the struggles between various interest groups to govern the police.[2] Elsewhere, the authors of this paper analyzed a portion of American police history in terms of its organizational strategy.[3] The following discussion of these elements of the police organizational strategy during the political era expands on that effort.

Legitimacy and Authorization

Early American police were authorized by local municipalities. Unlike their English counterparts, American police departments lacked the powerful, central authority of the crown to establish a legitimate, unifying mandate for their enterprise. Instead, American police derived both their authorization and resources from local political leaders, often as ward politicians. They were, of course, guided by the law as to what tasks to undertake and what powers to utilize. But their link to neighborhoods and local politicians was so tight that both Jordan[4] and Fogelson[5] refer to the early police as adjuncts to local political machines. The relationship was often reciprocal: political machines recruited and maintained police in office and on the beat, while police helped ward political leaders maintain their political offices by encouraging citizens to vote for certain candidates, discouraging them from voting for others, and, at times, by assisting in rigging elections.

The Police Function

Partly because of their close connection to politicians, police during the political era provided a wide array of services to citizens. Inevitably police departments were involved in crime prevention and control and order maintenance, but they also provided a wide variety of social services. In the late 19th century, municipal police departments ran soup lines; provided temporary lodging for newly arrived immigrant workers in station houses;[6] and assisted ward leaders in finding work for immigrants, both in police and other forms of work.

Organizational Design

Although ostensibly organized as a centralized, quasi-military organization with a unified chain of command, police departments of the political era were nevertheless decentralized. Cities were divided into precincts, and precinct-level managers often, in concert with the ward leaders, ran precincts as small-scale departments—hiring, firing, managing, and assigning personnel as they deemed appropriate. In addition, decentralization combined with primitive communications and transportation to give police officers substantial discretion in handling their individual beats. At best, officer contact with central command was maintained through the call box.

External Relationships

During the political era, police departments were intimately connected to the social and political world of the ward. Police officers were often recruited from the same ethnic stock as the dominant political groups in the localities, and continued to live in the neighborhoods they patrolled. Precinct commanders consulted often with local political representatives about police priorities and progress.

Demand Management

Demand for police services came primarily from two sources: ward politicians making demands on the organization and citizens making demands directly on beat officers. Decentralization and political authorization encouraged the first; foot patrol, lack of other means of transportation, and poor communications produced the latter. Basically, the demand for police services was received, interpreted, and responded to at the precinct and street levels.

Principal Programs and Technologies

The primary tactic of police during the political era was foot patrol. Most police officers walked beats and dealt with crime, disorder, and other problems as they arose, or as they were guided by citizens and precinct superiors. The technological tools available to police were limited. However, when call boxes became available, police administrators used them for supervisory and managerial purposes; and, when early automobiles became available, police used them to transport officers from one beat to another.[7] The new technology thereby increased the range, but did not change the mode, of patrol officers.

Detective divisions existed but without their current prestige. Operating from a caseload of "persons" rather than offenses, detectives relied on their caseload to inform on other criminals.[8] The "third degree" was a common means of interviewing criminals to solve crimes. Detectives were often especially valuable to local politicians for gathering information on individuals for political or personal, rather than offense-related, purposes.

Measured Outcomes

The expected outcomes of police work included crime and riot control, maintenance of order, and relief from many of the other problems of an industrializing society (hunger and temporary homelessness, for example). Consistent with their political mandate, police emphasized maintaining citizen and political satisfaction with police services as an important goal of police departments.

In sum, the organizational theory of the political era of policing included the following elements:

- Authorization—primarily political.

- Function—crime control, order maintenance, broad social services.

- Organizational design—decentralized and geographical.

- Relationship to environment—close and personal.

- Demand—managed through links between politicians and precinct commanders, and face-to-face contacts between citizens and foot patrol officers.

- Tactics and technology—foot patrol and rudimentary investigations.

- Outcome—political and citizen satisfaction with social order

The political strategy of early American policing had strengths. First, police were integrated into neighborhoods and enjoyed the support of citizens—at least the support of the dominant and political interests of an area. Second, and probably as a result of the first, the strategy provided useful services to communities. There is evidence that it helped contain riots. Many citizens believed that police prevented crimes or solved crimes when they occurred.[9] And the police assisted immigrants in establishing themselves in communities and finding jobs.

The political strategy also had weaknesses. First, intimacy with community, closeness to political leaders, and a decentralized organizational structure, with its inability to provide supervision of officers, gave rise to police corruption. Officers were often required to enforce unpopular laws foisted on immigrant ethnic neighborhood by crusading reformers (primarily of English and Dutch background) who objected to ethnic values[10] Because of their intimacy with the community, the officers were vulnerable to being bribed in return for nonenforcement or lax enforcement of laws. Moreover, police closeness to politicians created such forms of political corruption as patronage and police interference in elections[11] Even those few departments that managed to avoid serious financial or political corruption during the late 19th and early 20th centuries, Boston for example, succumbed to large-scale corruption during and after Prohibition.

Second, close identification of police with neighborhoods and neighborhood norms often resulted in discrimination against strangers and others who violated these norms, especially minority ethnic and racial groups. Often ruling their beats with the "ends of their nightsticks," police regularly targeted outsiders and strangers for rousting and "curbstone justice."[13]

Finally, the lack of organizational control over officers resulting from both decentralization and the political nature of many appointments to police positions caused inefficiencies and disorganization. The image of Keystone Cops—police as clumsy bunglers—was widespread and often descriptive of realities in American policing.

The Reform Era

Control over police by local politicians, conflict between urban reformers and local ward leaders over the enforcement of laws regulating the morality of urban migrants, and abuses (corruption, for example) that resulted from the intimacy between police and political leaders and citizens produced a continuous struggle for control over police during the late 19th and early 20th centuries.[14] Nineteenth-century attempts by civilians to reform police organizations by applying external pressures largely failed; 20th-century attempts at reform, originating from both internal and external forces, shaped contemporary policing as we knew it in the 1970's.[15]

Berkeley's police chief, August Vollmer, first rallied police executives around the idea of reform during the 1920's and early 1930's. Vollmer's vision of policing was the trumpet call: police in the post-flapper generation were to remind American citizens and institutions of the moral vision that had made America great and of their responsibility to maintain that vision.[16] It was Vollmer's protege, O.W. Wilson, however, who taking guidance from J. Edgar Hoover's shrewd transformation of the corrupt and discredited Bureau of Investigation into the honest and prestigious Federal Bureau of Investigation (FBI), became the principal administrative architect of the police reform organizational strategy.[17]

Hoover wanted the FBI to represent a new force for law and order, and saw that such an organization could capture a permanent constituency that wanted to an agency to take a stand against lawlessness, immorality, and crime. By raising eligibility standards and changing patterns of recruitment and training, Hoover gave the FBI agents stature as upstanding moral crusaders. By committing the organization to attacks on crimes such as kidnapping, bank robbery, and espionage—crimes that attracted wide publicity and required technical sophistication, doggedness, and a national jurisdiction to solve—Hoover established the organization's reputation for professional competence and power. By establishing tight central control over his agents, limiting their use of controversial investigation procedures (such as undercover operations) and keeping them out of narcotics enforcement, Hoover was also able to maintain an unparalleled record of integrity. That, too, fitted the image of a dogged, incorruptible crime-fighting organization. Finally, lest anyone fail to notice the important developments within the Bureau, Hoover developed impressive public relations programs that presented the FBI and its agents in the most favorable light. (For those of us who remember the 1940's, for example, one of the most popular radio phrases was, "The FBI in peace and war"—the introductory line in a radio program that portrayed a vigilant FBI protecting us from foreign enemies as well as villains on the "10 Most Wanted" list, another Hoover/FBI invention.)

Struggling as they were with reputations for corruption, brutality, unfairness, and downright incompetence, municipal police reformers found Hoover's path a compelling one. Instructed by O.W. Wilson's texts on police administration, they began to shape an organizational strategy for urban police analogous to the one pursued by the FBI.

Legitimacy and Authorization

Reformers rejected politics as the basis of police legitimacy. In their view, politics and political involvement was the *problem* in American policing. Police reformers therefore allied themselves with Progressives. They moved to end the close ties between political leaders and police. In some states, control over police was usurped by state government. Civil service eliminated patronage and ward influences in hiring and firing police officers. In some cities (Los Angeles and Cincinnati, for example), even the position of chief of police became a civil service position to be attained through examination. In others (such as Milwaukee), chiefs were given lifetime tenure by a police commission, to be removed from office only for cause. In yet others (Boston, for example), contracts for chiefs were staggered so as not to coincide with the mayor's tenure. Concern for separation of police from politics did not focus only on chiefs, however. In some cities, such as Philadelphia, it became illegal for patrol officers to live in the beats they patrolled. The purpose of all these changes was to isolate police as completely as possible from political influences.

Law, especially criminal law, and police professionalism were established as the principal bases of police legitimacy. When police were asked why they performed as they did, the most common answer was that they enforced the law. When they chose not to enforce the law— for instance, in a riot when police isolated an area rather than arrested looters—police justification for such action was found in their claim to professional knowledge, skills, and values which uniquely qualified them to make such tactical decisions. Even in riot situations, police rejected the idea that political leaders should make tactical decisions; that was a police responsibility.[18]

So persuasive was the argument of reformers to remove political influences from policing, that police departments became one of the most autonomous public organizations in urban government.[19] Under such circumstances, policing a city became a legal and technical matter left to the discretion of professional police executives under the guidance of law. Political influence of any kind on a police department came to be seen as not merely a failure of police leadership but as corruption in policing.

The Police Function

Using the focus on law as a basic source of police legitimacy, police in the reform era moved to narrow their functioning to crime control and criminal apprehension. Police agencies became *law enforcement* agencies. Their goal was to control crime. Their principal means was the use of criminal law to apprehend and deter offenders. Activities that drew the police into solving other kinds of community problems and relied on other kinds of responses were identified as "social work," and became the object of derision. A common line in police circles during the 1950's and 1960's was, "If only we didn't have to do social work, we could really do something about crime." Police retreated from providing emergency medical services as well—ambulance and emergency medical services were transferred to medical, private, or firefighting organizations.[20] The 1967 President's Commission on Law Enforcement and Administration of Justice ratified this orientation: heretofore, police had been conceptualized as an agency of urban government; the President's Commission reconceptualized them as part of the criminal justice system.

Organizational Design

The organization form adopted by police reformers generally reflected the *scientific* or *classical* theory of administration demonstrated by Frederick W. Taylor during the early 20th century. At least two assumptions attended classical theory. First, workers are inherently uninterested in work and, if left to their own devices, are prone to avoid it. Second, since workers have little or no interest in the substance of their work, the sole common interest between workers and management is found in economic incentives for workers. Thus, both workers and management benefit economically when management arranges work in ways that increase workers' productivity and link productivity to economic rewards.

Two central principles followed from these assumptions: division of labor and unity of control. The former posited that if tasks can be broken into components, workers can become highly skilled in particular components and thus more efficient in carrying out their tasks. The latter posited that the workers' activities are best managed by a *pyramid of control*, with all authority finally resting in one central office.

Using this classical theory, police leaders moved to routinize and standardize police work, especially patrol work. Police work became a form of crimefighting in which police enforced the law and arrested criminals if the opportunity presented itself. Attempts were made to limit discretion in patrol work: a generation of police officers was raised with the idea that they merely enforced the law.

If special problems arose, the typical response was to create special units (e.g., vice, juvenile, drugs, tactical) rather than to assign them to patrol. The creation of these special units, under central rather than precinct command, served to further centralize command and control and weaken precinct commanders.[21]

Moreover, police organizations emphasized control over workers through bureaucratic means of control: supervision, limited span of control, flow of instructions downward and information upward in the organization, establishment of elaborate record-keeping systems requiring additional layers of middle managers, and coordination of activities between various production units (e.g., patrol and detectives), which also required additional middle managers.

External Relationships

Police leaders in the reform era redefined the nature of a proper relationship between police officers and citizens. Heretofore, police had been intimately linked to citizens. During the era of reform policing, the new model demanded an impartial law enforcer who related to citizens in professionally neutral and distant terms. No better characterization of this model can be found than television's Sergeant Friday, whose response, "Just the facts, ma'am," typified the idea: impersonal and oriented toward crime solving rather than responsive the emotional needs of a victim.

The professional model also shaped the police view of the role of citizens in crime control. Police redefined the citizen role during an era when there was heady confidence about the ability of professionals to manage physical and social problems. Physicians would care for health problems, dentists for dental problems, teachers for educational problems, social workers for social adjustment problems, and police for crime problems. The proper role of citizens in crime control was to be relatively passive recipients of professional crime control services. Citizens' actions on their own behalf to defend themselves or their communities came to be seen as inappropriate, smacking of vigilantism. Citizens met their responsibilities when a crime occurred by calling police, deferring to police actions, and being good witnesses if called upon to give evidence. The metaphor that expressed that orientation to the community was that of the police as the "thin blue line." It connotes the existence of dangerous external threats to communities, portrays police as standing between that danger and good citizens, and implies both police heroism and loneliness.

Demand Management

Learning from Hoover, police reformers vigorously set out to sell their brand of urban policing.[22] They, too, performed on radio talk shows, consulted with media representatives about how to present police, engaged in public relations campaigns, and in other ways presented this image of police as crime fighters. In a sense, they began with an organizational capacity—anticrime police tactics—and intensively promoted it. This approach was more like selling than marketing. Marketing refers to the process of carefully identifying customer needs and then developing goods and services to meet those needs. Selling refers to having a stock of products or goods on hand irrespective of need and selling them. The reform strategy had as its starting point a set of police tactics (services) that police promulgated as much for the purpose of establishing internal control of police officers and enhancing the status of urban police as for responding to community needs or market demands.[23] The community "need" for rapid response to calls for service, for instance, was largely the consequence of police selling the service as efficacious in crime control rather than a direct demand from citizens.

Consistent with this attempt to sell particular tactics, police worked to shape and control demand for police services. Foot patrol, when demanded by citizens, was rejected as an outmoded, expensive frill. Social and emergency services were terminated or given to other agencies. Receipt of demand for police services was centralized. No longer were citizens encouraged to go to "their" neighborhood police officers or districts; all calls went to a central communications facility. When 911 systems were installed, police aggressively sold 911 and rapid response to calls for service as effective police service. If citizens continued to use district, or precinct, telephone numbers, some police departments disconnected those telephones or got new telephone numbers.[24]

Principal Programs and Technologies

The principal programs and tactics of the reform strategy were preventive patrol by automobile and rapid response to calls for service. Foot patrol, characterized as outmoded and inefficient, was abandoned as rapidly as police administrators could obtain cars.[25] The initial tactical reasons for putting police in cars had been to increase the size of the areas police officers could patrol and to take the advantage away from criminals who began to use automobiles. Under reform policing, a new theory about how to make the best tactical use of automobiles appeared.

O.W. Wilson developed the theory of preventive patrol by automobile as an anticrime tactic.[26] He theorized that if police drove conspicuously marked cars randomly through city streets and gave special attention to certain "hazards" (bars and schools, for example), a feeling of police omnipresence would be developed. In turn, that sense of omnipresence would both deter criminals and reassure good citizens. Moreover, it was hypothesized that vigilant patrol officers moving rapidly through city streets would happen upon criminals in action and be able to apprehend them.

As telephones and radios became ubiquitous, the availability of cruising police came to be seen as even more valuable: if citizens could be encouraged to call the police via telephone as soon as problems developed, police could respond rapidly to calls and establish control over situations, identify wrong-doers, and make arrests. To this end, 911 systems and computer-aided dispatch were developed throughout the country. Detective units continued, although with some modifications. The "person" approach ended and was replaced by the case approach. In addition, forensic techniques were upgraded and began to replace the old "third degree" or reliance on informants for the solution of crimes. Like other special units, most investigative units were controlled by central headquarters.

Measured Outcomes

The primary desired outcomes of the reform strategy were crime control and criminal apprehension.[27] To measure achievement of these outcomes, August Vollmer, working through the newly vitalized International Association of Chiefs of Police, developed and implemented a uniform system of crime classification and reporting. Later, the system was taken over and administered by the FBI and the *Uniform Crime Reports* became the primary standard by which police organizations measured their effectiveness. Additionally, individual officers' effectiveness in dealing with crime was judged by the number of arrests they made; other measures of police effectiveness included response time (the time it takes for a police car to arrive at the location of a call for service) and "number of passings" (the number of times a police car passes a given point on a city street). Regardless of all other indicators, however, the primary measure of police effectiveness was the crime rate as measured by the *Uniform Crime Reports*.

In sum, the reform organizational strategy contained the following elements:

- Authorization—law and professionalism.

- Function–crime control.

- Organizational design—centralized, classical.

- Relationship to environment—professionally remote.

- Demand—channeled through central dispatching activities.

- Tactics and technology—preventive patrol and rapid response to calls for service.

- Outcome—crime control.

In retrospect, the reform strategy was impressive. It successfully integrated its strategic elements into a coherent paradigm that was internally consistent and logically appealing. Narrowing police functions to crime fighting made sense. If police could concentrate their efforts on prevention of crime and apprehension of criminals, it followed that they could be more effective than if they dissipated their efforts on other problems. The model of police as impartial, professional law enforcers was attractive because it minimized the discretionary excesses which developed during the political era. Preventive patrol and rapid response to calls for service were intuitively appealing tactics, as well as means to control officers and shape and control citizen demands for service. Further, the strategy provided a comprehensive, yet simple, vision of policing around which police leaders could rally.

The metaphor of the thin blue line reinforced their need to create isolated independence and autonomy in terms that were acceptable to the public. The patrol car became the symbol of policing during the 1930's and 1940's; when equipped with radio, it was at the limits of technology. It represented mobility, power, conspicuous presence, control of officers, and professional distance from citizens.

During the late 1960's and 1970's, however, the reform strategy ran into difficulty. First, regardless of how police effectiveness in dealing with crime was measured, police failed to substantially improve their record. During the 1960's, crime began to rise. Despite large increases in the size of police departments and in expenditures for new forms of equipment (911 systems, computer-aided dispatch, etc.), police failed to meet their own or public expectations about their capacity to control crime or prevent its increase. Moreover, research conducted during the 1970's on preventive patrol and rapid response to calls for service suggested that neither was an effective crime control or apprehension tactic.[28]

Second, fear rose rapidly during this era. The consequences of this fear were dramatic for cities. Citizens abandoned parks, public transportation, neighborhood shopping centers, churches, as well as entire neighborhoods. What puzzled police and researchers was that levels of fear and crime did not always correspond: crime levels were low in some areas, but fear high. Conversely, in other areas levels of crime were high, but fear low. Not until the 1980's did researchers discover that fear is more closely correlated with disorder than with crime.[29] Ironically, order maintenance was one of those functions that police had been downplaying over the years. They collected no data on it, provided no training to officers in order maintenance activities, and did not reward officers for successfully conducting order maintenance tasks.

Third, despite attempts by police departments to create equitable police allocation systems and to provide impartial policing to all citizens, many minority citizens, especially blacks during the 1960's and 1970's, did not perceive their treatment as equitable or adequate. They protested not only police mistreatment, but lack of treatment—inadequate or insufficient services—as well.

Fourth, the civil rights and antiwar movements challenged police. This challenge took several forms. The legitimacy of police was questioned: students resisted police, minorities rioted against them, and the public, observing police via live television for the first time, questioned their tactics. Moreover, despite police attempts to upgrade personnel through improved recruitment, training, and supervision, minorities and then women insisted that they had to be adequately represented in policing if police were to be legitimate.

Fifth, some of the myths that undergirded the reform strategy—police officers use little or no discretion and the primary activity of police is law enforcement—simply proved to be too far from reality to be sustained. Over and over again research showed that use of discretion characterized policing at all levels and that law enforcement comprised but a small portion of police officers' activities.[30]

Sixth, although the reform ideology could rally police chiefs and executives, it failed to rally line police officers. During the reform era, police executives had moved to professionalize their ranks. Line officers, however, were managed in ways that were antithetical to professionalization. Despite pious testimony from police executives that "patrol is the backbone of policing," police executives behaved in ways that were inconsistent with classical organizational theory—patrol officers continued to have low status; their work was treated as if it were routinized and standardized; and petty rules governed issues such as hair length and off-duty behavior. Meanwhile, line officers received little guidance in use of discretion and were given few, if any, opportunities to make suggestions about their work. Under such circumstances, the increasing "grumpiness" of officers in many cities is not surprising, nor is the rise of militant unionism.

Seventh, police lost a significant portion of their financial support, which had been increasing or at least constant over the years, as cities found themselves in fiscal difficulties. In city after city, police departments were reduced in size. In some cities, New York for example, financial cutbacks resulted in losses of up to one-third of departmental personnel. Some, noting that crime did not increase more rapidly or that arrests decrease during the cutbacks, suggested that New York City had been overpoliced when at maximum strength. For those concerned about levels of disorder and fear in New York City, not to mention other problems, that came as a dismaying conclusion. Yet it emphasizes the erosion of confidence in that citizens, politicians, and academicians had in urban police—an erosion that was translated into lack of political and financial support.

Finally, urban police departments began to acquire competition: private security and the community crime control movement. Despite the inherent value of these developments, the fact that businesses, industries, and private citizens began to search for alternative means of protecting their property and persons suggests a decreasing confidence in either the capability or the intent of the police to provide the services citizens want.

In retrospect, the police reform strategy has characteristics similar to those that Miles and Snow[31] ascribe to a defensive strategy in the private sector. Some of the characteristics of an organization with a defensive strategy are (with specific characteristics of reform policing added in parentheses):

- Its market is stable and narrow (crime victims).

- Its success is dependent on maintaining dominance in a narrow, chosen market (crime control).

- It tends to ignore developments outside its domain (isolation).

- It tends to establish a single core technology (patrol).

- New technology is used to improve its current product or service rather than to expand its product or service line (use of computers to enhance patrol).

- Its management is centralized (command and control).

- Promotions generally are from within (with the exception of chiefs, virtually all promotions are from within).

- There is a tendency toward a functional structure with high degrees of specialization and formalization.

A defensive strategy is successful for an organization when market conditions remain stable and few competitors enter the field. Such strategies are vulnerable, however, in unstable market conditions and when competitors are aggressive.

The reform strategy was a successful strategy for police during the relatively stable period of the 1940's and 1950's. Police were able to sell a relatively narrow service line and maintain dominance in the crime control market. The social changes of the 1960's and 1970's, however, created unstable conditions. Some of the more significant changes included: the civil rights movement; migration of minorities into cities; the changing age of the population (more youths and teenagers); increases in crime and fear; increased oversight of police actions by courts; and the decriminalization and deinstitutionalization movements. Whether or not the private sector defense strategy properly applies to police, it is clear that the reform strategy was unable to adjust to the changing social circumstances of the 1960's and 1970's.

The Community Problem-Solving Era

All was not negative for police during the late 1970's and early 1980's, however. Police began to score victories which they barely noticed. Foot patrol remained popular, and in many cities citizens and political demands for it intensified. In New Jersey, the state funded the Safe and Clean Neighborhoods Program, which funded foot patrol in cities, often over the opposition of local chiefs of police.[32] In Boston, foot patrol was so popular with citizens that when neighborhoods were selected for foot patrol, politicians often made the announcements, especially during election years. Flint, Michigan, became the first city in memory to return to foot patrol on a citywide basis. It proved so popular there that citizens twice voted to increase their taxes to fund foot patrol—most recently by a two-thirds majority. Political and citizen demands for foot patrol continued to expand in cities throughout the United States. Research into foot patrol suggested it was more than just politically popular, it contributed to city life: it reduced fear, increased citizen satisfaction with police, improved police attitudes toward citizens, and increased the morale and job satisfaction of police.[33]

Additionally, research conducted during the 1970's suggested that one factor could help police improve their record in dealing with crime: information. If information about crimes and criminals could be obtained from citizens by police, primarily patrol officers, and could be properly managed by police departments, investigative and other units could significantly increase their effect on crime.[34]

Moreover, research into foot patrol suggested that at least part of the fear reduction potential was linked to the order maintenance activities of foot patrol officers.[35] Subsequent work in Houston and Newark indicated that tactics other than foot patrol that, like foot patrol, emphasized increasing the quantity and improving the quality of police-citizen interactions had outcomes similar to those of foot patrol (fear reduction, etc.).[36] Meanwhile, many other cities were developing programs, though not evaluated, similar to those in the foot patrol, Flint, and fear reduction experiments.[37]

The findings of foot patrol and fear reduction experiments, when coupled with the research on the relationship between fear and disorder, created new opportunities for police to understand the increasing concerns of citizens' groups about disorder (gangs, prostitutes, etc.) and to work with citizens to do something about it. Police discovered that when they asked citizens about their priorities, citizens appreciated the inquiry and also provided useful information—often about problems that beat officers might have been aware of, but about which departments had little or no official data (e.g., disorder). Moreover, given the ambiguities that surround both the definitions of disorder and the authority of police to do something about it, police learned that they had to seek authorization from local citizens to intervene in disorderly situations.[38]

Simultaneously, Goldstein's problem-oriented approach to policing[39] was being tested in several communities: Madison, Wisconsin; Baltimore County, Maryland; and Newport News, Virginia. Problem-oriented policing rejected the fragmented approach in which police deal with each incident, whether citizen- or police-initiated, as an isolated event with neither history nor future. Pierce's findings about calls for service illustrate Goldstein's point: 60 percent of the calls for service in any given year in Boston originated from 10 percent of the households calling the police.[40] Furthermore, Goldstein and his colleagues in Madison, Newport News, and Baltimore County discovered the following: police officers enjoy operating with a holistic approach to their work; they have the capacity to do it successfully; they can work with citizens and other agencies to solve problems; and citizens seem to appreciate working with police—findings similar to those of the foot patrol experiments (Newark and Flint)[41] and the fear reduction experiments (Houston and Newark).[42]

The problem confronting police, policymakers, and academicians is that these trends and findings seem to contradict many of the tenets that dominated police thinking for a generation. Foot patrol creates new intimacy between citizens and police. Problem solving is hardly the routinized and standardized patrol modality that reformers thought was necessary to maintain control of police and limit their discretion. Indeed, use of discretion is the *sine qua non* of problem-solving policing. Relying on citizen endorsement of order maintenance activities to justify police action acknowledges a continued or new reliance on political authorization for police work in general. And, accepting the quality of urban life as an outcome of good police service emphasizes a wider definition of the police function and the desired effects of police work.

These changes in policing are not merely new police tactics, however. Rather, they represent a new organizational approach, properly called a community strategy. The elements of that strategy are:

Legitimacy and Authorization

There is renewed emphasis on community, or political, authorization for many police tasks, along with law and professionalism. Law continues to be the major legitimating basis of the police function. It defines basic police powers, but it does not fully direct police activities in efforts to maintain order, negotiate conflicts, or solve community problems. It becomes one tool among many others. Neighborhood, or community, support and involvement are required to accomplish those tasks. Professional and bureaucratic authority, especially that which tends to isolate police and insulate them from neighborhood influences, is lessened as citizens contribute more to definitions of problems and identification of solutions. Although in some respects similar to the authorization of policing's political era, community authorization exists in a different political context. The civil service movement, the political centralization that grew out of the Progressive era, and the bureaucratization, professionalization, and unionization of police stand as counterbalances to the possible recurrence of the corrupting influences of ward politics that existed prior to the reform movement.

The Police Function

As indicated above, the definition of police function broadens in the community strategy. It includes order maintenance, conflict resolution, problem solving through the organization, and provision of services, as well as other activities. Crime control remains an important function, with an important difference, however. The reform strategy attempts to control crime directly through preventive patrol and rapid response to calls for service. The community strategy emphasizes crime control *and prevention* as an indirect result of, or an equal partner to, the other activities.

Organizational Design

Community policing operates from organizational assumptions different from those of reform policing. The idea that workers have no legitimate, substantive interest in their work is untenable when programs such as those in Flint, Houston, Los Angeles, New York City, Baltimore County, Newport News, and others are examined. Consulting with community groups, problem solving, maintaining order, and other such activities are antithetical to the reform ideal of eliminating officer discretion through routinization and standardization of police activities. Moreover, organizational decentralization is inherent in community policing: the involvement of police officers in diagnosing and responding to neighborhood and community problems necessarily pushes operational and tactical decisionmaking to the lower levels of the organization. The creation of neighborhood police stations (storefronts, for example), reopening of precinct stations, and establishment of beat offices (in schools, churches, etc.) are concrete examples of such decentralization.

Decentralization of tactical decisionmaking to precinct or beat level does not imply abdication of executive obligations and functions, however. Developing, articulating, and monitoring organizational strategy remain the responsibility of management. Within this strategy, operational and tactical decisionmaking is decentralized. This implies what may at first appear to be a paradox: while the number of managerial levels may decrease, the number of managers may increase. Sergeants in a decentralized regime, for example, have managerial responsibilities that exceed those they would have in a centralized organization.

At least two other elements attend this decentralization: increased participative management and increased involvement of top police executives in planning and implementation. Chiefs have discovered that programs are easier to conceive and implement if officers themselves are involved in their development through task forces, temporary matrix-like organizational units, and other organizational innovations that tap the wisdom and experience of sergeants and patrol officers. Additionally, police executives have learned that good ideas do not translate themselves into successful programs without executive involvement of the chief executive and his close agents in every stage of planning and implementation, a lesson learned in the private sector as well.[43]

One consequence of decentralized decisionmaking, participative planning and management, and executive involvement in planning is that fewer levels of authority are required to administer police organizations. Some police organizations, including the London Metropolitian Police (Scotland Yard), have begun to reduce the number of middle-management layers, while others are contemplating doing so. Moreover, as in the private sector, as computerized information gathering systems reach their potential in police departments, the need for middle managers whose primary function is data collection will be further reduced.

External Relationships

Community policing relies on an intimate relationship between police and citizens. This is accomplished in a variety of ways: relatively long-term assignment of officers to beats, programs that emphasize familiarity between citizens and police (police knocking on doors, consultations, crime control meetings for police and citizens, assignment to officers of "caseloads" of households with ongoing problems, problem solving, etc.), revitalization or development of Police Athletic League programs, educational programs in grade and high schools, and other programs. Moreover, police are encouraged to respond to the feelings and fears of citizens that result from a variety of social problems or from victimization.

Further, the police are restructuring their relationship with neighborhood groups and institutions. Earlier, during the reform era, police had claimed a monopolistic responsibility for crime control in cities, communities, and neighborhoods; now they recognize serious competitors in the "industry" of crime control, especially private security and the community crime movement. Whereas in the past police had dismissed these sources of competition or, as in the case of community crime control, had attempted to coopt the movement for their own purposes,[44] now police in many cities (Boston, New York, Houston, and Los Angeles, to name a few) are moving to structure working relationships or strategic alliances with neighborhood and community crime control groups. Although there is less evidence of attempts to develop alliances with the private security industry, a recent proposal to the National Institute of Justice envisioned an experimental alliance between the Fort Lauderdale, Florida, Police Department and the Wackenhut Corporation in which the two organizations would share responses to calls for service.

Demand Management

In the community problem-solving strategy, a major portion of demand is decentralized, with citizens encouraged to bring problems directly to beat officers or precinct offices. Use of 911 is discouraged, except for dire emergencies. Whether tactics include aggressive foot patrol as in Flint or problem solving as in Newport News, the emphasis is on police officers' interacting with citizens to determine the types of problems they are confronting and to devise solutions to those problems. In contrast to reform policing with its selling orientation, this approach is more like marketing: customer preferences are sought, and satisfying customer needs and wants, rather than selling a previously packaged product or service, is emphasized. In the case of police, they gather information about citizens' wants, diagnose the nature of the problem, devise possible solutions, and then determine which segments of the community they can best serve and which can be best served by other agencies and institutions that provide services, including crime control.

Additionally, many cities are involved in the development of demarketing programs.[45] The most noteworthy example of demarketing is in the area of rapid response to calls for service. Whether through the development of alternatives to calls for service, educational programs designed to discourage citizens from using the 911 system, or, as in a few cities, simply not responding to many calls for service, police actively attempt to demarket a program that had been actively sold earlier. Often demarketing 911 is thought of as a negative process. It need not be so, however. It is an attempt by police to change social, political, and fiscal circumstances to bring consumers' wants in line with police resources and to accumulate evidence about the value of particular police tactics.

Tactics and Technology

Community policing tactics include foot patrol, problem solving, information gathering, victim counseling and services, community organizing and consultation, education, walk-and-ride and knock-on-door programs, as well as regular patrol, specialized forms of patrol, and rapid response to emergency calls for service. Emphasis is placed on information sharing between patrol and detectives to increase the possibility of crime solution and clearance.

Measured Outcomes

The measures of success in the community strategy are broad: quality of life in neighborhoods, problem solution, reduction of fear, increased order, citizen satisfaction with police services, as well as crime control. In sum, the elements of the community strategy include:

- Authorization—community support (political), law, professionalism.

- Function—crime control, crime prevention, problem solving.

- Organizational design—decentralized, task forces, matrices.

- Relationship to environment—consultative, police defend values of law and professionalism, but listen to community concerns.

- Demand—channeled through analysis of underlying problems.

- Tactics and technology—foot patrol, problem solving, etc.

- Outcomes—quality of life and citizen satisfaction.

Conclusion

We have argued that there were two stages of policing in the past, political and reform, and that we are now moving into a third, the community era. To carefully examine the dimensions of policing during these eras, we have used the concept of organizational strategy. We believe that this concept can be used not only to describe the different styles of policing in the past and the present, but also to sharpen the understanding of police policymakers of the future.

For example, the concept helps explain policing's perplexing experience with team policing during the 1960's and 1970's. Despite the popularity of team policing with officers involved in it and with citizens, it generally did not remain in police departments for very long. It was usually planned and implemented with enthusiasm and maintained for several years. Then, with little fanfare, it would vanish—with everyone associated with it saying regretfully that for some reason it just did not work as a police tactic. However, a close examination of team policing reveals that it was a strategy that innovators mistakenly approached as a tactic. It had implications for authorization (police turned to neighborhoods for support), organizational design (tactical decisions were made at lower levels of the organization), definition of function (police broadened their service role), relationship to environment (permanent team members responded to the needs of small geographical areas), demand (wants and needs came to team members directly from citizens), tactics (consultation with citizens, etc.), and outcomes (citizen satisfaction, etc.). What becomes clear, though, is that team policing was a competing strategy with different assumptions about every element of police business. It was no wonder that it expired under such circumstances. Team and reform policing were strategically incompatible—one did not fit the other. A police department could have a small team policing unit or conduct a team policing experiment, but business as usual was reform policing.

Likewise, although foot patrol symbolizes the new strategy for many citizens, it is a mistake to equate the two. Foot patrol is a tactic, a way of delivering police services. In Flint, its inauguration has been accompanied by implementation of most of the elements of a community strategy, which has become business as usual. In most places, foot patrol is not accompanied by the other elements. It is outside the mainstream of "real" policing and often provided only as a sop to citizens and politicians who are demanding the development of different policing styles. This certainly was the case in New Jersey when foot patrol was evaluated by the Police Foundation.[46] Another example is in Milwaukee, where two police budgets are passed: the first is the police budget; the second, a supplementary budget for modest levels of foot patrol. In both cases, foot patrol is outside the mainstream of police activities and conducted primarily as a result of external pressures placed on departments.

It is also a mistake to equate problem solving or increased order maintenance activities with the new strategy. Both are tactics. They can be implemented either as part of a new organizational strategy, as foot patrol was in Flint, or as an "add-on," as foot patrol was in most of the cities in New Jersey. Drawing a distinction between organizational add-ons and a change in strategy is not an academic quibble; it gets to the heart of the current situation in policing. We are arguing that policing is in a period of transition from a reform strategy to what we call a community strategy. The change involves more than making tactical or organizational adjustments and accommodations. Just as policing went through a basic change when it moved from the political to the reform strategy, it is going through a similar change now. If elements of the emerging organizational strategy are identified and the policing institution is guided through the change rather than left blindly thrashing about, we expect that the public will be better served, policymakers and police administrators more effective, and the profession of policing revitalized.

A final point: the classical theory of organization that continues to dominate police administration in most American cities is alien to most of the elements of the new strategy. The new strategy will not accommodate to the classical theory: the latter denies too much of the real nature of police work, promulgates unsustainable myths about the nature and quality of police supervision, and creates too much cynicism in officers attempting to do creative problem solving. Its assumptions about workers are simply wrong.

Organizational theory has developed way beyond the stage it was at during the early 1900's, and policing does have organizational options that are consistent with the newly developing organizational strategy. Arguably, policing, which was moribund during the 1970's, is beginning a resurgence. It is overthrowing a strategy that was remarkable in its time, but which could not adjust to the changes of the recent decades. Risks attend the new strategy and its implementation. The risks, however, for the community and the profession of policing, are not as great as attempting to maintain a strategy that faltered on its own terms during the 1960's and 1970's.

Notes

[1] Kenneth R. Andrews, *The Concept of Corporate Strategy,* Homewood, Illinois, Richard D. Irwin, Inc. 1980.

[2] Robert M. Fogelson, *Big-City Police,* Cambridge, Harvard University Press, 1977; Samuel Walker, *A Critical History of Police Reform: The Emergence of Professionalism,* Lexington, Massachusetts, Lexington Books, 1977.

[3] Mark H. Moore and George L. Kelling, "To Serve and Protect: Learning From Police History," *The Public Interest,* 7, Winter 1983.

[4] K.E. Jordan, *Ideology and the Coming of Professionalism: American Urban Police in the 1920's and 1930's,* Dissertation, Rutgers University, 1972.

[5] Fogelson, *Big-City Police.*

[6] Eric H. Monkkonen, *Police in Urban America,* 1860-1920, Cambridge, Cambridge University Press, 1981.

[7] *The Newark Foot Patrol Experiment,* Washington, D.C., Police Foundation, 1981.

[8] John Eck, *Solving Crimes: The Investigation of Burglary and Robbery,* Washington, D.C., Police Executive Research Forum, 1984.

[9] Thomas A. Reppetto, *The Blue Parade,* New York, The Free Press, 1978.

[10] Fogelson, *Big-City Police*.

[11] Ibid.

[12] George L. Kelling, "Reforming the Reforms: The Boston Police Department," Occasional Paper, Joint Center for Urban Studies of M.I.T. and Harvard, Cambridge, 1983.

[13] George L. Kelling, "Juveniles and Police: The End of the Nightstick," in *From Children to Citizens, Vol. II: The Role of the Juvenile Court*, ed. Francis X. Hartmann, New York, Springer-Verlag, 1987.

[14] Walker, *A Critical History of Police Reform: The Emergence of Professionalism*.

[15] Fogelson, *Big-City Police*.

[16] Kelling, "Juveniles and Police: The End of the Nightstick."

[17] Orlando W. Wilson, *Police Administration*, New York: McGraw-Hill, 1950.

[18] "Police Guidelines," John F. Kennedy School of Government Case Program # C14-75-24, 1975.

[19] Herman Goldstein, *Policing a Free Society*, Cambridge, Massachusetts, Ballinger, 1977.

[20] Kelling, "Reforming the Reforms: The Boston Police Department."

[21] Fogelson, *Big-City Police*.

[22] William H. Parker, "The Police Challenge in Our Great Cities," *The Annals* 29 (January 1954): 5-13.

[23] For a detailed discussion of the differences between selling and marketing, see John L. Crompton and Charles W. Lamb, *Marketing Government and Social Services*, New York, John Wiley and Sons, 1986.

[24] Commissioner Francis "Mickey" Roache of Boston has said that when the 911 system was instituted there, citizens persisted in calling "their" police—the district station. To circumvent this preference, district telephone numbers were changed so that citizens would be inconvenienced if they dialed the old number.

[25] *The Newark Foot Patrol Experiment*.

[26] O.W. Wilson, *Police Administration*.

[27] A.E. Leonard, "Crime Reporting as a Police Management Tool," *The Annals* 29 (January 1954).

[28] George L. Kelling et al., *The Kansas City Preventive Patrol Experiment: A Summary Report*, Washington, D.C., Police Foundation, 1974; William Spelman and Dale K. Brown, *Calling the Police*, Washington, D.C., Police Executive Research Forum, 1982.

[29] *The Newark Foot Patrol Experiment*; Wesley G. Skogan and Michael G. Maxfield, *Coping with Crime*, Beverly Hills, California, Sage, 1981; Robert Trojanowicz, *An Evaluation of the Neighborhood Foot Patrol Program in Flint, Michigan*, East Lansing, Michigan State University, 1982.

[30] Mary Ann Wycoff, *The Role of Municipal Police Research as a Prelude to Changing It*, Washington, D.C., Police Foundation, 1982; Goldstein, *Policing a Free Society*.

[31] Raymond E. Miles and Charles C. Snow, *Organizational Strategy, Structure and Process*, New York, McGraw-Hill, 1978.

[32] *The Newark Foot Patrol Experiment*.

[33] *The Newark Foot Patrol Experiment*; Trojanowicz, *An Evaluation of the Neighborhood Foot Patrol Program in Flint, Michigan*.

[34] Tony Pate, et al., *Three Approaches to Criminal Apprehension in Kansas City: An Evaluation Report*, Washington, D.C., Police Foundation, 1976; Eck, *Solving Crimes: The Investigation of Burglary and Robbery*.

[35] James Q. Wilson and George L. Kelling, "Police and Neighborhood Safety: Broken Windows," *Atlantic Monthly*, March 1982: 29-38.

[36] Tony Pate et al., *Reducing Fear of Crime in Houston and Newark: A Summary Report*, Washington, D.C., Police Foundation, 1986.

[37] Jerome H. Skolnick and David H. Bayley, *The New Blue Line: Police Innovation in Six American Cities*, New York, The Free Press, 1986; Albert J. Reiss, Jr., *Policing a City's Central District: The Oakland Story*, Washington, D.C., National Institute of Justice, March 1985.

[38] Wilson and Kelling, "Police and Neighborhood Safety: Broken Windows."

[39] Herman Goldstein, "Improving Policing: A Problem-Oriented Approach," *Crime and Delinquency,* April 1979, 236-258.

[40] Glenn Pierce, et al., "Evaluation of an Experiment in Proactive Police Intervention in the Field of Domestic Violence Using Repeat Call Analysis," Boston, Massachusetts, The Boston Fenway Project, Inc., May 13, 1987.

[41] *The Newark Foot Patrol Experiment;* Trojanowicz, *An Evaluation of the Neighborhood Foot Patrol Program in Flint, Michigan.*

[42] Pate et al., *Reducing Fear of Crime in Houston and Newark: A Summary Report.*

[43] James. R. Gardner, Robert Rachlin, and H.W. Allen Sweeny, eds., *Handbook of Strategic Planning,* New York, John Wiley and Sons, 1986.

[44] Kelling, "Juveniles and Police: The End of the Nightstick."

[45] Crompton and Lamb, *Marketing Government and Social Services.*

[46] *The Newark Foot Patrol Experiment.*

Samuel Walker

"Broken Windows" and Fractured History: The Use and Misuse of History in Recent Police Patrol Analysis*

In a recent and provocative article entitled "Broken Windows," James Q. Wilson and George L. Kelling propose a new role orientation for the urban police force in America. They argue that the police should replace their current preoccupation with crime control and concentrate instead on dealing with small order maintenance problems. Their argument is based upon a synthesis of recent police research and an analysis of police history.

This article critiques the analysis of police history offered by Wilson and Kelling. It disputes their argument that American police officers enjoyed a high degree of legitimacy in the eyes of urban neighborhood residents in the years before the advent of the patrol car. It also offers a different interpretation of the impact of technological innovation upon patterns of police-citizen contacts during the past fifty years.

A fresh burst of creativity marks current thinking about police patrol in the United States. This revival follows a period of doubt and disorientation in the late 1970s when recent research shattered traditional assumptions about patrol strategy. The most notable proposal for a reorientation of police patrol is set forth in "Broken Windows" by James Q. Wilson and George L. Kelling. Drawing partly on recent patrol experiments and partly on a re-thinking of police history, Wilson and Kelling propose a return to what they see as an older "watchman" style of policing (Wilson and Kelling 1982).

Source: Samuel Walker (1984). "Broken Windows and Fractured History: The Use and Misuse of History in Recent Police Patrol Analysis," *Justice Quarterly*, 1:77-90. Reprinted courtesy of Samuel Walker, University of Nebraska at Omaha.

*The author would like to thank Lawrence W. Sherman and James Fyfe for their comments on an earlier draft of this article. A revised version was presented at the annual meeting of the American Society of Criminology, Denver, Colorado, November, 1983.

This paper examines the use of history by Wilson and Kelling in their proposal for reorienting police patrol. Because the historical analysis is central to their argument, its viability may well depend upon how well they have interpreted police history. Kelling develops his view of police history even more explicitly in a subsequent article co-authored with Mark H. Moore (Moore and Kelling 1983).

We shall argue here that Wilson, Kelling and Moore have misinterpreted police history in several important respects. Their proposal calls for a restoration—a return to a former tradition of police patrol. Joe McNamara, Chief of the San Jose police, has already responded to the "broken windows" thesis by arguing that the good old days weren't all that good (McNamara 1982). This paper elaborates upon that point and argues that the tradition of policing cited by Wilson, Kelling and Moore never existed. This does not necessarily mean that the broken windows thesis is completely invalid. But if there is merit in the style of police patrol Wilson and Kelling propose, that style will have to be created anew. There is no viable older tradition to restore. Obviously, this is a far more difficult and challenging proposition than they have suggested.

Policing and Broken Windows

Broken windows are a metaphor for the deterioration of neighborhoods. A broken window that goes unrepaired is a statement that no one cares about the quality of life in the neighborhood to bother fixing the little things that are wrong. While a broken window might be a small thing in and of itself, left unrepaired it becomes an invitation to further neglect. The result is a progressive deterioration of the entire neighborhood. Wilson and Kelling cite research in social psychology where abandoned cars were rapidly vandalized when some sign of prior vandalism invited further destructive acts (Zimbardo 1969).

Policing in America has failed, Wilson, Kelling and Moore argue, because it has neglected "the little things," the law enforcement equivalents of broken windows. This neglect is the product of the development of an efficiency-oriented, crime control-focused style of policing over the past fifty years. Eric Monkkonen argues that the shift toward crime control began even earlier and was substantially complete by 1920 (Monkkonen 1981).

Two developments in the 1930s launched a radical reorientation of police patrol. The first was the greatly increased use of the patrol car, which took the patrol officer off the street and isolated him from the public. The second was the development of the Uniform Crime Reports system which then became the basic measure of police "success."

By themselves, these two developments might not have exerted such a profound effect on policing. The crucial difference was the influence of O.W. Wilson who forged a coherent theory of police management in the late 1930s. Wilsonian theory emphasized the suppression of crime as the primary mission of policing. Fulfillment of this mission depended upon maximizing the efficiency of patrol coverage. The automobile allowed a patrol officer to cover his beat more often during one tour of duty, and to do so in a more unpredictable fashion than foot patrol.

Wilson became the leading proponent of one-officer cars, claiming that two single officer patrol cars were twice as efficient as one two-officer car. He recommended that patrol beats should be organized according to a workload formula which distributed the work evenly among patrol officers. Finally, he concluded that rapid response time would increase apprehensions and generally enhance public satisfaction with police service (Walker 1977; Fogelson 1977).

Wilson tirelessly propounded his gospel of efficiency from the late 1930s onward. His text *Police Administration* became "the bible" of police management and instructed an entire generation of police executives (Wilson and McLaren 1977). Police departments converted almost entirely from foot to automobile patrol, invested enormous sums of money in sophisticated communications equipment, and encouraged members of the public to avail themselves of their service.

Lost in this process were the personal aspects of routine policing. The car isolated officers from the people in the neighborhoods, which became nothing more than a series of "beat assignments" to the officers. The most professionalized departments, in fact, took extra measures to de-personalize policing. Frequent rotation of beat assignments was adopted as a strategy to combat corruption.

The crime control orientation meanwhile caused the police to concentrate on more serious crimes—primarily, the seven felonies that comprised the Crime Index. Significantly, the police actively adopted the UCR system as the measure of their performance. It was not something imposed on them (Manning 1977). The police lost interest in lesser violations of the law and routine nuisances because they just did not count. These nuisances included drunks, loud and intimidating groups of teenagers, public drug dealing, and the like.[1]

According to Wilson, Kelling and Moore, these nuisances are the "broken windows," the little things that convey the message that no one cares about the quality of life in this neighborhood. Wilson, Kelling and Moore base much of their argument on the recent Newark Foot Patrol Experiment (The Police Foundation 1981). The presence of officers on foot patrol did not reduce crime, but did make people feel safer.

---

[1] James Fyfe argues that prosecutorial and judicial indifference to minor "quality of life" offenses is also responsible for neighborhood deterioration and that the police should not be singled out as the major culprits. By implications, he suggests that reorienting the police role would be futile without simultaneously reorienting the priorities of prosecutors and judges. Personal correspondence, James Fyfe to Walker.

Officers were able to establish and enforce informal rules of behavior for the neighborhood. It was alright to be intoxicated in public but not to pass out in the gutter, for example. Wilson and Kelling also cite with apparent approval the technique used by some Chicago police officers to maintain order in public housing projects: if groups of teenagers were troublesome, the officers would simply chase them away. "We kick ass," one officer explained (Wilson and Kelling 1982:35).

The "Broken Windows" article argues that policing should be neighborhood-oriented. More officers should be deployed on foot, and those officers should concentrate less on catching criminals and more on enforcing neighborhood norms of behavior. To a certain extent it advocates a form of team policing, although with some important differences.

Team policing experiments in the 1970s did not emphasize foot patrol, gave insufficient attention to street-level patrol tactics, and maintained the traditional crime control focus. Indeed, the incompatibility of some elements of team policing with the prevailing organizational structure and management philosophy was one of the factors in the failure of early team policing experiments (Sherman 1973; U.S. Department of Justice 1977; Schwartz and Clarren 1977).

"Broken Windows" offers an alternative model precisely because it focuses on what officers would actually do. It characterizes the recommended style of policing as a return to an earlier (pre-1930s) style of "watchman" or "constabulary" policing. At this point we turn our attention to the historical analysis that underpins this argument.

The Historical Framework

The historical framework presented by Wilson, Kelling and Moore consists of three components: the near-term, which embraces the last fifteen years; the middle-term, which includes the last fifty years; and the long-term, which involves all of police history before the last fifty years.

Their reading of near-term history is excellent. One of the most important developments of the past fifteen years has unquestionably been the enormous expansion of our knowledge about all aspects of policing. We can now discuss in an informed fashion issues that were *terra incognita* to the staff of the President's Crime Commission (Walker 1983). The most important findings constitute a systematic demolition of the assumptions underlying O.W. Wilson's approach to police management. We have learned that adding more police or intensifying patrol coverage will not reduce crime and that neither faster response time nor additional detectives will improve clearance rates. Few authorities on policing today could endorse the basic Wilsonian idea that improved management in the deployment of patrol officers or detectives is likely to reduce the crime rate.

Wilson's, Kelling's and Moore's reading of the last fifty years of police history is mixed. They recognize the most significant developments in the period but misinterpret them in important respects. There are substantial implications of this misinterpretation for their proposed style of policing.

The development of American policing from the 1930s through the 1960s was a far more complex process than historians have led us to believe. Wilson, Kelling and Moore can be excused in large part because they have simply drawn upon the available historical scholarship. We will focus here on two aspects of police history since the 1930s which have not received sufficient attention. The first involves the impact of the patrol car and the second concerns the crime control orientation of policing.

The Technological Revolution

It is indeed true that American police departments largely converted from foot to automobile patrol between the 1930s and the present. We should, of course, be cognizant of the enormous variations that exist even today. Some departments are almost wholly motorized while others, primarily Eastern cities, sill make heavy use of foot patrol (Police Executive Research Forum 1981). And it is also true that car patrols remove officers from sidewalks, isolate them from casual contacts with ordinary citizens, and damage police-community relations. This analysis is part of the conventional wisdom about policing.

The impact of technology was paradoxical, however. The mid-century revolution in American policing involved not just the patrol car, but the car in conjunction with the telephone and the two-way radio. These served to bring police officers into far more intimate contact with people than ever before. While the patrol car isolated police officers in some respects, the telephone simultaneously increased the degree of contact in other respects. Let us examine this paradox in detail.

In the days of foot patrol, officers had extensive casual contacts with people. But they occurred primarily on the streets or in other public places. The police did not obtain entry to private residences. The reason for this is obvious: there was no mechanism whereby the ordinary citizen could effectively summon the police. The telephone radically altered that situation with profound ramifications for both policing and public expectations about the quality of life. Stinchcombe (1963) has discussed the impact of privacy considerations on routine police work.

The telephone made it possible for the ordinary citizen to summon the police, and the combination of the two-way radio and the patrol car allowed the police to respond quickly. As we know, the more professional departments acquired a fetish for responding as quickly as possible to all calls. The development of the 911 telephone number was simply the logical conclusion of this effort to advertise and encourage people to use police service. People have in fact availed themselves of this service. The number of calls for service has escalated to the point where serious attention has been given to the idea of restricting or otherwise managing those requests in the last few years (Gay 1977).

Technology radically alters the nature of police-citizen contacts. Most of those contacts now occur in private residences. Albert Reiss reports that 70% of all police-citizen contacts occur in private places, 12% in semi-public, and 18% in open public places (Reiss 1971:16). The police must not only gain access to private places, but observe the most intimate aspects of peoples' lives, and are asked to handle their most personal problems.

Research has confirmed that the bulk of police work involves domestic disputes and other problems arising from alcohol, drugs, mental illness, and poverty. Officers refer to all this as "bullshit" or "social work" because it is unrelated to what they believe to be their crime control mission.

Police-citizen contacts became increasingly skewed. The police lost contact with "ordinary" people and gained a great deal of contact with "problem" people, who included not just criminal offenders but those with multiple social problems. David Bayley and Harold Mendelsohn once observed that police officers had more direct knowledge about minorities than did the members of any other occupation. This knowledge was a direct product of the heavy demands upon police service placed by low-income and racial minorities (Bayley and Mendelsohn 1969:156).

Our understanding of the full impact of the telephone on policing remains problematic. Not all experts on policing accept the argument advanced here. Some argue that the police were indeed intimately involved in people's lives prior to the advent of the telephone.[2] Unfortunately, there is no empirical evidence that would permit the resolution of this question. Prior to the late 1950s, there were no observational studies of police patrol activities and thus we have no reliable evidence on what American police officers did on patrol in the pre-telephone era.[3]

The Revolution in Public Expectations

One consequence of the technological revolution in policing has been a parallel revolution in public expectations about the quality of life. The availability of police service created and fed a demand for

---

[2] Lawrence W. Sherman accepts this view and dissents from the argument advanced in this article. Personal correspondence, Lawrence W. Sherman to Walker.

[3] The debate is conducted largely on the basis of circumstantial evidence. Sherman, for example, believes that literary evidence is a reliable guide to past police practices and cites *A Tree Grows in Brooklyn* as one useful example. Personal Correspondence, Sherman to Walker.

those services. The establishment of the modern police in the early nine-teenth century was an initial phase of this process, which created the expectation that a certain level of public order would, or at least should, prevail (Silver 1967).

The technological revolution of the mid-twentieth century generat-ed a quantum leap in those expectations. Because there was now a mechanism for getting someone (the police) to "do something" about minor disorders and nuisances, people came to expect that they should not have to put up with such minor irritations. Thus, the general level of expectations about the quality of life—the amount of noise, the presence of "strange" or "undesirable" people—has undergone an enormous change. Three generations of Americans have learned or at least have come to believe that they should not have to put up with certain problems.

The police are both the source and the victims of this revolution. They have stimulated high levels of public expectations by their very presence and their policy of more readily available services. At the same time they are the prisoners of their own creation, swamped with an enormous service call workload. The recent effort to restrict or some-how manage this workload faces the problem of a public that expects rapid police response for any and every problem as a matter of right.

Documenting changes in public expectations concerning the police is difficult given the absence of reliable data about public attitudes or police practices prior to the late 1950s and early 1960s. Several indica-tors do provide evidence of short-term changes in public expectations. The development of three-digit (911) emergency phone numbers for the police increased the number of service calls. In Omaha, Nebraska, for example, the number of patrol car dispatches increased by 36% between 1969 and 1971, presumably as a result of a new 911 phone number (Walker 1983:110). These figures represent the dispatch of a patrol car, not the number of incoming calls. Omaha police officials estimate that about 35% of all calls do not result in a dispatch.

Additional evidence is found in data on the number of civilian com-plaints about police misconduct. In New York City, for example, the number of complaints filed with the Civilian Complaint Review Board (CCRB) increased from about 200 per year in 1960-62 to just over 2000 per year in 1967-68 and more than 3000 annually in 1971-74. It would be difficult to believe that the conduct of New York City police officers deteriorated by a factor of 10 or 15 during this period. Rather, the increase is probably the result of a lower threshold of tolerance for police misconduct on the part of citizens and the increased availability of an apparent remedy for perceived misconduct.

During the period under discussion, the procedures of the New York CCRB were reorganized several times. Each reorganization facili-tated complaint filing and at the same time heightened public awareness of this particular remedy (Kahn 1975:113). The data on civilian complaints supports the argument made herein concerning police services generally: the availability of a service or remedy stimulates demand for that service, thereby altering basic expectations.

The Mythology of Crime Control

The conventional wisdom states that police organize their efforts around the goal of crime control. Wilson, Kelling and Moore restate this conventional wisdom, but the matter is a bit more complex.

There is an important distinction between the self-image of the police and the day-to-day reality of routine policing (Goldstein 1977). The emphasis on crime control is and has been largely a matter of what the police say they are doing. Peter Manning argues persuasively that the police consciously created and manipulated this self-image as a way of establishing greater professional and political autonomy (Manning 1977).

As we have seen, however, the day to day reality of policing contradicted this self-image. The sharp contrast between the crime-fighting imagery of the police and the peacekeeping reality of police activities was one of the first and most important findings of the flood of police research that began in the 1960s. When Wilson, Kelling and Moore suggest that the police are completely crime control-oriented they seriously misrepresent the nature of contemporary policing.

The discrepancy between crime control imagery and operational reality also becomes evident when we look more closely at how police departments utilize their resources. The most recent Survey of Police Operational and Administrative Practices reveals enormous variations among departments (Police Executive Research Forum 1981). Many still distribute their patrol officers equally among three shifts, ignoring even the most rudimentary workload formulas, which were first developed by O.W. Wilson over forty years ago (Wilson and McLaren 1977: Appendix J). Departments typically do not revise the boundaries of their patrol districts on a regular basis. Districts remain unchanged for ten or twenty years, or longer. Meanwhile, the composition of the urban environment changes radically, as older areas are depopulated, new residential areas are created, and so on.

The Question of Legitimacy

The most important long-term development in American policing, according to Wilson, Kelling and Moore, has been the loss of political legitimacy. There can be little doubt that legitimacy, by which we mean acceptance of police authority by the public, is a major problem today.

The interpretation of police history offered by Wilson, Kelling and Moore, which purports to explain how that legitimacy was lost, is seriously flawed. The evidence completely contradicts the thrust of their argument.

The police in the nineteenth century were not merely the "adjuncts" of the machine, as Robert Fogelson (1977) suggests, but were central cogs in it. Wilson, Kelling and Moore maintain that this role offered certain benefits for the police, which reformers and historians alike have overlooked.

As cogs in the machine, the police served the immediate needs of the different neighborhood. Political control was highly decentralized and local city councilmen or ward bosses exercised effective control over the police. Thus, the police carried out a wide range of services. Historians have rediscovered the social welfare role of the police, providing food and lodging for vagrants (Walker 1977; Monkkonen 1981). The police also performed political errands and were the means by which certain groups and individuals were able to corrupt the political process. These errands included open electioneering, rounding up the loyal voters, and harassing the opponents. Police also enforced the narrow prejudices of their constituents, harassing "undesirables" or discouraging any kind of "unwelcome" behavior.

Wilson, Kelling and Moore concede that there was a lack of concern for due process, but argue that there was an important trade-off. By virtue of serving the immediate needs and narrow prejudices of the neighborhoods, the police gained an important degree of political legitimacy. They were perceived as faithful servants and enjoyed the resulting benefits. All of this was destroyed by the reforms of the twentieth century. The patrol car removed officers from the streets, while the new "professional" style dictated an impersonal type of policing. Legal concerns with due process denied officers the ability to use the tactics of rough justice by which they had enforced neighborhood community norms.

This historical analysis is central to the reorientation of policing presented in the "Broken Windows" article. Wilson, Kelling and Moore propose that the lost political legitimacy could be re-established by what they view as the older "watchman" style of policing. Unfortunately, this historical analysis is pure fantasy.

Historians are unanimous in their conclusion that the police were at the center of urban political conflict in the nineteenth century. In many instances policing was the paramount issue and in some cases the only issue. Historians disagree only on their interpretation of the exact nature of this political conflict. The many experiments with different forms of administrative control over the police were different forms of administrative control over the police (the last of which survives only in Missouri) were but one part of this long and bitter struggle for political control (Walker 1977; Fogelson 1977).

To say that there was political conflict over the police means that the police lacked political legitimacy. Their authority was not accepted by the citizenry. Wilson, Kelling and Moore are seriously in error when they suggest that the police enjoyed substantial legitimacy in the pre-technology era.

The lack of legitimacy is further illustrated by the nature of the conflicts surrounding the police. Non-enforcement of the various laws designed to control drinking was the issue that most often roused the so-called "reformers" to action. Alcohol consumption was a political issue with many dimensions. In some respects it was an expression of ethnic conflict, pitting sobersided Anglo Saxons against the heavy-drinking Irish and Germans. Drinking was also a class issue. Temperance and, later, prohibition advocates tended either to come from the middle class or at least define themselves in terms of the values of hard work, sobriety, thrift and upward mobility (Gusfield 1963). When nineteenth century Americans fought over the police and the enforcement of the drinking laws, that battle expressed the deepest social conflicts in American society.

In one of the finest pieces of historical scholarship on the American police, Wilbur Miller explores the question of legitimacy from an entirely different angle (Miller 1977). The great difference between the London and New York City police was precisely the extent to which officers in New York were denied the grant of legitimacy enjoyed by their counterparts in London. Miller further argues that the problem of legitimacy was individualized in New York City. Each officer faced challenges to his personal authority and had to assert his authority on a situational level.

Miller does not argue that challenges to police legitimacy were patterned according to class, ethnicity or race. Thus, an Irish-American cop was just as likely to be challenged by a fellow countryman as he was by someone of a different ethnic background. To be sure, the poor, political radicals, blacks, and other people deemed "undesirable" were victimized more often by the police than were other groups, but it does not follow that the police enjoyed unquestioned authority in the eyes of those people who were members of the same class and ethnic groups as police officers.

The Myth of the Watchman

With their argument that the nineteenth century police enjoyed political legitimacy, Wilson, Kelling and Moore have resurrected in slightly different garb the old myth of the friendly cop on the beat. They offer this older "watchman" style of policing as a viable model for contemporary policing. Quite apart from the broader question of political legitimacy, their argument turns on the issue of on-the-street police behavior.

Historians have not yet reconstructed a full picture of police behavior in the nineteenth century. At best, historians can make inferences about this behavior from surviving records. None of the historical accounts published to date presents a picture of policing that could be regarded as a viable model for the present.

What do we know about routine policing in the days before the patrol car? There is general agreement that officers did not necessarily do much work at all. Given the primitive state of communications technology, patrol officers were almost completely on their own and able to avoid effective supervision (Rubinstein 1974). Evidence suggests that evasion of duty was commonplace. We also know that corruption was the norm. Mark Haller (1976) suggests that corruption was possibly the primary objective of all of municipal government, not just the police department.

Wilbur Miller (1977), meanwhile, places the matter of police brutality in a new and convincing light. His argument that brutality was a response to the refusal of citizens to grant the police legitimacy speaks directly to the point raised by Wilson, Kelling and Moore.

Recently some historians have attempted to draw a more systematic picture of police law enforcement activities. The most convincing picture is drawn by Lawrence Friedman and Robert Percival (1981) in their study of the Oakland police between 1870 and 1910. They characterize police arrest patterns as a giant trawling operation. The typical arrestee was a white, working class adult male who was drunk and was arrested for intoxication, disturbing the peace, or some related offense. But there was nothing systematic about police operations. The people swept up into their net were simply unlucky—there was no reason why they should have been arrested rather than others whose behavior was essentially the same. Nor was it apparent, in Friedman's and Percival's view, that the police singled out any particular categories of people for especially systematic harassment.

The argument offered by Wilson, Kelling and Moore turns in part on the question of purpose: what the police saw themselves doing. Historians have established that police officers had a few purposes. The first was to get and hold the job. The second was to exploit the possibilities for graft that the job offered. A third was to do as little actual patrol work as possible. A fourth involved surviving on the street, which meant establishing and maintaining authority in the face of hostility and overt challenges to that authority. Finally, officers apparently felt obliged to go through the motions of "real" police work by arresting occasional miscreants.

We do not find in this picture any conscious purpose of fighting crime or serving neighborhood needs. That is precisely the point made

by Progressive era reformers when they indicted the police for inefficiency. Wilson, Kelling and Moore have no grounds for offering this as
a viable model for contemporary policing. Chief McNamara is right:
the good old days were not that good.

The watchman style of policing described by Wilson, Kelling and
Moore can also be challenged from a completely different perspective.
The idea that the police served the needs of local neighborhoods and
thereby enjoyed political legitimacy is based on a highly romanticized
view of nineteenth century neighborhood life. Urban neighborhoods
were not stable and homogenous little villages nestled in the city. They
were heterogeneous, and the rate of geographic mobility was even higher than contemporary rates. Albert Reiss (1971: 209-210) in *Police and
the Public* critiques recent "community control" proposals on these
very grounds: they are based on the erroneous impression that neighborhoods are stable, homogeneous and relatively well-defined.

Summary and Conclusions

In "Broken Windows," James Q. Wilson and George Kelling offer a
provocative proposal for reorienting police patrol. Their argument is
based primarily on an historical analysis of American policing. They
propose a return to a watchman style of policing, which they claim
existed before the advent of crime control oriented policing in the
1930s. This historical analysis is further developed in a subsequent article by Kelling and Moore (1983).

In this article we have examined the historical analysis used by these
three authors. We find it flawed on several fundamental points.

First, the depersonalization of American policing from the 1930s
onward has been greatly exaggerated. While the patrol car did isolate
the police in some respects, the telephone brought about a more intimate form of contact between police and citizen by allowing the police
officer to enter private residences and involving them in private disputes
and problems.

Second, the crime control orientation of the police has been greatly
exaggerated. Crime control is largely a matter police rhetoric and self-
image. Day-to-day policing is, on the other hand, primarily a matter of
peacekeeping.

Third, there is no historical evidence to support the contention that
the police formerly enjoyed substantial political legitimacy. To the contrary, all the evidence suggests that the legitimacy of the police was one
of the major political controversies throughout the nineteenth century
and well into the twentieth.

Fourth, the watchman style of policing referred to by Wilson,
Kelling and Moore is just as inefficient and corrupt as the reformers

accuse it of being. It does not involve any conscious purpose to serve neighborhood needs and hardly serves as a model for revitalized contemporary policing.

Where does this leave us? We should not throw the proverbial baby out with the bath water. The fact that Wilson and Kelling construct their "Broken Windows" thesis on a false and heavily romanticized view of the past does not by itself invalidate their concept of a revitalized police patrol. They correctly interpret the lessons of recent police research. Suppression of crime is a will-of-the-wisp which the police should no longer pursue. Enhancement of public feelings of safety, however, does appear to be within the grasp of the police. A new form of policing based on the apparent lessons of the Newark Foot Patrol Experiment, the failures of team policing experiments, and the irrelevance of most official police-community relations programs seems to be a goal that is both worth pursuing and feasible.

Our main point here is simply that such a revitalized form of policing would represent something entirely new in the history of the American police. There is no older tradition worthy of restoration. A revitalized, community-oriented policing would have to be developed slowly and painfully.

There should be no mistake about the difficulty of such a task. Among other things, recent research on the police clearly demonstrates the enormous difficulty in changing either police officer behavior and/or the structure and process of police organization. Yet at the same time, the history reviewed here does suggest that fundamental long-term changes in policing are indeed possible. Change is a constant; shaping that change in a positive way is the challenge.

References

Bailey, D. and Mendelsohn, H. (1969) *Minorities and the Police*. New York: The Free Press.

Fogelson, R. (1977) *Big City Police*. Cambridge: Harvard University Press.

Friedman, L.M. and Percival, R.V. (1981) *The Roots of Justice*. Chapel Hill: University of North Carolina Press.

Gay, W. (1977) *Improving Patrol Productivity*, Volume I, Routine Patrol. Washington: Government Printing Office.

Goldstein, H. (1977) *Policing a Free Society*. Cambridge: Ballinger.

Gusfield, J. (1963) *Symbolic Crusade: Status Politics and the American Temperance Movement*. Urbana: University of Illinois Press.

Haller M. (1976) "Historical Roots of Police Behavior: Chicago, 1890-1925," *Law and Society Review* 10 (Winter):303-324.

Kahn, R. (1975) "Urban Reform and Police Accountability in New York City, 1950-1974." In *Urban Problems and Public Policy*, edited by R.L. Lineberry and L.H. Masotti. Lexington, Lexington Books.

McNamara, J.D. (1982) "Dangerous Nostalgia for the Cop on the Beat." *San Jose Mercury-News,* May 2.

Manning, P.K. (1977) *Police Work.* Cambridge: MIT Press.

Miller, W. (1977) *Cops and Bobbies.* Chicago: University of Chicago Press.

Monkkonen, E. (1981) *Police in Urban America, 1860-1920.* Cambridge: Cambridge University Press.

Moore, M.H. and Kelling, G.L. (1983) "To Serve and Protect: Learning from Police History." *The Public Interest* 70: 49-65.

Police Executive Research Forum (1981) *Survey of Police Operational and Administrative Practices—1981.* Washington: Police Executive Research Forum.

Police Foundation (1981) *The Newark Foot Patrol Experiment.* Washington: The Police Foundation.

Reiss, A. (1971) *The Police and the Public.* New Haven: Yale University Press.

Rubinstein, J. (1974) *City Police.* New York: Ballantine Books.

Schwartz, A.I. and Clarren, S.N. (1977) *The Cincinnati Team Policing Experiment.* Washington: The Police Foundation.

Sherman, L.W. (1973) *Team Policing: Seven Case Studies.* Washington: The Police Foundation.

Silver, A. (1967) "The Demand for Order in Civil Society." In *The Police: Six Sociological Essays,* ed. by David J. Bordua. New York: John Wiley.

Stinchcombe, A. (1963) "Institutions of Privacy in the Determination of Police Administrative Practice." *American Journal of Sociology* 69 (September): 1501-60.

U.S. Department of Justice (1977) *Neighborhood Team Policing.* Washington: Government Printing Office.

Walker, S. (1983) *The Police in America: An Introduction.* New York: McGraw-Hill.

—— (1977) *A Critical History of Police Reform: The Emergence of Professionalization.* Lexington: Lexington Books.

Wilson, J.Q. and Kelling, G.L. (1982) "Broken Windows: Police and Neighborhood Safety." *Atlantic Monthly* 249 (March): 29-38.

Wilson, O.W. and McLaren, R.C. (1977) *Police Administration.* Fourth ed. New York: McGraw-Hill.

Zimbardo, P.G. (1969) "The Human Choice: Individuation, Reason, and Order versus Deindividuation, Impulse, and Chaos." In *Nebraska Symposium on Motivation,* edited by W. J. Arnold and D. Levine. Lincoln: University of Nebraska Press.

Egon Bittner

Popular Conceptions
about the Character of Police Work

The abandonment of the norm-derivative approach to the definition of the role of the police in modern society immediately directs attention to a level of social reality that is unrelated to the ideal formulations. Whereas in terms of these formulations police activity derives its meaning from the objectives of upholding the law, we find that in reality certain meaning features are associated with police work that are largely independent of the objectives. That is, police work is generally viewed as having certain character traits we take for granted, and which control dealings between policemen and citizens, on both sides. Though we are lacking in adequate evidence about these matters, the perceived traits we will presently discuss are universally accepted as present and the recognition of their presence constitutes a realistic constraint on what is expected of the police and how policemen actually conduct themselves. It is important to emphasize that even while some of these ideas and attitudes are uncritically inherited from the past they are far from being totally devoid of realism. In the police literature these matters are typically treated under either euphemistic or cynical glosses. The reason for this evasion is simple, the Sunday school vocabulary we are forced to employ while talking about any occupational pursuit as dignified, serious, and necessary forces us to be either hypocritical or disillusioned, and prevents us from dealing realistically with the facts and from being candid about opinion.

Among the traits of character that are commonly perceived as associated with police work, and which thus constitute in part the social reality within which the work has to be done, the following three are of cardinal importance.

1. Police work is a tainted occupation. The origins of the stigma are buried in the distant past and while much has been said and done to erase it, these efforts have been notably unsuccessful. Medieval watchmen, recruited from among the ranks of the destitute and subject to satirical portrayals, were perceived to belong to the world of shadows

Source: Egon Bittner (1967). Chapter 2, "Popular Conceptions About the Character of Police Work," pp. 6-14; Chapter 6, "The Capacity to Use Force as the Core of the Police Role," pp. 36-47. In *The Functions of Police in Modern Society*. Washington, DC: National Institute of Mental Health.

they were supposed to contain.[10] During the period of the absolute monarchy the police came to represent the underground aspects of tyranny and political repression, and they were despised and feared even by those who ostensibly benefited from their services. No one can say how much of the old attitude lives on; some of it probably seeps into modern consciousness from the continued reading of nineteenth century romantic literature of the Victor Hugo variety. And it cannot be neglected that the mythology of the democratic polity avidly recounts the heroic combat against the police agents of the old order. But even if the police officer of today did not evoke the images of the past at all, he would still be viewed with mixed feelings, to say the least. For in modern folklore, too, he is a character who is ambivalently feared and admired, and no amount of public relations work can entirely abolish the sense that there is something of the dragon in the dragon-slayer.[11] Because they are posted on the perimeters of order and justice in the hope that their presence will deter the forces of darkness and chaos, because they are meant to spare the rest of the people direct confrontations with the dreadful, perverse, lurid, and dangerous, police officers are perceived to have powers and secrets no one else shares. Their interest in and competence to deal with the untoward surrounds their activities with mystery and distrust. One needs only to consider the thoughts that come to mind at the sight of policemen moving into action: here they go to do something the rest of us have no stomach for! And most people naturally experience a slight tinge of panic when approached by a policeman, a feeling against which the awareness of innocence provides no adequate protection. Indeed, the innocent in particular typically do not know what to expect and thus have added, even when unjustified, reasons for fear. On a more mundane level, the mixture of fear and fascination that the police elicit is often enriched by the addition of contempt. Depending on one's position in society, the contempt may draw on a variety of sources. To some the leading reason for disparaging police work derives from the suspicion that those who do battle against evil cannot themselves live up fully to the ideals they presumably defend. Others make the most of the circumstance that police work is a low-paying occupation, the requirements for which can be met by men who are poorly educated. And some, finally, generalize from accounts of police abuses that come to their attention to the occupation as a whole.

It is important to note that the police do very little to discourage unfavorable public attitudes. In point of fact, their sense of being out of favor with a large segment of the society has led them to adopt a petu-

---

[10] Werner Dankert, *Unehrliche Menschen: Die Verfehmten Berufe,* Bern: Francke Verlag, 1963.

[11] G.S. McWatters wrote about the typical policeman, after many years of being one himself, "He is the outgrowth of a diseased and corrupted state of things, and is, consequently, morally diseased himself," quoted in Lane, *op. cit. supra,* Note 2 at p. 69.

lant stance and turned them to courting the kinds of support which, ironically, are nothing but a blatant insult. For the movement that is known by the slogan, "Support your local police," advocates the unleashing of a force of mindless bullies to do society's dirty work. Indeed, if there is still some doubt about the popular perception of police work as a tainted occupation, it will surely be laid to rest by pointing to those who, under the pretense of taking the side of the police, imply that the institution and its personnel are uniformly capable and willing to act out the baser instincts inherent in all of us.

In sum, the taint that attaches to police work refers to the fact that policemen are viewed as the fire it takes to fight fire, that they in the natural course of their duties inflict harm, albeit deserved, and that their very existence attests that the nobler aspirations of mankind do not contain the means necessary to insure survival. But even as those necessities are accepted, those who accept them seem to prefer to have no part in acting upon them, and they enjoy the more than slightly perverse pleasure of looking down on the police who take the responsibility of doing the job.

2. Police work is not merely a tainted occupation. To draw a deliberately remote analogy, the practice of medicine also has its dirty and mysterious aspects. And characteristically dealings with physicians also elicit a sense of trepidated fascination. But in the case of medicine, the repulsive aspects, relating to disease, pain and death, are more than compensated by other features, none of which are present in police work. Of the compensatory features, one is of particular relevance to our concerns. No conceivable human interest could be opposed to fighting illness; in fact, it is meaningless to suppose that one could have scruples in opposing disease. But the evils the police are expected to fight are of a radically different nature. Contrary to the physician, the policeman is always opposed to some articulated or articulable human interest. To be sure, the police are, at least in principle, opposed to only reprehensible interests or to interest lacking in proper justification. But even if one were to suppose that they never err in judging legitimacy—a farfetched supposition, indeed—it would still remain the cage that police work can, with very few exceptions, accomplish something *for* somebody only by proceeding against someone else. It does not take great subtlety of perception to realize that standing between man and man locked in conflict inevitably involves profound moral ambiguities. Admittedly, few of us are constantly mindful of the saying, "He that is without sin among you, let him cast the first stone . . .", but only the police are explicitly required to forget it. The terms of their mandate and the circumstances of their practices do not afford them the leisure to reflect about the deeper aspects of conflicting moral claims. Not only are they required to proceed forcefully against all appearances of transgression but they are also expected to penetrate the appearance of innocence to discover craftiness hiding under its cloak. While most of us

risk only the opprobrium of foolishness by being charitable or gullible, the policeman hazards violating his duty by letting generosity or respect for appearances govern his decisions.

Though it is probably true that persons who are characterologically inclined to see moral and legal problems in black and white tend to choose police work as a vocation more often than others, it is important to emphasize that the need to disregard complexity is structurally built into the occupation. Only after a suspect is arrested, or after an untoward course of events is stopped, is there time to reflect on the merits of the decision and, typically, that reflective judgment is assigned to other public officials. Though it is expected that policemen will be judicious and that experience and skill will guide them in the performance of their work, it is foolish to expect that they could always be both swift and subtle. Nor is it reasonable to demand that they prevail, where they are supposed to prevail, while hoping that they will always handle resistance gently. Since the requirement of quick and what is often euphemistically called aggressive action is difficult to reconcile with error-free performance, police work is, by its very nature, doomed to be often unjust and offensive to someone. Under the dual pressure to "be right" and to "do something," policemen are often in a position that is compromised even before they act.[12]

In sum, the fact that policemen are required to deal with matters involving subtle human conflicts and profound legal and moral questions, without being allowed to give the subtleties and profundities anywhere near the consideration they deserve, invests their activities with the character of crudeness. Accordingly, the constant reminder that officers should be wise, considerate, and just, without providing them with opportunities to exercise these virtues is little more than vacuous sermonizing.

3. The ecological distribution of police work at the level of departmentally determined concentrations of deployment, as well as in terms of the orientations of individual police officers, reflects a whole range of public prejudices. That is, the police are more likely to be found in places where certain people live or congregate than in other parts of the city. Though this pattern of manpower allocation is ordinarily justified by references to experientially established needs for police service, it inevitably entails the consequence that some persons will receive the dubious benefit of extensive police scrutiny merely on account of their membership in those social groupings which invidious social compar-

---

[12] Erle Stanley Gardner, the prolific detective story writer, reports being troubled by the apparent need for the "dumb" cop in fiction. When he attempted to remedy this and depicted a policeman in favorable colors in one of his books, bookdealers and readers rose in protest; see his "The Need for New Concepts in the Administration of Criminal Justice," *Journal of Criminal Law, Criminology and Police Science,* 50 (1959) 20-26; see also, G.J. Falk, "The Public's Prejudice Against the Police," *American Bar Association Journal,* 50 (1965) 754-757.

isons locate at the bottom of the heap.[13] Accordingly, it is not a paranoid distortion to say that police activity is as much directed to who a person is as to what he does.

As is well known, the preferred targets of special police concern are some ethnic and racial minorities, the poor living in urban slums, and young people in general.[14] On the face of it, this kind of focusing appears to be, if not wholly unobjectionable, not without warrant. Insofar as the above-mentioned segments of society contribute disproportionately to the sum total of crime, and are more likely than others to engage in objectionable conduct, they would seem to require a higher degree of surveillance. In fact, this kind of reasoning was basic to the very creation of the police; for it was not assumed initially that the police would enforce laws in the broad sense, but that they would concentrate on the control of individual and collective tendencies towards transgression and disorder issuing from what were referred to as the "dangerous classes."[15] What was once a frankly admitted bias is, however, generally disavowed in our times. That is, in and of itself, the fact that someone is young, poor, and dark-complexioned is not supposed to mean anything whatsoever to a police officer. Statistically considered, he might be said to be more likely to run afoul of the law, but individually, all things being equal, his chances of being left alone *are supposed* to be the same as those of someone who is middle aged, well-to-do, and fair-skinned. In fact, however, exactly the opposite is the case. All things being equal, the young-poor-black and the old-rich-white doing the very same things under the very same circumstances will almost certainly not receive the same kind of treatment from policemen. In fact, it is almost inconceivable that the two characters could ever appear or do something in ways that would mean the same thing to a policeman.[16] Nor is the policeman merely expressing personal or institutional prejudice by according the two characters differential treatment.

---

[13] V.W. Piersante, Chief Detective of the Detroit Police Department, has juxtaposed with remarkable perceptiveness the considerations which, on the one hand, lead to dense and suspicious surveillance of certain groups because of their disproportionate contribution to crime totals, while on the other hand, these tactics expose the preponderant majority of law-abiding members of these groups to offensive scrutiny. He stated, "in Detroit in 1964 a total of 83,135 arrests were made . . . of this 58,389 were Negroes . . . This means that 89 percent of the Negro population were never involved with the police . . ." quoted at p. 215 in Harold Norris, "Constitutional Law Enforcement is Effective Law Enforcement," *University of Detroit Law Journal,* 42 (1965) 203-234.

[14] Gilbert Geis, *Juvenile Gangs.* A Report Produced for the President's Committee on Juvenile Delinquency and Youth Crime, Washington, D.C.: U.S. Government Printing Office, June 1965; Carl Werthman and Irving Piliavin, "Gang Membership and the Police," in Bordua (ed.), *op. cit. supra,* Note 3 at pp. 56-98.

[15] Allan Silver, "The Demand for Order in Civilized Society: A Review of Some Themes in the History of Urban Crime, Police and Riot," in Bordua (ed.), *op. cit. supra,* Note 3 at pp. 1-24.

[16] J.Q. Wilson writes, "The patrolman believes with considerable justification that teenagers, Negroes, and lower-income persons commit a disproportionate share of all reported crimes; being in those population categories at all makes one, statistically, more suspect than other persons; but to be in those categories *and* to behave unconventionally is to make oneself a prime suspect.

Public expectations insidiously instruct him to reckon with these "factors." These facts are too well known to require detailed exposition, but their reasons and consequences deserve brief consideration.

In the first place, the police are not alone in making invidious distinctions between the two types.[17] Indeed the differential treatment they accord them reflects only the distribution of esteem, credit, and desserts in society at large. Second, because of their own social origins, many policemen tend to express social prejudices more emphatically than other members of society.[18] Third, policemen are not merely like everybody else, only more so; they also have special reasons for it. Because the preponderant majority of police interventions are based on mere suspicion or on merely tentative indications of risk, policemen would have to be expected to judge matters prejudicially even if they personally were entirely free of prejudice. Under present circumstances, even the most completely impartial policeman who merely takes account of probabilities, as these probabilities are known to him, will feel reasonably justified in being more suspicious of the young-poor-black than of the old-rich-white, and once his suspicions are aroused, in acting swiftly and forcefully against the former while treating the latter with reserve and deference. For as the policeman calculates risk, the greater hazard is located on the side of inaction in one case, and on the side of unwarranted action in the other.

That policemen deal differently with types of people who are thought always to be "up to something" than with people who are thought to have occasional lapses but can otherwise be relied upon to conduct their affairs legally and honorably, does not come as a surprise, especially if one considers the multiple social pressures that instruct the police not to let the unworthy get away with anything and to treat the rest of the community with consideration. But because this is the case, police work tends to have divisive effects in society. While their existence and work do not create cleavages, they do magnify them in effect.

Patrolmen believe that they would be derelict in their duty if they did not treat such persons with suspicion, routinely question them on the street, and detain them for longer questioning if a crime has occurred in the area. To the objection of some middle-class observers that this is arbitrary and discriminatory, the police are likely to answer: 'Have *you* ever been stopped and searched? Of course not. We can tell the difference; we have to tell the difference in order to do our job. What are you complaining about?'" at pp. 40-41 of his *Varieties of Police Behavior: The Management of Law and Order in Eight Communities,* Cambridge, Mass.: Harvard University Press, 1968.

[17] Of primary significance in this respect is that the courts make the same kinds of invidious distinctions even as they follow the law; see J.E. Carlin, Jan Howard, and S.L. Messinger, "Civil Justice and the Poor," *Law and Society,* 1 (1966) 9-89, and Jacobus ten-Broek (ed.), *The Law of the Poor,* San Francisco, California: Chandler Publishing Co., 1966.

[18] Reference is made to the evidence that persons of working class origin are more prone than others to harbor attitudes that are favorable to politics of prejudice and authoritarianism; see S.L. Lipset, "Democracy and Working Class Authoritarianism," *American Sociological Review,* 24 (1959) 482-501; "Social Stratification and Right Wing Extremism," *British Journal of Sociology,* 10 (1959) 346-382; "Why Cops Hate Liberals—and Vice Versa," *Atlantic Monthly,* (March 1969).

The police view of this matter is clear and simple—too simple, perhaps. Their business is to control crime and keep the peace. If there is some connection between social and economic inequality, on the one hand, and criminality and unruliness, on the other hand, this is not their concern. The problem is not, however, whether the police have any responsibilities with regard to social injustice. The problem is that by distributing surveillance and intervention selectively they contribute to already existing tensions in society. That the police are widely assumed to be a partisan force in society is evident not only in the attitudes of people who are exposed to greater scrutiny; just as the young poor-black expects unfavorable treatment, so the old-rich-white expects special consideration from the policeman. And when two such persons are in conflict, nothing will provoke the indignation of the "decent" citizen more quickly than giving his word the same credence as the word of some "ne'er-do-well."[19]

The three character traits of police work discussed in the foregoing remarks—namely, that it is a tainted occupation, that it calls for peremptory solutions for complex human problems, and that it has, in virtue of its ecological distribution, a socially divisive effect—are structural determinants. By this is meant mainly that the complex of reasons and facts they encompass are not easily amenable to change. Thus, for example, though the stigma that attaches to police work is often viewed as merely reflecting the frequently low grade and bungling personnel that is currently available to the institution, there are good reasons to expect that it would continue to plague a far better prepared and a far better performing staff. For the stigma attaches not merely to the ways policemen discharge their duties, but also to what they have to deal with. Similarly, while it is probably true that moral naiveté is a character trait of persons who presently choose police work as their vocation, it is unlikely that persons of greater subtlety of perception would find it easy to exercise their sensitivity under present conditions. Finally, even though discriminatory policing is to some extent traceable to personal bigotry, it also follows the directions of public pressure, which, in turn, is not wholly devoid of factual warrant.

The discussion of the structural character traits of police work was introduced by saying that they were independent of the role definitions formulated from the perspective of the norm derivative approach. The latter interprets the meaning and adequacy of police procedure in terms of a set of simply stipulated ideal objectives. Naturally these objectives

---

[19] Arthur Niederhoffer, a former ranking police official, writes, "The power structure and the ideology of the community, which are supported by the police, at the same time direct and set boundaries to the sphere of police action." at p. 13 of his *Behind the Shield: The Police in Urban Society,* New York: Anchor Books, 1969: Niederhoffer cites an even stronger statement to that effect from Joseph Lohman, a former sheriff of Cook County, Ill., and later Dean of the School of Criminology at the University of California at Berkeley.

are considered desirable; more importantly, however, the values that determine the desirability of the objectives are also used in interpreting and judging the adequacy of procedures employed to realize them. Contrary to this way of making sense of police work, the consideration of the structural character traits was meant to draw attention to the fact that there attaches a sense to police work that is not inferentially derived from ideals but is rooted in what is commonly known about it. What is known about the police is, however, not merely a matter of more or less correct information. Instead, the common lore furnishes a framework for judging and interpreting their work. In crudest form, the common lore consists of a set of presuppositions about the way things are and have to be. Thus, for instance, whatever people assume to be generally true of the police will be the thing that a particular act or event will be taken to exemplify. If it is believed that police work is crude, then within a very considerable range of relative degrees of subtlety, whatever policemen will be seen doing will be seen as crudeness.

In addition to the fact that the normative approach represents an exercise in formal, legal inference, while the structural character traits reflect an approach of informal, commonsense practicality, the two differ in yet another and perhaps more important aspect. The normative approach does not admit the possibility that the police may, in fact, not be oriented to those objectives. Contrary to this, the sense of police activity that comes to the fore from the consideration of the character traits assigned to it by popular opinion and attitude leaves the question open.[20]

Since we cannot rely on abstract formulation that implicitly rule out the possibility that they might be entirely wrong, or far too narrow, and since we cannot depend on a fabric of commonsense characterizations, we must turn to still other sources. Of course, we can no more forget the importance of the popularly perceived character traits than we can forget the formulas of the official mandate. To advance further in our quest for a realistic definition of the police role, we must now turn to the review of certain historical materials that will show how the police moved into the position in which they find themselves today. On the basis of this review, in addition to what was proposed thus far, we will be able to formulate an explicit definition of the role of the institution and its officials.

*   *   *

---

[20] The normative approach is perhaps best exemplified in Jerome Hall, "Police and Law in a Democratic Society," *Indiana Law Journal,* 2 (1953) 133-177, where it is argued that the structure of police work must be understood as decisively determined by the duty to uphold the law and every police action must be interpreted in relation to this objective. The man on the street, however, approaches police work from a different vantage point. He probably supposes that police work has something to do with law enforcement, but to him this is mainly a figure of speech which does not limit his freedom to decide what the police are really for from case to case.

The Capacity to Use Force as the Core of the Police Role

We have argued earlier that the quest for peace by peaceful means is one of the culture traits of modern civilization. This aspiration is historically unique. For example, the Roman Empire was also committed to the objectives of reducing or eliminating warfare during one period of its existence, but the method chosen to achieve the *Pax Romana* was, in the language of the poet, *debellare superbos,* i.e., to subdue the haughty by force. Contrary to this, our commitment to abolish the traffic of violence requires us to pursue the ideal by pacific means. In support of this contention we pointed to the development of an elaborate system of international diplomacy whose main objective it is to avoid war, and to those changes in internal government that resulted in the virtual elimination of all forms of violence, especially in the administration of justice. That is, the overall tendency is not merely to withdraw the basis of legitimacy for all forms of provocative violence, but even from the exercise of provoked force required to meet illegitimate attacks. Naturally this is not possible to a full extent. At least, it has not been possible thus far. Since it is impossible to deprive responsive force entirely of legitimacy, its vestiges require special forms of authorization. Our society recognizes as legitimate three very different forms of responsive force.

First, we are authorized to use force for the purpose of self-defense. Though the laws governing self-defense are far from clear, it appears that an attacked person can counterattack only after he has exhausted all other means of avoiding harm, including retreat, and that the counterattack may not exceed what is necessary to disable the assailant from carrying out his intent. These restrictions are actually enforceable because harm done in the course of self-defense does furnish grounds for criminal and tort proceedings. It becomes necessary, therefore, to show compliance with these restrictions to rebut the charges of excessive and unjustified force even in self-defense.[63]

The second form of authorization entrusts the power to proceed coercively to some specifically deputized persons against some specifically named persons. Among the agents who have such highly specific powers are mental hospital attendants and prison guards. Characteristically, such persons use force in carrying out court orders; but they may use force only against named persons who are remanded to their custody and only to the extent required to implement a judicial order of confinement. Of course, like everybody else, they may also act within

---

[63] "Justification for the Use of Force in the Criminal Law," *Stanford Law Review,* 13 (1961) 566-609.

the provisions governing self-defense. By insisting on the high degree of limited specificity of the powers of custodial staffs, we do not mean to deny that these restrictions are often violated with impunity. The likelihood of such transgressions is enhanced by the secluded character of prisons and mental institutions, but their existence does not impair the validity of our definition.

The third way to legitimize the use of responsive force is to institute a police force. Contrary to the cases of self-defense and the limited authorization of custodial functionaries, the police authorization is essentially unrestricted. Because the expression "essentially" is often used to hedge a point, we will make fully explicit what we mean by it. There exist three formal limitations of the freedom of policemen to use force, which we must admit even though they have virtually no practical consequences. First, the police use of deadly force is limited in most jurisdictions. Though the powers of a policeman in this respect exceed those of citizens, they are limited nevertheless. For example, in some jurisdictions policemen are empowered to shoot to kill fleeing felony suspects, but not fleeing misdemeanor suspects. It is scarcely necessary to argue that, given the uncertainties involved in defining a delict under conditions of hot pursuit, this could hardly be expected to be an effective limitation.[64] Second, policemen may use force only in the performance of their duties and not to advance their own personal interest or the private interests of other persons. Though this is rather obvious, we mention it for the sake of completeness. Third, and this point too is brought up to meet possible objections, policemen may not use force maliciously or frivolously. These three restrictions, and nothing else, were meant by the use of the qualifier "essentially." Aside from these restrictions there exist no guidelines, no specifiable range of objectives, no limitations of any kind that instruct the policeman what he may or must do. Nor do there exist any criteria that would allow the judgment whether some forceful intervention was necessary, desirable, or proper. And finally, it is exceedingly rare that police actions involving the use of force are actually reviewed and judged by anyone at all.

In sum, the frequently heard talk about the lawful use of force by the police is practically meaningless and, because no one knows what is meant by it, so is the talk about the use of minimum force. Whatever vestigial significance attaches to the term "lawful" use of force is confined to the obvious and unnecessary rule that police officers may not

---

[64] "At common law, the rule appears to have been that an officer was entitled to make a reasonable mistake as to whether the victim had committed a felony, but a private person was not so entitled. Thus strict liability was created for the private arrester, and he could not justifiably kill, if the victim had not actually committed a felony. Several modern cases have imposed this standard of strict liability even upon the officer by conditioning justification of deadly force on the victim's actually having committed a felony, and a number of states have enacted statutes which appear to adopt this strict liability. However, many jurisdictions, such as California, have homicide statutes which permit the police officer to use deadly force for the arrest of a person 'charged' with felony. It has been suggested that this requirement only indicates the necessity for reasonable belief by the officer that the victim has committed a felony." *Ibid.*, pp. 599-600.

commit crimes of violence. Otherwise, however, the expectation that they may and will use force is left entirely undefined. In fact, the only instructions any policeman ever receives in this respect consist of sermonizing that he should be humane and circumspect, and that he must not desist from what he has undertaken merely because its accomplishment may call for coercive means. We might add, at this point, that the entire debate about the troublesome problem of police brutality will not move beyond its present impasse, and the desire to eliminate it will remain an impotent conceit, until this point is fully grasped and unequivocally admitted. In fact, our expectation that policemen will use force, coupled by our refusals to state clearly what we mean by it (aside from sanctimonious homilies), smacks of more than a bit of perversity.

Of course, neither the police nor the public is entirely in the dark about the justifiable use of force by the officers. We had occasion to allude to the assumption that policemen may use force in making arrests. But the benefit deriving from this apparent core of relative clarity is outweighed by its potentially misleading implications. For the authorization of the police to use force is in no important sense related to their duty to apprehend criminals. Were this the case then it could be adequately considered as merely a special case of the same authorization that is entrusted to custodial personnel. It might perhaps be considered a bit more complicated, but essentially of the same nature. But the police authority to use force is radically different from that of a prison guard. Whereas the powers of the latter are incidental to his obligation to implement a legal command, the police role is far better understood by saying that their ability to arrest offenders is incidental to their authority to use force.

Many puzzling aspects of police work fall into place when one ceases to look at it as principally concerned with law enforcement and crime control, and only incidentally and often incongruously concerned with an infinite variety of other matters. It makes much more sense to say that the police are nothing else than a mechanism for the distribution of situationally justified force in society. The latter conception is preferable to the former on three grounds. First, it accords better with the actual expectations and demands made of the police (even though it probably conflicts with what most people would say, or expect to hear, in answer to the question about the proper police function); second, it gives a better accounting of the actual allocation of police manpower and other resources; and, third, it lends unity to all kinds of police activity. These three justifications will be discussed in some detail in the following.

The American city dweller's repertoire of methods for handling problems includes one known as "calling the cops." The practice to which the idiom refers is enormously widespread. Though it is more frequent in some segments of society than in others, there are very few people who do not or would not resort to it under suitable circumstances. A few illustrations will furnish the background for an explanation of what "calling the cops" means.[65]

Two patrolmen were directed to report to an address located in a fashionable district of a large city. On the scene they were greeted by the lady of the house who complained that the maid had been stealing and receiving male visitors in her quarters. She wanted the maid's belongings searched and the man removed. The patrolmen refused the first request, promising to forward the complaint to the bureau of detectives, but agreed to see what they could do about the man. After gaining entrance to the maid's room they compelled a male visitor to leave, drove him several blocks away from the house, and released him with the warning never to return.

In a tenement, patrolmen were met by a public health nurse who took them through an abysmally deteriorated apartment inhabited by four young children in the care of an elderly woman. The babysitter resisted the nurse's earlier attempts to remove the children. The patrolmen packed the children in the squad car and took them to Juvenile Hall, over the continuing protests of the elderly woman.

While cruising through the streets a team of detectives recognized a man named in a teletype received from the sheriff of an adjoining county. The suspect maintained that he was in the hospital at the time the offense alleged in the communication took place, and asked the officers to verify his story over their car radio. When he continued to plead innocence he was handcuffed and taken to headquarters. Here the detectives learned that the teletype had been cancelled. Prior to his release the man was told that he could have saved himself grief had he gone along voluntarily.

In a downtown residential hotel, patrolmen found two ambulance attendants trying to persuade a man, who according to all accounts was desperately ill, to go to the hospital. After some talk, they helped the attendants in carrying the protesting patient to the ambulance and sent them off.

In a middle-class neighborhood, patrolmen found a partly disassembled car, tools, a loudly blaring radio, and five beer-drinking youths at the curb in front of a single-family home. The homeowner complained that this had been going on for several days and the men had refused to take their activities elsewhere. The patrolmen ordered the youths to pack up and leave. When one sassed them they threw him into the squad car, drove him to the precinct station, from where he was released after receiving a severe tongue lashing from the desk sergeant.

---

[65] The illustrations are taken from field notes I have collected over the course of fourteen months of intensive field observations of police activity in two large cities. One is located in a Rocky Mountain State, the other on the West Coast. All other case vignettes used in the subsequent text of this report also come from this source.

In the apartment of a quarreling couple, patrolmen were told by the wife, whose nose was bleeding, that the husband stole her purse containing money she earned. The patrolmen told the man they would "take him in," whereupon he returned the purse and they left.

What all these vignettes are meant to illustrate is that whatever the substance of the task at hand, whether it involves protection against an undesired imposition, caring for those who cannot care for themselves, attempting to solve a crime, helping to save a life, abating a nuisance, or settling an explosive dispute, police intervention means above all making use of the capacity and authority to overpower resistance to an attempted solution in the native habitat of the problem. There can be no doubt that this feature of police work is uppermost in the minds of people who solicit police aid or direct the attention of the police to problems, that persons against whom the police proceed have this feature in mind and conduct themselves accordingly, and that every conceivable police intervention projects the message that force may be, and may have to be, used to achieve a desired objective. It does not matter whether the persons who seek police help are private citizens or other government officials, nor does it matter whether the problem at hand involves some aspect of law enforcement or is totally unconnected with it.

It must be emphasized, however, that the conception of the centrality of the capacity to use force in the police role does not entail the conclusion that the ordinary occupational routines consist of the actual exercise of this capacity. It is very likely, though we lack information on this point, that the actual use of physical coercion and restraint is rare for all policemen and that many policemen are virtually never in the position of having to resort to it. What matters is that police procedure is defined by the feature that it may not be opposed in its course, and that force can be used if it is opposed. This is what the existence of the police makes available to society. Accordingly, the question, "What are policemen supposed to do?" is almost completely identical with the question, "What kinds of situations require remedies that are non-negotiably coercible?"[66]

---

[66] By "non-negotiably coercible" we mean that when a deputized police officer decides that force is necessary, then, within the boundaries of this situation, he is not accountable to anyone, nor is he required to brook the arguments of opposition of anyone who might object to it. We set this forth not as a legal but as a practical rule. The legal question whether citizens may oppose policemen is complicated. Apparently resisting police coercion in situations of emergency is not legitimate; see Hans Kelsen, *General Theory of Law and State*, New York: Russel & Russel, 1961, pp. 278-279, and H.A.L. Hart, *The Concept of Law*, Oxford: Clarendon Press, 1961, pp. 20-21. Common law doctrine allows that citizens may oppose "unlawful arrest," 6 *Corpus Juris Secundum*, Arrest #13, p. 613; against this, the Uniform Arrest Act, drafted by a committee of the Interstate Commission on Crime in 1939, provides in Section 5, "If a person has reasonable grounds to believe that he is being arrested by a police officer, it is his duty to refrain from using force or any weapons in resisting arrest regardless of whether or not there is a legal basis for the arrest." S.B. Warner, "Uniform Arrest Act," *Vanderbilt Law Review*, 28 (1942) 315-347. At present, at least twelve states are governed by case law recognizing the validity of the Common Law doctrine, at least five have adopted

Our second justification for preferring the definition of the police role we proposed to the traditional law enforcement focus of the role requires us to review the actual police practices to see to what extent they can be subsumed under the conception we offered. To begin we can take note that law enforcement and crime control are obviously regarded as calling for remedies that are non-negotiably coercible. According to available estimates, approximately one-third of available manpower resources of the police are at any time committed to dealing with crimes and criminals. Though this may seem to be a relatively small share of the total resources of an agency ostensibly devoted to crime control, it is exceedingly unlikely that any other specific routine police activity, such as traffic regulation, crowd control, supervision of licensed establishments, settling of citizens' disputes, emergency health aids, ceremonial functions, or any other, absorb anywhere near as large a share of the remaining two-thirds. But this is precisely what one would expect on the basis of our definition. Given the likelihood that offenders will seek to oppose apprehension and evade punishment, it is only natural that the initial dealings with them be assigned to an agency that is capable of overcoming these obstacles. That is, the proposed definition of the role of the police as a mechanism for the distribution of nonnegotiably coercive remedies entails the priority of crime control by direct inference. Beyond that, however, the definition also encompasses other types of activities, albeit at lower level of priority.

Because the idea that the police are basically a crimefighting agency has never been challenged in the past, no one has troubled to sort out the remaining priorities. Instead, the police have always been forced to justify activities that did not involve law enforcement in the direct sense by either linking them constructively to law enforcement or by defining them as nuisance demands for service. The dominance of this view, especially in the minds of policemen, has two pernicious consequences. First, it leads to a tendency to view all sorts of problems as if they involved culpable offenses and to an excessive reliance on quasilegal methods for handling them. The widespread use of arrests without intent to prosecute exemplifies this state of affairs. These cases do not involve errors in judgment about the applicability of a penal norm but deliberate pretense resorted to because more appropriate methods of handling problems have not been developed. Second, the view that crime control is the only serious, important, and necessary part of police work has deleterious effects on the morale of those police officers

---

the rule contained in the Uniform Arrest Act, and at least six have case law or statutes that give effect to the Uniform Arrest Act rule. That the trend is away from the Common Law doctrine and in the direction of the Uniform Arrest Act rule is argued in Max Hochanadel and H.W. Stege, "The Right to Resist an Unlawful Arrest: An Outdated Concept?" *Tulsa Law Journal*, 3 (1966) 40-46. I am grateful for the help I received from 35 of the 50 State Attorney General Offices from whom I sought information concerning this matter.

in the uniformed patrol who spend most of their time with other matters. No one, especially he who takes a positive interest in his work, likes being obliged to do things day-in and day-out that are disparaged by his colleagues. Moreover, the low evaluation of these duties leads to neglecting the development of skill and knowledge that are required to discharge them properly and efficiently.

It remains to be shown that the capacity to use coercive force lends thematic unity to all police activity in the same sense in which, let us say, the capacity to cure illness lends unity to everything that is ordinarily done in the field of medical practice. While everybody agrees that the police actually engage in an enormous variety of activities, only a part of which involves law enforcement, many argue that this state of affairs does not require explanation but change. Smith, for example, argued that the imposition of duties and demands that are not related to crime control dilutes the effectiveness of the police and that the growing trend in this direction should be curtailed and even reversed.[67] On the face of it this argument is not without merit, especially if one considers that very many of those activities that are unrelated to law enforcement involve dealing with problems that lie in the field of psychiatry, social welfare, human relations, education, and so on. Each of these fields has its own trained specialists who are respectively more competent than the police. It would seem preferable, therefore, to take all those matters that belong properly to other specialists out of the hands of the police and turn them over to those to whom they belong. Not only would this relieve some of the pressures that presently impinge on the police, but it would also result in better services.[68]

Unfortunately, this view overlooks a centrally important factor. While it is true that policemen often aid sick and troubled people because physicians and social workers are unable or unwilling to take their services where they are needed, this is not the only or even the main reason for police involvement. In fact, physicians and social workers themselves quite often "call the cops." For not unlike the case of the administration of justice, on the periphery of the rationally ordered procedures of medical and social work practice lurk exigencies that call for the exercise of coercion. Since neither physicians nor social workers are authorized or equipped to use force to attain desirable objectives, the total disengagement of the police would mean allowing many a problem to move unhampered in the direction of disaster. But the non-law enforcement activities of the police are by no means confined to matters that are wholly or even mainly within the purview of some other institutionalized remedial specialty. Many, perhaps most, consist of addressing situations in which people simply do not seem to be able

[67] Smith, *op. cit. supra*, Note 1.
[68] The authors of the *Task Force Report: Police* note that little has been done to make these alternative resources available as substitutes for police intervention; *op. cit. supra*, Note 56 at p. 14.

to manage their own lives adequately. Nor is it to be taken for granted that these situations invariably call for the use, or the threat of the use, of force. It is enough if there is need for immediate and unquestioned intervention that must not be allowed to be defeated by possible resistance. And where there is a possibility of great harm, the intervention would appear to be justified even if the risk is, in statistical terms, quite remote. Take, for instance the presence of mentally ill persons in the community. Though it is well known that most live quiet and unobtrusive lives, they are perceived as occasionally constituting a serious hazard to themselves and others. Thus, it is not surprising that the police are always prepared to deal with these persons at the slightest indication of a possible emergency. Similarly, though very few family quarrels lead to serious consequences, the fact that most homicides occur among quarreling kin leads to the preparedness to intervene at the incipient stages of problems.

In sum, the role of the police is to address all sorts of human problems when and insofar as their solutions do or may possibly require the use of force at the point of their occurrence. This lends homogeneity to such diverse procedures as catching a criminal, driving the mayor to the airport, evicting a drunken person from a bar, directing traffic, crowd control, taking care of lost children, administering medical first aid, and separating fighting relatives.

There is no exaggeration in saying that there is topical unity in this very incomplete list of lines of police work. Perhaps it is true that the common practice of assigning policemen to chauffeur mayors is based on the desire to give the appearance of thrift in the urban fisc. But note, if one wanted to make as far as possible certain that nothing would ever impede His Honor's freedom of movement, he would certainly put someone into the driver's seat of the auto who has the authority and the capacity to overcome all unforeseeable human obstacles. Similarly, it is perhaps not too farfetched to assume that desk sergeants feed ice cream to lost children because they like children. But if the treat does not achieve the purpose of keeping the youngster in the station house until his parents arrive to redeem him, the sergeant would have to resort to other means of keeping him there.

We must now attempt to pull together the several parts of the foregoing discussion in order to show how they bring into relief the main problems of adjusting police function to life in modern society, and in order to elaborate constructively certain consequences that result from the assumption of the role definitions we have proposed.

At the beginning we observed that the police appear to be burdened by an opprobrium that did not seem to lessen proportionately to the acknowledged improvements in their practices. To explain this puzzling fact we drew attention to three perceived features of the police that appear to be substantially independent of particular work methods.

First, a stigma attaches to police work because of its connection with evil, crime, perversity, and disorder. Though it may not be reasonable, it is common that those who fight the dreadful end up being dreaded themselves. Second, because the police must act quickly and often on mere intuition, their interventions are lacking in those aspects of moral sophistication which only a more extended and more scrupulous consideration can afford. Hence their methods are comparatively crude. Third, because it is commonly assumed that the risks of the kinds of breakdowns that require police action are much more heavily concentrated in the lower classes than in other segments of society, police surveillance is inherently discriminatory. That is, all things being equal, some persons feel the sting of police scrutiny merely because of their station in life. Insofar as this is felt, police work has divisive effects in society.

Next, we argued that one cannot understand how the police "found themselves" in this unenviable position without taking into consideration that one of the cultural trends of roughly the past century-and-a-half was the sustained aspiration to install peace as a stable condition of everyday life. Though no one can fail being impressed by the many ways the attainment of this ideal has been frustrated, it is possible to find some evidence of partially effective efforts. Many aspects of mundane existence in our cities have become more pacific than they have been in past epochs of history. More importantly for our purposes, in the domain of internal statecraft, the distance between those who govern and those who are governed has grown and the gap has been filled with bureaucratically symbolized communication. Where earlier compliance was secured by physical presence and armed might, it now rests mainly on peaceful persuasion and rational compliance. We found the trend toward the pacification in governing most strongly demonstrated in the administration of justice. The banishment of all forms of violence from the criminal process, as administered by the courts, has as a corollary the legalization of judicial proceedings. The latter reflects a movement away from peremptory and oracular judgment to a method in which all decisions are based on exhaustively rational grounds involving the use of explicit legal norms. Most important among those norms are the ones that limit the powers of authority and specify the rights of defendants. The legalization and pacification of the criminal process was achieved by, among other things, expelling from its purview those processes that set it into motion. Since in the initial steps, where suspicions are formed and arrests are made, force and intuition cannot be eliminated entirely, purity can be maintained by not taking notice of them. This situation is, however, paradoxical if we are to take seriously the idea that the police is a law enforcement agency in the strict sense of legality. The recognition of this paradox became unavoidable as early as in 1914, in the landmark decision of *Weeks v. U.S.* In the following decades the United States Supreme Court issued a series of rulings affecting police procedure which foster the impression that the judiciary exercises control over the police. But this impression is misleading, for the rulings do not set forth binding norms for police work but merely provide that *if* the police propose to set the criminal process into motion, *then* they must proceed in certain legally restricted ways. These restrictions are, therefore, conditional, specifying as it were the terms of delivery and acceptance of a service and nothing more. Outside of this arrangement the judges have no direct concerns with police work and will take notice of its illegality, if it is illegal, only when offended citizens seek civil redress.

Because only a small part of the activity of the police is dedicated to law enforcement and because they deal with the majority of their problems without invoking the law, a broader definition of their role was proposed. After reviewing briefly what the public appears to expect of the police, the range of activities police actually engage in, and the theme that unifies all these activities, it was suggested that *the role of the police is best understood as a mechanism for the distribution of non-negotiably coercive force employed in accordance with the dictates of an intuitive grasp of situational exigencies.*

It is, of course, not surprising that a society committed to the establishment of peace by pacific means and to the abolishment of all forms of violence from the fabric of its social relations, at least as a matter of official morality and policy, would establish a corps of specially deputized officials endowed with the exclusive monopoly of using force contingently where limitations of foresight fail to provide alternatives. That is, given the melancholy appreciation of the fact that the total abolition of force is not attainable, the closest approximation to the ideal is to limit it as a special and exclusive trust. If it is the case, however, that the mandate of the police is organized around their capacity and authority to use force, i.e., if this is what the institution's existence makes available to society, then the evaluation of that institution's performance must focus on it. While it is quite true that policemen will have to be judged on other dimensions of competence, too—for example, the exercise of force against criminal suspects requires some knowledge about crime and criminal law—their methods as society's agents of coercion will have to be considered central to the overall judgment.

The proposed definition of the police role entails a difficult moral problem. How can we arrive at a favorable or even accepting judgment about an activity which is, in its very conception, opposed to the ethos of the polity that authorizes it? Is it not well nigh inevitable that this mandate be concealed in circumlocution? While solving puzzles of moral philosophy is beyond the scope of this analysis, we will have to address this question in a somewhat more mundane formulation: namely, on what terms can a society dedicated to peace institutionalize the exercise of force?

It appears that in our society two answers to this question are acceptable. One defines the targets of legitimate force as enemies and the coercive advance against them as warfare. Those who wage this war are expected to be possessed by the military virtues of valor, obedience and *esprit de corps*. The enterprise as a whole is justified as a sacrificial and glorious mission in which the warrior's duty is "not to reason why." The other answer involves an altogether different imagery. The targets of force are conceived as practical objectives and their attainment a matter of practical expediency. The process involves prudence, economy, and considered judgment, from case to case. The enterprise as a whole is conceived as a public trust, the exercise of which is vested in individual practitioners who are personally responsible for their decisions and actions.

Reflection suggests that the two patterns are profoundly incompatible. Remarkably, however, our police departments have not been deterred from attempting the reconciliation of the irreconcilable. Thus, our policemen are exposed to the demand of a conflicting nature in that their actions are supposed to reflect military prowess and professional acumen.

In the following, we will review certain well-known aspects of police organization and practice in an attempt to show that the adherence to the quasi-military model by our police forces is largely a self-defeating pretense. Its sole effect is to create obstacles in the development of a professional police system. On the basis of this review we will attempt to formulate an outline of a model of the police role in modern society that is recognizably in accord with existing practices but which contains safeguards against the existence and proliferation of those aspects of police work that are generally regarded as deplorable. In other words, the proposed suggestions will be innovative only in the sense that they will accent already existing strength and excise impeding ballasts.

Section II
POLICE DISCRETION

Introduction

Perhaps no topic in the police literature has received as much attention as police discretion. Discretion refers to the autonomy or freedom an officer has in choosing an appropriate course of action (Black, 1968; Davis, 1969). Since the police operate with limited resources, and since there is a great deal of uncertainty and complexity inherent in many police tasks, the exercise of discretion is an essential aspect of police work. There is little doubt that the scholarly effort devoted to developing an understanding of discretion is warranted given the desire for police accountability to the police organization and to the public they are supposed to serve. By seeking to identify the factors that influence the decisions of police officers, discretion may be better regulated and hence, the frequency of unequitable and unjust decisions may be minimized.

Scholars have developed and advanced various explanatory perspectives on police decisionmaking—research has examined the social-psychological, sociological, and organizational determinants of police officers' discretionary behavior. The social-psychological perspective focuses on the impact of individual characteristics (e.g., gender, race, educational level, attitudes) on officers' perceptions and behaviors. The sociological approach often highlights the importance of the structural characteristics of police-citizen encounters. Research that reflects the organizational perspective most clearly focuses on the influence of organizational structures, policies, incentive systems, social relationships, and the behaviors and styles of supervisors on officers' decisions. This section of *Classics in Policing* includes five readings that develop and reflect these three theoretical perspectives.

The first reading, an excerpt from William K. Muir Jr.'s text, *The Police: Street Corner Politicians,* most clearly reflects the social-psychological perspective of police discretion. On the basis of his ethnographic research, Muir explains that a "good" (i.e., "professional") police officer possesses two important qualities: passion and perspective. "Passion" refers to the belief in coercive power as a means to good ends and

131

to the willingness to invoke power to achieve these ends. "Perspective" refers to an objective understanding of human dignity. To develop his typology, Muir identifies three non-professional types of police officers: enforcers (those with passion but not perspective), reciprocators (those with perspective but not passion), and avoiders (those without passion or perspective). Muir discusses how an understanding of the qualities possessed by officers is important in explaining the discretionary behavior of officers.

The next two readings adopt a more sociological approach to understanding police discretion in that the discretionary decisions of police officers are portrayed as a function of the dynamics of police-citizen encounters. Donald Black, in his article "The Social Organization of Arrest," discusses the impact of various structural dimensions of the situations in which officers and citizens interact. He examines the influence of the evidence available, the seriousness of the crime, the complainant's preferences, the social relationship between the complainant and the suspect, the suspect's demeanor, and the suspect's race on police decisionmaking in law enforcement situations. On the basis of systematic observations of police-citizen encounters in three major cities, Black found each of the above factors (with the exception of suspect race) to influence officers' decisions to make arrests. The empirical generalizations offered by Black are strongly supported in the subsequent research that has examined the impact of these factors on police decisionmaking.

John Van Maanen, in "The Asshole," also takes a sociological approach in describing how the characteristics of citizens and the dynamics of police-citizen encounters form the basis for typifications developed and used by officers. The author explains that there are three ideal types of citizens as defined by officers: "suspicious persons" (those who may have committed a serious offense), "assholes" (those who do not accept the police definition of the situation and, accordingly, are viewed as deliberately disrespectful of the police), and "know-nothings" (everyone else). Given particular situational contingencies, an individual may come under police scrutiny as a "suspicious person." Given other situational dynamics and interactions, an individual may be cast as a morally repugnant "asshole." Van Maanen suggests that this classification scheme provides insight to the expectations, thoughts, and feelings of police officers as they organize their day-to-day work world. The author further explains how these ascribed labels guide police actions during street encounters.

The last two readings in this section place the discretionary decisions of police officers in the context of the organizational setting. These readings make it clear that an adequate understanding of police discretion can only be developed if the importance of organizational dynamics are explicitly considered. James Q. Wilson, in an excerpt from his book *Varieties of Police Behavior,* describes three organizational styles of policing—the "watchman style" where officers consider the violator and different standards of conduct in pursuing the proper course of action but generally "ignore the little stuff" (p. 145) and "follow the path of least resistance" (p. 144)—the "legalistic style" where only one standard of conduct is considered and consequently, many arrests and citations are produced—and the "service style" where intervention is often to provide services to citizens. According to Wilson, the predominate style of policing in a police organization is most attributable to the preferences and desires of the chief, and these preferences often correspond to the wishes and priorities of citizens in the community.

The final article of this section portrays administrative policy as an organizational constraint on police decisionmaking. In his article titled "Administrative Interventions on Police Shooting Discretion," James Fyfe provides an empirical analysis of the effect of administrative guidelines on the frequency of shootings in New York City. His analyses show that upon implementation of policies that limited the use of firearms, the frequency of shooting incidents dramatically declined.

While the readings included in this section represent some of the most influential works on police discretion, individually none of the readings provide a sufficient understanding of the issue. Each reading, as it represents a perspective on police discretionary behavior, is a piece of a much larger puzzle. As such, only when one appreciates the different levels and perspectives on which the decisions of police officers can be analyzed can a more thorough understanding of the complexities of police discretion be attained.

References

Black, Donald (1968) The Social Organization of Arrest. *Stanford Law Review* 23:1087-1111.

Davis, Kenneth C. (1969) *Discretionary Justice.* Baton Rouge: Louisiana State University Press.

William Ker Muir Jr.

The Professional Political Model of the Good Policeman

He who lets himself in for politics, that is, for power and force as a means, contracts with diabolical powers and for his action it is not true that good can follow only from good and evil only from evil, but that often the opposite is true. Anyone who fails to see this, is, indeed, a political infant.

Max Weber
"Politics as a Vocation"
1918

At this point I reveal myself in my true colours, as a stick-in-the-mud. I hold a number of beliefs that have been repudiated by the liveliest intellects of our time. I believe that order is better than chaos, creation better than destruction. I prefer gentleness to violence, forgiveness to vendetta. On the whole I think that knowledge is preferable to ignorance, and I am sure that human sympathy is more valuable than ideology. I believe that in spite of the recent triumphs of science, men haven't changed much in the last two thousand years; and in consequence, we must still try to learn from history. History is ourselves. I also hold one or two beliefs that are more difficult to put short. For example, I believe in courtesy, the ritual by which we avoid hurting other people's by satisfying our own egos. And I think we should remember that we are part of a great whole, which for convenience we call nature. All living things are our brothers and sisters. Above all, I believe in the God-given genius of certain individuals, and I value a society that makes their existence possible.

Kenneth Clark
Civilization
1969

Source: William Ker Muir Jr. (1977). *The Police: Streetcorner Politicians.* "The Professional Political Model of the Good Policeman" (Chapter 4), pp. 47-58. Chicago, IL: The University of Chicago Press. Reprinted by permission of The University of Chicago Press.

I

Coercion, the power of the sword, is not the only means of power. There are the power of the purse and the power of the word as well. We should keep these two other fundamental techniques of controlling others, reciprocity and exhortation, in mind to get a perspective on the moral implications of coercion.

Reciprocity is a distinct kind of power relationship. Instead of resorting to threats, one individual overcomes the resistance of another by making an attractive exchange. He gives up something he values less and gets in return something he thinks has a greater worth to him. His exchange partner, meanwhile, because his scale of values is different, receives something that he desires more than what he has to surrender. Thus, both are reciprocally enriched.

There is something extremely civilized about the notion of reciprocity. Persons with different possessions and diverse value systems exchange voluntarily in fair and mutually satisfactory trades. Because there is no antagonism on either side, the motives to welsh on a deal or to resist the terms of reciprocity are inhibited by the prospects of continuing the profitable relationship. Diversity, trustworthiness, constructiveness, empathy, self-improvement—all these virtues have their rewards in reciprocal relationships.

The other technique of power is exhortation. Individuals act, not because they are coerced or tempted, but because they think their action is right, because they are persuaded by the "truth" of the matter that they have a duty to fulfill. They will sacrifice gladly, even kill or be killed, for a cause they believe in, even though, without that dedication, they would have resisted the tortures of the barbarian and the blandishments of the devil. Exhortation is a noble form of human control. There is something inspiring about persons working harmoniously, coordinated by their inner convictions, identifying with the well-being of the larger group, bound by words of honor, certain of purpose. When one thinks of the exhortative relationship between a leader and his followers, numerous virtues leap to mind—solidarity, community, selflessness, conscience, inspiration.

Of the three techniques of power—trade and "truth" and threat—only the last, the means we call coercion, seems on first acquaintance mean and barbaric. To be sure, reciprocity and exhortation are not unmitigated goods. In fact, if the powers of the purse or word were to be examined in detail, they would present as many paradoxical and troublesome aspects as does the power of the sword. Each promotes, in the extreme, highly questionable qualities—for example, selfishness (reciprocity) and conformity (exhortation).

But coercion seems of a different order. The human qualities which appear to be required for the practice of coercion seem incompatible with any civilized notion of the good. The moral realm of the person who must recurrently deal with the paradoxes of dispossession, detachment, face, and irrationality is turned topsy-turvy. Coercion creates a situation in which what is effective is at odds on every point with what Lord Acton called "the inflexible integrity of the moral code."[1] The gap between being a good man and a good practitioner of coercion appears unbridgeable. Even if the person in authority would prefer to act in conventionally fair and gentle ways, he can be sure that self-minimization, detachment, remorselessness, and ignorance will be practiced against him, necessitating his self-defense and more, if his desires to put his authority to good purpose are to avail. The tendency of coercive power to corrupt its wielder seems nearly unavoidable.

II

But are there ways to prevent persons in authority from becoming wicked? In his essay, "Politics as a Vocation," the German social theorist Max Weber (1864-1920) probed that question.[2] He framed the problem of coercive power and personality as follows: "He who lets himself in for politics, that is, for power and force as means, contracts

---

[1] Lord John Emerich Edward Dalberg-Acton was born the year before Queen Victoria took the throne and died a year after her death. He believed passionately both in the inherent weakness and wickedness of mankind and in the uses of history to hold mankind accountable. For Acton, history recorded the deeds and misdeeds of individuals; it taught future generations about the evil consequences of doing evil; and it punished in perpetuity those men who had escaped punishment too long during their lives. Among the targets he attacked most devoutly were men of politics and men of the cloth; state and church alike, in his eyes, had done immeasurable disservice to mankind.

When Acton's friend Mandell Creighton concluded, in his *History of the Papacy during the Reformation,* that the late-medieval papacy had "been tolerant and benevolent," Acton disputed the point in a review submitted to the *English Historical Review,* of which Creighton was the editor. Creighton's kindly nature made him willing to publish the review despite its "ill-natured" quality, and in the correspondence between the two men concerning some revisions prior to its publication in 1887, Acton remarked, "Power tends to corrupt and absolute power corrupts absolutely." The tenor of Acton's argument is revealed in these excerpts: "I cannot accept your canon that we are to judge Pope and King unlike other men, with a favourable presumption that they did no wrong. . . . Historical responsibility has to make up for the want of legal responsibility . . .; if what one hears is true, then Elizabeth asked the gaoler to murder Mary, and William III ordered his Scots minister to extirpate a clan. Here are the greater names coupled with the greater crimes. . . . I would hang them, higher than Haman; for reasons of quite obvious justice still more, still higher, for the sake of historical science. . . . The inflexible integrity of the moral code is, to me, the secret of the authority, the dignity, the utility of history. If we may debase the currency for the sake of genius, or success, or rank, or reputation, we may debase it for the sake of a man's influence, of his religion, of his party, or the good cause which prospers by his credit and suffers by his disgrace. Then history ceases to be a science, an arbitration of controversy, a guide to the wanderer, the upholder of the moral standard which the powers of earth and religion itself tend constantly to depress. . . . Then history . . . serves where it ought to reign, and it serves the worst cause better than the purest."

[2] Max Weber, "Politics as a Vocation," in *From Max Weber: Essays in Sociology,* ed. and trans. H. Gerth and C. Wright Mills (New York: Oxford University Press, 1946), pp. 77-128.

with diabolical powers and for his action it is *not* true that good can follow only from good and evil only from evil, but that often the opposite is true. Anyone who fails to see this is, indeed, a political infant."[3] Or, as Weber said elsewhere in the essay, "Whosoever contracts with violent means for whatever ends—and every politician does," exposes himself to the "ethical paradoxes of coercion" and "endangers the 'salvation of the soul.' "Those paradoxes, summed up by Weber as the "irreconcilable conflict" between the "demon of politics" and the "god of love," produce consequences "for his inner self, to which he must helplessly submit, unless he perceives them." If political persons do not anticipate them, if those who undertake coercive power 'do not fully realize what they take upon themselves," then the consequence is bitterness, banal self-acceptance, or flight.[4]

Weber constructed a model of "a *mature* man," one who would not "crumble" under the ethically paradoxical pressures which afflict the "professional politician." For purposes of reference, I shall call this construct the professional political model, using "political" in Weber's limited sense to refer to matters involving coercive threats and violence, and professional to indicate that the encounters with coercion occur so recurrently as to become routine. Weber's model of a professional politician had two characteristics which in combination reduced the chances of corruption. Weber called them the virtues of "passion and perspective."

1. *Passion: a capacity to "integrate" coercion into morals.* Weber insisted that the "genuine man," the professional political model, harmonized his standards of innocence and his willingness to "stand up arms-in-hand" for the general welfare. He did not suffer disabling pangs of guilt about the harmful consequences which flowed from recourse to threats and violence. He reconciled the irreconcilable. He felt good about coercive power; he made the consequences of his recourse to threats consistent with those moral codes which regulated and gave value to the conduct of his total life; he knew that his involvement in violence was "principled." Having accomplished "the integration of violence into ethics, the professional political model achieved the "passion" necessary to endure the antagonisms aroused by politics, by coercive power. (The ethical basis for coercion lay in the "causes" served by it and not attainable without it.)

2. *Perspective: intellectual "objectivity."* But an ethic of "principled violence as a means" was not enough, since moral equanimity about coercive means could be achieved not by reconciling but by rejecting

---

[3] Ibid., p. 123.
[4] Weber summed up these three harmful developments this way: "Will you be bitter or banausic? Will you simply and dully accept world and occupation? Or will the third and by no means the least frequent possibility be your lot: mystic flight from reality . . . ?" (Ibid.. p. 128.)

the ethical concerns of civilization. Then there would be no guilt because there would be no conscience. For Weber such fundamental moral rejection led to a "really radical Machiavellianism," in which the world was distorted to appear hateful, thereby justifying the violence being used against it. In a word, cynicism was possible.

The model professional politician, however, fought the temptation to distort by cultivating "objectivity." By this Weber meant "the knowledge of tragedy with which all action, but especially political action, is truly interwoven." The professional political model possessed a sense of the meaning of human conduct—a comprehension of the suffering of each inhabitant of the earth, a sensitivity to man's yearning for dignity, and, ultimately, "some kind of faith" that no individual is worthless. In short, the professional political model nurtured a persistent contact with reality. He developed a cognitive efficiency, a "perspective," a capacity for seeing rich implications of meager cues. He developed an inner understanding of the motives of men, a sense of life's rhythms of cause-and effect, and a self-suspicion that drove him to find out for himself when what he had been told by frighteners and flatterers did not square with his inner "knowledge of tragedy."

The secret of avoiding corruption by coercive power—i.e., wickedness, banality, or cowardice—was to combine passion with perspective. Once again, to resort to Weber's language, the "good" politician was defined by an ability to forge together "warm passion and a cool sense of proportion . . . in one and the same soul."

III

What is the point of discussing Weber's professional political model in a book on policemen? It turns out to be of the utmost utility in solving the crucial methodological problem inherent in this study. I ask the reader's patience to indulge me in a short excursion into technical matters which may strike him or her as a bit pedantic. I think the point is important enough to take the time.

Recall that what I am trying to do is to explain the development of good policemen. The reader and I both know that to derive any value from such an inquiry, we must come up with a sensible definition of what we mean by "good." The problem is a sticky one. Any solution to it is both pivotal and also most deserving of critical scrutiny.

I urge that a reasonable definition of "good" will have to satisfy three criteria: (1) *Independence*—is the definition grounded in terms of a relatively broad range of social concerns and as free of police organizational bias as practical? (2) *Realism*—would a reasonable policeman agree that any assessment made of him in terms of the definition was taking into consideration many of the substantial constraints affecting him? and (3) *Timeliness*—assuming the definition was relatively independent and realistic, could a researcher gather evidence on how a policeman currently measured up to the definition?

In view of these three standards, let me explain why I flirted with, but ultimately rejected, five apparent solutions to the problem of defining the good policeman.

1. *Good is what a policeman's supervisors say it is.* Performance ratings by supervisors were made annually in the Laconia Police Department. Each supervisor reviewed them with both the rated officers and his own superior. The evaluations tended to be knowledgeable and were taken seriously by all parties. The merit of an inside, informed appraisal, however, was undermined by its lack of independence. In making ratings, policemen were writing their own report cards, not only in the sense that an officer's promising development reflected well on the supervisor's abilities but also, and more important, because the evaluations were based on the Laconia Police Department's criteria and not demonstrably on the larger society's.

Under ideal circumstances the administrator's definition of good police work might have been appropriate for the larger society. But it was not necessarily so. In any organization a tendency exists to displace the needs of its clientele for its own good, and the Laconia Police Department was unlikely to be an exception to this general rule. To know whether the organization's goals were congruent with the social welfare, it ultimately was necessary to anchor the evaluative standard outside the organization. For these two reasons, self-inflation and self-deception, I rejected supervisors ratings as a measure of good police work.

2. *Good is measured by a policeman's performance in recruit school.* Recruit-school grades of the individual patrolmen were tempting because they were so precise in appearance and the recruit school was, to me, so sophisticated. The grades, however, lacked timeliness (as well as independence). Unless one presupposed that good trainees eventually made good police officers, classroom performance was either obsolete or irrelevant. In fact, one of the inquiries made in this research was whether good trainees turned into good police officers.

3. *Good is standing at one extreme or another on a scale created by the police organization for other reasons.* Certain secondary indicators had the merit of automatic and timely collection. Injuries on the job, days of absence from work, censures and awards, and public complaints about police misconduct were recorded systematically in the department. The difficulty in using these statistics as gauges of merit was their empirical remoteness to the quality of police work. For exam-

ple, both good and bad policemen could be injured. Injuries were often explicable in terms of beat assignment (and selection for a tough beat, at least arguably, was related to the quality of a police officer). Absences resulted as much from a good officer's having an unbearable supervisor as an unbearable officer's having a good supervisor. And so on. No matter what the secondary indicator, every policeman I met thought it too remote or too equivocal in the individual case to be a decisive measure of police work.

4. *Good is the number of arrests a policeman makes.* The Laconia Police Department required each policeman to summarize his accomplishments on weekly activity sheets. However, it limited the recordable activities to issuing tickets and making arrests. This indicator of activity obviously lacked comprehensiveness. Ticketing and arresting were not the quintessence of police work in most men's minds. The activity sheets omitted to record the family beefs handled well, the crime prevented, the information gathered, the stolen goods recovered, the friends made, the potential delinquents set straight, the commercial relationships ameliorated, the racial cleavages bridged, the hope infused, the help given. Such activities, which frequently animated the policeman, never were tabulated administratively. The activity sheets were, in a word, unrealistic.

5. *Good is a psychiatrist's finding of "not being abnormal."* Psychiatric examinations were made of Laconia policemen initially when they were recruited and followed up a year or two later. The reports of the psychiatrist resulting from this series of examinations overcame some of the liabilities of the first four definitions of a "good" policeman. They were more independent than the ratings of supervisors, more timely than recruit-school grades, more decisive than secondary indicators, and more comprehensive in assessing the whole policeman than the department's activity sheets.

A psychiatric evaluation was based upon a medical "model" of a "bad" man. A Laconia police officer was deemed "bad" if he approached the sick state of schizophrenia, "good" if he was not so sick. The "model" was sensitive to the individual's attitudes, not to his behavior. It searched out his understandings and emotions, and if they resembled those of the "sick" psychiatric model, then he was considered problematic and hence a problem cop. If he saw things with an "unrealism," if he evaluated matters too autonomously, without an adequate appreciation of the complex interrelationships of others around him, then his resemblance to the psychiatric model of the schizophrenic was marked, and he was characterized as abnormal, hence "bad."

Problems with the psychiatric model, however, occurred in two directions. Defining a bad policeman in terms of whether or not he was a sick man was at once too broad and too narrow. Too broad, because it presupposed that "bad" men would be "bad" policemen, that unhealthy attitudes would produce socially destructive behavior. Conceivably, however, "unrealistic" ideas and autonomous value systems might produce beneficial behavior. Martin Luther and Mahatma Gandhi might well have looked sick to the psychiatrists of their day. This is the problem of the attitude/behavior relationship, and we shall come back to it in the next section.

Even more important, the definition of a "bad" policeman was too narrow. By confining itself to detecting "bad" men, it might not identify a great many "bad" policemen. Arguably, the police job could be so demanding that more than a nonsick condition would be required of an individual if he were to do good police work over the long haul. An individual adequate to manage his own affairs might prove inadequate to govern the lives of others. A good man, as determined by civilized standards, able to cope well within the reciprocal and moral conventions of civilization, might be out of his depth in the uncushioned and frightening circumstances of the coercive world. Thus, application of the psychiatric model failed the test of realism.

IV

That is where the professional political model came in. By accepting Weber's assertions, I could identify a "good" policeman in terms of how his "passion and perspective" resembled the qualities of the professional politician. If he felt morally reconciled to using coercion and at the same time he reflected empathetically upon the condition of mankind, he measured up to being a professional, a good policeman.

To be sure, the professional political model was no less based on attitudes than the psychiatric model, which we have just rejected, had been. It did not solve the problem of the attitude/behavior relationship any better. Singling out "passion and perspective" as important assumed, but never proved, that the personal attitudes of a policeman and the actual results of his public actions were somehow positively related. I think there are both logical connections and a factual correlation between the two, but the reader should remain skeptical. Comparing the professional political model with the psychiatric model, however, I must repeat one point. They are both attitude models. The question is, which is the better attitude model for assessing policemen?

The professional political model had some virtues. It was independent of organizational bias, capable of using timely information, and, above all, realistic. Every policeman I asked insisted that the critical and recurrent part of his job occurred when he was the object of the threats of others and when he, in turn, had to influence people to do those things they were little inclined to do of their own accord—to desist from an antisocial act, to give humiliating information, to go to jail. At those times, he could give little in the way of positive inducements to compensate the citizens for their pains. He had only his authority, the threat to harm, to defend or assert himself. He had to extort cooperation because often he could not obtain it by any other means. In that a Laconia policeman often had to rely on his power to harm to prevent himself from being harmed by others, Weber's model of the professional politician seemed to fit the problem of measuring the man to the police job.

Moreover, a further advantage of the two-dimensional professional political model was that it could, theoretically at least, generate three types of nonprofessional policemen: (1) enforcers—police who had passion, but lacked perspective; (2) reciprocators—police who had perspective, but lacked passion; and (3) avoiders—police who lacked both passion and perspective.

V

I carefully analyzed the contents of the first interview of each police officer, young man and old-timer alike. I characterized his attitudes about the motives of mankind and the acceptability of coercion. I looked for clues particularly, but not exclusively, in his answers to these five questions.

1. Now let me get a feeling for what it is like being a police officer in Laconia today. Can you tell me about a particular incident which turned out to be one of the more difficult spots you've been in as a policeman in the field in Laconia?

2. Did anyone ever tell you how to deal with bullies—a pal or a minister or teacher or father or someone?

3. Let me shift gears a minute. I was reading a story of a first-year New York policeman named Gene Radano, and he told of an incident when he pulled over a car, an expensive-looking car, for running a stoplight. Radano said to the young guy who was driving, "I'm sorry, sir, but you just went through that red light. Can I have your license, please?"

   The driver was pretty rude, but the policeman kept on being polite and said, "I'm sorry, but from where I was standing you had ample time to stop." The driver wouldn't turn over his license and told Officer Radano to go ahead and arrest him; his father who was a bigwig would have his job. A crowd gathered—about eight or nine people, and when the driver even refused to give his name, Radano decided to take him to the station to be booked. Well, it turned out the guy who was arrested had claustrophobia, a fear of closed places, but nobody knew about it, including him, and when he refused to cooperate even at the station, the lieutenant decided to lock him up and cool him off. When the kid saw the bars of the lockup, however, he began fighting hysterically. In the fight a couple of officers got hurt, but, of course, the young fellow got hurt worst of all, and he ended up in the hospital. Radano's reaction was to blame himself. "If only I'd spoken with more authority in the beginning. Maybe if I'd been stern, it might not have happened. Maybe my courtesy was interpreted by the man as a sign of weakness. Maybe that was what started the snowball rolling downhill. " One thing that interested me was the way Officer Radano felt about himself. What do you think of the way he blamed himself for what happened?

4. I have heard policemen talk about each other, and invariably they seem to talk about how one group of men will do things differently from other groups of police officers. What are the different types of police officers which you see, and what are they like, and how do they differ?

5. Let me ask you a personal question: Have you ever had a tough problem in your police work where a decision of yours was right from one angle but wrong from another: say, from a personal or religious viewpoint it may have been right to do something, but from a police angle it was wrong, or the other way around: right from a police angle but not from a personal one.

Among the twenty-eight young policemen, ten (36%) appeared to be professionals. They resembled Jay Justice, whom we met in chapter 2, with his general notion about the dignity and tragedy of human nature and his ability to integrate the use of "proportionate" force into his principles of morality. Five (18%) could be characterized as enforcers. In their first interviews, at least, they resembled John Russo, whom we saw earlier as thoroughly confident in the efficacy of force but somewhat cynical about human society. Six (21%) could be typed as reciprocators, officers like Bob Ingersoll, who had moral conflicts over the necessity of coercion ("hated it," Ingersoll said) and were sympathetic with the citizenry. Finally, seven (25%) fell into the category of avoider. Bill Tubman, with his suspicion, cognitive bluntness toward the subtleties of human detail, and puzzlement about the ethics of force, illustrated this group of policemen.

A tabulation of the twenty-eight young officers would look like table 1.

In the course of this book, you will become acquainted with most of these individual policemen. Before you do get to know them better, let me utter two essential reservations about the classifications.

First, some men did not readily fall into categories. Some officers were uncertain about their perspectives. Rockingham, for example, a giant motorcycle-riding ex-military policeman with a musician's sensibilities, was still trying to make sense of a hazy world filled with human suffering and he wavered almost day to day. Because he had not resolved this conflict in comprehension, his perspective was treated as if it were cynical. Some officers who usually felt good about exercising coercive power (and hence were labeled as having an integrated passion) still evinced considerable discomfort about coercion in some situations. And vice versa: some officers usually troubled by force could take coercive action without the slightest qualm when the conditions were right.

Table 1
Classification According to Professional Political Model

| | Morality of Coercion | |
	Integrated	Conflicted
Tragic Perspective	*Professional* Justice Andros Bentham Chacon Douglas Patch Peel Rolfe Tennison Wilkes	*Reciprocator* Ingersoll Haig Hooker Hughes Lancaster Wrangel
Cynical Perspective	*Enforcer* Russo Bacon Carpasso Kane Kip	*Avoider* Tubman Booth Garfield Longstreet Nary Rockingham Thayer

Second, these men were young and, by and large, developing. Some had just begun the domesticating experience of having their own families. Some were taking college courses and confronting systems of ideas in their sociology and history courses that allowed them to recompose their perspectives. Each was increasing in police skills, and each was encountering new aspects of the city and of humanity. Some were likely to encounter difficulties which were going to overwhelm and destroy their development as professionals. Others, like John Russo, thanks to maturation, reassignment, and accident, appeared to change their outlooks and moralities so perceptibly in the several years I observed them as to begin the transformation into professionals .

This last point is the essential one to recall. Development and change were not easy, yet paradoxically were very likely. Development occurred daily; some was constructive, some destructive. One object of this book will be to identify a few of the crucial factors affecting this development.

VI

We have just begun the inquiry by measuring twenty-eight young policemen against the professional political model. Assuming for sake of argument that this typology is "correct" in some way, I want to emphasize that it is still nothing more than a starting point. We need to discover three things.

First, we have to know whether the typology is *useful.* Do policemen whose attitudes place them in these different categories behave differently? Specifically, did the professional policeman, the "good" cop, perform differently (and in some sense, respond more desirably) from the nonprofessional officer? This question, as we shall soon see, produces some very complex answers, and some readers may believe (as I do) that, sometimes, in some situations, the professional may behave *less* desirably than the nonprofessional policeman.

Second, there is the question of *explanation.* What is the dynamic process by which the recurrent use of coercive means produces the perspectives and passion to which the professional political model is sensitive? How does the resort to force build and destroy the attributes measured by Weber's scheme?

And third is the question of *engineering.* How can the corrupting effects of confronting recurrent coercive situations be modulated by human artifice so that desirable development will more probably occur and bad effect will be less likely? Those three questions—usefulness, explanation, and manipulation—constitute the final three parts of this book.

Donald J. Black

The Social Organization
of Arrest[*]

This article offers a set of descriptive materials on the social conditions under which policemen make arrests in routine encounters. At this
level, it is a modest increment in the expanding literature on the law's
empirical face. Scholarship on law-in-action has concentrated upon
criminal law in general and the world of the police in particular.[1] Just
what, beyond the hoarding of facts, these empirical studies will yield,
however, is still unclear. Perhaps a degree of planned change in the
criminal justice system will follow, be it in legal doctrine or in legal
administration. In any event, evaluation certainly appears to be the purpose, and reform the expected outcome, of much empirical research.
This article pursues a different sort of yield from its empirical study: a
sociological theory of law.[2] The analysis is self-consciously inattentive
to policy reform or evaluation of the police; it is intentionally bloodless
in tone. It examines arrest in order to infer patterns relevant to an
understanding of all instances of legal control.

Source: Donald J. Black (1971). "The Social Organization of Arrest," *Stanford Law Review*, 23:1087-
1092; 1104-1111. © 1971 by the Board of Trustees of the Leland Stanford Junior University.

*The article's findings derive from a larger research project under the direction of Professor Albert
J. Reiss, Jr., Department of Sociology and Institute of Social Science, Yale University. The project
was coordinated at the Center for Research on Social Organization, Department of Sociology, University of Michigan. It was supported by Grant Award 006, Office of Law Enforcement Assistance,
U.S. Department of Justice, under the Law Enforcement Assistance Act of 1965, and by grants
from the National Science Foundation and the Russell Sage Foundation.

[1] *See generally* E. SCHUR, LAW AND SOCIETY (1968); Skolnick, *The Sociology of Law in America:
Overview and Trends,* in LAW AND SOCIETY 4 (1965) (supplement to 13 SOCIAL PROBLEMS (1965));
Bordua & Reiss *Law Enforcement,* in THE USES OF SOCIOLOGY 275 (1967); Manning, *Observing
the Police,* in OBSERVING DEVIANCE (J. Douglas ed., forthcoming). The empirical literature is so
abundant and is expanding so rapidly that these published bibliographic discussions are invariably
inadequate.

[2] It should be noted that the article's approach to legal life differs quite radically from the
approach of Philip Selznick, one of the most influential American sociologists of law. Selznick's
sociology of law attempts to follow the path of natural law; my approach follows the general
direction of legal positivism. In Lon Fuller's language, Selznick is willing to tolerate a confusion of
the *is* and *ought,* while I am not. L. FULLER, THE LAW IN QUEST OF ITSELF 5 (1940). *See* P. SELZNICK,
LAW, SOCIETY, AND INDUSTRIAL JUSTICE (1969); Selznick, *The Sociology of Law,* 9 INTERNATIONAL
ENCYCLOPEDIA OF THE SOCIAL SCIENCES 50 (D.L. Sills ed., 1968); Selznick, *Sociology and Natural
Law,* 6 NATURAL L.F. 84 (1961).

The empirical analysis queries how a number of circumstances affect the probability of arrest. The factors considered are: the suspect's race, the legal seriousness of the alleged crime, the evidence available in the field setting, the complainant's preference for police action, the social relationship between the complainant and suspect, the suspect's degree of deference toward the police, and the manner in which the police come to handle an incident, whether in response to a citizen's request or through their own initiative. The inquiry seeks to discover general principles according to which policemen routinely use or withhold their power to arrest, and thus to reveal a part of the social organization of arrest.[3]

The article begins with a skeletal discussion of the field method. Next follows a brief ethnography of routine police work designed to place arrest within its mundane context. The findings on arrest are then presented, first for encounters involving both a citizen complainant and a suspect, and second for police encounters with lone suspects. The article finally speculates about the implications of the empirical findings at the level of a general theory of legal control, the focus shifting from a sociology of the police to a sociology of law.

I. Field Method

The data were collected during the summer of 1966 by systematic observation of police-citizen transactions in Boston, Chicago, and Washington, D.C.[4] Thirty six observers—persons with law, social science, and police administration backgrounds—recorded observations of encounters between uniformed patrolmen and citizens. The observers' training and supervision was, for all practical purposes, identical in the three cities. Observers accompanied patrolmen on all work shifts on all days of the week for seven weeks in each city. Proportionately more of our manhours were devoted to times when police activity is comparatively high, namely evening shifts, and particularly weekend evenings. Hence, to a degree the sample overrepresents the kinds of social disruptions that arise more on evenings and weekends than at other times. The police precincts chosen as observation sites in each city were select-

---

[3] As used in this article, the broad concept "social organization" refers to the supraindividual principles and mechanisms according to which social events come into being, are maintained and arranged, change, and go out of existence. Put another way, social organization refers to the descriptive grammar of social events.

[4] At this writing, the data are over four years old. However, there has been little reform in routine patrol work since 1966. This is in part because of the police work in question—everyday police contact with citizens—is not as amenable to planned change as other forms of police work, such as crowd or riot control, traffic regulation, or vice enforcement. Moreover, the data have value even if they no longer describe contemporary conduct, since they remain useful for developing a theory of law as a behavior system. A general theory of law has no time limits. Indeed, how fine it would be if we possessed more empirical data from legal life past.

ed to maximize scrutiny of lower socio-economic, high crime rate, racially homogeneous residential areas. Two precincts were used in both Boston and Chicago, and four precincts were used in Washington, D.C. The Washington, D.C. precincts, however, were more racially integrated than were those in Boston and Chicago.

Observers recorded the data in "incident booklets," forms structurally similar to interview schedules. One booklet was used for each incident. A field situation involving police action was classified as an "incident" if it was brought to the officer's attention by the police radio system, or by a citizen on the street or in the police station, or if the officer himself noticed a situation and decided that it required police attention. Also included as incidents were a handful of situations in which the police noticed themselves but which they chose to ignore.

The observers did not fill out incident booklets in the presence of policemen. In fact, the line officers were told that the research was not concerned with police behavior but only with citizen behavior toward the police and the kinds of problems citizens make for the police.

The observers recorded a total of 5,713 incidents, but the base for present analysis is only a little more than 5 percent of the total. This attrition results primarily from the general absence of opportunities for arrest in patrol work, where most of the incidents involve non-criminal situations or criminal situations for which there is no suspect. Traffic encounters also were excluded, even though technically any traffic violation presents an opportunity for arrest. Other cases were eliminated because they involved factors that could invisibly distort or otherwise confuse the analysis. The encounters excluded were those initiated by citizens who walked into a police station to ask for help (6 percent of the total) or who flagged down the police on the street (5 percent). These kinds of encounters involve peculiar situational features warranting separate treatment, though even that would be difficult, given their statistically negligible number. For similar reasons encounters involving participants of mixed race and mixed social-class status[5] were eliminated. Finally, the sample of encounters excludes suspects under 18 years of age—legal juveniles in most states—and suspects of white-collar status.[6] Thus, it investigates arrest patterns in police encounters with predominantly blue-collar adult suspects.

---

[5] This means that encounters involving a complainant and suspect of different races were excluded. Similarly, the sample would not include the arrest of a black man with a white wife. However, it does not mean the exclusion of encounters where the policeman and suspect were not of the same race.

[6] Because field observers occasionally had difficulty in judging the age or social class of a citizen, they were told to use a "don't know" category whenever they felt the danger of misclassification. Two broad categories of social class, blue-collar and white-collar were employed. Since the precincts sampled were predominantly lower class, the observers labeled the vast majority of the citizen participants as blue-collar. In fact, not enough white-collar cases were available for separate analysis. The small number of adults of ambiguous social class were combined with the blue-collar cases into a sample of "predominantly blue-collar" suspects. The observers probably were reasonably accurate in classifying suspects because the police frequently interviewed suspects about their age and occupation.

II. Routine Police Work

In some respects, selecting arrest as a subject of study implicitly mis-represents routine police work. Too commonly, the routine is equated with the exercise of the arrest power, not only by members of the general public but by lawyers and even many policemen as well. In fact, the daily round of the patrol officer infrequently involves arrest[7] or even encounters with a criminal suspect. The most cursory observation of the policeman on the job overturns the imagery of a man who makes his living parceling citizens into jail.

Modern police departments are geared to respond to citizen calls for service; the great majority of incidents the police handle arise when a citizen telephones the police and the dispatcher sends a patrol car to deal with the situation. The officer becomes implicated in a wide range of human troubles, most not of his own choosing, and many of which have little or nothing to do with criminal law enforcement. He transports people to the hospital, writes reports of auto accidents, and arbitrates and mediates between disputants—neighbors, husbands and wives, landlords and tenants, and businessmen and customers. He takes missing-person reports, directs traffic, controls crowds at fires, writes dogbite reports, and identifies abandoned autos. He removes safety hazards from the streets, and occasionally scoops up a dead animal. Policemen disdain this kind of work, but they do it every day. Such incidents rarely result in arrest; they nevertheless comprise nearly half of the incidents uniformed patrolmen encounter in situations initiated by phone calls from citizens.[8] Policemen also spend much of their time with "juvenile trouble," a police category typically pertaining to distinctively youthful disturbances of adult peace—noisy groups of teenagers on a street corner, ball-playing in the street, trespassing or playing in deserted buildings or construction sites, and rock-throwing. These situations, too, rarely result in arrest. Some officers view handling juvenile trouble as work they do in the service of neighborhood grouches. The same may be said of ticketing parking violations in answer to citizen complaints. All these chores necessitate much unexciting paperwork.

Somewhat less than half of the encounters arising from a citizen phone call have to do with crime—a felony or a misdemeanor other than juvenile trouble. Yet even criminal incidents are so constituted situationally as to preclude arrest in the majority of cases, because no sus-

---

[7] In this article, "arrest" refers only to transportation of a suspect to a police station. It does not include the application of restraint in field settings, and it does not require formal booking of a suspect with a crime. See W. LAFAVE, ARREST: THE DECISION TO TAKE A SUSPECT INTO CUSTODY 4 (1965).

[8] D. Black, Police Encounters and Social Organization: An Observation Study, 51-57, Dec. 15, 1968 (unpublished dissertation in Department of Sociology, University of Michigan). See also Cumming, Cumming & Edell, Policeman as Philosopher, Guide and Friend, 12 SOCIAL PROBLEMS 276 (1965).

pect is present when the police arrive at the scene. In 77 percent of the felony situations and in 51 percent of the misdemeanor situations the only major citizen participant is a complainant.[9] In a handful of other cases the only citizen present is an informant or bystander. When no suspect is available in the field setting, the typical official outcome is a crime report, the basic document from which official crime statistics are constructed and the operational prerequisite of further investigation by the detective division.

The minority of citizen-initiated crime encounters where a suspect is present when the police arrive is the appropriate base for a study of arrest. In the great majority of these suspect encounters a citizen complainant also takes part in the situational interaction, so any study of routine arrest must consider the complainant's role as well as those of the police officer and the suspect.[10]

Through their own discretionary authority, policemen occasionally initiate encounters that may be called *proactive* police work, as opposed to the *reactive,* citizen-initiated work that consumes the greater part of the average patrol officer's day.[11] On an evening shift (traditionally 4 p.m. to midnight) a typical work-load for a patrol car is 6 radio-dispatched encounters and one proactive encounter. The ratio of proactive encounters varies enormously by shift, day of week, patrol beat or territory, and number of cars on duty. An extremely busy weekend night could involve 20 dispatches to a single car. Under these rushed conditions the officers might not initiate any encounters on their own. At another time in another area a patrol car might receive no dispatches, but the officers might initiate as many as 8 or 10 encounters on the street. During the observation study only 13 percent of incidents came to police attention without the assistance of citizens.[12] Still, most officers as well as citizens probably think of proactive policing as the form that epitomizes the police function.

The police-initiated encounter is a bald confrontation between state and citizen. Hardly ever does a citizen complainant take part in a proactive field encounter and then only if a policeman were to discover an incident of personal victimization or if a complainant were to step subsequent to the officer's initial encounter with a suspect. Moreover, the array of incidents policeman handle—their operational jurisdiction—is quite different when they have the discretion to select situa-

---

[9] D. Black, *supra* note 8 at 94.

[10] In fact, of all the felony cases the police handle in response to a citizen request by telephone, including cases where only a complainant, informant, or bystander is present in the situation, a mere 3% involve a police transaction with a lone suspect. D. black, *supra* note 8, at 94.

[11] The concepts "reactive" and "proactive" derive from the origins of individual action, the former referring to actions originating in the environment, the latter to those originating within the actor. *See* Murray, *Toward a Classification of Interactions,* in TOWARD A GENERAL THEORY OF ACTION 434 (1967).

[12] This proportion is based upon the total sample of 5,713 incidents.

tions for attention compared to what it is when that discretion is lodged in citizens. In reactive police work they are servants of the public, with one consequence being that the social troubles they oversee often have little if anything to do with criminal law. Arrest is usually a situational impossibility. In proactive policing the officer is more a public guardian and the operational jurisdiction is a police choice; the only limits are in law and in departmental policy. In proactive work, arrest is totally a matter of the officer's own making. Yet the reality of proactive police work has an ironic quality about it. The organization of crime in time and space deprives policemen on free patrol of legally serious arrests. Most felonies occur in off-street settings and must be detected by citizens. Even those that occur in a visible public place usually escape the policemen's ken. When the police have an opportunity to initiate an encounter, the occasion is more likely than not a traffic violation. Traffic violations comprise the majority of proactive encounters, and most of the remainder concern minor "disturbances of the peace."[13] In short, where the police role is most starkly aggressive in form, the substance is drably trivial, and legally trivial incidents provide practically all of the grist for arrest in proactive police operations.

Perhaps a study of arrest flatters the legal significance of the everyday police encounter. Still, even though arrest situations are uncommon in routine policing, invocation of the criminal process accounts for more formal-legal cases, more court trials and sanctions, more public controversies and conflicts than any other mechanism in the legal system. As a major occasion of legal control, then, arrest cries out for empirical study.[14]

* * *

[13] Much proactive patrol work involves a drunken or disorderly person. Typically, however, arrest occurs in these cases only when the citizen is uncooperative; ordinarily the policeman begins his encounter by giving an order such as "Move on," "Take off," or "Take it easy." Arrest is an outcome of interaction rather than a simple and direct response of an officer to what he observes as an official witness.

[14] Earlier observational studies have neglected patterns of arrest in the everyday work of uniformed patrolmen. Emphasis has instead been placed upon detective work, vice enforcement, policing of juveniles, and other comparatively marginal aspects of police control. *See* J. SKOLNICK, JUSTICE WITHOUT TRIAL (1966) (patterns of arrest in vice enforcement); Bittner, *The Police on Skid-Row: A Study of Peace-Keeping*, 32 AM. SOC. REV. 699 (1967); Black & Reiss, *Police Control of Juveniles*, 35 AM. SOC. REV. 63 (1970); Piliavin & Briar, *Police Encounters with Juveniles*, 70 AM. J. SOC. 206 (1964). Several observational studies emphasizing other dimensions of police work also are directly relevant. *See* L. TIFFANY, D. MCINTYRE, & D. ROTENBERG, DETECTION OF CRIME (1967); Reis & Black, *Interrogation and the Criminal Process*, 374 ANNALS OF THE AM. ACADEMY OF POL. & SOC. SCI. 47 (1967); Project, *Interrogations in New Haven: The Impact of Miranda*, 76 YALE L.J. 1519 (1967). There also have been a number of studies based upon official arrest statistics. *See* N. Goldman, THE DIFFERENTIAL SELECTION OF JUVENILE OFFENDERS FOR COURT APPEARANCE (1963); J. WILSON, VARIETIES OF POLICE BEHAVIOR (1968); Green, *Race, Social Status, and Criminal Arrest*, 35 AM. SOC. REV. 476 (1970); Terry, *The Screening of Juvenile Offenders*, 58 J. CRIM. L.C. & P.S. 173 (1967). For a more speculative discussion *see* Goldstein, *Police Discretion Not to Invoke the Criminal Process: Low-Visibility Decisions in the Administration of Justice*, 69 YALE L.J. 543 (1960). *See generally* W. LAFAVE, *supra* note 7.

V. Generalizations

This section restates the major findings of this study in the form of empirical generalizations which should provide a manageable profile of police behavior in routine situations where arrest is a possibility. When appropriate, inferences are drawn from these materials to more abstract proponents at the level of a general theory of legal control. Arrest patterns may reveal broad principles according to which legal policy is defined, legal resources mobilized, and dispositions made.[19]

A. Mobilization

Most arrest situations arise through citizen rather than police initiative. In this sense, the criminal law is invoked in a manner not unlike that of private-law systems that are mobilized through a reactive process, depending upon the enterprise of citizen claimants in pursuit of their own interests. In criminal law as in other areas of public law, although the state has formal, proactive authority to bring legal actions, the average criminal matter is the product of a citizen complaint.

One implication of this pattern is that most criminal cases pass through a moral filter in the citizen population before the state assumes its enforcement role. A major portion of the responsibility for criminal-law enforcement is kept out of police hands. Much like courts in the realm of private law, the police operate as moral servants of the citizenry. A further implication of this pattern of reactive policing is that the deterrence function of the criminal process, to an important degree, depends upon citizen willingness to mobilize the criminal law, just at the deterring function of private law depends so much on citizen plaintiffs.[20] Sanctions cannot deter illegal behavior if the law lies dormant because of an inefficient mobilization process.[21] In this sense all legal systems rely to a great extent upon private citizens.

---

[19] These three functional foci of legal control—prescription, mobilization, and disposition—correspond roughly to the legislative, executive, and judicial dimensions of government, though they are useful in the analysis of subsystems of legal control as well as total systems. For instance, the police can be regarded as the major mobilization subsystem of the criminal justice system. Yet the police subsystem itself can be approached as a total system involving prescription, mobilization, and disposition subsystems. *Cf.* H. LASSWELL, THE DECISION PROCESS 2 (1956).

[20] Contemporary literature on deterrence is devoted primarily to the role of sanctions in criminal law. *See*, e.g., Andenaes, *The General Preventive Effects of Punishment,* 114 U. PA. L. REV. 949 (1966). *But see* R. VON JHERING, THE STRUGGLE FOR LAW (1879).

[21] Roscoe Pound concludes that the contingent nature of legal mobilization is one of the major obstacles to the effectiveness of law as a social engineering device. *See* Pound, *The Limits of Effective Legal Action,* 27 INT'L J. ETHICS 150 (1917). *See also* H. JONES, THE EFFICACY OF LAW 21-26 (1969); Bohannan, *The Differing Realms of the Law,* in THE ETHNOGRAPHY OF LAW 33 (1965) (supplement to 67 AM. ANTHROPOLOGIST 33 (1965)).

B. Complainants

Arrest practices sharply reflect the preferences of citizen complainants, particularly when the desire for leniency and also, though less frequently, when the complainant demands arrest. The police are an instrument of the complainant, then, in two ways: Generally they handle what the complainant wants them to handle and they handle the matter in the way the complainant prescribes.

Often students of the police comment that a community has the kind of police it wants, as if the community outlines the police function by some sort of *de facto* legislative process.[22] That view is vague, if not mistaken. Instead, the police serve an atomized mass of complainants far more than they serve an organized community. The greater part of the police workload is case-by-case, isolated contacts between individual policemen and individual complainants. In this sense the police serve a phantom master who dwells throughout the population, who is everywhere but nowhere at once. Because of this fact, the police are at once an easy yet elusive target for criticism. Their field work evades planned change, but as shifts occur in the desires of the atomized citizenry who call and direct the police, changes ripple into policemen's routine behavior.

The pattern of police compliance with complainants gives police work a radically democratic character. The result is not, however, uniform standards of justice, since the moral standards of complainants doubtlessly vary to some extent across the population. Indeed, by complying with complainants the police in effect perpetuate the moral diversity they encounter in the citizen mass.[23] In this respect again, a public-law system bears similarity to systems of private law.[24] Both types seem organized, visibly and invisibly, so as to give priority to the demands of their dispersed citizens. Whoever may prescribe the law and however the law is applied, many sovereigns call the law to action.[25] Public-law sys-

---

[22] *See, e.g.,* P. SLATER, THE PURSUIT OF LONELINESS: AMERICAN CULTURE AT THE BREAKING POINT 49 (1970).

[23] This generalization does not apply to proactive police operations such as vice control or street harassment, which seldom involve a citizen complainant. By definition, street harassment is the selective and abrasive attention directed at people who are, at best, marginally liable to arrest—for example, a police command to "move on" to a group of unconventional youths. Proactive policing may involve an attack on particular moral subcultures. *Compare* J. CLEBERT, THE GYPSIES 87-119 (1963) *with* Brown, *The Condemnation and Persecution of Hippies,* TRANS-ACTION, Sept. 1969 at 33, *and* W. HAGAN, INDIAN POLICE AND JUDGES (1966).

[24] *See* Pashukanis, *The General Theory of Law and Marxism* in SOVIET LEGAL PHILOSOPHY III (H. Babb transl. 1951).

[25] This is true historically as well; legal systems usually have made the citizen complainant the *sine qua non* of legal mobilization, except under circumstances posing a direct threat to political order. A well-known example was the Roman legal process, where even extreme forms of personal violence required the initiative of a complainant before government sanctions were imposed. *See generally* A. LINTOTT, VIOLENCE IN REPUBLICAN ROME (1968). A theory of legal control should treat as problematic the capacity and willingness of government to initiate cases and sanction violators in the absence of an aggrieved citizen demanding justice. *See generally* S. RANULF, MORAL INDIGNATION AND MIDDLE CLASS PSYCHOLOGY: A SOCIOLOGICAL STUDY (1938).

tems are peculiar in that their formal organization allows them to initiate and pursue cases without complainants as sponsors. Still, the reality of public-law systems such as the police belies their formal appearance. The citizenry continually undermines uniformity in public- as well as private-law enforcement. Perhaps democratic organization invariably jeopardizes uniformity in the application of legal controls.[26]

C. Leniency

The police are lenient in their routine arrest practices; they use their arrest power less often than the law would allow. Legal leniency, however, is hardly peculiar to the police. Especially in the private-law sector[27] and also in other areas of public law,[28] the official process for redress of grievances is invoked less often than illegality is detected. Citizens and public officials display reluctance to wield legal power in immediate response to illegality, and a sociology of law must treat as problematic the fact that legal cases arise at all.

D. Evidence

Evidence is an important factor in arrest. The stronger the evidence in the field situation, the more likely is an arrest. When the police themselves witness a criminal offense they are more likely to arrest the suspect than when they only hear about the offense from a third party. Rarely do the police confront persons as suspects without some evidence; even more rarely are arrests unsupported by evidence. The importance of situational evidence hardly constitutes a major advance in knowledge. Evidence has a role in every legal process. It is the definition of evidence, not whether evidence is required, that differs across legal system. It should be emphasized that even when the evidence

---

[26] The norm of universalism reflected in systems of public law in advanced societies is a norm of impersonalism: The police are expected to enforce the law impersonally. But by giving complainants a strong role in the determination of outcomes, the police personalize the criminal law. This pattern allows fellow family members and friends to mobilize the police to handle their disputes with little danger that the police will impose standards foreign to their relationships. At the level of disputes between strangers, however, the same pattern of police compliance with complaints can, given moral diversity, result in a form of discriminatory enforcement. A law enforcement process that takes no account of the degree of intimacy between complainant and suspect may also upset the peculiar balance of close social relationships. *See* Kawashima, *Dispute Resolution in Contemporary Japan,* in LAW IN JAPAN: THE LEGAL ORDER IN A CHANGING SOCIETY 41 (A. von Mehren ed. 1964).

[27] *See, e.g.,* Macaulay, *Non-Contractual Relations in Business: A Preliminary Study,* 28 AM. SOC. REV. 55 (1963).

[28] *See, e.g.,* M. Mileski, *Policing Slum Landlords: An Observation Study of Administrative Control,* June 14, 1971 (unpublished dissertation in Department of Sociology, Yale University).

against a suspect is very strong, the police frequently take action short of arrest. Evidence alone, then, is a necessary but not a sufficient basis for predicting invocation of the law.

E. Seriousness

The probability of arrest is higher in legally serious crime situations than in those of a relatively minor nature. This finding certainly is not unexpected, but it has theoretical significance. The police levy arrest as a sanction to correspond with the defined seriousness of the criminal event in much the same fashion as legislators and judges allocate punishments. The formal legal conception of arrest contrasts sharply with this practice by holding that arrest follows upon detection of any criminal act without distinguishing among levels of legal seriousness. Assuming the offender population is aware that arrest represents legislation and adjudication by police officers, arrest practices should contribute to deterrence of serious crime, for the perpetrator whose act is detected risks a greater likelihood of arrest as well as more severe punishment. The higher the risk of arrest, once the suspect confronts the police, may help to offset the low probability of detection for some of the more serious crimes.[29]

F. Intimacy

The greater the relational distance between a complainant and a suspect, the greater is the likelihood of arrest. When a complainant demands the arrest of a suspect the police are most apt to comply if the adversaries are strangers. Arrest is less likely if they are friends, neighbors, or acquaintances, and it is least likely if they are family members. Policeman also write official crime reports according to the same differential.[30] Relational distance likewise appears to be a major factor in the probability of litigation in contract disputes[31] and other private-law contexts.[32] One may generalize that in all legal affairs relational distance between the adversaries affects the probability of formal litiga-

---

[29] *See* Black, *Production of Crime Rates,* 35 AM. SOC. REV. 733, 735 (1970) (remarks on detection differentials in police work).

[30] Black, *supra* note 29, at 740. Jerome Hall hypothesizes that relational distance influences the probability of criminal prosecution. J. HALL, THEFT, LAW AND SOCIETY 318 (2d ed. 1952).

[31] Macaulay, *supra* note 27, at 56.

[32] For example, in Japan disputes that arise across rather than within communities are more likely to result in litigation. *See* Kawashima, *supra* note 26, at 45. In American chinatowns disputes that arise between Chinese and non-Chinese are far more likely to result in litigation than disputes between Chinese. *See* Grace, *Justice, Chinese Style,* CASE & COM., Jan.-Feb., 1970, at 50. The same is true of disputes between gypsies and non-gypsies as compared to disputes between gypsies.

tion. If the generalization is true, it teaches that legal control may have comparatively little to do with the maintenance of order between and among inmates.

Yet the findings on relational distance in police arrest practices may merely reflect the fact that legal control operates only when sublegal control is unavailable.[33] The greater the relational distance, the less is the likelihood that sublegal mechanisms of control will operate. This proposition even seems a useful principle for understanding the increasing salience of legal control in social evolution.[34] Over time the drift of history delivers proportionately more and more strangers who need the law to hold them together and apart. Law seems to bespeak an absence of community, and law grows ever more prominent as the dissolution of community proceeds.[35]

G. Disrespect

The probability of arrest increases when a suspect is disrespectful toward the police. The same pattern appears in youth officer behavior,[36] patrol officer encounters with juveniles,[37] and in the use of illegal violence by the police.[38] Even disrespectful complainants receive a penalty of sorts from the police, as their complaints are less likely to receive official recognition.[39] In form, disrespect in a police encounter is much the same as "contempt" in a courtroom hearing. It is a rebellion against

---

See J. CLEBERT, *supra* note 23, at 90. Likewise, in the United States in the first half of the 19th century, crimes committed between Indians generally were left to the tribes. *See* F. PRUCHA, AMERICAN INDIAN POLICY IN THE FORMATIVE YEARS: THE INDIAN TRADE AND INTERCOURSE ACTS 188-212 (1962). In medieval England the same sort of pattern obtained in the legal condition of the Jews. Ordinary English rules applied to legal dealings between Jews and the King and between Jews and Christians, but disputes between Jew and Jew were heard in Jewish tribunals and decided under Jewish law. *See* I F. POLLOCK & F. MAITLAND, THE HISTORY OF ENGLISH LAW 468-475 (2d ed. 1898).

[33] *See* L. PEATTIE, THE VIEW FROM THE BARRIO 54-62 (1968) (for a stark illustration of this pattern). *See generally* R. POUND, SOCIAL CONTROL THROUGH LAW 18-25 (1942); S. VAN DER SPRENKEL, LEGAL INSTITUTIONS IN MANCHU CHINA: A SOCIOLOGICAL ANALYSIS (1962); Cohen, *Chinese Mediation on the Eve of Modernization*, 54 CALIF. L. REV. 1201 (1966); Nader, *An Analysis of Zapotec Law Cases*, 3 ETHNOLOGY 404 (1964); Nader & Metzger, *Conflict Resolution in Two Mexican Communities*, 65 AM. ANTHROPOLOGIST 584 (1963); Schwartz, *Social Factors in the Development of Legal Control: A Case Study of Two Israeli Settlements*, 63 YALE L.J. 471 (1954); notes 26, 30-31 *supra*.

[34] It is at this level that Pound posits his thesis concerning the priority of sublegal control. R. POUND, *supra* note 33, at 33. *See also* Fuller, *Two Principles of Human Association*, II NOMOS 3 (1969); Selznick, *Legal Institutions and Social Controls*, 17 VAND. L. REV. 79 (1963).

[35] *See* F. TONNIES, COMMUNITY AND SOCIETY 202 (C. Loomis transl. 1957).

[36] Piliavin & Briar, *supra* note 14, at 210.

[37] Black & Reiss, *Police Control of Juveniles, supra* note 14, at 74-75.

[38] P. CHEVIGNY, POLICE POWER: POLICE ABUSES IN NEW YORK CITY 51-83 (1969); Reiss, *Police Brutality—Answers to Key Questions*, TRANS-ACTION, July-Aug., 1968, at 18; Westley, *Violence and the Police*, 59 AM. J. SOC. 34 (1954).

[39] Black, *supra* note 29, at 742-44.

the processing system. Unlike the judge, however, the policeman has no special legal weapons in his arsenal for dealing with citizens who refuse to defer to his authority at a verbal or otherwise symbolic level. Perhaps as the legal system further differentiates, a crime of "contempt of police" will emerge. From a radically behavioral standpoint, indeed, this crime has already emerged; the question is when it will be formalized in the written law.

All legal control systems, not only the police and the judiciary, defend their own authority with energy and dispatch. To question or assault the legitimacy of a legal control process is to invite legal invocation, a sanction, or a more serious sanction, whatever is at issue in a given confrontation. Law seems to lash out at every revolt against its own integrity. Accordingly, it might be useful to consider disrespect toward a policeman to be a minor form of civil disorder, or revolution the highest form of disrespect.

H. Discrimination

No evidence exists to show that the police discriminate on the basis of race. The police arrest blacks at a comparatively high rate, but the difference between the races appears to result primarily from the greater rate at which blacks show disrespect for the police. The behavioral difference thus lies within the citizen participants, not the police.[40] This finding conflicts with some ideological conceptions of police work, but it is supported by the findings of several studies based upon direct observation of the police.[41] These findings should be taken as a caveat that in general improper or illegal behavior toward blacks does not in itself constitute evidence of discrimination against blacks. A finding of discrimination or of nondiscrimination requires a comparative analysis

---

[40] Of course, "discrimination" can be defined to include any *de facto* unequal treatment, regardless of its causes. *See* L. MAYHEW, LAW AND EQUAL OPPORTUNITY 59-60 (1968). The evidence in the article simply indicates that blacks are treated differently not because they are blacks, but because they manifest other behavioral patterns, such as disrespect for the police, more frequently than whites. The question of why blacks disproportionately show disrespect for the police cannot be addressed with the observational data. We could speculate, for example, that in anticipation of harsh treatment blacks often behave disrespectfully toward the police, thereby setting in motion a pattern that confirms their expectations.

Despite the article's finding of nondiscrimination the police officers observed did reveal considerable prejudice in their attitude toward blacks. *See generally* Black & Reiss, *Patterns of Behavior in Police and Citizen Transactions,* in 2 PRESIDENT'S COMMISSION ON LAW ENFORCEMENT AND ADMINISTRATION OF JUSTICE, STUDIES IN CRIME AND LAW ENFORCEMENT IN MAJOR METROPOLITAN AREAS 132-139. *See also* Deutscher, *Words and Deeds: Social Science and Social Policy,* 13 SOCIAL PROBLEMS 235 (1966).

[41] *See generally* W. LAFAVE, *supra* note 7; J. SKOLNICK, *supra* note 14, at 83-88; L. TIFFANY, D. MCINTYRE, & D. ROTENBERG, *supra* note 14; Piliavin & Briar, supra note 14 (despite innuendos to the contrary); Project, *supra* note 14, at 1645; n.9. These studies do not report evidence of discrimination or fail altogether to mention race as an analytically important variable.

of behavior toward each race with other variables such as level of respect held constant. No study of citizen opinions or perceptions[42] or of official statistics[43] can hold these variables constant.

In closing this Section it is important to note that the findings on racial discrimination by the police should not remotely suggest that law is oblivious to social rank. On the contrary, broader patterns in the form and substance of legal control seem at any one time to reflect and to perpetuate existing systems of social stratification. That the degradation of arrest is reserved primarily for the kinds of illegality committed by lower status citizens exemplifies this broader tendency of the law in action.

VI. Concluding Remarks

A major commitment of this article is to dislodge the discussion from its grounding in empirical findings and to raise the degree of abstraction to the level of general theory. Statements at this level ignore the boundaries and distinctions that ordinarily contain and constrain generalization about law as a social phenomenon. The various subsystems of law—criminal law, torts, contracts, constitutional law, family law, property law, criminal procedure, administrative law—are assumed to contain common elements. As if this aim were too faint-hearted, a general theory of legal control also seeks to discover patterns present in several functional dimensions of law: prescription, mobilization, and disposition; or respectively, the articulation of legal policy, the engagement of legal cases by legal organizations, and the situational resolution of legal disputes. This sort of sociology of law shares with jurisprudence the inclusiveness of its subject matter. Each discipline acts upon a longing for a universal understanding of law. For each, the past shares the relevance of the present, and other legal systems illustrate our own. Unlike jurisprudence, however, sociology of law abjures problems of a normative character; unlike sociology of law, jurisprudence bypasses the ordeal of concrete description.

A closing note should state what the article has not done. Arrest might be examined from a number of other perspectives that have their own vocabulary suited to their own special kind of discourse. For example, arrest may usefully be conceived as one stage in an elaborate processing network, an assembly line of inputs and outputs. This technocratic metaphor has been popular in recent studies of the criminal justice system. Another perspective might see every arrest as a political event. When and how the arrest power is used says much about the

---

[42] E.g., Werthman & Piliavin, *Gang Members and the Police,* in THE POLICE: SIX SOCIOLOGICAL ESSAYS 56 (D. Bordua ed. 1967).

[43] *See* N. GOLDMAN, *supra* note 14, at 45; J. WILSON, *supra* note 14, at 113; Green, *supra* note 14, at 481.

nature of a political system and the quality of life within it. Then, too, arrest is part of a job. It is a role performance of a bureaucratic functionary. Police work may be contemplated as it arises from its rich occupational subculture with standards and values that policemen share and enforce among their peers. And every arrest is enveloped by the police bureaucracy. Not surprisingly, therefore, the arrest practices of individual officers are under some degree of surveillance from their superiors as well as their peers. Finally, a study of arrest can inform and benefit from the sociology of face-to-face interaction. The police encounter is a small group with its own morphology, its own dynamics. What happens in an encounter may have less to do with crime and law than with the demands of situational order, with social etiquette or the pressures of group size or spatial configuration. An arrest may be the only means available to a policeman bent on restoring order to field situation, yet other time sit is the surest way to undermine order by making a situation disintegrate.

Some encouragement may be taken from the development of social science to the point where a subject such as arrest can occasion so many diverse perspectives. Diversity of this degree, nevertheless, casts a film of arbitrariness over whatever theoretical framework is chosen. Although the many perspectives available to a study of arrest surely mirror the empirical nature of arrest itself, its theoretical identity is precarious and unstable. Here it is sanction and justice; there, input, coercion, expectation, job, criterion, or gesture. Any single theoretical view of arrest is inevitably incomplete.

John Van Maanen

The Asshole

"I guess what our job really boils down to is not letting the assholes take over the city. Now I'm not talking about your regular crooks . . . they're bound to wind up in the joint anyway. What I'm talking about are those shitheads out to prove they can push everybody around. Those are the assholes we gotta deal with and take care of on patrol. . . . They're the ones that make it tough on the decent people out there. You take the majority of what we do and its nothing more than asshole control."

A veteran patrolman[1]

I. Police Typifications

The asshole—creep, bigmouth, bastard, animal, mope, rough, jerkoff, clown, scumbag, wiseguy, phony, idiot, shithead, bum, fool, or any of a number of anatomical, oral, or incestuous terms—is a part of every policeman's world.[2] Yet the grounds upon which such a figure stands have never been examined systematically. The purpose of this essay is to display the interactional origins and consequences of the

---

Source: John Van Maanen (1978). "The Asshole." In P.K. Manning and John Van Maanen (eds.) *Policing: A View from the Street*, pp. 221-238. Santa Monica, CA: Goodyear. Reprinted courtesy of John Van Maanen, Erwin Schell Professor of Organizational Studies, M.I.T.

[1] All police quotes are taken from field notes I compiled of conversations and observations taking place during a year of participant observation in what I have referred to anonymously in my writings as the Union City Police Department (a large, metropolitan force employing over 1,500 uniformed officers). The quotes are as accurate as my ear, memory, and notes allow (see Epilogue—eds.) I should note, also, that in this essay I use the terms "police," "police officer," "patrolman," and "policemen" somewhat interchangeably. However, unless I indicate otherwise, my comments are directed solely toward the street-level officer—the cop on the beat—and not toward his superiors, administrators, or colleagues in the more prestigeful detective bureaus.

[2] I chose the term "asshole" for the title of this essay simply because it is a favorite of working policemen (at least in Union City). The interested reader might check my assumption by a casual glance at what several others have to say about this linguistic matter. Most useful in this regard are the firsthand account police have themselves provided and can be found, for example, in Terkel (1968, 1974); Drodge, (1973); Mass (1972); Olsen (1974); Whittemore (1973); Walker (1969). I should note as well that such labeling proceeds not only because of its functional use to the police but also because it helps officers to capture perceptual distinctions (i.e., labels are "good to think"). Thus assholes are conceptually part of the ordered world of police—the statuses, the rules, the norms, and the contrasts that constitute their social system.

label asshole as it is used by policemen, in particular, patrolmen, going about their everyday tasks. I will argue that assholes represent a distinct but familiar type of person to the police and represent, therefore, a part of their commonsense wisdom as to the kinds of people that populate their working environment. From this standpoint, assholes are analytic types with whom the police regularly deal. More importantly, however, I will also argue that the label arises from a set of situated conditions largely unrelated to the institutional mandate of the police (i.e., to protect life and property, arrest law violators, preserve the peace, etc.) but arises in response to some occupational and personal concerns shared by virtually all policeman.

According to most knowledgeable observers, nothing characterizes policing in America more than the widespread belief on the part of the police themselves that they are primarily law enforcers—perpetually engaged in a struggle with those who would disobey, disrupt, do harm, agitate, or otherwise upset the just order of the regime. And, that as policemen, they and they alone are the most capable of sensing right from wrong; determining who is and who is not respectable; and, most critically, deciding what is to be done about it (if anything). Such heroic self-perceptions reflecting moral superiority have been noted by numerous social scientists concerned with the study of the police. Indeed, several detailed, insightful, and thoroughly accurate mappings of the police perspective exist.[3] For instance, learned discussions denote the various "outgroups" perceived by the police (e.g., Harris, 1973; Bayley and Mendelsohn, 1969); or the "symbolic assailants" which threaten the personal security of the police (e.g., Skolnick, 1966; Niederhoffer, 1967; Rubinstein, 1973); or the "suspicious characters" recognized by the police via incongruous (nonordinary) appearances (e.g., Sacks, 1972; Black, 1968). These reports provide the background against which the pervasive police tropism to order the world into the "for us" and "against us" camps can most clearly be seen.

Yet these studies have glossed over certain unique but together commonsensical properties of the police situation with the attendant consequence of reifying the police position that the world is in fact divided into two camps. Other than noting the great disdain and disgust held by many police officers toward certain predefined segments of the population they presumably are to serve, these studies fail to fully describe and explain the range and meaning attached to the various labels used by the police themselves to affix individual responsibility for particular

---

[3] See, for example: Rubinstein's (1973) report on the Philadelphia police; Westley's (1970) study of a midwestern police department in the late 1940s; Wilson's (1968) global of accounting of the police perspective; Reiss's (1971) research into police-community interactions; LaFave's (1965) treatment of the police decision to arrest; Cain's (1973) and Banton's (1964) observations on the British police; and Berkley's (1969) cross-cultural view of policing in democratic societies. What comes out of these excellent works is tantamount to a reaffirmation of Trotsky's famous dictum, "There is but one international and that is the police."

actions occurring within their normal workaday world. Furthermore, previous studies do not provide much analytic aid when determining how the various typifications carried by the police are recognized as relevant and hence utilized as guides for action by a police officer in a particular situation. In short, if police typifications are seen to have origins as well as consequences, the popular distinction between "suspicious" or "threatening" and the almost mythologized "normal" or "respectable" is much too simple. It ignores not only the immediate context in which street interactions take place, but it also disregards the critical signs read by the police within the interaction itself which signify to them both the moral integrity of the person with whom they are dealing and the appropriate recipe they should follow as the interaction proceeds.[4] Therefore, any distinction of the "types" of people with whom the police deal must include an explicit consideration of the ways in which the various "types" are both immediately and conditionally identified by the police. Only in this fashion is it possible to accurately depict the labels the police construct to define, explain, and take action when going about their routine and nonroutine tasks.

To begin this analysis, consider the following typology which suggests that the police tend to view their occupational world as comprised exhaustively of three types of citizens (Van Maanen, 1974). These ideal types are: (1) "suspicious persons"—those whom the police have reason to believe may have committed a serious offense; (2) "assholes"—those who do not accept the police definition of the situation; and (3) "know nothings"—those who are not either of the first two categories but are not police and therefore, according to the police, cannot know what the police are about.

This everyday typification scheme provides a clue to the expectations, thoughts, feelings, and behaviors of the police. For example, "suspicious persons" are recognized on the basis of their appearance in public surroundings. Such an appearance is seen as a furtive, nonroutine, *de trop,* or, to use Sacks's (1972) nicely turned phrase, "dramatically torturous." Crucially, such persons, when they provide the police reason to stop and interrogate them, are treated normally in a brisk, though thoroughly professional, manner. It is not their moral worth or identity which is at issue, but rather it is a possible illegal action in their immediate or not-so-immediate past which is in question. From the patrolman's point of view, he is most interested in insuring that formal procedural issues are observed. Hence the personal production of a pro-

---

[4] For example, Skolnick's (1966) idea that policemen are "afraid" of certain categories of persons distorts the nature of the occupational perspective. More to the point, policemen are disgusted by certain people, envious of others, and ambivalent toward most. At times they may even vaguely admire certain criminals—those that the British police call "good villians" (Cain, 1971). Fear must of course be given its due, but the occasion of fear hangs more upon unforeseen situational contingencies (the proverbial dark alley, desolate city park, or underlife tavern) than upon certain individuals.

fessional police performance is called for and is presented—at least initially.[5] On the other end of the continuum reside the "know nothings," the "average" citizens, who most generally come under police scrutiny only via their request for service; The "know nothing" may be the injured or wronged party or the seeker of banal information and as such is treated with a certain amount of deference and due respect by the patrolman.

"Assholes," by way of contrast, are stigmatized by the police and treated harshly on the basis of their failure to meet police expectations arising from the *interaction situation itself*. Of course, street interaction may quickly transform suspicious persons into know nothings and know nothings into assholes, or any combination thereof. But it is the asshole category which is most imbued with moral meaning for the patrolman—establishing for him a stained or flawed identity to attribute to the citizen upon which he can justify his sometimes malevolent acts. Consequently, the asshole may well be the recipient of what the police call "street justice"—a physical attack designed to rectify what police take as personal insult. Assholes are most vulnerable to street justice, since they, as their title implies, are not granted status as worthy human beings. Their actions are viewed by the police as stupid or senseless and their feelings as incomprehensible (if they can even be said to have feelings). Indeed, as I will show, the police consistently deny an asshole a rationale or ideology to support their actions, insisting that the behavior of an asshole is understandable only as a sudden or lifelong character aberration. On the other hand, suspicious persons are less likely candidates for street justice because, in the majority of cases, their guilt may still be in question, or, if their guilt has been in fact established, their actions are likely to seem at least comprehensible and purposeful to the police (i.e., a man steals because he needs money; a man shoot his wife because she "two-timed" him; etc.). Also, there are incentives for the suspicious person to cooperate (at least nominally) when subject to police attention. The suspicious person may well be the most cooperative of all the people with whom the police deal on a face-to-face basis. This is, in part, because he is most desirous of pre-

---

[5] Certainly this may not always be the case. For example, some "suspected persons," due to the nature of their alleged crime (e.g., child molestation, drug dealing, indecent exposure, political sabotage, assault [or worse] upon a police officer, etc.) are likely to provide a strong sense of moral indignation on the part of the arresting (or stopping) officers. In such cases, once identity has been established to the satisfaction of the police (and it should be noted that errors are not unknown—particularly in these volatile cases) the person suspected is transformed immediately into an asshole and is subject to a predictably harsh treatment. Thus, in effect the label arises from an offense which occurred outside the immediate presence of the officers. However, since the spoiled identity must be reestablished anew in the immediate surroundings, the properties of the "affront" correspond analytically to the more familiar case outlines in the text. And while the distinction has theoretical value regarding the norms of the police culture (i.e., that it is not the denounced per se that is important, but rather it is the denouncer that matters—"say's who?"), its practical implications are questionable because patrolmen rarely encounter such situations.

senting a normal appearance (unafraid, unruffled, and with nothing to hide), and, in part, because if he is in fact caught he does not want to add further difficulty to his already difficult position. Finally, know nothings are the least likely candidates for street justice since they represent the so-called client system and are therefore those persons whom the police are most interested in impressing through a polished, efficient, and courteous performance.

At this point, I should note that the above ideal types are anything but precise and absolute. One purpose of this paper is to make at least one of these categories more explicit. But since I am dealing primarily with interior, subjective meanings negotiated in public with those whom the police interact, such typifications will always be subject to severe situational, temporal, and individually idiosyncratic restriction. Hence, an asshole in one context may be a know nothing in another, and vice versa. In other words, I am not arguing in this essay that a general moral order is shared by all policemen as their personalized but homomorphic view of the world. Indeed, the moral order subscribed to by police is complex, multiple, and continually shifts back and forth between that which is individual and that which is collective. What I will argue, however, is that particular situational conditions (i.e., provocations) predispose most policemen toward certain perceptions of people which lead to the application of what can be shown to be rule-governed police action. My objective, then, is simply to begin teasing out the underlying structure of police thought and to denote the features of what might be called the secondary reality of police work.

The remainder of this essay is divided into four sections. The next section, "Patrol Work," describes very briefly certain understandings shared by street-level patrolmen as to what is involved in their work. In a sense, these understandings are akin to behavioral rules that can be seen to mobilize police action; hence they represent the grounds upon which the figure of the asshole is recognized. The following section, "Street Justice," deals with the characteristic processes involved in discovering, distinguishing, and treating the asshole. Some conclusions revolving around the relationship between the police and the asshole are suggested in the next section. And, finally, a few of the broad implications that flow from this analysis are outlined in the last section.

II. Patrol Work

Policing city streets entails what Hughes (1958) refers to as a "bundle of tasks." Some of these tasks are mundane; many of them are routine; and a few of them are dangerous. Indeed, patrol work defies a general job description since it includes an almost infinite set of activities—dogcatching, first-aid, assisting elderly citizens, breaking up family fights, finding lost children, pursuing a fleeing felon, directing traffic, and so forth. Yet, as in other lines of endeavor, patrolmen develop certain insider notions about their work that may or may not reflect what outsiders believe their work to be. Such notions are of course attached firmly to the various experientially based meanings the police learn to regularly ascribe to persons, places, and things—the validity of which is established, sustained, and continually reaffirmed through everyday activity. Because these meanings are, to some degree, shared by patrolmen going about similar tasks, their collective representation can be detailed and linked to certain typical practices engaged in on the street by the police. Thus, to understand the police perspective on, and treatment of, the asshole, it is necessary also to understand the manner in which the policeman conceives of his work. Below is a very short summary of certain interrelated assumptions and beliefs that patrolmen tend to develop regarding the nature of their job.

Real Police Work

Many observers have noted the pervasive police tendency to narrowly constrict their perceived task to be primarily—and to the exclusion of other alternatives—law enforcement. As Skolnick and Woodworth (1967:129) suggest evocatively, "when a policeman can engage in real police work—act out the symbolic rites of search, chase and capture—his self-image is affirmed and morale enhanced." Yet, ironically, opportunities to enact this sequence are few and far between. In fact, estimates of the time police spend actually in real police work while on patrol vary from 0 percent (as in the case of the quiet country policeman for whom a street encounter with a bona fide "criminal" would be a spectacular exception to his daily tour of duty) to about 10 or 16 percent (as in the case of the busy urban patrolman who works a seamy cityside district in which the presence of pimps, dealers, cons, and burglars among others, are the everyday rule). Nonetheless, most of the policeman's time is spent performing rather dry, monotonous, and relatively mundane activities of a service nature—the proverbial clerk in a patrol car routinely cruising his district and awaiting dispatched calls (see Cain, 1971; Reiss, 1971; Webster, 1970; and Cummings, Cummings and Edell, 1965 for further discussion on how the police, spend their time).

Within these boundaries, notions of real police work develop to provide at least a modicum of satisfaction to the police. To a patrolman, *real police work* involves the use of certain skills and special abilities he believes he possesses by virtue of his unique experience and training. Furthermore, such a perspective results in minimizing the importance of other activities he is often asked regularly to perform. In fact, an ethos of "stay-low-and-avoid-trouble-unless-real-police-work-is-called-for" permeates police organizations (Van Maanen, 1973, 1974, 1975). Only tasks involving criminal apprehension are attributed symbolic importance. For the most part, other tasks, if they cannot be avoided, are performed (barring interruption) with ceremonial dispatch and disinterest.

Territoriality

A central feature of policing at the street level is the striking autonomy maintained (and guarded jealously) by patrolmen working the beat. All patrol work is conducted by solo officers or partnerships (within a squad to whom they are linked) responsible for a given plot of territory. Over time, they come to know, in the most familiar and penetrating manner, virtually every passageway—whether alley, street, or seldom-used path—located in their sector. From such knowledge of this social stage comes the corresponding evaluations of what particular conditions are to be considered good or bad, safe or unsafe, troubled or calm, usual or unusual, and so on. Of course, these evaluations are also linked to temporal properties associated with the public use of a patrolman's area of responsibility. As Rubinstein (1973) suggests, the territorial perspective carried by patrolmen establishes the basic normative standard for the proper use of place. And those perceived by patrolmen to be beyond the pale regarding their activities in space and time are very likely to warrant police attention.

Maintaining the Edge

Charged with enforcing ambiguous generalized statutes and operating from an autonomous, largely isolated position within the city, it is not surprising that police have internalized a standard of conduct which dictates that they must control and regulate all situations in which they find themselves. At one level, police feel they have the right to initiate, terminate, or otherwise direct all encounters with members of the public. Yet such perceptions penetrate more broadly into the social scheme of things, for police feel furthermore that the public order is a product of their ability to exercise control. The absence of trouble on their beat becomes, therefore, a personalized objective providing intimate feedback as to one's worth as a patrolman. Activity which may threaten the perceived order becomes intolerable, for it signifies to the patrolman that his advantage over the conduct of others (his "edge") is in question. It is a source of embarrassment in front of a public audience, and sometimes it is considered a disgrace to the police uniform if it is viewed by one's peers or departmental superiors. Clearly, such activity cannot be allowed to persist, for it may indicate both to a patrolman's colleagues and to his superiors that the officer no longer cares for his job and has, consequently, lost the all-important respect of those he polices (endangering, it is thought, other policemen who might work the same district). Hence, to "maintain one's edge" is a key concept vis-à-vis the "how to" of police work. And, as all policemen know, to let down the facade (for they do recognize the contrived nature of the front) is to invite disrespect, chaos, and crime.

The Moral Mandate

In light of the above three features of the police frame, it should be clear that police are both representatives of the moral order and a part of it. They are thus committed ("because it is right") to maintain their collective face as protectorates of the right and respectable against the wrong and the not-so respectable. Situations in which this face is challenged—regardless of origin—are likely to be responded to in unequivocal terms. For example, Cain (1971) writes that when the authority of an officer is questioned by a member of the nonpolice public, the officer has three broad responses available to him. He may (1) physically attack the offender; (2) swallow his pride and ignore the offender; or (3) manufacture a false excuse for the arrest of the offender. What this suggests is a highly personalized view on the part of the police as to their moral position and responsibility, one in which an attempt on the part of the citizen to disregard the wishes of a policeman may be viewed by the police as a profaning of the social and legal system itself. Such an act can also be seen to provoke moral and private indignation on the part of the officer as an individual, thus providing him with another *de rigueur* excuse to locate an appropriate remedy. Since the police personally believe that they are capable of making correct decisions regarding the culpability of an involved party, justice is likely, in the case of an offense to the moral sensibilities of a police officer, to be enacted quickly, parsimoniously, and self-righteously—whether it be the relatively trivial swift kick in the pants or the penultimate tragedy involved in the taking of a life. Thus, the moral mandate felt by the police to be their just right at the societal level is translated and transformed into occupational and personal terms and provides both the justification and legitimation for specific acts of street justice.

This truncated picture of the occupational frame involved in the doing of police work provides the rubric upon which we now can examine the making of an asshole. As one would expect, assholes are not afforded the protection of the more structured relationships police maintain with other of their categories of persons—the suspicious and the know nothings. Rather, they fall outside this fragile shelter, for their actions are seen as "senseless," so "aimless" and "irrational" that recognizable and acceptable human motives are difficult for the police to discover (i.e., from the patrolmen's perspective, there are not legitimate reasons to distrust, disagree with, make trouble for, or certainly hate the police). In this sense, it is precisely the "pointlessness" of an individual's behavior that makes him an asshole and subjects him to the police version of street justice.

III. Street Justice

> Policeman to motorist stopped for speeding:
>   "May I see your driver's license, please?
> Motorist:
>   "Why the hell are you picking on me and not somewhere else looking for some real criminals?"
> Policeman:
>   "Cause you're an asshole, that's why . . . but I didn't know that until you opened your mouth."

The above sea story represents the peculiar reality with which patrolmen believe they must contend. The world is in part (and, to policemen, a large part) populated by individuals to whom an explanation for police behavior cannot be made, for, as the police say, "assholes don't listen to reason." The purpose of this section is to explore the commonplace and commonsense manner in which the tag asshole arises, sticks, and guides police action during a street encounter. This stigmatization process is divided into three stages which, while analytically distinct, are highly interactive and apt to occur in the real world of policing almost simultaneously. For convenience only, then, these phases are labeled *affront, clarification,* and *remedy.*

Throughout this discussion it should be remembered that the asshole is not necessarily a suspected law violator—though the two often overlap, thus providing double trouble, so to speak, for the labeled. Importantly, the police view of the asshole as deviant is a product of the immediate transaction between the two and not a product of an act preceding the transaction. This is not to say, however, that certain classes in society—for example, the young, the black, the militant, the homosexual—are not "fixed" by the police as a sort of permanent asshole grouping. Indeed, they are. Yet such bounded *a priori* categories can do policemen little good—except perhaps when dealing with the racial or bohemian obvious—for such stereotyping are frequently misleading and dysfunctional (e.g., the "hippie" who is a detective's prized informant; the black dressed in a purple jumpsuit who happens to be a mayor's top aide; the sign carrying protestor who is an undercover FBI agent). And, even in cases in which *a priori character* judgments are a part of the decision to stop an individual, the asshole label, if it is to play a determining role in the encounter, must arise anew. That is to say, if the asshole distinction is to have a *concrete* as opposed to abstract meaning, it must in some manner be tied fundamentally and irresolutely to observable social action occurring in the presence of the labeling officer.

Certainly, a policeman's past experience with an individual or with a recognizable group will influence his street behavior. For example, a rookie soon discovers (as a direct consequence of his initiation into a department) that blacks, students, Mexicans, reporters, lawyers, welfare workers, researchers, prostitutes, and gang members are not to be trusted, are unpredictable, and are usually "out-to-get-the-police." He may even sort these "outsiders" into various categories indicative of the risk he believes they present to him or the implied contrast they have with his own life-style and beliefs. Yet, without question, these categories will never be exhaustive—although the absolute size of what patrolmen call their "shit lists" may grow over the years. Consequently, to understand the police interpretation and meaning of the term "asshole" we must look directly into the field situations in which it originates.

Affront: Challenge

When a police officer approaches a civilian to issue a traffic citation or to inquire as to the whys and wherefores of one's presence or simply to pass the time of day, he directly brings the power of the state to bear on the situation and hence makes vulnerable to disgrace, embarrassment, and insult that power. Since the officer at the street level symbolizes the presence of the Leviathan in the everyday lives of the citizenry, such interactions take on dramatic properties far different from ordinary citizen-to-citizen transactions (Manning, 1974a; Silver, 1967). In a very real sense, the patrolman-to-citizen exchanges are moral contests in which the authority of the state is either confirmed, denied, or left in doubt. To the patrolman, such contests are not to be taken lightly, for the authority of the state is also his personal authority, and is, of necessity, a matter of some concern to him. To deny or raise doubt about his legitimacy is to shake the very ground upon which his self-image and corresponding views are built.

An affront, as it is used here, is a challenge to the policeman's authority, control, and definition of the immediate situation. As seen by the police, an affront is simply a response on the part of the other which indicates to them that their position and authority in the interaction are not being taken seriously. It may occur with or without intent.

Whether it is the vocal student who claims to "know his rights," the stumbling drunk who says he has had "only two beers," or the lady of the evening who believes she is being questioned only because she is wearing "sexy clothes," the police will respond in particular ways to those who challenge or question their motive or right to intervene in situations that they believe demand police intervention. Clearly, overt and covert challenges to police authority will not go unnoticed. In fact, they can be seen to push the encounter to a new level wherein any further slight to an officer, however subtle, provides sufficient evidence to a patrolman that he may indeed be dealing with a certifiable asshole and that the situation is in need of rapid clarification. From this standpoint, an affront can be seen, therefore, as disrupting the smooth flow of the police performance. The argumentative motorist, the pugnacious drunk, the sometimes ludicrous behavior of combatants in a "family beef" all interfere, and hence make more difficult, the police task. Of course, some officers relish such encounters. In this sense, ironically, the asshole gives status to the police rather than takes it away. However, since the label is itself a moral charge (and it need not be made salient or verbally expressed), it is open theoretically for rebuttal and evidence may or may not be forthcoming which will substantiate or contradict the charge. Such evidence is gathered in the next analytic stage.

Clarification: Confrontation

Based upon a perceived affront, the patrolman must then attempt to determine precisely the kind of person with whom he is engaged. It is no longer an idle matter to him in which his private conceptions of people can be kept private as he goes about his business. But the patrolman is now in a position wherein he may discover that his taken-for-granted authority on the street is not exactly taken for granted by another. Two commonsensical issues are critical at this point in an encounter. *First,* the officer must determine whether or not the individual under question could have, under the present circumstance, acted in an alternative fashion. To wit, did the perceived affront occur by coercion or accident through no fault of the person? Did the person even know he was dealing with a police officer? Was he acting with a gun at his head? And so on. *Second,* and equally important, given that the person could have acted differently, the officer must determine whether or not the individual was aware of the consequences that might follow his action. In other words, was the action frivolous, naive, unserious, and not meant to offend? Did the person know that his actions were likely to be interpreted offensively by the police? The answers to these two questions, provide patrolmen with material (or lack of it) to construct and sustain an asshole definition. Let us examine in some depth these questions, for they raise the very issue of personal responsibility which is at the nexus of the asshole definition.[6]

McHugh (1969) argues persuasively that the social construction of deviant categories is a matter of elimination which proceeds logically through a series of negotiated offers and responses designed to fix responsibility for a perceived deviant act (i.e., a deviant act requires a charge before it can be said to have happened). Police follow a similar paradigm when filling, emptying, or otherwise attending to their person categories. Again, the first item to be determined in this process is the issue of whether or not the person had alternative means available to him of which he could reasonably be expected to be aware. For example, the speeding motorist who, when pulled to the side of the road, could be excused for his abusive language if it were discovered by the officer that the motorist's wife was at the same time in the back seat giving birth to a child. Similarly, juveniles "hanging out" on a public street corner at certain times of the day may be sometimes overlooked if the police feel that "those kids don't have anyplace to go." On the other hand, if it can be determined that there is no unavoidable reason behind the affronting action, the individual risks being labeled an asshole. The drunken and remorseless driver, the wife who harangues the police officer for mistreating her husband after she herself requested police service to break up a family fight, or the often-warned teenager who makes a nuisance of himself by flagrantly parading in public after curfew are all persons whom the police believe could have and should have acted differently. Their acts were not inevitable, and it could be expected that they had available to them conventional alternatives.

Given that there are no compelling deterministic accounts readily available to the patrolman to excuse a particular affront, the officer must still make a judgment about the offender's motive. In other words, as the second issue listed above suggests, the policeman must decide whether or not the person knows what he is doing. Could the person be expected to know of the consequences which follow an affront to an officer of the law? Indeed, does the person even realize that what he is doing is likely to provoke police action? Could this particular person be expected to know better? All are questions related to the establishment of a motive for action. For example, the stylized and ceremonial upright third finger when attached to the hand of a thirty-year-old man is taken by the police very differently from the same gesture attached to the hand of a four-year-old child. Loud and raucous behavior in some parts of a city may be ignored if the police feel "the people there don't know any better." Or the claim that one is Jesus Christ resurrected and is out to do battle with the wages of sin may indicate to the police that they

---

[6] In most regards, the asshole is a classic case of the deviant—although not transituationally so. See Matza (1969), Becker (1963), and Cohen (1965) for a systematic elaboration of the ideas which underpin this analysis.

are either in the presence of a "dope-crazed radical hippie freak" or a "soft-brained harmless mental case," depending, perhaps, on the offender's age. If the person is young, for instance, responsibility is likely to be individualized—"it is his fault"; however, if the person is old, responsibility is likely to be institutionalized—"he can't help it, he's a nut."

Summarily, the police have available to them two principles of clarification. One concerns the means available to a person guilty of an affront, and the other concerns the purposes behind the affront itself. If the affront is viewed as unavoidable or unintended, the person is unlikely to be subjected to shabby or harsh treatment at the hands of the police. The asshole, however, is one who is viewed as culpable and blameworthy for his affronting action, and, as the next section details, he will be dealt with by the police in ways they feel appropriate.

Remedy: Solution

The above portrait of the clarification principles utilized by police in labeling assholes suggests that certain typical police responses can be displayed by a simple fourfold typology. Figure 1 depicts the relationship between the police officer's assessment of responsibility for the affront and denotes, within each cell, the typical police response given the various possible assessments.

Cell A represents the subject case of this essay since it involves a flagrant (inexcusable) disregard for the sentiments of the police. To the police, those falling into this category are unmistakably assholes and are therefore prominent candidates to be the recipients of street justice—the aim of which is to punish or castigate the individual for a moral transgression. Persons placed in this category are also the most likely to be placed under questionable arrest. This is not so because of the original intent of the encounter (which often, by itself, is trivial) but rather because of the serious extralegal means utilized by the police to enforce their particular view of the situation upon the recalcitrant asshole—"hamming-up" or "thumping" (beating).[7] And, as Reiss (1971) suggests, the use of force is not a philosophical question to the police but rather one of who, where, when, and how much.

The use of such means require of course that the officer manufacture post facto a legally defensible account of his action in order to, in the vernacular of the day, "cover his ass."[8] Such accounts in legalese

---

[7] By the term "extralegal" I am merely implying that the formal police mandate excludes such moral considerations from actions inducing decisions made by officers on the street. The notion of professional policing makes this explicit when it is suggested that patrolmen must act impersonally without regard to individual prejudice.

[8] The "cover-your-ass" phenomena associated with urban policing is described in more depth in Van Maanen (1974). See also Manning (1974b) for a theoretical view of the more general construct, the police lie; and Chevigny (1968) for a presentation of numerous disturbing case studies.

Figure 1

	DOES THE PERSON KNOW WHAT HE IS DOING?	
	YES	NO
COUGH THE PERSON ACT DIFFERENTLY UNDER THE CIRCUMSTANCES?	YES A Castigate	B Teach
	NO C Ignore	D Isolate

most often take the form of "disorderly conduct," "assaulting a police officer," "the use of loud and abusive language in the presence of women and children," "disturbing the peace," or the almost legendary—due to its frequent use—"resisting arrest." The asshole from this position is subject to a police enactment of double jeopardy—justice without trial in the streets and justice, perhaps with trial, in the courts. And regardless of the outcome in the latter case, there is usually only one loser. I should emphasize, however, that I am not saying the behavior of the asshole may not be brutish, nasty, and itself thoroughly vicious. I am simply suggesting that behavior violating extralegal moral codes used by police to order their interactions—whether it be inconsiderate, barbarous, or otherwise—will be responded to in what police believe to be appropriate ways.

Cell B of Figure 1 also represents serious affront to police integrity, and it too may be an affront which calls for an extra-legal response. An illustration provided by the remarks of a patrolman is useful in this context:

> Those goddamn kids got to learn sooner or later that we won't take a lot of shit around Cardoza (a local college campus). Next time I see one of I those punks waving a Viet Cong flag I'm gonna negotiate the little bastard back into an alley and kick his rosy red ass so hard he ain't gonna carry nothing for awhile. Those kids gotta be made to see that they can't get away with this type of thing.

Whether or not such a prediction was actually carried out does not matter, for the quotation itself indicates that "teaching" occupies a particularly prominent position in the police repertoire of possible responses. Thus, the uncooperative and surly motorist finds his sobriety rudely questioned, or the smug and haughty college student discovers himself stretched over the hood of a patrol car and the target of a mortifying and brusque body search. The object of such degradation ceremonies is simply to reassert police control and demonstrate to the citizen that his behavior is considered inappropriate. Teaching techniques are numerous, with threat, ridicule, and harassment among the more widely practiced. Other examples are readily available, such as the morally-toned lectures meted out to those who would attempt to bribe, lie, or otherwise worm their way out of what a policeman sees to be a legitimate traffic citation, the traditional—but vanishing—"kick in the ass" administered to a youngster caught stealing an apple or cutting school. The intent in all these cases is clear. The person must be taught a lesson. And whether the teaching occurs in public or in the back of an alley, the person must be shown the error of his ways. He has acted perhaps out of ignorance, but nevertheless the police feel they must demonstrate that they will not casually overlook the action. However, I should note that the person in this category will remain an asshole in the eyes of the police until he has apparently learned his lesson to the satisfaction of the officers on the scene. Here a display of remorse is no doubt crucial to the police.[9]

Cell C represents the case in which the police are likely to excuse the affront due to the extenuating circumstances surrounding the affront. When it is clear to the police that there are indeed mitigating conditions, their response is to ignore the error—to pretend, as it were, that such an affront never happened. For example, it is understandable to the police that the victim of a mugging may be somewhat abusive toward them when they interrogate him just after the crime (although there is a fine line to be drawn here). Similarly, if a teenage male vigorously defends the chaste and virtuous intentions of he and his girl friend while questioned by the police in a concealed and cozy corner of a public park, it is understood by the police that the boy has few other acceptable alternative lines available. The police response is typically to adopt a somewhat bemused tolerance policy toward actions which under different circumstances may have produced the orb and scepter.

Finally, cell D in Figure 1 concerns the case of an affront which police take to lie beyond the responsibility of the actor. While such action cannot normally be allowed to continue, the moral indignation felt by police is tempered by the understanding that the person is not aware nor could be easily made aware of the rule-breaking nature of his actions. The police response is to isolate the offender, not to punish him. Thus, the "mental case" is shipped to the county hospital for observation and treatment; the "foul-mouthed child" is returned to those responsible for his behavior; the out of-state tourist prowling an area close to his hotel but frequented by prostitutes is informed of his "oversight" and told in unmistakable terms to vacate the territory. It is impor-

---

[9] Arrests are, of course, sometimes used to teach someone a lesson. However, police believe that in many cases the asshole will arrange his release before the patrolman will have completed the paperwork necessitated by the arrest. And since the affront was moral the legal justification to "make the case" in court may be lacking. Thus, the classroom more often than not is in the street. Given the opportunity to teach the asshole either by "turning him in" or "doing him in," most police would choose the latter.

tant to note that police feel justified in using only enough force or coercive power to seal off the offender from public (and, by implication; their own) view. To use more force would be considered unreasonable.

It has been my purpose here to suggest that much of what the general public might see as capricious, random, or unnecessary behavior on the part of the police is, in fact, governed by certain rather pervasive interpretive rules which lie close enough to the surface such that they can be made visible. Certain police actions, following the model presented above, can be seen, then, to be at least logical if not legal. Furthermore, much of the power of these rules stems from their tacit or taken-for-granted basis. Indeed, were the rules to be questioned, the game could not continue. However, while these rules are applied in a like fashion by all police in a given interactional episode, the specific situated behavior of a citizen that is taken as a sign which leads to isolating, ignoring, teaching, or castigating a given individual is no doubt quite different across patrolmen. Here, the police game continues as it does because, in part, the asshole label swallows up and hides whatever individual differences exist across patrolmen. Thus, language neatly solves the problem of misunderstanding that would arise among the police were the rules to be articulated and standards sought as to how they should be applied.

IV. Some Conclusions

It is possible, of course, to see the preceding ritualized sequence as an isolated and rarely indulged propensity of the police. However, in this section, I will argue that indeed such a sequence and the corresponding identification and treatment of the asshole is intimately related to the police production and represents an aspect of policing that is near the core of the patrolman's definition of his task. In essence, the existence of an asshole demonstrates and confirms the police view of the importance and worth of themselves both as individuals and as members of a necessary occupation. However, several other, somewhat more practical and everyday features of police work insure the ominous presence of the asshole in the police world.

First, the labeling of individuals as assholes can be seen as a technique (although invisible to most) useful to patrolmen in providing distance between themselves and their segmented audiences—to be liked by the people in the street is, in the defensive rhetoric of patrolmen, a sign of a bad cop. By profaning and degrading the actions of another, social distance can be established and maintained—a guarantee, so to speak, that the other will not come uncomfortably close. Thus, the asshole simplifies and orders the policeman's world and continually verifies his classification scheme regarding those who are "like him" and those who are "unlike him." Relatedly the labeling serves also as an immediate call to action, denoting a consensually approved, (by the police culture) means for remedying "out-of-kilter" situations.

Second, the label not only describes and prescribes but it also explains and makes meaningful the statements and actions of others. In fact, an entire set of action expectations (i.e., "they are out to make the police look bad") can be ascribed as motives to the asshole. In this sense, the police function in street interaction is not unlike that of a psychiatrist diagnosing a patient. Both explain perceived deviancy in terms of a characterological genesis. Hence, the label implies that a different, inappropriate, and strange motivational scheme is used by the "type of person" known as an asshole. In this manner, an act is made understandable by stripping away whatever meaning might be attributed to it by the actor. Thus, to make sense of the act is to assume that it does not make sense—that it is stupid, irrational, wrong, deranged, or dangerous. Any other assumption would be too threatening.

Third, the labeling process must be viewed as serving an occupational purpose. I suggested previously that the urban policeman is primarily a keeper of the peace yet he defines his job in terms of law enforcement. Furthermore, as others have noted, many patrolmen try to convert peacekeeping situations to those of law enforcement (e.g., Bittner, 1967, 1970; Wilson, 1969; Piliavin and Briar, 1964). Since real police work is seldom available, marginally legitimate arrests of assholes provide a patrolman excitement and the opportunity to engage one's valued skills. Perhaps the police cliché, "a good beat is full of deadbeats," reflects structural support for the asshole-labeling phenomena.

Fourth, the discovery and subsequent action taken when the police encounter the asshole provides an expressive outlet—almost ceremonial in its predictability—for much of the frustration policing engenders. To the patrolman, one particular asshole symbolizes all those that remain "out there" untouched, untaught, and unpunished. Such emotional outbursts provide, therefore, a reaffirmation of the moral repugnance of the asshole. Whether the officer responds by placing the handcuffs on the person's wrists such that they cut off circulation (and not incidentally cause intense, almost excruciating pain) or pushes a destitute soul through a shop window, these actions release some of the pent-up energies stored up over a period in which small but cumulative indignities are suffered by the police at the hands of the community elites, the courts, the politicians, the uncaught crooks, the press, and numerous others. The asshole stands, then, as a ready ersatz for those whom the police will never—short of a miracle—be in a position to directly encounter and confront.

Finally, the asshole can be seen as a sort of reified other, representing all those persons who would question, limit, or otherwise attempt to control the police. From this standpoint, knowing that there are assholes at large serves perhaps to rally and solidify police organizations around at least one common function. Thus, the police are, to a limited degree, unified by their disdain of those who would question their activities. Perhaps one could say that the police represent what Simmel (1950) referred to as an "invisible church" in which the faithful are fused together through their common relation to an outside phenomenon.

Consequently, assholes are not simply obscure and fanciful figments of the bedeviled imagination of the police. On the contrary, they define to a surprising degree what the police are about. And while the internal satisfaction and rewards involved in "slamming around" an asshole may seem esoteric if not loathsome to the outsider, to the patrolman who makes his living on the city streets it is not.

V. Postscript

The foregoing description and explanation of an overlooked aspect of urban policing highlights the fact that the police officer is anything but a Weberian bureaucrat whose discretion and authority are checked rigidly. The collective myth surrounding the rulebound "policeman-as-public-servant" has no doubt never been very accurate. By virtue of their independence from superiors, their carefully guarded autonomy in the field, their deeply felt notions about real police work and those who would interfere with it, and their increasing isolation from the public they serve (as a result of mobile patrol, rotating shifts, greater specialization of the police, and the growing segmentation of the society at large with its own specialized and emerging subcultures), police-community "problems" will not disappear. And, since the police view their critics as threatening and as persons who generally should be taught or castigated, one could argue that the explosive potential of citizen-police encounters will grow.

Additionally, if the police become more sensitive to public chastisement, it could be expected that something of a self-fulfilling prophecy may well become a more important factor in the street than it is presently. That is to say, if the police increasingly view their public audience as foes—whose views are incomprehensible if not degenerate or subversive—it is likely that they will also magnify clues which will sustain the stereotype of citizen-as-enemy escalating therefore the percentage of street interactions which result in improper arrest and verbal or physical attack. Thus, the fantasy may well become the reality as stereotypes are transformed into actualities. In fact, the future may make prophetic Brendan Behan's half-jesting remark that he had never seen a situation so bad that a policeman couldn't make it worse.

To conclude, this essay has implied that there is a virtual—if unintended—license in this society granted to police. In particular, when it comes to the asshole, police actions are not governed at all, given the present policies of allowing the watchers to watch themselves. It would seem that something is amiss, and, if the practical morality in urban areas is not exactly inverted, it is at least tilted. If the asshole is indeed a critical aspect of policing, then there is serious risk involved in the movement to "professionalize" the police. As other observers have remarked, successful occupational professonalization inevitably leads to increased autonomy and ultimately increased power for members of the occupation (Becker, 1962; Hughes, 1965). Professonalism may well widen the police mandate in society and therefore amplify the potential of the police to act as moral entrepreneurs. From this perspective, what is required at present is not professional police but accountable police.

References

Banton Michael, (1964) *The Policeman in the Community.* New York: Basic Books.

Bayley P. H. and H. Mendelsohn, (1969) *Minorities and the Police: Confrontation in America.* New York: Free Press.

Becker, Howard S., (1962) "The Nature of a Profession," in *Education for the Professions,* 61st Yearbook of the Society for the Study of Education, Part 2. Chicago: University of Chicago Press. (1963) *Outsiders.* New York: Free Press.

Berkeley, George E., (1969) *The Democratic Policeman,* Boston: Beacon Press.

Bittner, Egon, (1970) *The Functions of the Police in Modern Society.* Washington, D.C.: United States Government Printing Office. (1967) "The Police on Skid Row," 32, *American Sociological Review,* 699-715.

Black, Donald, (1968) "Police Encounters and Social Organization: An Observational Study." Unpublished Ph.D. dissertation, University of Michigan.

Cain, Maureen, (1973) *Society and the Policeman's Role.* London: Kegan Paul. (1971) "On the Beat: Interactions and Relations in Rural and Urban Police Forces," in S. Cohen (ed.) *Images of Deviance.* Middlesex, England: Penguin Books.

Chevigny, Paul, (1968) *Police Power: Police Abuses in New York.* New York: Pantheon.

Cohen, Albert K., (1965) "The Sociology of the Deviant Act," 30, *American Sociological Review,* 5-14.

Cumming, E., I. Cumming and L. Edell, (1965) "The Policeman as Philosopher, Guide and Friend," 12, *Social Problems,* 276-286.

Drodge, Edward F., (1973) *The Patrolman: A Cop's Story.* New York: New American Library

Harris, Richard N., (1973) *The Police Academy: An Inside View.* New York: John Wiley and Sons.

Hughes, Everett C., (1965) "Professions," in K. S. Lynn (ed.) *Professions in America.* Boston: Beacon Press. (1958) *Men and Their Work.* Glencoe, Ill. Free Press.

LaFave, W. R., (1965) *Arrest: The Decision to Take a Suspect into Custody.* Boston: Little, Brown and Company.

Manning, Peter K., (1971) "The Police: Mandate, Strategies and Appearances," in J. Douglas (ed.) *Crime and Justice in America.* Indianapolis: Bobbs-Merrill. (1974a) "Dramatic Aspects of Policing: Selected Propositions." *Sociology and Social Research.* 59 (October). (1974b) "Police Lying." *Urban Life* 3 (October).

Maas, Peter, (1973) *Serpico*. New York: The Viking Press.

Matza, David, (1969) *Becoming Deviant*. Englewood Cliffs, N.J.: Prentice-Hall.

McHugh, Peter, (1969) "A Common-Sense Perception of Deviancy," in J. Douglas (ed.) *Deviance and Respectability*. New York: Basic Books.

Niederhoffer, Arthur, (1969) *Behind the Shield*. Garden City, N.Y.: Doubleday, 1967.

Olsen, Jack, (1974) *Sweet Street*. New York: Simon and Schuster.

Piliavin, I. and S. Briar, (1964) "Police Encounters with Juveniles." 70, *American Journal of Sociology* 206-214.

Reiss, Albert J., (1971) *The Police and the Public*. New Haven, Conn.: Yale University Press.

Rubinstein, Jonathan, (1973) *City Police*. New York: Farrar, Straus and Giroux.

Sacks, Harvey, (1972) "Notes on Police Assessment of Moral Character," in D. Sudnow (ed.) *Studies in Social Interaction*. New York: The Free Press.

Silver, Allen, (1967) "The Demand for Order in Civil Society," in D. Bordua (ed.) *The Police: Six Sociological Essays*. New York: John Wiley and Sons.

Simmel, Georg, (1950) *The Sociology of Georg Simmel*. Translated, edited, and with an introduction by Kurt H. Wolff. New York: The Free Press.

Skolnick, Jerome, (1966) *Justice Without Trial*, New York: John Wiley and Sons.

Skolnick, Jerome and J. R. Woodworth, (1967) "Bureaucracy, Information and Social Control," in D. Bordua (ed.) *The Police: Six Sociological Essays*. New York: John Wiley and Sons.

Terkel, Studs, (1968) *Division Street: America*. New York: Random House. (1974) *Working*. New York: Pantheon.

Van Maanen, John, (1972) "Pledging the Police: A Study of Selected Aspects of Recruit Socialization in a Large Police Department." Unpublished Ph.D. dissertation, University of California, Irvine.(1973) "Observations on the Making of Policemen," 32, *Human Organizations*, 407-418. (1974) "Working the Street: A Developmental View of Police Behavior," in H. Jacobs (ed.) *Reality and Reform: The Criminal Justice System*, Beverly Hills, California: Sage Publications.(1975) Police Socialization. *Administrative Science Quarterly*, 20, 207-228.

Walker, T. Mike, (1969) *Voices from the Bottom of the World: A Policeman's Journal*. New York: Grove Press.

Webster, J. A., (1970) "Police Task and Time Study," 61 *Journal of Criminal Law, Criminology and Police Science,* 94-100.

Westley, William, (1970) *Violence and the Police*. Cambridge, Mass.: MIT Press (originally a Ph.D. dissertation, University of Chicago, 1951).

Whittemore, L. H., (1973) *The Super Cops*. New York: Stein and Day.

Wilson, James, Q., (1967) "Police Morale, Reform and Citizen Respect: The Chicago Case," in D. Bordua (ed.) *The Police: Six Sociological Essays*. New York John Wiley and Sons. (1968) *Varieties of Police Behavior*. Cambridge, Mass.: Harvard University Press.

James Q. Wilson

The Watchman Style

In some communities, the police in dealing with situations that do not involve "serious" crime act as if order maintenance rather than law enforcement were their principal function. What is the defining characteristic of the patrolman's role thus becomes the style or strategy of the department as a whole because it is reinforced by the attitudes and policies of the police administrator. I shall call this the "watchman" style, employing here for analytical purposes a term that was once—in the early nineteenth century—descriptive generally of the mission of the American municipal police.[1]

In every city, of course, all patrolmen display a watchman style, that is, a concern for the order maintenance aspect of their function, some of the time, but in a few places this style becomes the operating code of the department. To the extent the administrator can influence the discretion of his men, he does so by allowing them to ignore many common minor violations, especially traffic and juvenile offenses, to tolerate, though gradually less so, a certain amount of vice and gambling, to use the law more as a means of maintaining order than of regulating conduct, and to judge the requirements of order differently depending on the character of the group in which the infraction occurs. Juveniles are "expected" to misbehave, and thus infractions among this group— unless they are serious or committed by a "wise guy"—are best ignored or treated informally. Negroes are thought to want, and to deserve, less law enforcement because to the police their conduct suggests a low level

Source: James Q. Wilson (1968). Chapter 5, "The Watchman Style," pp. 140-145; Chapter 6, "The Legalistic Style," pp. 172-175; Chapter 7, "The Service Style," pp. 200-201. In *Varieties of Police Behavior: The Management of Law and Order in Eight Communities*. Cambridge, MA: Harvard University Press. Copyright © 1971 by the Board of Trustees of the Leland Stanford Junior University. Reprinted by permission.

[1] A social scientist reading this and the next two chapters will understand that any typology is an abstraction from reality that is employed, not to describe a particular phenomenon, but to communicate its essential or "ideal" form—in this case, the "flavor" or "style" of the organization. The lay reader should bear this in mind and guard against assuming that because two or three police departments are grouped together they are identical in all respects. They are not. Furthermore, a typology can only suggest, it cannot prove, that a particular operating style is associated with certain organizational characteristics. Finally, merely because it was found convenient in this study to group these departments together into three styles, no one should assume that these are the only police styles or that every police department in the country displays one or the other of them. I assume if enough departments were studied that one would probably learn of other styles in addition to these and that one would certainly learn that many, if not most, departments display a combination of two or more styles.

of public and private morality, an unwillingness to cooperate with the police or offer information, and widespread criminality. Serious crimes, of course, should be dealt with seriously; further, when Negroes offend whites, who, in the eyes of the police, have a different standard of public order, then an arrest must be made. Motorists, unless a departmental administrator waits to "make a record" by giving a few men the job of writing tickets, will often be left alone if their driving does not endanger or annoy others and if they do not resist or insult police authority. Vice and gambling are crimes only because the law says they are; they become problems only when the currently accepted standards of public order are violated (how accurately the political process measures those standards is another question). Private disputes—assaults among friends or family—are treated informally or ignored, unless the circumstances (a serious infraction, a violent person, a flouting of police authority) require an arrest. And disputes that are a normal business risk, such as getting a bad check, should be handled by civil procedures if possible. With exceptions to be noted, the watchman style is displayed in Albany, Amsterdam, and Newburgh.

The police are watchman-like not simply in emphasizing order over law enforcement but also in judging the seriousness of infractions less by what the law says about them than by their immediate and personal consequences, which will differ in importance depending on the standards of the relevant group—teenagers, Negroes, prostitutes, motorists, families, and so forth. In all cases, circumstances of person and condition are taken seriously into account—community notables are excused because they have influence and, perhaps, because their conduct is self-regulating; Negroes are either ignored or arrested, depending on the seriousness of the matter, because they have no influence and their conduct, except within broad limits, is not thought to be self-regulating. But no matter what his race, if a man's actions are "private" (gambling, for instance, or driving while intoxicated) or if they involve only another person with whom he has a dispute (an assault or a petty larceny), then, unless the offense is a "serious" one, the police tend to overlook the violation, to handle it informally (by a reprimand, for example), or to allow the two aggrieved parties to resolve it between themselves as if it were a private matter (a storekeeper getting restitution from a shoplifter or an assault victim bringing a civil action). If, on the other hand, the public peace has been breached—creating a disturbance in a restaurant, bothering passers-by on a sidewalk, insulting an officer, causing a crowd to collect, endangering others, or publicly offending current standards of propriety, then the officer is expected to restore order. If order cannot be restored or respect for authority elicited in any other way, an arrest is appropriate.

This "privatization" of the law defining misdemeanors and offenses and the emphasis on keeping order in public places is squarely within the nineteenth-century tradition of American law enforcement. As Lane notes in his history of the Boston police, the present-day force grew out of men appointed as part-time watchmen to keep the streets clear of obstructions, human and material, and to supervise a number of ordinances pertaining to health, lighting, and animals running loose. Vagabondage, raucous behavior, public lewdness, and street fights were the "criminal" matters handled by the watchmen and later by the police. *Real* crime—theft, robbery, murder, a private assault—was not in their province at all; detecting the perpetrators was essentially a private matter. If the victim could learn the identity of the thief or assailant, he applied for a warrant, which was then served, for a fee, by a constable. Later, detectives added to the force aided in the apprehension of criminals, but still on a fee-for-service basis: they were paid with a share of the recovered loot. The object of the process was not so much punishment as restitution.[2] Prostitution flourished, as did illegal drinking establishments; when they became too noxious—that is to say, when their toleration became impolitic—a "descent" (in modern terms, a raid) was carried out, never to eliminate the nuisance but to contain it.[3] As late as 1863, a Boston alderman, the aristocratic Thomas Coffin Amory, objected to proposals that the police play a more aggressive role in enforcing laws, especially those against drinking, and proclaimed: "It is the duty of the police officer to serve . . . warrants, when directed to him. It is nowhere made his duty to initiate prosecutions."[4] A few years later, Alderman Jonas Fitch rejected complaints against detective procedures and argued instead for a return to purely private enterprise.[5] When a visitor to Albany or Newburgh remarks that the city appears to be still in the nineteenth century, he is making a more significant observation than he may realize.

Cities where the police follow a watchman style will not thereby have identical standards of public order and morality. The quality of law enforcement depends not simply on how the police make judgments, but also on the socioeconomic composition of the community, the law enforcement standards set, implicitly or explicitly, by the political systems, and the special interests and concerns of the police chief. A

---

[2] Roger Lane, *Policing the City: Boston, 1822-1885* (Cambridge, Mass. Harvard University Press, 1967), pp. 7, 56, 57, 150. See also Seldon D. Bacon, "The Early Development of American Municipal Police," unpublished Ph.D. dissertation, Yale University (1939), p. 784. Professor Herbert Jacob suggests another way in which the law may become privatized. In his study of bankruptcy and wage garnishment proceedings in four Wisconsin cities, he found that in some, such as Green Bay, there is relatively little inclination to invoke the legal processes to handle debts, while in others, such as Madison, there is a strong inclination. Green Bay prefers to settle such matters privately, Madison to settle them formally and publicly. Herbert Jacob, "Wage Garnishment and Bankruptcy Proceedings in Four Cities," in James Q. Wilson, ed., *City Politics and Public Policy* (New York: John Wiley & Sons, 1968).

[3] Lane, *Policing the City,* pp. 115-116.

[4] Quoted in *ibid.,* p. 130.

[5] Quoted in *ibid.,* p. 154.

city like Amsterdam with almost no Negroes and few derelict drunks obviously cannot ignore petty Negro crime or chronic alcoholics. Whether or not a city is "wide open" with respect to vice and gambling depends as much on what the political leadership will allow as on what the police are willing to ignore. And although the police in all three cities tend to make very few misdemeanor or juvenile arrests and issue very few traffic tickets, there are exceptions—the Albany police arrest drunks in large numbers, the Newburgh police issue many more speeding tickets.

The police style in these cities is watchman-like because, with certain exceptions dictated by the chief's policies or the city's expectations, the patrolman is allowed—and even encouraged— to follow the path of least resistance in carrying out his daily, routine assignments. His desire "to keep his nose clean" is reinforced by the department's desire "not to rock the boat." The police handle the problem of an adversary relationship with the public by withdrawing from as many such relationships as possible. As in all cities, these departments are highly sensitive to complaints from the public, though they differ in their handling of them. There is no formal complaint procedure nor any internal review or inspection system; instead, the chief handles such matters personally. Depending on the kind of political system of which he is a part, he may defend the department vocally, or hush the matter up quietly, or, if an influential person or segment of opinion has been offended, "throw the man to the wolves" by suspending or discharging him. (There were cases of officers dismissed in all three cities.) The chief tries to avoid such difficulties, however, by tightly restricting the discretionary authority of his patrolmen ("don't stick your neck out" unless you can make a "good pinch") and by having them refer all doubtful matters to the sergeants, the lieutenant, or even the chief himself.

In none of the three cities did even the critics of the police allege that serious crime was overlooked, nor did anyone deny that police tolerance of vice and gambling had declined somewhat over the years. All three communities were once a good deal gaudier and there is still a lot of life left in Albany and Newburgh. But all have become, at least publicly, more decorous, and this was accomplished without any significant change in the police—it was simply understood that the politicians and the community and church leaders wanted things a bit quieter, a process aided in Albany by the fact that the governor tore down the wooliest part of the city. (As in all land clearance programs, a large proportion of small businessmen, illegitimate as well as legitimate, never survive the relocation process.)

To a watchman-like department, the penal law is a device empowering the police to maintain order and protect others while a serious infraction has occurred; the exact charge brought against the person is not so important—or rather, it is important mostly in terms of the extent to which that particular section of the law facilitates the uncomplicated exercise of police power and increases the probability of the court sustaining the action. The charges of public intoxication and disorderly conduct are useful, and thus frequently used, in this regard—they are general, they are difficult to dispute, they carry relatively light penalties and thus are not likely to be resisted, and they are not technically, in New York, "crimes" that might hurt a man's record.

In these cities, the patrolman is expected to ignore the "little stuff" but to "be tough" where it is important. For example, the police have essentially a "familial" rather than law enforcement view of juvenile offenders. Their policy is to ignore most infractions ("kid's will be kids") and to act *in local parentis* with respect to those that cannot be ignored: administer a swift kick or a verbal rebuke, have the boy do some chores ("Tom Sawyer justice"), or turn him over to his parents for discipline. An Albany probation officer who handles many young people told an interviewer that "sometimes a cop has to do things that aren't strictly legal, like taking a kid into the back room . . . The parents should do it, but don't."

The Legalistic Style

In some departments, the police administrator uses such control as he has over the patrolmen's behavior to induce them to handle commonplace situations as if they were matters of law enforcement rather than order maintenance. He realizes, of course, that the officer cannot always act as if his duty were merely to compare observed behavior

with a legal standard and make an arrest if that standard has been violated—the law itself, especially that governing misdemeanor arrests,
does not always permit the application of its sanctions. But whenever
he acts on his own initiative or to the extent he can influence the outcome of disorderly situations in which he acts on the initiative of the
citizen, the patrolman is expected to take a law enforcement view of his
role. Such a police style will be called "legalistic," and it can be found
in varying degrees in Oakland and Highland Park and to a growing
extent in Syracuse.

A legalistic department will issue traffic tickets at a high rate,
detain and arrest a high proportion of juvenile offenders, act vigorously against illicit enterprises, and make a large number of misdemeanor
arrests even when, as with petty larceny, the public order has not been
breached. The police will act, on the whole, as if there were a single
standard of community conduct—that which the law prescribes—
rather than different standards for juveniles, Negroes, drunks, and the
like. Indeed, because such persons are more likely than certain others
to commit crimes, the law will fall heavily on them and be experienced
as "harassment."

The Oakland and Highland Park police departments began functioning this way in about the mid-1950's; Oakland continues to do so,
and Highland Park has modified its policies only slightly since the
appointment of a new chief in 1965. Syracuse began moving in this
direction in 1963, with the arrival of a "reform" police chief and
deputy chief; it is too early to tell how far it will proceed. For now, it
has only some of the earmarks of a legalistic department—and these
primarily in the field of traffic enforcement.

The concept "legalistic" does not necessarily imply that the police
regard all laws as equally important or that they love the law for its
own sake. In all the cities here discussed, officers distinguish between
major and minor crimes, feel that private disputes are usually less
important than public disorders, and are willing to overlook some
offenses and accept some excuses. Indeed, because the "normal" tendency of police officers, for reasons explained in Chapter 2, is to underenforce the law, a legalistic police style is necessarily the result of rather
strenuous administrative efforts to get patrolmen to do what they might
not otherwise do; as such, it is never completely successful. Though
there may be a few zealots in a watchman-like department, they will be
few indeed and will probably concentrate their efforts more on making
"good pinches," which in any department are rewarded, than on
"pushing paper" (that is, writing tickets or citing juveniles). In a legalistic department, there is likely to be a sizable number of patrolmen with
comparatively little zeal— typically older officers, or officers "left over"
from a previous and different administration, or officers of any age
who do not regard the benefits (in terms of promotions, official recog-

nition, or good duty assignments) of zealousness as worth the costs in effort and possibly adverse citizen relations.

The legalistic style does mean that, on the whole, the department will produce many arrests and citations, especially with respect to those matters in which the police and not the public invoke the law; even when the police are called by the public to intervene, they are likely to intervene formally, by making an arrest or urging the signing of a complaint, rather than informally, as through conciliation or by delaying an arrest in hopes that the situation will take care of itself.

Though in many cases they are required by law to rely on citizen arrests, the police in following the legalistic style do not try to privatize the handling of disputes and minor offenses. Citizen arrests are facilitated, prosecution of shoplifters is encouraged, juveniles are handled formally, and drunks are arrested "for their own protection." Prostitutes are arrested (but drug-store pornography, because the law affords few grounds for an arrest, is pretty much left alone). Even in Highland Park, though a small town, drunks and juveniles have been handled more formally since the mid-1950's and bad-check passers are often prosecuted even when the merchant is willing to drop charges. As the chief told an interviewer, "Once we get that check, we'll sign a complaint and we'll prosecute. We've got the check with their name on it and the date, and it's marked 'insufficient funds,' so we've got all the evidence we need. A lot of the stores would just as soon not prosecute, I suppose, but . . . we're not a collection agency." At the same time, as Highland Park *is* a small and affluent town, the police are hardly eager to intervene in domestic disputes—to be precise, wife beatings—which, unlike the barroom brawls of the big city, are rich in opportunities for an officer to get himself in trouble. The police once handled such dilemmas occasionally by calling the local magistrate (until recently, an elected magistrate handled all local cases) and asking him to try informally to reach a settlement and, of course, to take responsibility. This is no longer the case; now, the victim would be asked to sign a complaint ticket.

Though the legalistic department will issue a large number of traffic tickets, not every department with a high ticketing rate can be called legalistic. Because he has an unambiguous performance measure, the police administrator can obtain almost any level of ticketing he wishes without necessarily altering the way the police conceive their function, as when ticketing is delegated to a specialized traffic enforcement unit. A legalistic department will typically go beyond this, however, and put *all* patrolmen, not just traffic specialists, under some pressure to "produce." To the extent this policy is followed, some change in the patrolman's conception of his function ensues. Sometimes, however, the opposite occurs. In Highland Park, the chief responsible for the heavy emphasis on traffic enforcement was replaced, in 1965, by a chief who shifted the department's strategy without greatly affecting its ticket productivity and without abandoning its general law enforcement orientation. He did this by substituting specialization for quotas—easing somewhat the pressure to produce on the force as a whole and giving the task to one or two officers who would do little else.[1]

A better test for the existence of the legalistic style can be found in those situations where the administrator's control of his subordinates' conduct is less certain and where therefore greater and more systematic efforts must be made to achieve the desired behavior. The handling of juvenile offenders is just such a case. In Oakland and Highland Park, and perhaps to a growing extent in Syracuse, the police take a law enforcement rather than familial view of their responsibilities in delinquency cases. Perhaps "institutional" view would be more correct, because the police in none of these cities feel their task is simply to make an arrest whenever possible. Indeed, the officers are keenly aware of the importance of the family and spend considerable time talking to parents, but the relationship between officer and juvenile or officer and parent is formal and institutional—the officer seeks to invoke specialized, professional services (probation officers, judges, child guidance clinics) rather than to apply his own form of discipline or to resort to appeals to clergymen or others presumed to wield "moral" influence. Of course, to take advantage of the professional services the community provides, the juvenile must be brought into these institutions—and that, typically, requires an arrest.

---

[1] When the specialized enforcement strategy replaced the quota system, the morale of the Highland Park patrolmen improved. But the new methods did not substantially reduce the chance that a motorist would be ticketed. In 1965, though the new chief was in office for about nine months, the number of moving violation tickets issued was about the same as the average for the preceding three years when the former chief, and thus the quota system, prevailed.

The Service Style

In some communities, the police take seriously all requests for either law enforcement or order maintenance (unlike police with a watchman style) but are less likely to respond by making an arrest or otherwise imposing formal sanctions (unlike police with a legalistic style). The police intervene frequently but not formally. This style is often found in homogeneous, middle-class communities in which there is a high level of apparent agreement among citizens on the need for and definition of public order but in which there is no administrative demand for a legalistic style. In these places, the police see their chief responsibility as protecting a common definition of public order against the minor and occasional threats posed by unruly teenagers and "outsiders" (tramps, derelicts, visiting college boys). Though there will be family quarrels, they will be few in number, private in nature, and constrained by general understandings requiring seemly conduct. The middle-class character of such communities makes the suppression of illegal enterprises both easy (they are more visible) and necessary (public opinion will not tolerate them) and reduces the rate of serious crime committed by residents; thus, the police will be freer to concentrate on managing traffic regulating juveniles, and providing services.

Such a police policy will be called the "service" style, and it can be found especially in Brighton and Nassau County. In such communities, which are not deeply divided along class or racial lines the police can act as if their task were to estimate the "market" for police services and to produce a "product" that meets the demand. For patrolmen especially, the pace of police work is more leisurely (there are fewer radio messages per tour of duty than in a community with a substantial lower class)[1] and the community is normally peaceful, thus apparent threats to order are more easily detected. Furthermore, the citizenry expects its police officers to display the same qualities as its department store salesmen, local merchants, and public officials—courtesy, a neat appearance, and a deferential manner. Serious matters—burglaries, robberies, assaults—are of course taken seriously and thus "suspicious" persons are carefully watched or questioned. But with regard to minor infractions of the law, arrests are avoided when possible (the rates at which traffic tickets are

---

[1] During the first week of June 1965, the Brighton police sent 124 nonadministrative radio messages to patrol cars and the Newburgh police sent 173; the towns are approximately equal in population, but the median income in Brighton is twice that in Newburgh. Furthermore, a substantially higher fraction of the Newburgh calls (8.9 percent) were for "crimes in progress" than of the Brighton calls (3.2 percent).

issued and juveniles referred to Family Court will be much lower than in legalistic departments) but there will be frequent use of informal, nonarrest sanctions (warnings issued to motorists, juveniles taken to headquarters or visited in their homes for lectures).

Because the two departments which most clearly—and, to some extent, by their own admission—display the "service" style are Nassau and Brighton, one might suppose that they are merely watchman-style police departments with a different, less divided, or more demanding clientele: prosperous suburbanites want to be left alone with respect to their own minor indiscretions, to have "undesirables" kept away, and the peace maintained. To some extent this is true, but it is not the whole story. The Albany Police Department, if transplanted to Nassau, probably would not—and certainly without major internal changes, could not—begin to serve this new and different constituency in accordance with its demands. Those matters about which the Nassau police believe, no doubt rightly, that Nassau residents feel strongly—residential burglaries, teenage narcotics, juvenile misconduct, personal and courteous "service"—are best dealt with by specialized police units and a certain type of officer.

James J. Fyfe

Administrative Interventions on Police Shooting Discretion: An Empirical Examination

In August, 1972, the New York City Police Department promulgated administrative shooting guidelines and shooting incident review procedures far more restrictive than former statutory "defense of life" and "fleeing felon" justifications for police shooting. Using a data base that includes all reported New York City police firearms discharges and serious assaults from 1971 to 1975, this article examines the effects of the new guidelines and procedures on shooting frequencies, patterns, and consequences.

Great decreases in "fleeing felon" shootings, "warning shots," and shooting-opponent injuries and deaths were found to be associated with the new rules. This change also appeared to have a favorable effect on line-of-duty officer deaths and serious injuries. The implications of these findings are discussed.

Perhaps the major paradox of the American system of justice is the discretionary latitude it allows many of its police officers in the use of their firearms as a means of "deadly force." While the system—and the society—argue and agonize over the death penalty, police shootings generally draw little attention. It is likely, in fact, that the 1977 execution of Gary Gilmore generated more publicity and debate than did the more than 2500 police shooting deaths that occurred during the ten-year period between that event and the last previous court-ordered exercise of deadly force (Milton et al., 1977:33).

It is true that police use of deadly force differs dramatically from court-ordered death sentences. Police often use their firearms as the last resort against real and imminent peril; they often have no choice but to shoot. Judges who elect to impose the death penalty, in contrast, usually select it from among a range of alternatives after lengthy deliberation in the safety of their chambers. Despite these differences, it is ironic that the system has devised rigid devices to control and review court-ordered

Source: James J. Fyfe (1979). "Administrative Interventions on Police Shooting Discretion." *Journal of Criminal Justice*, 7:309-323. Reprinted by permission of Elsevier Science Ltd., Pergamon Imprint, Oxford, England.

death sentences, but has generally maintained a hands-off policy where police decisions to shoot are concerned. Indeed, the system zealously controls the court's power to take lives on evidence of guilt beyond a reasonable doubt, but frequently gives its police a blank check in deciding whether or not to shoot at those they have probable cause to arrest.

Police Shootings

Legal Controls and Review Procedures

While Milton et al., (1977:41-43) detect both a "recent eagerness of the judiciary to impose restraints upon police conduct" and an increase in the number of civil actions alleging excessive police force, police shooting discretion in many jurisdictions is limited only by the broad common law fleeing-felon and defense-of-life rules (National Advisory Commission, 1973:18). In addition, police shooting is often subjected to review procedures of questionable effectiveness (Harding and Fahey, 1973).

The fleeing-felon rule is very briefly, but accurately, described by Wilson as police "authority to use deadly force to prevent escape from any felony charge" (1972). Milton et al., (1977:39) note that this principle was defensible when "virtually all felonies were punishable by death," but question its wisdom in an era in which the death penalty is all but extinct.

An only slightly lengthier definition of the defense-of-life rule is offered by Rhine (1968:834):

> [It is the police officer's] general right to use deadly force for defense of self and others against threats of death and serious bodily action. In addition, law enforcement authorities never have a duty to retreat before using deadly force, and may always use this for defense of others solely upon reasonable belief that they are being threatened with death or serious bodily harm.

The most striking features of these guidelines are brevity and breadth. Further, while many states have supplemented them by legislating more narrow and clearly delineated statutory limits on police shooting discretion, the record suggests that police officers are rarely penalized for violating them.[1] The adjudication of violations of either codified common law principles or more restrictive legislative guidelines requires that they be subjected to the criminal process. Here, one finds that, even among those cases that do come before the courts,[2] often the only civilian eyewitness to a police shooting is its subject—if surviving.

The only version of a police shooting that comes to court attention, therefore, is likely to be that of the police officer involved. Further, even where alternative versions are offered, the prosecutor must decide to take action if a case is to go to trial. Several reasons have been proposed to explain the reluctance of district attorneys to take these cases to trial. Rhine (1968:856) suggests that it is very difficult to prove criminal intent in police killings. Harding and Fahey (1973:298, 299) point out that elected prosecutors may find that both constituent concern with law and order and the need to maintain a cooperative relationship with police militate against such prosecution.

Administrative Controls and Review Procedures

The broad nature of legal restrictions on police shooting discretion and the difficulties of enforcing them have led many to argue that police agencies should formulate narrower administrative guidelines and internal procedures for the review of shootings (President's Commission, 1967:189, 190; American Bar Association, 1973:125-131). Milton et al, (1977:45-57) report a "clear trend" toward the adoption of such policies. They note, also, however, that where administrative standards are operative, they vary widely and are frequently contradictory or (perhaps intentionally) vague. As a result, "their impact on the conduct of police officers is questionable." Further, the adoption of administrative guidelines and review procedures is often resisted by police who perceive such rules as arbitrary restrictions on their ability to defend themselves (Berkley, 1969; McKiernan, 1973). This argument is based on the premise that such regulations would promote police reluctance to shoot when necessary for self-defense out of fear that their split-second, life-or-death decisions will be subject to leisurely second-guessing (Rubinstein, 1973:333).

New York City: A Test Case

One agency that has adopted clearly delineated administrative shooting guidelines and review procedures is the New York City Police Department. In August, 1972, that department promulgated Temporary Operating Procedure 237 (T.O.P. 237), a directive that narrowed officer shooting discretion considerably more than did New York's statutory provisions. In addition, T.O.P. 237 established a high-level Firearms Discharge Review Board (FDRB) to investigate and adjudicate all officer firearm discharges.

T.O.P. 237 refined New York's penal law restrictions on police shooting (which are based on the American Law Institute's 1962 Model

Penal Code and permit officer use of deadly force to "defend life" or to arrest for several specified "violent felonies") by providing that:

a. In all cases, only the minimum amount of force will be used which is consistent with the accomplishment of a mission. Every other reasonable means will be utilized for arresting, preventing, or terminating a felony or for the defense of oneself or another before a police officer resorts to the use of his firearm.

b. A firearm shall not be discharged under any circumstances where lives of innocent persons may be endangered.

c. The firing of a warning shot is prohibited.

d. The discharging of a firearm to summon assistance is prohibited, except where the police officer's safety is endangered.

e. Discharging a firearm at or from a moving vehicle is prohibited unless the occupants of the other vehicle are using deadly physical force against the officer or another, by means other than the vehicle. (NYPD, 1972:1)

Except for some minor changes in 1973 (NYPD, 1973:2), these provisions have been in effect since 1972. So too, has the FDRB, which is chaired by the Chief of Operations (the department's highest ranking officer), and which also includes as members two deputy police commissioners and the supervisor of the Police Academy's Firearms Unit. FDRB is empowered to conduct hearings at which it may question civilian witnesses, the officer involved, the officer's commander, or any other officers. Its findings are submitted in the form of recommendations to the commander of the officer involved. These, a review of case dispositions reveals, fall into one or more of the following categories:

1. The discharge was in accordance with law and department policy.

2. The discharge was justifiable, but the officer should be given additional training in the use of firearms or in the law and department policy.

3. The shooting was justifiable under law, but violated department policy and warrants department disciplinary action.

4. The shooting was in apparent violation of law and should be referred to the appropriate prosecutor if criminal charges had not already been filed.

5. The officer involved should be transferred (or offered the opportunity to transfer) to a less sensitive assignment.

6. The officer involved should be the subject of psychological testing or alcoholism counseling.[3]

T.O.P. 237 became the core of this study, which attempts to examine the impact of that directive on the frequency, nature, and consequences of police shooting in New York City.

Data Sources

The primary data for this study consist of 4,904 Firearms Discharge/Assault Reports, (FDAR) or all of those filed by officers who had reported discharging their firearms (N = 3,827) or being the subjects of serious assaults (assaults with deadly weapons that may have resulted in officer death or serious injury) between January 1, 1971 and December 31, 1975. These FDAR reports, supplemented by various personnel records, were converted to computer data and analyzed using the Statistical Package for the Social Sciences (Nie et al., 1975).

We would have preferred to have included in this data set reports on shootings and assaults on officers that occurred during the two or three years immediately preceding 1971. While this endeavor might have strengthened our analysis by providing a clearer description of shooting frequencies and patterns before the promulgation of T.O.P. 237, we were precluded from undertaking it by the unsystematic and incomplete shooting and assault data available. Of necessity, therefore, we contented ourselves with the inclusion of data on shootings and assaults on officers reported during the nineteen months preceding T.O.P. 237.

A potential weakness of this data base (or of any other that consists of incident reports) involves the degree to which events have not been reported or have been inaccurately reported. Because officers who fired justifiably would not be disciplined for shooting but would be charged for failing to report, we concluded that missing data would most often include shootings of questionable justifiability. Even in violative cases, however, officers would be unlikely to omit reports of shootings in which they had (or thought they might have) hit someone or something. They would also be unlikely to omit reports of shootings perceived as likely to be brought to official attention by third parties, including their colleagues. Because of New York City's population density and because its police rarely work alone, it is unlikely that more than a very few police could fail to file incident reports in confidence that their shootings would not otherwise come to light. We concluded that the problem of missing data was of minimal import.

The problem of inaccurate reports was viewed as more substantive. Following the T.O.P. 237 ban on warning shots, for example, we had found a great and unexpected increase in reported accidental "shots in the air" fired by police who "tripped on curbs" while pursuing fleeing suspects (Fyfe, 1978:316-328). FDRB generally recommends disciplinary action against officers who fire warning shots, but usually refers accidental shooters to nonpunitive tactical retraining classes. It is probably, therefore, that this specific pattern change reflects altered reporting behavior rather than changes in actual field behavior. To minimize the effects of this and any other distortions, we attempted to limit our analysis to variables reasonably immune to reporting bias.[4]

Analysis

Shootings and Intra-Community Violence

In related research (Fyfe, 1978:32-106), we had found strong correlations among the geographic distributions of shooting incidents, arrests for felonies against the person, and reported murders and nonnegligent manslaughters (Pearson's r = +.062 and +0.78 respectively). Therefore, we commenced the present investigation by examining the relationships between those variables over the five years studied. If we found that these associations also existed over time, it would be reasonable to conclude that changes in shooting frequencies were at least in part attributable to these nonorganizational variables.

Table 1, which contrasts annual shooting incidents (which may include one or more officer shooters who fired at the same time and place) with reported criminal homicides and arrests for felonies against the person, presents strong evidence to the contrary. After peaking in 1972, homicides remain fairly constant over the period studied (the relatively large 1973-1974 decrease is only a 7.5 percent decline), while arrests register a regular annual increase and firearms discharge incidents decline annually after a large increase between 1971 and 1972. More specifically, columns four and five reveal considerable variation in annual ratios of homicides/shootings and arrests/shootings before and after the promulgation of T.O.P. 237. In 1971, there were 2.33 reported criminal homicides for every police shooting in New York City; this ratio declines slightly (to 2.11) in 1972, then increases considerably over 1973 and 1974 to a high of 3.67 in 1975. Perhaps most significant for the purposes of police administrators, the table indicates that the annual ratio of arrests/shootings has been nearly doubled over the five years studied (from 47.62 in 1971 to 86.88 in 1975).

Table 1
Violent Crimes and Police Shootings By Year, 1971-1975

Year	Reported Homicides[a]	Felony Arrests[a,b]	Police Shootings	Ratios Homicides/ Shootings	Ratios Arrests/ Shootings
1971	18.2% (1466)	17.1% (30002)	21.5% (630)	2.33	47.62
1972	21.0% (1691)	18.9% (33070)	27.5% (803)	2.11	41.18
1973	20.9% (1680)	20.1% (35163)	19.6% (574)	2.93	61.26
1974	19.3% (1554)	21.7% (37971)	16.1% (471)	3.30	80.62
1975	20.5% (1645)	22.2% (38922)	15.3% (448)	3.67	86.88
Totals	100.0% (8036)	100.0% (175128)	100.0% (2926)	2.75	59.85

[a]Calculated from: New York City Police Department (December, 1971-1975). *Monthly arrest report.*
[b]Includes murder, non-negligent manslaughter, forcible rape, robbery, felonious assault.
NOTE: Subcell percentages may not total 100.0 due to rounding.

T.O.P. 237

The decline in reported shooting incidents in the face of a continuing increase in arrests in 1972 suggests the intervention of another variable. A logical first subject of investigation in looking for such an event is T.O.P. 237, which became effective in late 1972, after which the relationship seems to have changed. Our examination of the association of T.O.P. 237 with decreased shooting frequencies commenced by dividing the five years under study into two-month periods and displaying the number of reported officer shooters and shooting incidents for each, as shown in Figure 1. The two-month observation periods were chosen to refine the trend as far as possible without losing information: they reduce the total of observations from sixty to thirty and allow for the data to be cut September 1, close in time to T.O.P. 237 (August 18, 1972) and its slightly altered successor, I.O. 118 (August 27, 1973).

The chart and the overall r's of –0.62 and –0.64 for office shooters and shooting incidents, indicate that both phenomena have fluctuated somewhat, but have been declining steadily since the period during which T.O.P. 237 became effective; "officer shooters" show a peak of 210 during May and June, 1972, decline to 175 during July and

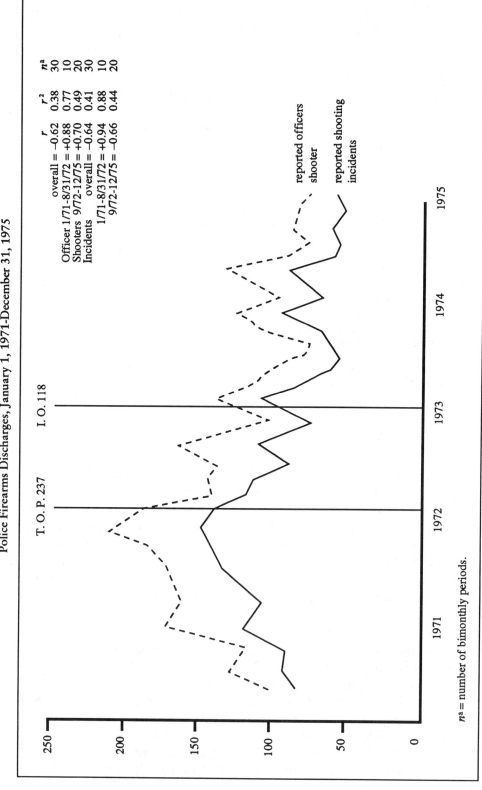

Figure 1
Police Firearms Discharges, January 1, 1971–December 31, 1975

n[a] = number of bimonthly periods.

August, 1972, and never again reach either level. Similarly, "shooting incidents" peak at 149 during the May-June, 1972 period, decline to 141 during July-August, 1972, and remain below those levels for the duration of the period studied.

One cannot argue, of course, that incident declines are entirely attributable to T.O.P. 237. Indeed, the "shooter" and "incident" r^2 values of 0.38 and 0.41 serve notice that fewer than half these variations are explained by the passage of time. Many other variables over which the department has little or no control (e.g., economic and social conditions, the numbers of officers available for street duty) are certain to have affected these frequencies. On the other hand, splitting the chart at September 1, 1972 produces Pearson's r values of +0.88 (officer shooters) and +0.94 (shooting incidents) for the earlier period and respective r's of –0.70 and –0.66 for the latter. It is evident, therefore, that T.O.P. 237 was accompanied by rather dramatic changes in the frequencies with which New York City police officers reported discharging their firearms.

I.O. 118

The second department firearms policy statement was I.O. 118, which was issued on August 27, 1973. The major purposes of this directive were to clarify T.O.P. 237's ambiguities and to establish decentralized "area level" review boards,[5] but the document appears at the beginning of a six-month decline in shooting incident frequencies and an eight-month decline in officer shooting frequencies. Some percentage of these decreases may be attributable to a cold weather slump. But the declines continued in the absence of other possible explanations (e.g., the department was, at that time, adding to its ranks; reported homicides and arrests for violent crime did not show similar declines), and are at least as severe and as long as those that followed the issuance of T.O.P. 237.

Because so few observations are included in this second period, it was decided not to attempt to test their possible significance statistically. It would be interesting, however, to continue following the frequencies of shooting incidents and reported shooters consequent to other clarifications, procedural alterations, and minor discretionary changes. If further declines occurred, one might postulate that substantial influence is exerted on shooting frequencies by continuing emphasis on limits to individual officer discretion or the institution of decentralized reporting and review procedures.

Weekly Means

The two-month periods studied thus far are, of course, rather inexact and may be criticized if used as a basis for comparison because they include varying numbers of days. July/August periods, for example, encompass sixty-two days, while January/February includes only fifty-nine (in all years except 1972, which was a leap year). In addition, bimonthly figures do not allow the data to be split precisely at the effective date of T.O.P. 237 (August 18, 1972).

To provide comparable figures, the five years under study were therefore split at midnight August 18, 1972, and means of reported officer reason for shooting were computed weekly for each period (period 1 weeks = 85.1; period 2 = 175.7). The results are presented in Table 2. Its column totals reveal that a weekly mean of 18.4 officers reported discharging their firearms prior to T.O.P 237 and that this figure dropped to 12.9 officers after the directive was put into force (this represents a decrease of 29.9 percent). Further, the table shows important changes in the reasons given by officers in reported discharging of firearms ($p = 0.001$; $v = 0.28$). Indeed, while the weekly mean reported "defense of life" shootings has decreased (from 11.9 to 9.0), the pre-T.O.P. 237 percentage of these shootings (65.8 percent) has increased since the order (to 70.6 percent). Concomitantly, both the weekly mean and percentage of "prevent/terminate crime" shootings (usually fleeing-felon situations) have decreased substantially (from 3.9 and 21.4 percent to 0.6 and 4.6 percent, respectively). Conversely Table 2 demonstrates that both the weekly means and percentage of suicide attempts have remained relatively constant. As one would expect, T.O.P. 237 has little effect in deterring suicides.

Warning Shots

While Table 2 demonstrates reduced shooting frequencies and varying reported reasons for shooting, it leaves unanswered many questions about other consequences of T.O.P. 237. Its frequencies, for example, are confounded because they include warning shots, which were not treated separately but were coded on the basis of the officer shooter's reported intent. If, for example, a police officer fired a shot into the air in an attempt to stop a fleeing burglary suspect, the shooting would be classified as "prevent/terminate crime" and would be included in Table 2. What Table 2 does *not* provide, therefore, is a measure of T.O.P. 237's effect in reducing shots fired *at* fleeing burglars or other opponents. Instead, it indicates that before T.O.P. 237, 3.9 officers per week reported discharging their firearms to prevent or terminate crimes, regardless of whether or not they fired at or over the heads of suspects, and that this mean has subsequently declined to 0.6. Since, in addition to mandating the use of "every other reasonable means . . . for arresting preventing, or terminating a felony . . . before a police officer resorts to the use of a firearm," T.O.P. 237 flatly prohibits warning shots, one might expect that much of the decrease discussed above is attributable to lower warning shot frequencies rather than to reduced number of shootings at human targets.

Table 2
Officer-Reported Reason for Shooting

	Pre-T.O.P. 237	Weekly Mean	Post-T.O.P. 237	Weekly Mean	Totals	Weekly Mean
Defense of Life	65.8% (1016)	11.9	70.6% (1582)	9.0	67.9% (2598)	10.0
Prevent or Terminate Crime	21.4% (330)	3.9	4.6% (103)	0.6	11.3% (433)	1.7
Destroy Animal	4.4% (68)	0.8	11.4% (255)	1.5	8.4% (323)	1.2
Suicide Attempt	0.7% (11)	0.1	0.8% (18)	0.1	0.8% (29)	0.1
Accidental	3.6% (56)	0.7	9.0% (201)	1.2	6.7% (257)	1.0
Other	4.1% (63)	0.7	3.7% (83)	0.5	3.8% (146)	0.6
Totals	40.8% (1562)	18.4	59.2% (2265)	12.9	100.0% (1827)[a]	14.7

NOTE: Chi-squared = 318.82; $p = 0.001$; $v = 0.28$. Subcell percentages may not total 100.0 due to rounding.
[a] All column totals include 18 pre-T.O.P. 237 and 23 post-T.O.P. 237 cases in which reason for shooting was not reported.

To control for this possibility and to better measure relative frequencies of officers who shot at targets (except, obviously, accidental shooters), Table 3, which excludes all officers who reported firing only warning shots, was calculated. This table presents some important differences from the data in Table 2. Its total (3,413 shooters) indicates that 414 of the shooters reported in the previous table had fired only warning shots. Further, most of the reported warning shots (304 of the 414) took place during the period preceding T.O.P. 237. Consequently, the weekly mean number of officers who reported firing "in defense of life" during the early period has declined from 10.6 and the weekly mean "prevent/terminate crime" shooters is almost halved from 3.9 to 2.0). While this table's exclusion of "warning shots" still leaves significant pre- post-T.O.P. 237 differences in the mean weekly frequencies of reported reasons for shootings, the differences shrink considerably; indeed, the relative percentage of reported "defense of life" shootings decreases.[6] In terms of weekly shots fired at people, however, this table also demonstrates significant decreases following T.O.P. 237.

Table 3
Officer Reported Reason for Shooting, Excluding Warning Shots

Reason	Pre-T.O.P. 237	Weekly Mean	Post-T.O.P. 237	Weekly Mean	Totals	Weekly Mean
Defense of Life	72.7% (902)	10.6	70.7% (1536)	8.7	71.5% (2438)	9.0
Prevent or Terminate Crime	13.9% (172)	2.0	4.3% (93)	0.5	7.8% (265)	1.0
Destroy Animal	5.5% (68)	0.8	11.7% (254)	1.4	9.4% (322)	1.2
Suicide Attempt	0.9% (11)	0.1	0.8% (18)	0.1	0.8% (29)	0.1
Accidental	4.5% (56)	0.7	9.2% (201)	1.2	7.5% (257)	1.0
Other	2.5% (31)	0.4	3.3% (71)	0.4	3.0% (102)	0.4
Totals	36.3% (1240)	14.6	63.7% (2173)	12.3	100.0% (3413)	13.1[a]

NOTE: Chi-squared = 102.62; $p = 0.001$; $v = 0.17$
[a]Total weekly mean includes 36 cases in which a reason for shooting was not reported.

T.O.P. 237 and Firearms Discharge/Assault Generated Injury

In measuring the impact of T.O.P. 237 on officer injury, we chose to include in our analysis only injuries and deaths sustained in the line of duty. In this manner, we eliminated from consideration injuries on which one might reasonably expect that T.O.P. 237 would have no impact (e.g., officer suicides, injuries accidentally suffered while handling or cleaning weapons). This does not, however, limit the analysis to injuries sustained by on-duty officers. Off-duty officers hurt while "taking police action" (e.g., while attempting arrests, stopping and questioning suspicious persons) are defined by the department to have been injured in the line of duty. Thus, for example, an off-duty officer who is shot while attempting to apprehend the perpetrators of a robbery that the officer witnesses is deemed to have been injured only because his or her status and actions as a police officer. The injury was sustained in response to "duty's call." If, conversely, whether the officer is off or on duty when injured in circumstances that do not involve the performance of a police function or that involve negligence on the officer's part, the injury is defined as non-line of duty. As a case in point, an officer stabbed in a street robbery by individuals who do not know that he or she is a police officer is regarded as having been injured as would any citizen in similar circumstances. The injury, therefore, is classified as non-line of duty. Similarly, an on-duty officer who is injured by, for example, the accidental discharge of a carelessly handled weapon while not engaged in a specific police action, is also recorded as having suffered a non-line of duty injury.

Table 4, which presents comparative frequencies of FDAR-generated, officer-line-of-duty injury and death before and after T.O.P. 237, demonstrates that the injury vs. death percentages remained fairly constant across the two periods. Once again, however, one finds that weekly means for injured and killed officers vary considerably. Before T.O.P. 237, 4.4 officers a week suffered nonfatal FDAR-generated, line-of-duty injuries; after T.O.P. 237, the figure declines to 2.5. Similarly, the frequency with which officers are killed in the line of duty drops from 0.2 (one every five weeks) to 0.1 (one every ten weeks).

Table 4
Reported Line-of-Duty Injuries Sustained by Officers in Firearms
Discharge/Assault Incidents[a]

Officer Injury	Pre-T.O.P. 237	Weekly Mean	Post-T.O.P. 237	Weekly Mean	Totals	Weekly Mean
Injured	95.9% (376)	4.4	96.9% (438)	2.5	96.4% (814)	3.1
Killed	4.1% (16)	0.2	3.1% (14)	0.1	3.6% (30)	0.1
Totals	46.4% (392)	4.6	53.6% (452)	2.6	100.0% (844)	3.2

NOTE: Chi-squared = 0.14; p = 0.70; Q = 0.14
[a]Excludes incidents not involving confrontations with human opponents (e.g., destroying injured animal).

Table 5, which presents frequencies of known shooting incidents opponent degree of injury for the pre- and post-T.O.P. 237 periods, shows reductions in these frequencies as well. Again, one finds that the relative chances of opponent injury have remained fairly constant across the five years studied. Of opponents whose degree of injury was

Table 5
Known Injuries Sustained by Opponents in Police Shooting Incidents

Opponent Injury	Pre-T.O.P. 237	Weekly Mean	Post-T.O.P. 237	Weekly Mean	Totals	Weekly Mean
None	69.0% (1043)	12.3	70.9% (1435)	8.2	70.1% (2478)	9.5
Injured	21.8% (329)	3.9	20.0% (405)	2.3	20.8% (734)	2.8
Killed	9.2% (139)	1.6	9.1% (184)	1.0	9.1% (323)	1.2
Totals	42.7% (1511)	17.8	57.3% (2024)	11.5	100.0% (3535)	13.5

NOTE: Chi-squared = 0.03; $p = 0.99$; $v = 0.01$.

known to the police, approximately seventy percent suffered no injury, slightly more than twenty percent were wounded and just over nine percent were killed during both periods.

But in examining the weekly means, we again find considerable reductions in all our categories following T.O.P. 237. Most specifically, Table 5 shows that New York City police wounded a weekly average of 3.9 opponents and that they killed 1.6 prior to T.O.P. 237; during the period between that intervention and December 31, 1975, these means fell to 2.3 and 1.0, respectively.

While both tables 4 and 5 present rather striking differences between the pre-and post-T.O.P. 237 periods, several considerations prevent our concluding that these differences are entirely attributable to that directive and that they limit the degree to which equivalent reductions might be predicted for other agencies. Simply stated, the reduced frequencies that are presented in both tables are based on two observations made over a five-year period, during which other variables might have been expected to influence police and citizen injuries. Those other variables (e.g., injuries resulting from the unprovoked police assassination attempts by the radical "Black Liberation Army," which were most frequent during the pre-T.O.P. 237 period; police personnel deployment), however, are beyond the scope of the present inquiry.[7] We elected, therefore, to more clearly identify the effect of T.O.P. 237 on police and citizen injury by increasing the number of observations in our examination of those phenomena during the five years studied.

Figure 2 contrasts the bimonthly frequency of civilian FDAR-generated deaths and injuries (classified as one entity on the premise that degree of injury is subject to chance variations) with the frequency with which officers were shot or stabbed in the line of duty (including only what are generally the most serious injuries). This figure demonstrates a general decrease in both these phenomena between 1971 and 1975. In addition, the figure reveals that the relationship between citizen injuries and officer shot or stabbed frequencies is subject to considerable variation. In some periods, citizen injuries far outweigh officer shot or stabbed frequencies, while in others, the gap is closed considerably: during May and June, 1973, officer injuries even exceeded citizen injuries. Again, except for these periods, and despite the gross incident and injury reductions cited earlier, the relative risk of FDAR-generated officer or citizen injury or death looks relatively stable.

Figure 2
Police Opponent Injuries and Deaths and Police Officers
Shot or Stabbed in the Line of Duty, (N = 30)

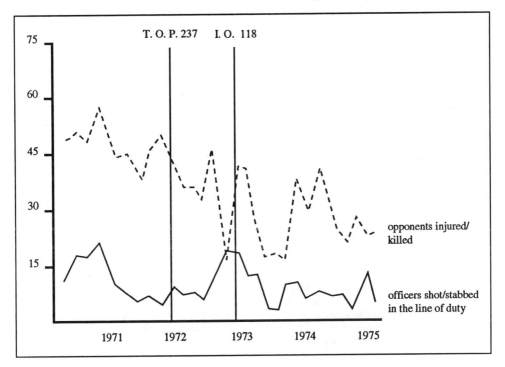

Conclusions

Our examination has demonstrated that a considerable reduction in the frequency of police shooting accompanied New York City's direct intervention on the firearms discretion of its police officers. Further, our data indicate that this reduction was greatest among the most controversial shooting incidents: shootings to prevent or terminate crimes, which frequently involve police shots at fleeing felons. To the extent that this New York experience may be generalized to other agencies, therefore, an obvious consequence of the implementation of clear shooting guidelines and their stringent enforcement is a reduction of injuries and deaths sustained by suspects who would face far less severe penalties even if convicted after trial.

Of equal significance to the police administrator is the fact that these shooting decreases were not accompanied by increased officer injury or death. Conversely, since both these phenomena appear to be associated with the frequency of shooting incidents and related citizen injury, both declined pursuant to T.O.P. 237.

In the most simple terms, therefore, the New York City experience indicates that considerable reductions in police shooting and both officer and citizen injury and death are associated with the establishment of clearly delineated guidelines and procedures for the review of officer shooting discretion.

Notes

This paper is a revision of a paper presented at the Annual Meeting of the American Society of Criminology, Atlanta, Georgia, November, 1977.

[1] Kobler (1975:164) reports that only three of the 1,500 police shooters he studied were criminally punished for their actions.

[2] It is probable that officers who do violate statutory provisions (e.g., by shooting at fleeing misdemeanants) but who both miss and fail to apprehend their targets do not often come to court attention.

[3] Firearms Discharge Review Board cases disposed of with recommendations that include more than one of these categories most typically involve shootings deemed to have violated departmental guidelines and to have indicated that transfers from sensitive (and often desirable) assignments are appropriate. Narcotics officers and other plainclothes personnel who shoot in violation of departmental policy, for example, are often recommended for transfers to administrative assignments or to patrol duty in outlying areas where the chances of encountering circumstances provocative of weapons use are slight. In such cases, we considered the board's recommendation for disciplinary action to be its major and most severe finding and coded dispositions under that single heading. Similarly, because we regarded criminal charges to be the major and most severe finding in all cases in which they resulted, we included such cases in that single category, although they also invariably involved some departmental disciplinary action. Cases involving criminal charges are held in abeyance by FDRB pending court disposition: officers convicted of criminal use of firearms are then summarily dismissed from the department; all officers acquitted of such criminal charges during the period we studied were subsequently subjected to departmental trials for their actions.

By the time the data collection for this report ceased (August, 1976), the Firearms Discharge Review Board had adjudicated 2,155 shootings. Their major recommendations in these cases were as follows;

Within law and departmental guidelines:	70.8%	(1525)
Retraining in law or tactics	18.3%	(395)
Disciplinary action	7.7%	(167)
Criminal charges	1.2%	(26)
Transfer	0.6%	(13)
Psychological or alcoholic counselling	1.3%	(29)
Total	100.0%	(2155)

[4] This attempt was not always successful. In the absence of information to the contrary (e.g., FDRB or judicial findings), we accepted "officer reported reason for shooting" at face value. This exception, however, affects only our examination of changes in the nature of shootings. It has little or no significance as far as total shooting frequencies are concerned.

[5] I.O. 118's only new discretionary parameter was the statement that "(t)he discharge of a firearm at dogs or other animals should be an action employed ONLY when no other means to bring the animal under control exists."

[6] A good part of this percentage decrease, however, is due to the great increase in frequency in reported "destroy animal" shootings. Had these remained constant at their pre-T.O.P. 237 level (0.8 per week), the post-T.O.P. 237 "defense of life shots at people" percentage would have been 74.6 percent.

[7] We concluded detailed examinations of the effects of several other variables on shooting frequency, type, and consequences in Fyfe (1978) and found that they did not significantly alter the findings reported in this study.

References

American Bar Association Project on Standards for Criminal Justice (1973). *Standards relating to the urban police function.* New York: American Bar Association.

Berkley, G.E. (1969). *The democratic policeman.* Boston: Beacon Press.

Fyfe, J.J. (1978). *Shots fired: An examination of New York City police firearms discharges.* Ph.D. dissertation, State University of New York at Albany.

Harding, R.W. and Fahey, R.P. (1973). Killings by Chicago police, 1969-70; An empirical study. 4 *Southern California law review,* 6:284-315.

Kobler, R.M. (1975). Police homicide in a democracy. *Journal of social issues,* 31:163-181.

McKiernan, R.M. (1973). Police shotguns: Devastating to the animals. *The New York Times,* February 7:35.

Milton, C.H.; Halleck, J.W.; Lardiner, J.; and Abrecht, G.L. (1977). *Police use of deadly force.* Washington, DC: Police Foundation.

National Advisory Commission on Criminal Justice Standards and Goals (1973). *Police.* Washington, DC: U.S. Government Printing Office.

New York City Police Department (1973). *Interim order 118.*

———, (1972). Temporary Operating Procedure 237.

———, Crime Analysis Unit (1971-1975). *Monthly arrest report.* December.

Nie, N.H.; Hull, C.H.; Jenkins, J.G.; Steinbrenner, K.; and Bent, D.H. (1975). *Statistical package for the social sciences.* New York: McGraw-Hill.

President's Commission on Law Enforcement and Administration of Justice (1967). *Task force report: The police.* Washington, DC: U.S. Government Printing Office.

Rhine, B. (1968). Kill or be killed: Use of deadly force in the riot situation. 56 *California law review:* 829.

Rubinstein, J. (1973). *City police.* New York: Farrar, Strauss and Giroux.

Wilson, J.V. (1972). Deadly force. *Police chief,* December: 44-46.

Section III
POLICE STRATEGIES

Introduction

Organizations develop and implement strategies in order to reach their goals. A primary official goal of the police organization is the control of crime; accordingly, many of the most significant operational strategies of the police have crime control as the outcome upon which success is measured. This section of *Classics in Policing* presents many of the most significant studies on the operational strategies of the police (preventive patrol, criminal investigation, arrest in domestic violence situations, team policing, and community/problem oriented policing).

As a starting point, the first reading provides a critical analysis of what the police say they do and how they say they do it. According to Peter K. Manning in his article "The Police: Mandate, Strategies, and Appearances," the police have "an impossible mandate." According to Manning (1978), the police have staked out crime control as their territory and the ideological dimension that provides legitimacy to the organization. In turn, the public has come to equate the police organization with crime control and evaluates it on crime control criteria. As a result, the police further internalize this conception and act in accordance with it, thus further re-enforcing public beliefs. The problem is that the police have extremely limited capabilities in controlling crime, hence the "impossible mandate." As a result, according to Manning, the police have resorted to the use of symbols and the manipulation of appearances to perpetuate the belief that the police influence crime. According to Manning, many operational strategies of the police (like those discussed below) are displayed to convey the impression that the police are able to control crime when in actuality they cannot.

Indeed, as demonstrated by many of the readings included here, studies that have examined the effectiveness of the major operational strategies of the police have shown that they have little impact on crime. Perhaps the most significant study that has come to this conclusion is the Kansas City Preventive Patrol Experiment, a summary of which is included here. In 1972 George Kelling and his colleagues conducted an experimental study to test the almost sacred assumption that routine preventive patrol reduces crime. In comparing the extent of crime across areas with different levels of police patrol, the researchers found few significant differences. These findings led the researchers to the conclusion that preventive patrol may not affect crime as previously thought. Although certainly not without criticism (see Larson, 1975), the study represents a critical piece of knowledge on police strategies and has been the catalyst (at least in part) for innovations in the patrol function, or, as Manning (1978) would likely argue, for more manipulation of appearances.

Like the Kansas City study on preventive patrol, Jan Chaiken and her colleagues in "The Criminal Investigation Process: A Summary Report" examine another core strategy of the police: criminal investigation. A major finding of Chaiken et al. (1977) was that the overwhelming majority of solved crimes are solved because of arrests by patrol officers or because the identity of the perpetrator is known when the crime report reached the detective, not because of detective work. In essence, circumstances of the criminal event largely determine the case outcome, and the police do not control these circumstances. These findings directly contradict popular images of detectives as highly skilled investigators who are able to solve any crime through the use of complex and extraordinary methods. While subsequent research has been critical of some of their findings (e.g., Eck, 1982; Brandl and Frank, 1994), the study represents an important inquiry into the criminal investigation process.

In the fourth reading, Lawrence Sherman and Richard Berk report on an experimental study that was designed to test the effects of arrest for minor domestic violence. In the Minneapolis Domestic Violence study, the researchers compared recidivism of spouse abusers who received various treatments (arrest, separation, mediation) and found arrest to be the most effective at reducing repeat violence. Like the other studies included here, this investigation had direct policy implications. Specifically, based on their finding that arrest was most effective in reducing repeat violence, the authors recommended presumptive arrest policies. However, since the publication of this study, replications have been conducted in several jurisdictions but, with few exceptions, the other studies have found arrest to be no more effective than the other treatments (see Sherman, 1992 for a discussion of these studies). The Sherman and Berk study has ignited the smoldering debate on the role of social science research in formulating public policy (see Binder and Meeker, 1988; Sherman and Cohn, 1989). (The summary included here is from a publication of the Police Foundation, an organization devoted to funding and conducting research on police policy issues, and was written with the police administrator in mind. For a more scholarly report of the study, see Sherman and Berk, 1984).

The final three readings discuss team policing and community policing. As discussed earlier in this text, the police in this country operated under the "professional model" of policing until the late 1960s. This philosophy of policing had at its core the conviction that the police can enjoy the greatest degree of organizational efficiency only if allowed to operate on an autonomous basis, free from outside "political" intervention. Further, it was argued that enhanced organizational efficiency would lead to the more effective control of crime. However, as a result of the turbulent 1960s, this philosophy of operation came under close scrutiny. Scholars and police practitioners alike began to realize the undesirable outcomes of such a belief—namely, police alienation from the communities they supposedly serve and the corresponding disintegration of public support. To remedy these problems, particularly as manifested within the minority community, police departments began to "experiment" with several strategies such as community relations bureaus and team policing.

Sherman, Milton, and Kelly (1973), in an excerpt from their book *Team Policing: Seven Case Studies*, describe team policing as it looked in several police departments in the 1970s. They define team policing as the decentralization of command where small groups of officers are permanently assigned to particular neighborhoods in order to improve the control of crime. The authors also discuss the major supports and obstacles to the development and implementation of team policing. History showed that team policing was difficult to implement and its effectiveness was unproven. In the mid-1970s, team policing died. It was viewed as a failure and no longer the "thing to do" in policing.

With the demise of team policing, community policing emerged in the 1980s as another hopeful means. Unlike team policing and the other strategies discussed here, community policing is commonly described as an operational *philosophy*, as a belief in the way the police should approach their responsibilities, not as a particular means to achieve certain goals. It is an effort that encapsulates the "community era" of policing.

Herman Goldstein's 1979 article "Improving Policing: A Problem-Oriented Approach" set the stage for the development of community-oriented policing. Goldstein describes the "means over ends" syndrome where the police essentially become preoccupied with internal management and correspondingly ignore the objectives or outcomes police activities are supposed to achieve. Goldstein identifies a new way of approaching the police function—one that focuses directly on the ends of policing, one oriented around the identification of problems and the development of solutions to these problems. Although there is little specific reference to "community policing" in this article, this approach lies at the conceptual core of the community policing effort.

The next reading, an excerpt from Robert Trojanowicz and Bonnie Bucqueroux's (1990) text *Community Policing*, presents a thumbnail sketch of the definitional complexities of community policing. According to these authors, community policing is an organizational philosophy of policing that promotes a cooperative relationship between citizens and the police in order to address problems of crime, fear of crime, and physical and social disorder. To promote these cooperative relationships, police officers are placed in specific neighborhoods on a long-term basis and are removed from the patrol car that engenders isolation and anonymity. The police are a resource to residents and the catalyst for citizen responsibility.

The final reading, James Q. Wilson and George Kelling's 1982 piece "The Police and Neighborhood Safety: Broken Windows," provides a theoretical backdrop for community policing. They describe the process in which one "broken window" becomes many, and how the process may be interrupted by certain police activities. Specifically, the authors argue that disorder (e.g., broken windows, panhandlers, abandoned cars) and anonymity among residents and between police and residents encourages illegal behaviors. Residents who live in areas of disorder will feel that the area is unsafe. In turn, these feelings reinforce the anonymity among residents, and residents avoid one another. According to the authors, such areas are most vulnerable to serious crime, although the linkage between disorder and crime is not automatic. In such an environment, criminals may believe that the chances of apprehension are relatively slim. It follows then that police efforts directed at reaffirming informal controls, thus providing for the maintenance of order, would lead not only to the reduction of disorder, but also to a reduction in actual crime and fear of it. Community policing is portrayed as such an effort.

References

Binder, Arnold and James W. Meeker (1988). "Experiments as Reforms" *Journal of Criminal Justice* 16:347-358.

Brandl, Steven G. and James Frank (1994). "The Relationship Between Evidence, Detective Effort, and the Disposition of Burglary and Robbery Investigations" *American Journal of Police* 13:149-168.

Eck, John E. (1982). *Solving Crimes: The Investigation of Burglary and Robbery*. Washington D.C.: Police Executive Research Forum.

Larson, Richard C. (1975). "What Happened to Patrol Operations in Kansas City? A Review of the Kansas City Preventive Patrol Experiment" *Journal of Criminal Justice* 3:267-297.

Sherman, Lawrence W. (1992). *Policing Domestic Violence: Experiments and Dilemmas*. New York: The Free Press.

_____ and Richard A. Berk (1984). "The Specific Deterrent Effects of Arrest for Domestic Assault" *American Sociological Review* 49:261-272.

_____ and Ellen G. Cohn (1989). "The Impact of Research on Legal Policy: The Minneapolis Domestic Violence Experiment" *Law and Society Review* 23: 117-144.

Peter K. Manning

The Police:
Mandate, Strategies and Appearances

I. Introduction

All societies have their share of persistent, chronic problems—problems of life, of death, problems of property and security, problems of man's relationship to what he consecrates. And because societies have their quota of troubles, they have developed ways in which to distribute responsibility for dealing with them. The division of labor that results is not only an allocation of functions and rewards, it is a moral division as well. In exchange for money, goods, or services, these groups—such as lawyers or barbers or clergymen or pharmacists—have a *license* to carry out certain activities that others may not. This license is a legally defined right, and no other group or groups may encroach upon it.[1]

The right to perform an occupation may entail the permission to pick up garbage or to cut open human bodies and transfer organs from one to another. What it always involves, however, is a series of tasks and associated attitudes and values that set apart a specialized occupational group from all the others. Further, the licensed right to perform an occupation may include a claim to the right to define the proper conduct of others toward matters concerned with the work. The claim, if granted, is the occupation's *mandate*. The mandate may vary from a right to live dangerously to the right to define the conditions of work and functions of related personnel.

The professional mandate is not easily won, of course, for clients are often unwilling to accept the professional definition of their problem. Professions claim a body of theory and practice to justify their right to discover, define, and deal with problems. The medical profes-

Source: Peter K. Manning (1978). "The Police: Mandate, Strategies, and Appearances." In Peter K. Manning and John Van Maanen (eds.) *Policing: A View from the Street*, pp. 7-31. Santa Monica, CA: Goodyear. Reprinted by permission of Peter K. Manning.

*I would like to thank Howard S. Becker, Jerome H. Skolnick, and Jack D. Douglas for helpful comments and criticism on this essay.

[1] See Everett C. Hughes, *Men and Their Work* (New York: The Free Press, 1958), chap. 6; idem, "The Study of Occupations," in *Sociology Today*, ed. R. K. Merton, Leonard Broom, and L. S. Cottrell (New York: Basic Books, 1959), pp. 442-458 (footnotes renumbered—eds.).

sion, for example, is usually considered the model of a vocation with a secure license and mandate. Yet even in medicine the client may refuse to accept the diagnosis; he may change physicians or fail to follow doctor's orders or insist upon defining his troubles as the product of a malady best cured by hot lemonade or prayer. The contraction and expansion of an occupation's mandate reflects the concerns society has with the services it provides, with its organization, and with its effectiveness. In times of crisis, it is the professions that are questioned first.[2]

Some occupations are not as fortunate as others in their ability to delimit a societal "trouble" and deal with it systematically. The more power and authority a profession has, the better able it is to gain and maintain control over the symbolic meanings with which it is associated in the public's mind. As we have become less concerned with devils and witches as causes of mental illness, clergymen have lost ground to psychiatrists who have laid claim to a secular cure for madness; in this sense, mental illness is a product of the definitions supplied by psychiatry. A profession, therefore, must not only compete with its clientele's definitions, it must also defend itself against the definitions of competing groups. Is a backache better treated by a Christian Scientist, an osteopath, a chiropractor, a masseuse, or an M.D.? Professional groups whose tools are less well-developed, whose theory is jerry-built or unproved, and who are unable to produce results in our consumer-oriented society will be beset with public doubt, concern, and agitation. In other words, these are the groups that have been unable to define their mandate for solving social "troubles" in such a way that it can be accomplished with ease and to the satisfaction of those they intend to serve.

The police have trouble. Among the many occupations now in crisis, they best symbolize the shifts and strains in our changing sociopolitical order. They have been assigned the task of crime prevention, crime detection, and the apprehension of criminals. Based on their legal monopoly of violence, they have staked out a mandate that claims to include the efficient, apolitical, and professional enforcement of the law. It is the contention of this essay that the police have staked out a vast and unmanageable social domain. And what has happened as a result of their inability to accomplish their self-proclaimed mandate is that the police have resorted to the manipulation of *appearances*.

We shall attempt to outline the nature of the police mandate, or their definition of social trouble, their methods of coping with this trouble, and the consequences of their efforts. After developing a sociological analysis of the paradoxes of police work and discussing the heroic attempt—*strategies*—by police to untangle these paradoxes, we shall also consider the recommendations of the President's crime

---

[2] Hughes, *op. cit.*

commission[3] and assess their value as a means of altering and improving the practical art of managing public order.

To turn for the moment to "practical matters," the same matters to which we shall return before concluding, the troubles of the police, the problems and paradoxes of their mandate in modern society, have become more and more intense. Police today may be more efficient in handling their problems than were the first bobbies who began to patrol London in 1829. Or they may not be. There may or may not be more crime. Individual rights may or may not be greatly threatened by crime or crime-fighters, and the enforcement of law in view of recent Supreme Court decisions may or may not be a critical issue in crime control . The police may or may not have enough resources to do their job, and they may or may not be allocating them properly. Peace-keeping rather than law enforcement may or may not be the prime need in black communities, and the police may or may not need greater discretionary powers in making an arrest. But however these troubles are regarded, they exist. They are rooted deeply in the mandate of the police.

Some Sociological Assumptions

This essay makes several assumptions about occupations, about people as they execute occupational roles, about organizations as loci or structures for occupational activities, and about the nature of society. Not all activity taking place "on the job" can be construed as "work"; goldbricking is not unknown in American society and some professionals have even been known to use their places of work to conduct business somewhat outside the mandate of their organization. An individual's "organizational" behavior varies with what the organization is said to require or permit, with his particular place in the organizational hierarchy, and with the degree of congruence between the individual's personal definition of his role and the organization's definition of his role. In a given situation, then, organizational rules and regulations may be important sources of meanings ("He's working hard"), or other criteria may provide more relevant meanings of behavior ("He can't be expected to work. His wife just had a baby"). The ways in which people explain or account for their own organizational activities and those of others are problematic. How do people refer to their organizational roles and activities? How do they construct their moral obligations to the organization? What do they think they owe the organization? How

---

[3] The President's Commission on Law Enforcement and Administration of Justice (hereafter cited as President's Commission). *The Challenge of Crime in a Free Society* (Washington, D.C.: U.S. Government Printing Office, 1967); and idem. *Task Force Report: The Police* (Washington, D C.: United States Government Printing Office, 1967).

does this sense of obligation and commitment pattern or constrain them in another role—the role of golfer or father or politician?

People as they perform their roles are actors. They are alert to the small cues that indicate meaning and intention—the wink, the scowl, the raised eyebrow. Those who attend to these behavioral clues are the audience. All actors try to maximize the positive impression they make on others, and both experience and socialization provide them with a repertoire of devices to manage their appearance.

People as actors in roles must also make assumptions about their audience. The politician, for example, must make certain assumptions about his constituency, the lawyer certain assumptions about clients. Assumptions are an important part of urban life. Some actors with white faces, for instance, may make certain assumptions about others with black faces, that they will be ill-mannered or badly educated and that any request for directions is a prelude to a holdup. Assumptions are not simply individual in nature; they are shared, patterned, and passed on from one social group to the next.

One of the most important aspects of assumptions, however, is that they are the basis for strategies.[4] Strategies arise from the need of organizations and individuals to cope with persistent social problems about which assumptions have been made. Strategies are often a means of survival in a competitive environment; they can be inferred from the allocation of resources or from the behavior and pronouncements of an organization. In short, strategies assist any organization within the society in managing its appearance and in controlling the behavior of its audience.

All organizations and individuals, we assume, are bent on maximizing their impressions in order to gain control over an audience.[5] The audience for the police is diverse; it should be considered many audiences. For the police must convince the politicians that they have used their allocated resources efficiently; they must persuade the criminals that they are effective crimefighters; they must assure the broader public that they are controlling crime. Rather than a single rhetoric—the "use of words to form attitudes or induce actions in other human agents"[6]—directed toward convincing one audience, the police must develop many rhetorics. Linguistic strategies to control audiences are only one of many ploys used by the police organization to manage its impression. Not all the results of the use of rhetorics are intended; the consequence of the rhetorical "war on crime" in Detroit in the fall of 1969, to cite one example, was a continued advance in the city's downtown crime rate. Moreover, rhetoric can take on different meanings

---

[4] The important, sociological notions of "strategy" and "tactics" come from military theory and game theory. See, for example, Erving Goffman, *The Presentation of Self in Everyday Life* (Garden City, N.Y.: Doubleday, 1959).

[5] *Ibid.*

[6] Kenneth Burke, *A Grammar of Motives and a Rhetoric of Motives* (New York: Meridian Books, 1962), p. 565.

even within the organizational hierarchy. To patrolmen, the term "professionalism" means control over hours and salary and protection from arbitrary punishment from "upstairs"; to the chief and the higher administrators, it relates to the public-administration notions of efficiency, technological expertise, and standards of excellence in recruitment and training.

Tactics are the means by which a strategy is implemented. If the strategy is to mount a war on crime, then one tactic might be to flood the downtown area with scooter-mounted patrolmen. Tactics, in other words, are the ways in which one group of people deals with others in face-to-face encounters. How does the policeman handle a family quarrel in which the wife has the butcher knife and the husband already knows how sharp it is? Strategies pertain to general forms of action or rhetoric while tactics refer to the specific action or the specific words used to best meet a specific, problematic situation.[7] The tactic of flattery may be far more effective—and safer—in wresting the butcher knife than a leap over the kitchen table.

All occupations possess strategies and tactics, by means of which they attempt to control their most significant audiences. However, our analysis must do more than describe the existence of such means of creating impressions. So far as the police are concerned, impression management, or the construction of appearances, cannot substitute for significant control of crime. To maintain the dramaturgic metaphor, we suggest that there are significant flaws and contradictions in the performance of the police that cast a serious doubt on the credibility of their occupational mandate.

The mandate of the police is fraught with difficulties, many of them, we shall argue, self-created. They have defined their task in such a way that they cannot, because of the nature of American social organization, hope to honor it to the satisfaction of the public. We will argue that the appearances that the police create—that they control crime and that they attain a high level of efficiency—are transparent on close examination, that they may, in fact, be created as a sop to satisfy the public's impossible expectations for police performance. By utilizing the rhetoric of crime control, the police claim the responsibility for the social processes that beget the illegal acts. They cannot control these social processes that are embedded in American values, norms and cultural traditions. Creating the appearance of controlling them is only a temporizing policy; it is not the basis for a sound, honorable mandate.

The police mandate and the problems it creates in American society are our central concern. We will rely on the concepts of actor, organization, and audience, of mandate, and of strategy and appearances. We

---

[7] D.W. Ball makes this distinction between rhetoric and what he terms "situated vocabularies" in "The Problematics of Respectability," in Jack D. Douglas, ed., *Deviance and Respectability* (New York: Basic Books, 1970).

will show that the police mandate, as presently defined, is full of contradictions. We will further demonstrate that the strategies and tactics of the American police are failing in a serious way to meet the need of controlling crime.

The Occupational Culture of the Police

Before beginning an analysis of the police mandate, a brief comment is necessary about the occupational culture of our law enforcers. The American police act in accord with their assumptions about the nature of social life, and their most important assumptions originate with their need to maintain control over both their mandate and their self-esteem. The policeman's self is an amalgam of evaluations made by the many audiences before whom he, as social actor must perform: his peers, his family, his immediate superiors and the higher administrators, his friends on and off duty. His most meaningful standards of performance are the ideals of his *occupational culture*. The policeman judges himself against the ideal policeman as described in police occupational lore and imagery. What a "good policeman" does is an omnipresent standard. The occupational culture, however, contains more than the definition of a good policeman. It contains the typical values, norms, attitudes, and material paraphernalia of an occupational group.

An occupational culture also prompts the *assumptions* about everyday life that become the basis for organizational strategies and tactics. Recent studies of the occupational culture of the police allow the formulation of the following postulates or assumptions, all of which are the basis for police strategies to be discussed later:

1. People cannot be trusted; they are dangerous.

2. Experience is better than abstract rules.

3. You must make people respect you.

4. Everyone hates a cop.

5. The legal system is untrustworthy; policemen make the best decisions about guilt or innocence.

6. People who are not controlled will break laws.

7. Policemen must appear respectable and be efficient.

8. Policemen can most accurately identify crime and criminals.

9. The major jobs of the policeman are to prevent crime and
    to enforce laws.

10. Stronger punishment will deter criminals from repeating
    their errors.[8]

Some qualifications about these postulates are in order. They apply primarily to the American noncollege-educated patrolman. They are less applicable to administrators of urban police departments and to members of minority groups within these departments. Nor do they apply accurately to nonurban, state, and federal policemen.

We shall now describe the paradoxes of the police mandate, the strategies of the police in dealing with their troubles, and some of the findings and recommendations of the President's crime commission as they bear on the current attempt by the police to make a running adjustment to their problems.

II. The "Impossible" Mandate

The police in modern society are in agreement with their audiences—which include their professional interpreters, the American family, criminals, and politicians—in at least one respect: they have an "impossible" task. Certainly, all professionals have impossible tasks insofar as they try to surmount the problems of collective life that resist easy solutions. The most "successful" occupations, however, have managed to construct a mandate in terms of their own vision of the world. The policeman's mandate, on the other hand, is defined largely by his publics—not, at least at the formal level, in his own terms.

Several rather serious consequences result from the public's image of the police. The public is aware of the dramatic nature of a small portion of police work, but it ascribes the element of excitement to all police activities. To much of the public, the police are seen as alertly ready to respond to citizen demands, as crime-fighters, as an efficient, bureaucratic, highly organized force that keeps society from falling into

---

[8] These postulates have been drawn from the work of Michael Banton, *The Policeman in the Community* (New York: Basic Books, 1965), the articles in *The Police: Six Sociological Essays*, ed. David Bordua (New York: John Wiley & Sons, 1967), esp. those by Albert J. Reiss and David Bordua, and John H. McNamara; Arthur Niederhoffer, *Behind the Shield* (Garden City, N.Y.: Doubleday, 1967); Jerome Skolnick, *Justice Without Trial* (New York: John Wiley & Sons, 1966); and William A. Westley, "Violence and the Police," *American Journal of Sociology*, 59 (July 1953) 34 41; idem, "Secrecy and the Police," *Social Forces*, 34 (March 1956), 254-257; idem "The Police: Law, Custom and Morality," in Peter I. Rose, ed. *The Study of Society* (New York: Random House, 1967). See also James Q. Wilson, *Varieties of Police Behavior: The Management of Law and Order in Eight Communities* (Cambridge, Mass.: Harvard University Press, 1968), idem, "The Police and Their Problems: A Theory," *Public Policy*, 12 (1963), 189-216, idem, in "Generational and Ethnic Differences Among Police Officers," *American Journal of Sociology*, 69 (March 1964), 522-528.

chaos. The policeman himself considers the essence of his role to be the dangerous and heroic enterprise of crook-catching and the watchful prevention of crimes.[9] The system of positive and negative sanctions from the public and within the department encourages this heroic conception. The public wants crime prevented and controlled; that is, it wants criminals caught. Headlines herald the accomplishments of G-Men and F.B.I. agents who often do catch dangerous men, and the reputation of these federal authorities not infrequently rubs off on local policemen who are much less adept at catching criminals.

In an effort to gain the public's confidence in their ability, and to insure thereby the solidity of their mandate, the police have encouraged the public to continue thinking of them and their work in idealized terms, terms, that is, which grossly exaggerate the actual work done by police. They do engage in chases, in gunfights, in careful sleuthing. But these are rare events. Most police work resembles any other kind of work: it is boring, tiresome, sometimes dirty, sometimes technically demanding, but it is rarely dangerous. Yet the occasional chase, the occasional shoot-out, the occasional triumph of some extraordinary detective work have been seized upon by the police and played up to the public. The public's response has been to demand even more dramatic crook-catching and crime prevention, and this demand for arrests has been converted into an index for measuring how well the police accomplish their mandate. The public's definitions have been converted by the police organization into distorted criteria for promotion, success, and security. Most police departments promote men from patrol to detective work, a generally more desirable duty, for "good pinches"—arrests that are most likely to result in convictions.[10] The protection of the public welfare, however, including personal and property safety, the prevention of crime, and the preservation of individual civil rights, is hardly achieved by a high pinch rate. On the contrary, it might well be argued that protection of the public welfare could best be indexed by a low arrest rate. Because their mandate automatically entails mutually contradictory ends—protecting both public order and individual rights—the police resort to managing their public image and the indexes of their accomplishment. And the ways in which the police manage their appearance are consistent with the assumptions of their occupational culture, with the public's view of the police as a social-control agency, and with the ambiguous nature of our criminal law.

---

[9] Although the imagery of the police and their own self-definition coincide on the dangers of being a policeman, at least one study has found that many other occupations are more dangerous. Policemen kill six times as many people as policemen are killed in the line of duty. In 1955, Robin found that the rate of police fatalities on duty, including accidents, was 33 per 100,000, less than the rate for mining (94), agriculture (55), construction (76), and transportation (44). Between 1950 and 1960, an average of 240 persons were killed each year by policemen—approximately six times the number of policemen killed by criminals. Gerald D. Robin, "Justifiable Homicide by Police Officers," *Journal of Criminal Law, Criminology and Police Science*, 54 (1963), 225-231.

[10] Niederhoffer, *Behind the Shield*, p. 221.

The Problematic Nature of Law and Order

The criminal law is one among many instrumentalities of social control. It is an explicit set of rules created by political authority; it contains provisions for punishment by officials designated with the responsibility to interpret and enforce the rules which should be uniformly applied to all persons within a politically defined territory.[11] This section discusses the relationships between the laws and the mores of a society, the effect of the growth of civilized society on law enforcement, and the problematic nature of crime in an advanced society. The differential nature of enforcement will be considered as an aspect of peace-keeping, and will lead to the discussion of the police in the larger political system.

A society's laws, it is often said, reflect its customs; it can also be said that the growth of the criminal law is proportionate to the decline in the consistency and binding nature of these mores. In simpler societies, where the codes and rules of behavior were well known and homogeneous, sanctions were enforced with much greater uniformity and predictability. Social control was isomorphic with one's obligations to family, clan, and age group, and the political system of the tribe. In a modern, differentiated society, a minimal number of values and norms are shared. And because the fundamental, taken-for-granted consensus on what is proper and respectable has been blurred or shattered, or, indeed, never existed, criminal law becomes a basis of social control. As Quinney writes, "Where correct conduct cannot be agreed upon, the criminal law serves to control the behavior of all persons within a political jurisdiction."[12]

Social control through the criminal law predominates in a society only when other means of control have failed. When it does predominate, it no longer reflects the mores of the society. It more accurately reflects the interest of shifting power groups within the society. As a result, the police, as the designated enforcers of a system of criminal laws, are undercut by circumstances that accentuate the growing differences between the moral order and the legal order.

One of these complicating circumstances is simply the matter of social changes, which further stretch the bond between the moral and the legal. The law frequently lags behind the changes in what society deems acceptable and unacceptable practice. At other times, it induces changes, such as those pertaining to civil rights, thereby anticipating acceptable practice. The definition of crime, then, is a product of the relationship between social structure and the law. Crime, to put it another way, is not a homogeneous entity.

---

[11] See Richard Quinney, "Is Criminal Behavior Deviant Behavior?" *British Journal of Criminology,* 5 (April 1965), 133. The material in this section draws heavily from Quinney. See also R C. Fuller, "Morals and the Criminal Law," *Journal of Criminal Law, Criminology and Police Science,* 32 (March-April 1942), 624-630.

[12] Quinney *op. cit.,* p. 133.

The perspective of the patrolman as he goes about his daily rounds is a legalistic one. The law and the administrative actions of his department provide him with a frame of reference for exercising the mandate of the police. The of crime, then, is a product of the relationship between social structure and the citizen, on the other hand, does not live his life in accordance with a legalistic framework; he defines his acts in accordance with a moral or ethical code provided him by his family, his religion, his social class. For the most part, he sees law enforcement as an intervention in his private affairs.

No matter what the basis for actions of private citizens may be, however, the patrolman's job is one of practical decision-making within a legalistic pattern. His decisions are expected to include an understanding of the law as a system of formal rules, the enforcement practices emphasized by his department, and a knowledge of the specific facts of an allegedly illegal situation. The law includes little formal recognition of the variation in the private arrangement of lives. Even so, the policeman is expected to take these into account also. No policeman can ever be provided with a handbook that could tell him, at a moment's notice, just what standards to apply in enforcing the law and in maintaining order. Wilson summarizes the difficulty inherent in law enforcement as follows:

> Most criminal laws define *acts* (murder, rape, speeding, possessing narcotics), which are held to be illegal; people may disagree as to whether the act should be illegal, as they do with respect to narcotics, for example, but there is little disagreement as to what the behavior in question consists of. Laws regarding disorderly conduct and the like assert, usually by implication, that there is a condition ("public order") that can be diminished by various actions. The difficulty, of course, is that public order is nowhere defined and can never be defined unambiguously because what constitutes order is a matter of opinion and convention, not a state of nature. (An unmurdered person, an unraped woman, and an unpossessed narcotic can be defined so as to be recognizable to any reasonable person.) An additional difficulty, a corollary of the first, is the impossibility of specifying, except in the extreme case, what degree of disorder is intolerable and who is to be held culpable for that degree. A suburban street is quiet and pleasant; a big city street is noisy and (to some) offensive; what degree of noise and offense, and produced by whom, constitutes disorderly conduct"?[13]

The complexity of law enforcement stems from both the problem of police "discretion" and the inherent tensions between the maintenance

---

[13] Wilson, *op. cit.*, pp. 21-22.

of order and individual rights. The law contains rules on how to maintain order, it contains substantive definitions of crime, penalties for violations, and the conditions under which the commission of a crime is
said to have been intended.[14] Further, the law contains procedures for
the administration of justice and for the protection of the individual.
The complexities of law enforcement notwithstanding, however, the
modern policeman is frequently faced with the instant problem of
defining an action as either legal or illegal, of deciding, in other words,
whether to intervene and, if so, what tactic to use. He moves in a dense
web of social action and social meanings, burdened by a problematic,
complex array of ever-changing laws. Sometimes the policeman must
quickly decide very abstract matters. Though a practitioner of the legal
arts, his tools at hand are largely obscure, ill-developed, and crude.
With little formal training, the rookie must learn his role by absorbing
the theories, traditions, and personal whims of experienced patrolmen.

Police Work as Peace Keeping[15]

The thesis of two recent major works on the police, Wilson's *The
Varieties of Police Behavior* and Skolnick's *Justice Without Trial*, can be
paraphrased as follows: the policeman must exercise discretion in matters involving life and death, honor and dishonor, and he must do so in
an environment that he perceives as threatening, dangerous, hostile,
and volatile. He sees his efficiency constrained by the law and by the
police organization. Yet, he must effectively manage "disorder" in a
variety of unspecified ways, through methods usually learned and practiced on the job. As a result of these conditions, the policeman, in
enforcing his conception of order, often violates the rights of citizens.

Many observers of police work regard the primary function of a
policeman as that of a *peace-keeper*, not a *law enforcer*. According to
this view, police spend most of their time attending to order-maintain-
ing functions, such as finding lost children, substituting as ambulance
drivers, or interceding in quarrels of one sort or another. To these
observers, the police spend as little as 10 to 15 per cent of their time on
law enforcement—responding to burglary calls or trying to find stolen
cars. The large-scale riots and disorders of recent years accounted for
few police man-hours. Wilson illustrates the peace-keeping (order maintenance) and law-enforcement distinction this way:

[14] [This footnote was missing from Peter K. Manning and John Van Maanen's (eds.) *Policing: A
View from the Street*, pp. 7-31. Santa Monica, CA: Goodyear.]

[15] This perspective on police work is emphasized by Wilson *op. cit.*; Banton, *op. cit.*; and Skolnick,
op. cit. In addition, see the more legalistically oriented work of Wayne R. LaFave, *Arrest*, ed. F. J.
Remington (Boston: Little, Brown, 1965); Joseph Goldstein. "Police Discretion Not to Invoke the
Legal Process: Low-Visibility Decisions in the Administration of Justice." *Yale Law Journal*, 69
(1960), 543-594, and Herman Goldstein, "Police Discretion: The Ideal Versus the Real," *Public
Administration Review*, 23 (September 1963), 140-148.

The difference between order maintenance and law enforcement is not simply the difference between "little stuff" and "real crime" or between misdemeanors and felonies. The distinction is fundamental to the police role, for the two functions involve quite dissimilar police actions and judgments. Order maintenance arises out of a dispute among citizens who accuse each other of being at fault; law enforcement arises out of the victimization of an innocent party by a person whose guilt must be proved. Handling a disorderly situation requires the officer to make a judgment about what constitutes an appropriate standard of behavior; law enforcement requires him only to compare a person's behavior with a clear legal standard. Murder or theft is defined, unambiguously, by statutes; public peace is not. Order maintenance rarely leads to an arrest; law enforcement (if the suspect can be found) typically does. Citizens quarreling usually want the officer to "do something," but they rarely want him to make an arrest (after all, the disputants are usually known or related to each other). Furthermore, whatever law is broken in a quarrel is usually a misdemeanor, and in most states, an officer cannot make a misdemeanor arrest unless one party or the other will swear out a formal complaint (which is even rarer).[16]

The complexity of the law and the difficulty in obtaining a complainant combine to tend to make the policeman underenforce the law—to overlook, ignore, dismiss, or otherwise erase the existence of many enforceable breaches of the law.

Some researchers and legalists have begun to piece together a pattern of the conditions under which policemen have a tendency not to enforce the law. From a study of police in three Midwestern states, LaFave has concluded that two considerations characterize a decision not to arrest. The first is that the crime is unlikely to reach public attention—for example, that it is of a private nature or of low visibility—and the second is that underenforcement is unlikely to be detected or challenged.[17] Generally, the conditions under which policemen are less likely to enforce the law are those in which they perceive little public consensus on the law, or in which the law is ambiguous. LaFave found that policemen are not apt to enforce rigorously laws that are viewed by the public as dated, or that are used on the rare occasions when the public order is being threatened.

There is a certain Benthamic calculus involved in all arrests, a calculus that is based on pragmatic considerations such as those enumerated by LaFave. Sex, age, class, and race might also enter into the calculus of whether the law should be enforced. In a case study of the policeman

---

[16] James Q. Wilson, "What Makes a Better Policeman?" *Atlantic*, 223 (March 1969), 131.
[17] LaFave, *op. cit.*

assigned to skid row, Bittner illustrates the great degree of discretion exercised by the policeman. Yet the law, often reified by the policeman, is rarely a clear guide to action—despite the number of routine actions that might be termed "typical situations that policemen perceive as *demand conditions* for action without arrest."[18]

In the exercise of discretion, in the decision to enforce the law or to underenforce, the protection of individual rights is often at stake. But individual rights are frequently in opposition to the preservation of order, as a totalitarian state exemplifies in the extreme. The police try to manage these two contradictory demands by emphasizing their peace-keeping functions. This emphasis succeeds only when a consensus exists on the nature of the order (peace) to be preserved. The greater the difference in viewpoint between the police and the public on the degree and kind of order to be preserved, the greater will be antagonism between the two; the inevitable result of this hostility will be "law breaking."

The resolution of the contradictions and complexities inherent in the police mandate, including the problems of police discretion, of individual rights, of law enforcement and peace-keeping, is not helped, however, by the involvement of police in politics. Politics only further complicates the police mandate. The law itself is a political phenomenon, and at the practical level of enforcing it, the local political system is yet another source of confusion.

The Police in the Political System

In theory, the American police are apolitical. Their own political values and political aims are supposed to be secondary to the institutional objective of law enforcement. In practice, however, police organizations function in a political context; they operate in a public political arena and their mandate is defined politically. They may develop strategies to create and maintain the appearance of being apolitical in order to protect their organizational autonomy, but they are nonetheless a component of American political machinery. There are three reasons why the police are inextricably involved in the political system, the first and most obvious being that the vast majority of the police in this nation are locally controlled.

> [Among the 40,000 law-enforcement agencies in the United States], there are only 50 . . . on the federal level . . . 200 on the state level. The remaining 29,750 agencies are dispersed throughout the many counties, cities, towns, and villages that form our local governments. . . . Only 3,050 agencies are

---

[18] Egon Bittner, "The Police on Skid-Row: A Study of Peace-Keeping." *American Sociological Review*, 32 (October 1967), 699-715.

located in counties and 3,700 in cities. The great majority of
the police forces—33,000—are distributed throughout boroughs, towns, and villages.[19]

In 1966 there were 420,000 full- and part-time law-enforcement
officers and civilians employed by police agencies in the United States.
Most of them—371,000—were full-time employees; about 11 per cent—
46,000—were civilians. Of the full-timers, 23,000 served at the federal
level of government, 40,000 at the state level, and the remaining
308,000, or 83 per cent of the total, were divided between county and
local political jurisdictions. Of the 308,000, somewhat more than
197,000 were employees of counties, cities under 250,000, townships,
boroughs, and villages; the balance of 110,500 served in the 55 American cities with populations of more than 250,000. The number of police
personnel in any one type of political division varied widely, of course.
For example, on the county level of government, the roster of the 3,050
sheriffs offices in the United States ranged from a one-man force in Put-
nam County, Georgia, to a 5,515-man force in Los Angeles County.

What all these figures indicate is the massive dispersal of police
authority—and political authority—throughout the nation. What these
figures also indicate is the existence of overlapping laws governing law
enforcement. Further, they show that the responsibility for maintaining
public order in America is decentralized, and that law-enforcement officers are largely under the immediate control of local political authorities.

The second reason why the police are an integral part of the political system is this: law is a political entity, and the administration of
criminal law unavoidably encompasses political values and political
ends. The police are directly related to a political system that develops
and defines the law, itself a product of interpretations of what is right
and proper from the perspective of different politically powerful segments within the community.

The third reason why the police are tied to the political system
emanates from the second: the police must administer the law. Many
factors pattern this enforcement, but they all reflect the political organization of society. The distribution of power and authority, for example,
rather than the striving for justice, or equal treatment under the law,
can have a direct bearing on enforcement.

Because law enforcement is for the most part locally controlled, sensitivity to local political trends remains an important element in police
practice. Since the police are legally prohibited from being publicly
political, they often appeal to different community groups, and participate sub rosa in others, in order to influence the determination of public policy. Community policy, whether made by the town council or the
mayor or the city manager, affects pay scales, operating budgets, per-

---

[19] President's Commission, *Task Force Report: The Police*, pp. 7, 8-9

sonnel, administrative decisions, and, to some extent, organizational structure. The police administrator must, therefore, be responsive to these controls, and he must deal with them in an understanding way. He must be sensitive to the demands of the local politicians—even while maintaining the loyalty of the lower ranks through a defense of their interests.

There are several direct effects of the political nature of the police mandate. One is that many policemen become alienated; they lose interest in their role as enforcers and in the law as a believable criterion. The pressures of politics also erode loyalty to the police organization and not infrequently lead to collusion with criminals and organized crime.

The policeman's exposure to danger, his social background, low pay, low morale, his vulnerability in a repressive bureaucracy all conspire to make him susceptible to the lures of the underhanded and the appeals of the political. Studies summarized by Skolnick[20] reveal a political profile of the policeman as a conservative, perhaps reactionary, person of lower-class or lower-middle-class origin, often a supporter of radical right causes, often prejudiced and repressive, often extremely ambivalent about the rights of others. The postulates or assumptions of the police culture, the suspiciousness, fear, low self-esteem, and distrust of others are almost diametrically opposed to the usual conception of the desirable democratic man.

Thus, the enforcement of some laws is personally distasteful. Civil-rights legislation, for example, can be anathema. Or truculence can be the reaction to an order relaxing controls in ghettos during the summer months. It is the ambivalence of policemen toward certain laws and toward certain local policies that fragments loyalty within a department and causes alienation.

There is another consequence of the political nature of the police mandate: the police are tempted. They are tempted not to enforce the law by organized crime, by the operators of illegal businesses such as prostitution, and by fine "law-abiding," illegally parked citizens. All too frequently, the police submit to temptations, becoming in the process exemplars of the corruption typical of modern society, where the demand for "criminal services" goes on at the station house.[21]

Police and politics within the community are tightly interlocked. The sensitivity of the police to their political audiences, their operation within the political system of criminal justice, and their own personal political attitudes undermine their efforts to fulfill their contradictory mandate and to appear politically neutral.

---

[20] Jerome Skolnick, ed., *The Politics of Protest* (New York: Simon & Schuster, 1969), pp. 252-253.
[21] There are several popular treatments of police corruption, none of them very good. Ralph L. Smith, *The Tarnished Badge* (New York: Thomas Y. Crowell, 1965); Ed Cray, *The Big Blue Line* (New York: Coward-McCann, 1967).

The Efficient, Symptom-Oriented Organization

The Wickersham report, the Hoover administration's report on crime and law enforcement in the United States, was published in 1931. This precursor of the Johnson administration's *The Challenge of Crime in a Free Society* became a rallying point for advocates of police reform. One of its central themes was the lack of "professionalism" among the police of the time—their lack of special training, their corruption, their brutality, and their use of illegal procedures in law enforcement. And one of its results was that the police, partly in order to demonstrate their concern with scientific data gathering on crime and partly to indicate their capacity to "control" crime itself, began to stress crime statistics as a major component of professional police work.

Crime statistics, therefore—and let this point be emphasized—became a police construction. The actual amount of crime committed in a society is unknown—and probably unknowable, given the private nature of most crime. The *crime rate,* consequently, is simply a construction of police activities. That is, the crime rate pertains only to "crimes known to the police," crimes that have been reported to or observed by the police and for which adequate grounds exist for assuming that a violation of the law has, in fact, taken place. (The difference between the *actual* and *known crimes* is often called the "dark figure of crime.") Of course, the construction of a crime rate placed the police in a logically weak position in which they still find themselves. If the crime rate is rising, they argue that more police support is needed to fight the war against crime; if the crime rate is stable or declining, they argue that they have successfully combated the crime menace—a heads-I-win-tails-you-lose proposition.

In spite of their inability to control the commission of illegal acts (roughly, the actual rate), since they do not know about all crime, the police have claimed responsibility for crime control, using the crime rate as an index of their success. This use of the crime rate to measure success is somewhat analogous to their use of a patrolman's arrest rate as an indication of his personal success in law enforcement. Questions about the actual amount of crime and the degree of control exercised are thus bypassed in favor of an index that offers great potential for organizational or bureaucratic control. Instead of grappling with the difficult issue of defining the ends of police work and an operational means for accomplishing them, the police have opted for "efficient" law-enforcement defined in terms of fluctuations of the crime rate. They have transformed concern with undefined ends into concern with available means. Their inability to cope with the causes of crime—which might offer them a basis for defining their ends—shifts their "organizational focus" into symptomatic concerns, that is, into a preoccupation with the rate of crime, not its reasons.

This preoccupation with the symptoms of a problem rather than with the problem itself is typical of all bureaucracies. For one characteristic of a bureaucracy is goal-displacement. Bureaucratic organizations tend to lose track of their goals and engage in ritual behavior, substituting means for ends. As a whole, bureaucracies become so engrossed in pursuing, defending, reacting to, and, even, in creating immediate problems that their objective is forgotten. This tendency to displace goals is accelerated by the one value dear to all bureaucracies—efficiency. Efficiency is the be-all and end-all of bureaucratic organizations. Thus, they can expend great effort without any genuine accomplishment.

The police are burdened with the "efficiency problem." They claim to be an efficient bureaucratic organization, but they are unable to define for themselves and others precisely what it is they are being efficient about. In this respect, they do not differ from other paper-shuffling organizations. The police's problem is that the nature of their work is uncertain and negatively defined. It is uncertain in the absence of a consensus not only between the police and the public but also among themselves as to what the goals of a police department should be. It is defined in the negative because the organization punishes its members—patrolmen—for violating departmental procedures but offers no specifications on what they should do or how they should do it.

What do the police do about the problematic nature of law, about the problems arising from their involvement with politics, about their preoccupation with the symptoms of crime rather than the causes? Do they selectively adopt some strategies at the expense of others? Do they vacillate? Are the roles of the organization's members blurred? Before answering these questions, let us examine how the police, through various strategies, manage their appearance before the public. The questions will then be easier to answer.

III. Major Strategies of the Police

The responsibilities of the police lead them to pursue contradictory and unattainable ends. They share with all organizations and occupations, however, the ability to avoid solving their problems. Instead, they concentrate on managing them through strategies. Rather than resolving their dilemmas, the police have manipulated them with a professional eye on just how well the public accepts their dexterity. Thus, law enforcement becomes a self-justifying system. It becomes more responsive to its own needs, goals, and procedures than to serving society. In this section, we will show the ways in which the police have followed the course of most other bureaucratic institutions in society, responding to their problems by merely giving the appearance of facing them while simultaneously promoting the trained incapacity to do otherwise.

The two primary aims of most bureaucracies, the police included, are the maintenance of their organizational autonomy and the security of their members. To accomplish these aims, they adopt a pattern of institutional action that can best be described as "professionalism." This word, with its many connotations and definitions, cloaks all the many kinds of actions carried out by the police.

The guise of professionalism embodied in a bureaucratic organization is the most important strategy employed by the police to defend their mandate and thereby to build self-esteem, organizational autonomy and occupational solidarity or cohesiveness. The professionalization drives of the police are no more suspect than the campaigns of other striving, upwardly mobile occupational groups. However, since the police have a monopoly on legal violence, since they are the active enforcers of the public will, serving theoretically in the best interests of the public, the consequences of their yearnings for prestige and power are imbued with far greater social ramifications than the relatively harmless attempts of florists, funeral directors, and accountants to attain public stature. Disinterested law enforcement through bureaucratic means is an essential in our society and in any democracy, and the American police are certainly closer to attaining this ideal than they were in 1931 at the time of the Wickersham report. Professionalism qua professionalism is unquestionably desirable in the police. But if in striving for the heights of prestige they fail to serve the altruistic values of professionalism, if their professionalism means that a faulty portrait of the social reality of crime is being painted, if their professionalism conceals more than it reveals about the true nature of their operations, then a close analysis of police professionalism is in order.

Police professionalism cannot be easily separated in practice from the bureaucratic ideal epitomized in modern police practice. The bureaucratic ideal is established as a means of obtaining a commitment from personnel to organizational and occupational norms. This bureaucratic commitment is designed to supersede commitments to competing norms, such as obligations to friends or kin or members of the same racial or ethnic group. Unlike medicine and law, professions that developed outside the context of bureaucracies, policing has always been carried out, if done on a full-time basis, as a bureaucratic function.

Modern police bureaucracy and modern police professionalism are highly articulated, although they contain some inherent stresses that are not our present concern. The strategies employed by the police to manage their public appearance develop from their adaptation of the bureaucratic ideal. These strategies incorporate the utilization of *technology* and *official statistics* in law enforcement, of *styles of patrol* that attempt to accommodate the community's desire for public order with the police department's preoccupation with bureaucratic procedures, of *secrecy* as a means of controlling the public's response to their operations, of *collaboration* with criminal elements to foster the appearance of a smoothly run, law-abiding community, and of a *symbiotic relationship* with the criminal justice system that minimizes public knowledge of the flaws within this largely privately operated system.

IV. The Effectiveness of Police Strategies

The police have developed and utilized the strategies outlined above for the purpose of creating, as we have said, the appearance of managing their troublesome mandate. To a large extent, they are facilitated in the use of these strategies, in being able to project a favorable impression, by a public that has always been apathetic about police activity. Moreover, what activity the public does observe is filtered through the media with its own special devices for creating a version of reality. The public's meaning of police action is rarely gathered from first-hand experience, but from the constructed imagery of the media—which, in turn, rely upon official police sources for their presentation of the news. The police for their part, understandably, manipulate public appearances as much as they possibly can in order to gain and maintain public support.

The specific strategies used by the police to create a publicly suitable image were described in Section III: the guise of professionalism; the implementation of the bureaucratic ideal of organization; the use of technology, official statistics, and various styles of patrol; secrecy; collaboration with corrupt elements; and the establishment of a symbiotic relationship with the courts. This section will present evidence by which to evaluate these strategies. The term "effectiveness" is used only in the context of how well these devices accomplish the ends which the public and the police themselves publicly espouse; the recommendations and evaluations of the President's crime commission will be central in making judgments of police effectiveness. This appraisal of how well the police manipulate their appearance will also be a guideline for evaluating the recommendations of the commission's task force report on the police.

Professionalism and the Bureaucratic Ideal

The assumptions of professionalism and of a bureaucratic organization include a devotion to rational principles and ends that may then be translated into specific work routines having predictable outcomes. The police are organized in a military command fashion, with rigid rules and a hierarchy governing operations. However, the patrolman, the lowest man in the hierarchy—and usually the least well-trained and educated—is in the key position of exercising the greatest amount of discretion on criminal or possibly criminal activities. Especially in his peace-keeping role and in dealing with minor infractions (misdemeanors), the patrolman has wide discretionary power concerning if, when, why, and how to intervene in private affairs.

Police work must both rely on discretion and control it. Excessive inattention and excessive attention to infractions of the law are equally damaging to a community. However, the complexity of the law, its dynamic and changing properties, the extensiveness of police department regulations, policies, and procedures, and the equivocal, relativistic nature of crime in regard to certain situations, settings, persons, and groups make it impossible to create a job description that would eliminate the almost boundless uncertainty in police patrol.

Neither professionals nor bureaucrats, however, have yet found an effective means of controlling discretion. If an organization cannot control those of its members with the greatest opportunity to exercise discretion, it flounders in its attempts to accomplish its stated purposes. Two general principles suggest why the police have not been able to control discretion. The first has to do with the general problem of control and the second with the specific nature of police work.

Men are unwilling to submit completely to the will of their organizational superiors. Men will always attempt to define and control their own work. Control means the right to set the pace, to define mistakes, to develop standards of "good" production and efficiency. But as surely as superiors seek to control the quality and the extent of work performed by their subordinates in a hierarchy, just as surely will they meet with attempts to reshape and subvert these controls.

In the specific instance of police bureaucracies, the patrolman conceives of himself as a man able to make on-the-spot decisions of guilt or innocence. He does not think of himself as a bureaucratic functionary nor as a professional. Further, since the police organization itself has become far more interested in efficiency than in purpose, since it is unable to specify its overall objectives, the patrolman finds it difficult, if not impossible, to demonstrate that necessary devotion to rational ends required of professionalism and bureaucratic organizations. Until police departments are able to control the amount and kind of discretion exercised by their members, and until the police are able, with the help of lawyers and other citizens, to develop positive means of motivation and reward in line with clear, overall policy directives, the failure of what we have called the professionalism-bureaucracy strategy is an absolute certainty.

Technology, Statistics, and the Crime Rate

This section will evaluate the strategy of technology in the control and prevention of crime, the use of statistics, and the significance of the so-called crime rate. Given the sociological nature of crime, let it be said immediately that present technology deals with unimportant crime and that the F.B.I. Index of crimes, by which we base judgments of police effectiveness, is biased and an unrealistic reflection of the actual crime rate.

One of the striking aspects of the President's crime commission report is the thoroughly sociological nature of the document. The discussion of the causes of crime in the first two chapters points to the growth of urbanism, anonymity, the breakdown in social control, and the increasing numbers of frustrated and dissatisfied youth who have always constituted the majority of known lawbreakers. There are no labels such as "evil people," "emotionally disturbed," "mentally ill," or "criminally insane." The first set of recommendations under prevention in the summary pages of the report are "sociological": strengthen the family, improve slum schools, provide employment, reduce segregation, construct housing. All these matters are patently and by definition out of the control of the police.

There is every evidence that the police themselves subscribe to a thoroughly social, if not sociological, definition of the causes of crime—that is, that crime is the manifestation of long-established social patterns and structures which ensnare and implicate the police and the criminals as well as the general public. And they are doubtless correct.

Surveys done by the President's crime commission revealed that there are always contingencies in the information police receive about a crime even before they are able to investigate it. These contingencies involve such matters as the nature of the relationship between the victim and the offender and whether or not the victim believes the police are competent to investigate and solve the crime. Computer technology depends on informational "input." On that point, the police seem both unable to define what sort of information would be useful and unable to obtain, and probably never can obtain in a democratic society, information that would make them better able to enforce the law.

The facts in the problem of "crime prevention" overwhelmingly doom the present professionally based notion that the application of science and technology will begin to ease the distress the police feel as they face the escalating demands of their audiences. Also, it would be easier to assess the value of the technology strategy if we were able to define exactly to what end the technology would be applied and in what ways it could be expected to work.

Styles of Patrol

Police strategy is subject to many contingencies. It is a basic principle of public administration that policy made at the higher echelons of an organization will be effective only if each successively lower level of the organization complies with that policy and is capable of carrying it out. It is also a truism that participants at the lowest level in the hierarchy are the most "difficult" to mobilize and integrate into the organization. A style of patrol is basically the manner in which an administrative police policy is executed. The policy may prescribe that the patrolman overlook certain types of illegal acts; it may order that he minimally enforce particular laws or be sensitive to and strictly enforce others. If the administrative order setting a patrol style does not win the cooperation of the patrolman it is certain to fail. Thus, the success of any high-echelon policy that involves the performance of the patrolman is contingent upon his compliance with that policy. If the administrator's orders are not binding on the patrolman, no distinctive style of patrol will result; all that will be demonstrated will be the responses of the patrolman to other aspects of his social environment, especially, how his fellow patrolmen perform.

The success of this strategy is dependent upon the capacity of the administrator to create loyalty to his internal policies. With the rise of police unions, the discontent of the black patrolman, low pay, and relatively less security for the policeman, organizational control is a major problem in all the large police departments of the country—with Los Angeles possibly the single exception.

The effectiveness of the watchman, legalistic, and service styles of patrol will also depend on the degree of political consensus among the community groups patrolled, the clarity of the boundaries of community neighborhoods, competition between the police and self-help or vigilante groups, and the relative importance of nonoccupational norms in enforcement practices—that is, the importance of racial or ethnic similarities between the patrolman and the people in his neighborhood. If a clear social consensus on the meaning of the law and what is expected of the police can be established within a community, a well-directed policy of control over police patrol is the most logical and rational approach to police work. In some communities, largely suburban and middleclass, the police can carry out what their public demands and a degree of harmony exists. This consensus is absent in our inner cities.

Secrecy and Collaboration

The use of secrecy by the police is, as we have pointed out, a strategy employed not only to assist them in maintaining the appearance of political neutrality but to protect themselves against public complaints. Secrecy also helps to forestall public efforts to achieve better police service aimed to secure political accountability for police policy. Police collaboration with criminal elements corruption, in other words—has much the same effect since it decreases the pressure to enforce "unenforceable" laws against certain segments of the police's clientele.

These two strategies were among the major concerns of the President's crime commission task force on police. The task force's report devoted major attention to the fact that political forces influence police actions and policies. The report affirmed the political nature of police work; what concerned the writers of the report was the nature and type of political influence on police actions. Their recommendations, furthermore, were based on their recognition of the fact that the police have been fairly successful in managing the appearance of being apolitical.

There are several reasons why the police strategies of secrecy and collaboration will continue in force: (1) as long as the client—the public—is seen as the enemy, the police will treasure their secrecy and use it to engineer public consent to their policies and practices; (2) as long as a new political consensus is not formed on the nature and type of police control necessary in society as a whole, the organized, self-serving survival aims of police organizations will emerge victorious. Any well-organized consensual, secretive organization can resist the efforts of an unorganized public, managed by rhetoric and appearances, to reform it; (3) as long as there remains a lack of consensus on the enforcement of many of our "moralistic" laws, police corruption and selective law enforcement will continue. Collaboration to reduce adversary relationships with the criminal segment of society will always be an effective strategy—providing a sudden upsurge in public morality doesn't temporarily subject the police to a full-scale "housecleaning." Replacements would, of course, be subject to the same pressures and would, in all likelihood, eventually take the same line of least resistance.

One solution to corruption is said to be better educated, more professional policemen. By recruiting better educated men, the more professionalized police departments also seek to diminish the expression of political attitudes on the job and the tendency of policemen to form political power groups based on their occupation. These are also assumptions made by the crime commission's task force on police. There is, however, no evidence that college-educated or better paid policemen are "better policemen"; nor is there any evidence that "better men" alone will solve the essentially structural problems of the occupation.

We can tentatively conclude from this review that corruption will remain with us as long as laws remain which stipulate punishments for actions on which a low public consensus exists. It will remain when there is likely to be a low visibility of police performance, and it will remain while there is a high public demand for illegal services—gambling, prostitution, abortion—and the concomitant need of the police for information on these services from the practitioners themselves.

Symbiosis and Justice

Although the police have the principal discretion in the field with reference to the detection, surveillance, and appraisal of alleged offenders, the final disposition of a criminal case must be made in the courts. The police are thus dependent on the courts in a very special way for their successes. The ideal model of the criminal justice system makes the police essentially the fact gatherers and apprehenders, while the courts are to be the decision-makers.

The police attempt to appear efficient has led them as we have noted before, to seek the good pinch, the arrest that will stand up in court. With victimless crimes, such as those involving gambling or drugs or prostitution, the police control the situation since they alone decide whether an offense has been committed and whether they have a legal case against the offender. To control the success rate in these cases, the police create a gaggle of informants, many of whom are compelled to give the police evidence in order to stay free of a potential charge against themselves for a violation similar to the one they are providing information about. In the case of more serious crimes, the problems are more complex; in these cases the police must rely on other informants, and their discretion on arrests and charges are more often exercised by administrators and prosecuting attorneys.

In the prosecution stage, the bureaucratic demands of the court system are paramount. Abraham Blumberg describes these demands and the tension between efficiency and "due process":

> The dilemma is frequently resolved through bureaucratically ordained shortcuts, deviations and outright rule violations by the members of the courts, from judges to stenographers, in order to meet production norms. Because they fear criticism on ethical as well as legal grounds, all the significant participants in the court's social structure are bound into an organized system of complicity. Patterned, covert, informal breaches, and evasions of "due process" are accepted as routine—they are institutionalized—but are nevertheless denied to exist.[22]

The net effect of this strain within the court system is to produce a higher rate of convictions by means of encouraging a plea of guilty to a lesser charge. As far as the police are concerned, then, the strategy of symbiosis is sound.

There are several undesirable effects of this symbiosis. First, it encourages corruption by permitting the police to make decisions about the freedom of their informants; it gives them an illegal hold and power over them, and thus it undercuts the rule of law. Second, many offend-

---

[22] Abraham Blumberg, *Criminal Justice* (Chicago: Quadrangle Press, 1967), p. 69.

ers with long criminal records are either granted their freedom as informants or allowed to plead guilty to lesser charges in return for the dismissal of a more serious charge. Skolnick calls this the "reversal of the hierarchy of penalties," because the more serious crimes of habitual criminals are prosecuted less zealously than the minor violations of first offenders. Third, it helps blur the distinction between the apprehension and prosecution aspects of our criminal justice system.

V. Conclusions and Proposed Reforms

The allocation of rewards in a society represents both its division of labor and its configuration of problems. Ironically, the allocation of rewards is also the allocation of societal trouble. Societal trouble in a differentiated society is occupational trouble. The ebb and flow of rewards emanating from the division of labor becomes structured into persistent patterns that are sustained by continuous transactions among organizations and occupational groups. Occupational structures reflect societal structures, but they reflect them in ways that have been negotiated over time. The negotiation is based upon the universal human proclivity to differentiate roles, organizations, and occupations. The more dependent an organization is upon its environment for rewards, the more likely it is to rely on the management and presentation of strategies to establish the appearance of autonomy.

Organizations without a high degree of autonomy in the environments in which they operate are greatly constrained by the internal pressure of competing aims and roles of members. The agreement on problems, goals, values, and self-concepts that emerges from occupational socialization and functioning is a strong basis for influencing organizational direction. The occupational standards in this case subvert the rule of law as a system of norms outside the informal norms of the occupation. The policeman's view of his role and his occupational culture are very influential in determining the nature of policing. The basic source of police trouble is the inability of the police to define a mandate that will minimize the inconsistent nature of their self-expectations and the expectations of those they serve.

The problems derived from a contradictory mandate remain unaffected by the efforts of the institution to solve them; they do, however, take the shape into which they have been cast by institutional functionaries. Cooley long ago discussed the process of institutional ossification, the process by which institutions stray from serving the needs of their members and their publics, thereby losing the loyalty of those within and the support of those without. The consequences of institutional ossification as related to the police are twofold. First, the police begin to search for a so-called higher order of legitimacy; they make appeals to morality, to patriotism, to "Americanism," and to "law and order" to shore up eroded institutional charters and to accelerate their attempts to control and manipulate their members and clients. Second, the police, as they develop a far greater potential for controlling those they serve through their presentational strategies, come to serve themselves better than ever before.

The problem of the police is, essentially, the problem of the democratic society, and until the central values and social structures of our society are modified (and I think we are seeing such a modification), there can be no real change in the operation of social control. The needed changes are, by and large, not those dealt with in the crime commission report. And this is telling. For an eminently sociological document, it did not focus on the heart of the problem: our anachronistic, moralistic laws, with which the police are burdened, and our dated political system, which is unable to bring political units into a state of civil accountability. The focus of the report and recommendations was predictably on symptoms of crime, not on causes of crime. The "managerial focus" of the report, or its public-administration bias, outlined needed reforms, but not ways in which to implement them, and the problem of efficiency was never really faced.

Not surprisingly for a political document having a variety of public functions, the report has little to say about the nature of the present criminal laws. It dwells, like the police themselves, on means, not ends. As Isidore Silver points out in a critique of the report, more than one-half the crimes committed do not harm anyone: more than one-third are for drunkenness, and a small but important portion are for other "crimes without victims." Most crimes are committed by juveniles who inexplicably "grow out" of their criminality. In 1965, 50 per cent of the known burglaries and larcenies were committed by youths under 18.[23] The report does note what was a central point of our discussion of the political nature of crime, that police corruption is, in almost every instance, a consequence of trying to enforce admittedly unenforceable laws. The demand for services provided by homosexuals, by gamblers, prostitutes, and abortionists is high, and the supply is legally made unavailable to anyone who wants to remain in the so-called "law-abiding" category. The laws, in effect, create the crime and the criminals.

Changes in laws to reduce their absolutistic element and to free people who deviate with little harm to others from the onus of criminalization cannot be accomplished without a parallel change in the nature of police accountability. As we have seen, the strategies of secrecy and rhetoric used by the police play on the fears of society and provide a basis for police control. The managerial reforms contained in the task

---

[23] Isidore Silver, *Introduction to The Challenge of Crime in a Free Society* (New York: Avon Books, 1968), p. 25. The President's Commission, *Task Force Report: The Courts,* discusses substantive criminal law, however, and does make some suggestions for legal change.

force report—more public debate on and greater internal and external control over police actions—are needed. Even more urgently required are specific ways in which the cities can control the police and make them strictly accountable for their actions—methods, that is, which go a good deal further than merely disposing of the chief or convening a judicial review board. To give city governments this kind of control over the police, however, entails the reorganization of police departments themselves so that their goals are clear and defined and so that the occupational rewards within the police organization are aligned with public goals.

Three interrelated organizational changes must be made to insure that police attend to the job of maintaining public order. One is to reorganize police departments along functional lines aimed at peace-keeping rather than law enforcement; the second is to allocate rewards for keeping the peace rather than for enforcing the law; the third is to decentralize police functions to reflect community control without the diffusion of responsibility and accountability to a central headquarters.

Present police departments are organized in a military fashion; orders move down the line from the chief to departmental sections assigned law enforcement functions. These sections usually include such divisions as traffic, patrol, records, detective, juvenile, intelligence, crime-lab, and communications. The principal basis for the assignment of functions, however, is law enforcement;[24] what is needed is a new set of organizational premises so that the basis for the assignment of functions is not law enforcement but the maintenance of order. As Wilson explains:

> If order were the central mission of the department, there might be a "family disturbance squad," a "drunk and derelict squad," a "riot control squad," and a "juvenile squad"; law enforcement matters would be left to a "felony squad." Instead, there is a detective division organized, in the larger departments, into units specializing in homicide, burglary, auto theft, narcotics, vice, robbery, and the like. The undifferentiated patrol division gets everything else. Only juveniles tend to be treated by specialized units under both schemes, partly because the law requires or encourages such specialization. The law enforcement orientation of most departments means that new specialized units are created for every offense about which the public expresses concern or for which some special technology is required.[25]

What is called for, then, is a new organizational pattern that will provide a domestic unit (as is now being tried in New York City), a

---

[24] President's Commission, *Task Force Report: The Police*, charts on pp. 46-47.
[25] Wilson, *op. cit.*, p. 69.

juvenile unit, and a drunk unit with a detoxification center, all with a peace-keeping orientation and peace-keeping functions. Only a felony squad and perhaps a riot squad should be used to enforce the law.

One of the obvious ways in which to improve the morale of the patrolman is to let him do a greater amount of investigative work and to take on the responsibility for "solving" some of the crimes originating with his patrol. Rewards could then be allocated in accord with the more limited ends of peace-keeping—for instance, in rewarding a patrolman for a decline in the number of drunks who reappear in court. Since no comprehensive policy can be imagined to guide order maintenance, limited ends for various departments must be developed and subjected to public review. The key is to allow the policeman to develop judgment about the motives and future intentions of people with whom he comes in contact, and to reward him for peace-keeping, not "good pinches" alone.

This reappraisal of the allocation of rewards means, of course, that there must be greater coordination of police and other agencies within the criminal justice system in order to increase the benefits to the client (the offender or the criminal) and break down the isolation of the police.[26] To allow the policeman to assume greater peace-keeping responsibilities would allow him to play a functional role parallel to that of the better general practitioner of medicine: the referral specialist, the coordinator of family health, the source of records and information, and the family friend and counselor. Such an organizational change in the policemen's function would, naturally enough, make community control of the police a greater possibility. It would begin to bridge the chasm between the police and many hostile segments within the public, a process that could be facilitated by the creation of a community-relations division within police departments.

The third needed modification of the present structure of police work is the development of decentralized operations. One of the major social trends of the last ten years has been the increase in the lack of attachment people have for their major institutions. Police today suffer from a crisis of legitimacy, and this crisis is heightened by their failure to promote a sense of commitment to their operations by the citizens they serve. One way in which to introduce commitment and a sense of control over the police by members of a community is to make the police more accessible. St. Louis, for example, has experimented with "storefront" police stations, staffed by a few men who are available as advisers, counselors, protectors, and friends of the people in the immediate neighborhood. If the police should begin to differentiate the role of the patrolman to include the functions of a peace-keeping communi-

---

[26] See John P. Clark, "The Isolation of the Police: A Comparison of the British and American Situations," in John Scanzoni ed., *Readings in Social Problems* (Boston: Allyn & Bacon, 1967), pp. 384-410. See also David Bordua, "Comments on Police-Community Relations," mimeographed (Urbana: University of Illinois, n.d.).

ty agent, the control of these agents should reside in the community. Thus public participation in the decision-making processes of the police would begin at the precinct or neighborhood level; it would not be simply in the form of a punitive civilian review board or a token citizen board at headquarters.

We began with the notion of trouble, police trouble, the troublesome mandate of the policeman. There will be little succor for him as long as our social structure remains fraught with contradictory value premises, with fragmented political power and the consequent inadequate control of the police, with the transformation of public trusts into institutional rights. There will be little succor for him as long as our political agencies resist moving to de-moralize our criminal laws. As it is, we can expect that the management of crime through police strategies and appearances will continue to be a disruptive element in American society.

George L. Kelling, Tony Pate, Duane Dieckman & Charles E. Brown

The Kansas City
Preventive Patrol Experiment:
A Summary Report

I. Introduction and Major Findings

Ever since the creation of a patrolling force in 13th century Hang-chow, preventive patrol by uniformed personnel has been a primary function of policing. In 20th century America, about $2 billion is spent each year for the maintenance and operation of uniformed and often superbly equipped patrol forces. Police themselves, the general public, and elected officials have always believed that the presence or potential presence of police officers on patrol severely inhibits criminal activity.

One of the principal police spokesmen for this view was the late O.W. Wilson, former Chief of the Chicago Police Department and a prominent academic theorist on police issues. As Wilson once put it, "Patrol is an indispensable service that plays a leading role in the accomplishment of the police purpose. It is the only form of police service that directly attempts to eliminate opportunity for misconduct. . . ." Wilson believed that by creating the impression of police omnipresence, patrol convinced most potential offenders that opportunities for successful misconduct did not exist.

To the present day, Wilson's has been the prevailing view. While modern technology, through the creation of new methods of transportation, surveillance and communications, had added vastly to the tools of patrol, and while there have been refinements in patrol strategies based upon advanced probability formulas and other computerized methods, the general principle has remained the same. Today's police recruits, like virtually all those before them, learn from both teacher and textbook that patrol is the "backbone" of police work.

No less than the police themselves, the general public has been convinced that routine preventive patrol is an essential element of effective

Source: George L. Kelling, Tony Pate, Duane Dieckman, Charles E. Brown (1974). *The Kansas City Preventive Patrol Experiment: A Summary Report.* Washington, D.C.: Police Foundation. (Note: Complete report except for tables and reference to them—see document.) Reprinted by permission of The Police Foundation.

policing. As the International City Management Association has pointed out, "for the greatest number of persons, deterrence through ever-
present police patrol, coupled with the prospect of speedy police action
once a report is received, appears important to crime control." Thus, in
the face of spiraling crime rates, the most common answer urged by
public officials and citizens alike has been to increase patrol forces and
get more police officers "on the street." The assumption is that
increased displays of police presence are vitally necessary in the face of
increased criminal activity. Recently, citizens in troubled neighborhoods
have themselves resorted to civilian versions of patrol.

Challenges to preconceptions about the value of preventive police
patrol were exceedingly rare until recent years. When researcher Bruce
Smith, writing about patrol in 1930, noted that its effectiveness "lacks
scientific demonstration," few paid serious attention.

Beginning in 1962, however, challenges to commonly held ideas
about patrol began to proliferate. As reported crime began to increase
dramatically, as awareness of unreported crime became more common,
and as spending for police activities grew substantially, criminologists
and others began questioning the relationship between patrol and
crime. From this questioning a body of literature has emerged.

Much of this literature is necessarily exploratory. Earlier researchers
were faced with the problem of obtaining sufficient and correct data,
and then devising methodologies to interpret the data. The problems
were considerable, and remain so.

Another problem facing earlier investigators was the natural reluctance of most police departments to create the necessary experimental
conditions through which definitive answers concerning the worth of
patrol could be obtained. Assigned the jobs of protecting society from
crime, of apprehending criminals, and of carrying out numerous other
services such as traffic control, emergency help in accidents and disasters, and supervision of public gatherings, police departments have been
apprehensive about interrupting their customary duties to experiment
with strategies or to assist in the task evaluation.

It was in this context that the Kansas City, Missouri, Police Department, under a grant from the Police Foundation, undertook in 1972 the
most comprehensive experiment ever conducted to analyze the effectiveness of routine preventive patrol.

From the outset the department and the Police Foundation evaluation team agreed that the project design would be as rigorously experimental as possible, and that while Kansas City Police Department data
would be used, as wide a data base as possible, including data from
external measurements, would be generated. It was further agreed that
the experiment would be monitored by both department and foundation representatives to insure maintenance of experimental conditions.
Under the agreement between the department and the foundation, the

department committed itself to an eight-month experiment provided that reported crime did not reach "unacceptable" limits within the experimental area. If no major problems developed, the experiment would continue an additional four months.

The experiment is described in detail later in this summary. Briefly, it involved variations in the level of routine preventive patrol within 15 Kansas City police beats. These beats were randomly divided into three groups. In five "reactive" beats, routine preventive patrol was eliminated and officers were instructed to respond only to calls for service. In five "control" beats, routine preventive patrol was maintained at its usual level of one car per beat. In the remaining five "proactive" beats, routine preventive patrol was intensified by two to three times its usual level through the assignment of additional patrol cars and through the frequent presence of cars from the "reactive" beats.

For the purposes of measurement, a number of hypotheses were developed, of which the following were ultimately addressed:

1. crime, as reflected by victimization surveys and reported crime data, would not vary by type of patrol;

2. citizen perception of police service would not vary by type of patrol;

3. citizen fear and behavior as a result of fear would not vary by type of patrol;

4. police response time and citizen satisfaction with response time would vary by experimental area; and

5. traffic accidents would increase in the reactive beats.

The experiment found that the three experimental patrol conditions appeared not to affect crime, service delivery and citizen feelings of security in ways the public and the police often assume they do. For example,

- as revealed in the victimization surveys, the experimental conditions had no significant effect on residence and non-residence burglaries, auto thefts, larcenies involving auto accessories, robberies, or vandalism—crimes traditionally considered to be deterrable through preventive patrol;

- in terms of reporting crime to the police, few differences and no consistent patterns of differences occurred across experimental conditions;

- in terms of departmental reported crime, only one set of differences across experimental conditions was found and this one was judged likely to have been a random occurrence;

- few significant differences and no consistent pattern of differences occurred across experimental conditions in terms of citizen attitudes toward police services;

- citizen fear of crime, overall, was not affected by experimental conditions;

- there were few differences and no consistent pattern of differences across experimental conditions in the number and types of anti-crime protective measures used by citizens;

- in general, the attitudes of businessmen toward crime and police services were not affected by experimental conditions;

- experimental conditions did not appear to affect significantly citizen satisfaction with the police as a result of their encounters with police officers;

- experimental conditions had no significant effect on either police response time or citizen satisfaction with police response time;

- although few measures were used to assess the impact of experimental conditions on traffic accidents and injuries, no significant differences were apparent;

- about 60 percent of a police officer's time is typically non-committed (available for calls); of this time, police officers spent approximately as much time on non-police related activities as they did on police-related mobile patrol; and

- in general, police officers are given neither a uniform definition of preventive patrol nor any objective methods for gauging its effectiveness; while officers tend to be ambivalent in their estimates of preventive patrol's effectiveness in deterring crime, many attach great importance to preventive patrol as a police function.

Some of these findings pose a direct challenge to traditionally held beliefs. Some point only to an acute need for further research. But many point to what those in the police field have long suspected—an extensive disparity between what we want the police to do, what we often believe they do, and what they can and should do.

The immediate issue under analysis in the preventive patrol experiment was routine preventive patrol and its impact on crime and the community. But a much larger policy issue was implied; whether urban police departments can establish and maintain experimental conditions, and whether such departments can, for such experimentation, infringe upon that segment of time usually committed to routine preventive patrol. Both questions were answered in the affirmative, and in this respect the preventive patrol experiment represents a crucial first step, but just one in a series of such steps toward defining and clarifying the police function in modern society.

What the experiment did not address was a multitude of other patrol issues. It did not, for example, study such areas as two-officer patrol cars, team policing, generalist-specialist models, or other experiments currently underway in other departments. The findings of this experiment do not establish that the police are not important to the solution of crime or that police presence in some situations may not be helpful in reducing crime. Nor do they automatically justify reduction in the level of policing. They do not suggest that because the majority of a police officer's time is typically spent on non-crime related matters, the amount of time spent on crime is of any lesser importance.

Nor do the findings imply that the provision of public services and maintenance of order should overshadow police work on crime. While one of the three patrol conditions used in this experiment reduced police visibility in certain areas, the condition did not withdraw police availability from those areas. The findings in this regard should therefore not be interpreted to suggest that total police withdrawal from an area is an answer to crime. The reduction in routine police patrol was but one of three patrol conditions examined, and the implications must be treated with care.

It could be argued that because of its large geographical area and relatively low population density, Kansas City is not representative of the more populous urban areas of the United States. However, many of the critical problems and situations facing Kansas City are common to other large cities. For example, in terms of aggravated assault, Kansas City ranks close to Detroit and San Francisco. The rate of murder and manslaughter per 100,000 persons in Kansas City is similar to that of Los Angeles, Denver and Cincinnati. And in terms of burglary, Kansas City is comparable to Boston and Birmingham. Furthermore, the experimental area itself was diverse socio-economically, and had a population density much higher than Kansas City's average, making the experimental area far more representative and comparative than Kansas City as a whole might be. In these respects, the conclusions and implications of this study can be widely applied.

II. Description of the Preventive Patrol Experiment

The impetus for an experiment in preventive patrol came from within the Kansas City Police Department in 1971. While this may be surprising to some, the fact is that by that year the Kansas City department had already experienced more than a decade of innovation and improvement in its operations and working climate and had gained a reputation as one of the nation's more progressive police departments.

Under Chief Clarence M. Kelley, the department had achieved a high degree of technological sophistication, was receptive to experimentation and change, and was peppered with young, progressive and professional officers. Short- and long-range planning had become institutionalized, and constructive debates over methods, procedures and approaches to police work were commonplace. By 1972, this department of approximately 1,300 police officers in a city of just over half a million—part of a metropolitan complex of 1.3 million—was open to new ideas and recommendations, and enjoyed the confidence of the people it served.

As part of its continuing internal discussions of policing, the department in October of 1971 established a task force of patrol officers and supervisors in each of its three patrol divisions (South, Central and Northeast), as well as in its special operations division (helicopter, traffic, tactical, etc.). The decision to establish these task forces was based on the beliefs that the ability to make competent planning decisions existed at all levels within the department and that if institutional change was to gain acceptance, those affected by it should have a voice in planning and implementation.

The job of each task force was to isolate the critical problems facing its division and propose methods to attack those problems. All four task forces did so. The South Patrol Division Task Force identified five problem areas where greater police attention was deemed vital: burglaries, juvenile offenders, citizen fear, public education about the police role, and police-community relations.

Like the other task forces, the South task force was confronted next with developing workable remedial strategies. And here the task force met with what at first seemed an insurmountable barrier. It was evident that concentration by the South Patrol Division on the five problem areas would cut deeply into the time spent by its officers on preventive patrol. At this point a significant thing happened. Some of the members of the South task force questioned whether routine preventive patrol was effective, what police officers did while on preventive patrol duty, and what effect police visibility had on the community's feelings of security.

Out of these discussions came the proposal to conduct an experiment which would test the true impact of routine preventive patrol. The Police Foundation agreed to fund the experiment's evaluation.

As would be expected, considerable controversy surrounded the experiment, with the central question being whether long-range benefits outweighed short-term risks. The principal short-term risk was seen as the possibility that crime would increase drastically in the reactive beats; some officers felt the experiment would be tampering with citizens' lives and property.

The police officers expressing such reservations were no different from their counterparts in other departments. They tended to view patrol as one of the most important functions of policing, and in terms of time allocated, they felt that preventive patrol ranked on a par with investigating crimes and rendering assistance in emergencies. While some admitted that preventive patrol was probably less effective in preventing crime and more productive in enhancing citizen feelings of security, others insisted that the activities involved in preventive patrol (car, pedestrian and building checks) were instrumental in the capture of criminals and, through the police visibility associated with such activities, in the deterrence of crime. While there were ambiguities in these attitudes toward patrol and its effectiveness, all agreed it was a primary police function.

Within the South Patrol Division's 24-beat area, nine beats were eliminated from consideration as unrepresentative of the city's socioeconomic composition. The remaining 15-beat, 32-square mile experimental area encompassed a commercial-residential mixture, with a 1970 resident population of 148,395 persons and a density of 4,542 persons per square mile (significantly greater than that for Kansas City as a whole, which in 1970 with only 1,604 persons per square mile, was 45th in the nation). Racially, the beats within this area ranged from 78 percent black to 99 percent white. Median family income of residents ranged from a low of $7,320 for one beat to a high of $15,964 for another. On the average, residents of the experimental area tended to have been in their homes from 6.6 to 10.9 years.

Police officers assigned to the experimental area were those who had been patrolling it prior to the experiment, and tended to be white, relatively young, and somewhat new to the police department. In a sample of 101 officers in the experimental area taken across all three shifts, 9.9 percent of the officers were black, the average age of the officers was 27 years, and average time on the force was 3.2 years.

The 15 beats in the experimental area were computer matched on the basis of crime data, number of calls for service, ethnic composition, median income and transiency of population into five groups of three each. Within each group, one beat was designated reactive, one control, and one proactive. In the five reactive beats, there was no preventive patrol as such. Police vehicles assigned to these beats entered them only in response to calls for service. Their non-committed time (when not answering calls) was spent patrolling the boundaries of the reactive beats or patrolling in adjacent proactive beats. While police availability was closely maintained, police visibility was, in effect, withdrawn (except when police vehicles were seen while answering calls for service).

In the five control beats, the usual level of patrol was maintained at one car per beat. In the five proactive beats, the department increased police patrol visibility by two to three times its usual level both by the assignment of marked police vehicles to these beats and the presence of units from adjacent reactive beats.

Other than the restrictions placed upon officers in reactive beats (respond only to calls for service and patrol only the perimeter of the beat or in an adjacent proactive beat), no special instructions were given to police officers in the experimental area. Officers in control and proactive beats were to conduct preventive patrol, as they normally would.

It should be noted, however, that the geographical distribution of beats (see Figure 1) avoided clustering reactive beats together or at an unacceptable distance from proactive beats. Such clustering could have resulted in lowered response time in the reactive beats.

Figure 1
Schematic Representation of the 15-Beat Experimental Area

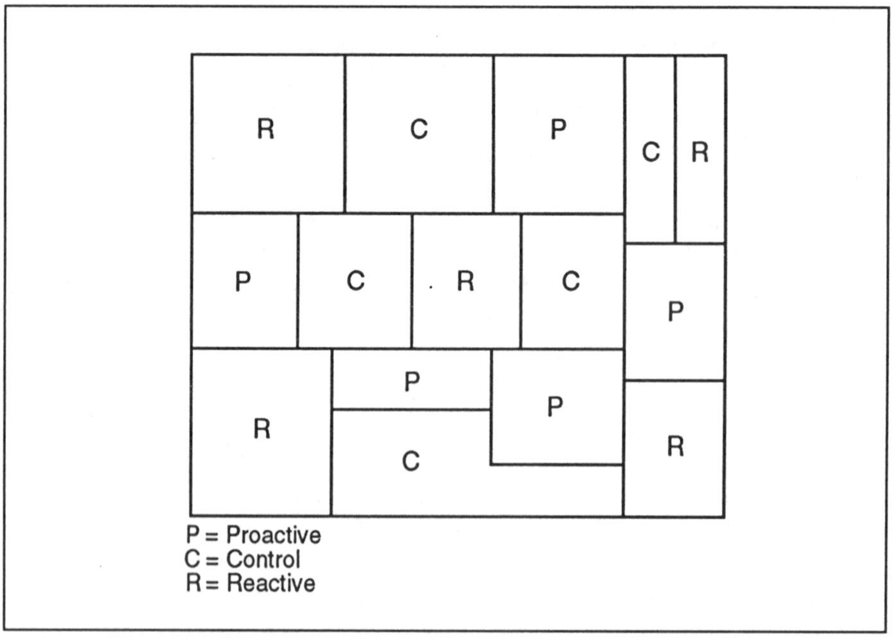

P = Proactive
C = Control
R = Reactive

It should also be noted that patrol modification in the reactive and proactive beats involved only routine preventive patrol. Specialized units, such as tactical, helicopter and K-9, operated as usual in these beats but at a level consistent with the activity level established the preceding year. This level was chosen to prevent infringement of these specialized units upon experimental results.

Finally, it should be noted that to minimize any possible risk through the elimination of routine preventive patrol in the reactive beats, crime rate data were monitored on a weekly basis. It was agreed that if a noticeable increase in crime occurred within a reactive beat, the experiment would be suspended. This situation, however, never materialized.

While the Kansas City experiment began on July 19, 1972, both department and Police Foundation monitors recognized by mid-August that experimental conditions were not being maintained, and that several problems had arisen. Chief Kelly then saw to it that these problems were rectified during a suspension of the experiment.

One problem was manpower, which in the South Patrol Division had fallen to a dangerously low level for experimental purposes. To correct this problem additional police officers were assigned to the division and an adequate manpower level restored. A second problem involved violations of the project guidelines. Additional training sessions were held, and administrative emphasis brought to bear to ensure adherence to the guidelines. A third problem was boredom among officers assigned to reactive beats. To counter this, guidelines were modified to allow an increased level of activity by reactive-assigned officers in proactive beats. These revisions emphasized that an officer could take whatever action was deemed necessary, regardless of location, should a criminal incident be observed. The revised guidelines also stressed adherence to the spirit of the project rather than to unalterable rules.

On October 1, 1972, the experiment resumed. It continued successfully for 12 months, ending on September 30, 1973. Findings were produced in terms of the effect of experimental conditions on five categories of crime traditionally considered to be deterrable through preventive patrol (burglary, auto theft, larceny—theft of auto accessories, robbery and vandalism) and on five other crime categories (including rape, assault, and other larcenies). Additional findings concerned the effect of experimental conditions on citizen feelings of security and satisfaction with police service, on the amount and types of anti-crime protective measures taken by citizens and businessmen, on police response time and citizen satisfaction with response time, and on injury/fatality and non-injury traffic accidents. The experiment also produced data concerning police activities during tours of duty, and police officer attitudes toward preventive patrol.

III. Data Sources

In measuring the effects of routine patrol, it was decided to collect as wide a variety of data from as many diverse sources as possible. By so doing, it was felt that overwhelming evidence could be presented to prove or disprove the experimental hypothesis.

To measure the effects of the experimental conditions on crime, a victimization survey, departmental reported crime, departmental arrest data, and a survey of businesses were used. While reported crime has traditionally been considered the most important indicator of police effectiveness, the accuracy of both reported crime and arrest data as indicators of crime and police effectiveness has come under scrutiny in recent years. Both types of data are subject to wide degrees of conscious and unconscious manipulation, and to distortion and misrepresentation. Because of these, a criminal victimization survey was used as an additional source of data.

Victimization surveys were first used by the President's Commission on Law Enforcement and Administration of Justice. These surveys revealed that as much as 50 percent of crime was unreported by victims, either from neglect, embarrassment, or a feeling that the crimes were not worth reporting. Although victimization surveys also have their limitations, they can be an important way of measuring crime. Thus a victimization survey was used by the experiment to measure this key outcome variable.

To measure the impact of experimental conditions on community attitudes and fear, attitudinal surveys of both households and businesses (in conjunction with the victimization surveys) and a survey of those citizens experiencing direct encounters with the police were administered. Estimates of citizen satisfaction with police services were also recorded by participant observers.

Overall, in collecting data for the experiment, the [sources listed on the opposite page] were used.

Because many of these sources were used to monitor the degree to which experimental conditions were maintained or to identify unanticipated consequences of the experiment, only findings derived from the following data are presented in this report.

Community Survey

The community survey, which measured community victimization, attitudes and fear, was taken on a before and after basis. A sample of 1,200 households in the experimental area (approximately 80 per beat) was randomly selected and interviewed in September of 1972. In September of 1973, 1,200 households were again surveyed, approximately 600 chosen from the same population as the 1972 survey (for a repeated sample) and 600 chosen randomly from the experimental area (for a non-repeated sample). Since 11 cases had to be excluded because of missing data, the 1973 sample totaled 1,189.

Commercial Survey

The commercial survey involved interviews conducted both in 1972 and 1973 with a random sample of 110 businesses in the experimental area to measure victimization rates and businessmen's perceptions of and satisfaction with police services.

Encounter Survey
(Both Citizen and Participant Observers)

Because household surveys tend to interview relatively few citizens who have experienced actual contact with the police, citizens in the three experimental areas who experienced direct encounters with police officers were interviewed. Although three survey instruments were developed (one to elicit the response of citizens, a second for the police officers, and a third for the observers riding with the officers) only the

Surveys and questionnaires

1 Community Survey
  victimization
  attitudes
  rates of reporting
	5 Encounter Survey—Observers
	  attitudes
	  perceptions

2 Commercial Survey
  victimization
  attitudes
  rates of reporting
	6 Noncommitted Time Survey
	7 Response Time Survey
	  observers

3 Encounter Survey—Citizens
  attitudes
  perceptions
	8 Response Time Survey
	  citizens
	9 HRD Survey

4 Encounter Survey—Officers
  attitudes
  perceptions
	10 Officer Questionnaire

Interviews and recorded observations

1 "Player" Observations 2 Officer interviews	3 Participant Observer Interviews 4 Participant Observer Transaction Recordings

Departmental data

1 Reported Crime 2 Traffic Data 3 Arrest Data	4 Computer Dispatch Data 5 Officer Activity Analysis Data 6 Personnel Records

observer and citizen responses were analyzed. Identical questions were used as often as possible. The survey was conducted over a four-month period (July through October, 1973). Interviewed were 331 citizens who were involved in either an officer-initiated incident (car check, pedestrian check or a traffic violation) or citizen-initiated incident (one in which the citizen called for police service: burglary, robbery, larceny, assault, etc.).

Participant Observer Transaction Recordings

While the community encounter survey focused on the location of the police-citizen contact, the observer transaction recordings focused on police-citizen interactions in terms of the assignment of the officer involved (reactive, control or proactive beats). These data were obtained by observers while riding with officers assigned to the experimental area, and involved observer estimates of citizen satisfaction as a result of direct contact with the police. Observations covered all three watches in all 15 beats. As a result, 997 incidents of police-citizen transactions were systematically recorded.

Reported Crime

Monthly totals for reported crime by beat over the October 1968 through September 1972 (pre-experimental) period and over the October 1972 through September 1973 (experimental) period were retrieved from departmental records. Time-series analyses were then performed on these data to produce the findings.

Traffic Data

Two categories of traffic accidents were monitored: non-injury and injury/fatality. Monitoring was maintained over two time periods, October 1970 through September 1972 for the pre-experimental period, and October 1972 through September 1973 for the experimental period.

Arrest Data

Arrest data by month and beat for the experimental year and the three preceding years were obtained from departmental records.

Response Time Survey

Police response time in the experimental area was recorded between May and September 1973 through the use of a response time survey completed by the participant observers and those citizens who had called the police for service. In measuring the time taken by the police in responding to calls, emphasis was placed on field response time (i.e., the amount of time occurring between the time a police unit on the street received a call from the dispatcher and the time when the unit contacted the citizen involved). In measuring citizen satisfaction with response time, the entire range of time required for the police to answer a call was considered (i.e., including time spent talking with the police department operator, police dispatcher, plus field response time).

Methodology and Maintenance of Experimental Conditions

Because multiple dimensions of the possible effects of the experiment were examined, differing methods of analysis were applied to the data generated. Detailed discussions of these and other factors concerning the experiment's methodology, including a discussion of the sampling error, can be found in the technical report and its appendices. A discussion of the methods used to determine the extent to which desired levels of patrol coverage were achieved, the degree to which experimental conditions were maintained, and whether the criminal world realized that routine patrol strategies had been modified and to what extent patterns of behavior changed as a result can be found in Chapter III of the technical report. In summary, the data sources used to analyze these factors point to the overall maintenance of experimental conditions.

Spillover Effect

One major concern in an experiment of this type is the so-called spillover or displacement theory, i.e., that as crime decreases in one area due to increased police presence, it will increase in other, usually contiguous, areas. This would mean that the effect of the experiment within the experimental area would be offset by counter-effects in other areas. To test this, various correlations between contiguous beats were calculated and analyzed. Except for auto theft, there were no noticeable alterations in the correlations of crime levels. These results, combined with an examination of the actual monthly figures, tend to indicate that, in general, there was no spillover effect. Results of the calculations can be found in the appendices to the technical report.

IV. Experimental Findings

The essential finding of the preventive patrol experiment is that decreasing or increasing routine preventive patrol within the range tested in this experiment had no effect on crime, citizen fear of crime, community attitudes toward the police on the delivery of police service, police response time, or traffic accidents. Given the large amount of data collected and the extremely diverse sources used, the evidence is overwhelming. Of the 648 comparisons made to produce the 13 major findings that follow, statistical significance occurred only 40 times between pairs, or in approximately 6 percent of the total. Of these 40, the change was greater 15 times in reactive beats, 19 times in control beats, and 6 times in proactive beats.

Findings of the experiment are presented in terms of the impact that the range of variation in preventive patrol used in this experiment had upon the following:

- community vicitimization

- departmental reported crime

- rates of reporting crime to police

- arrest trends

- citizen's fear of crime

- protective measures used by citizens

- protective measures used by businesses

- community attitudes toward the police and the delivery of police services

- businessmen's attitudes toward the police and the delivery of police services

- citizen attitudes toward the police as a result of encounters with the police

- estimation of citizen-police transactions

- police response time

- traffic incidents

The tables used in this document to illustrate the findings are summary tables which compress elaborate amounts of data. Presentation of the data in this form presents numerous problems in that much information is lost in summary. For example, actual numbers, direction of the findings, and discussion of those methodologies used for analyses are not included. Because of this, the findings are considered in their most generalized form; the sole issues are statistical significance and whether or not routine preventive patrol, within the range of variation tested, had an impact on the experimental area. The details of that impact are not presented. Consequently, as mentioned earlier, the findings outlined here cannot be used for specific planning purposes.

On the other hand, presentation in this manner allows for an overview, and focuses on only the most significant findings. Given the importance of the issue and the difficulties inherent in proving the effects of such experiments, emphasis is placed on the large amounts of data collected from diverse sources, and the overwhelming tendency of the data to point in a single direction.

* * *

Effects on Crime, Reporting and Arrests

Finding 1: Victimization

The Victimization Survey found no statistically significant differences in crime in any of the 69 comparisons made between reactive, control and proactive beats.

This finding would be expected for such categories as rape, homicide and common or aggravated assault. For one thing, these are typically impulsive crimes, usually taking place between persons known to each other. Furthermore, they most often take place inside a building, out of sight of an officer on routine preventive patrol. The spontaneity and lack of high visibility of these crimes, therefore, make it unlikely that they would be much affected by variations in the level of preventive patrol.

Given traditional beliefs about patrol, however, it is surprising that statistically significant differences did not occur in such crimes as commercial burglaries, auto theft and robberies.

Nonetheless, as measured by the victimization survey, these crimes were not significantly affected by changes in the level of routine preventive patrol.

Finding 2: Departmental Reported Crime

Departmental Reported Crimes showed only one statistical difference among 51 comparisons drawn between reactive, control and proactive beats.

Statistical significance occurred only in the category of "Other Sex Crimes." This category, separate from "Rape," includes such offenses as molestation and exhibitionism. Since this category is not traditionally considered to be responsive to routine preventive patrol, however, it appears likely that this instance of significance was a statistically random occurrence.

Finding 3: Rates or Reporting Crime

Crimes citizens and businessmen said they reported to the police showed statistically significant difference between reactive, control and proactive beats in only five of 48 comparisons, and these differences showed no consistent pattern.

Of the five instances of statistical significance, three involved vandalism and two residence burglary. But where statistical significance was found, no consistent pattern emerged. On two occasions the change was greater in the control beats, on two occasions greater in the proactive beats, and once it was greater in the reactive beats. Given the low number of statistically significant findings combined with a lack of consistent direction, the conclusion is that rates of reporting crimes by businessmen and citizens were unaffected by the experimental changes in levels of patrol.

* * *

Finding 4: Arrest Patterns

Police arrests showed no statistically significant differences in the 27 comparisons made between reactive, control and proactive beats.

While arrest totals for 16 categories of crime were determined, it will be noted that in seven categories—common assault, larceny-purse snatch, homicide, non-residence burglary, auto theft, larceny-auto accessory, and larceny-bicycle—either the number of arrests was too small to allow for statistical analysis, or the pre-experimental pattern of arrests was so distorted that statistical significance could not be determined. On the basis of the comparisons that could be made, however, the conclusion is that arrest rates were not significantly affected by changes in the level of patrol.

Effects on Community Attitudes

Citizen Fear of Crime

The experiment measured community attitudes toward many aspects of crime and police performance to determine whether varying degrees of routine preventive patrol—reactive, control, proactive—had any significant effect upon these attitudes. Previous investigators, including Roger Parks and Michael Maltz, have shown that citizens can recognize, or at least sense, changes in levels of service or innovations in policing.

Thus, through the Community and Commercial Surveys which provided the victimization information used in the previous section of this summary, citizen attitudes toward crime and police were also measured before and after the experiment.

The first attitude measured was citizen fear of crime, determined by (1) a series of questions in the Community Survey designed to probe levels of fear; (2) a series of questions in the Community Survey regarding protective and security measures taken by citizens; and (3) questions in the Commercial Survey about protective and security measures used by businessmen at their place of business.

* * *

Finding 5: Citizen Fear of Crime

Citizen fear of crime was not significantly affected by changes in the level of routine preventive patrol.

In the Community Survey, citizen estimates of neighborhood safety and perceptions of violent crimes were obtained. Citizens were then asked what they thought the probability was that they might be involved in various types of crime, including robbery, assault, rape, burglary and auto theft.

Of the 60 comparisons made between experimental areas, statistical significance was found in only five cases. Three involved the probability of being raped, one the probability of being robbed, and one the probability of being assaulted. The change in the level of fear was greater in reactive beats four times and greater in proactive beats once.

Yet when statistical significance is found, the patterns are inconsistent. For example, all cases in which the change in reactive beats are significantly higher than in other beats are found in the repeated sample. These findings are not confirmed by the non-repeated sample, however. The one area in which control registered the higher change occurs in the non-repeated sample, but this is not confirmed by the repeated sample.

The findings thus lead to the conclusion that citizen fear is not affected by differences in the level of routine preventive patrol.

* * *

Finding 6: Protective Measures (Citizens)

Protective and security measures taken by citizens against the possibility of being involved in crime were not significantly affected by variations in the level of routine preventive patrol.

The questions asked of citizens in the Community Survey on this subject dealt with the installation of such devices as bars, alarms, locks and lighting, the keeping of various types of weapons or dogs for protection, and the taking of certain actions, such as staying inside, as preventive measures.

Here, 84 comparisons were made between experimental areas, with statistical significance occurring 11 times. The significance occurred most often (6 times) in those beats where preventive patrol had not changed, that is, in control beats. The change in the reactive beats showed significance three times, and in the proactive beats twice. There is no apparent explanation for the fact that the use of protective measures supposedly increased in the control beats relative to the other two conditions. For the most part, the findings are inconsistent and occur either in the non-repeated sample or the repeated sample but never uniformly in both.

Thus, as measured by the use of protective and security measures, experimental preventive patrol conditions did not significantly affect citizen fear of crime.

Finding 7: Protective Measures (Businesses)

Protective and security measures taken by businesses in the experimental area to protect offices of other places of business did not show significant differences due to changes in the level of routine preventive patrol.

In the Commercial Survey, businessmen were asked such questions as whether they had installed alarm systems or reinforcing devices such as bars over windows, whether they had hired guards, or whether they kept watchdogs or firearms in their places of business.

All told, 21 comparisons were made and statistical significance was found once, where the change in the control beats was the greater as compared with the reactive beats.

Because this was a telephone survey, however, some problems with the findings were evident. Briefly, some businessmen were reluctant to talk about protective measures over the phone to persons unknown to them. This is discussed more fully in the technical report.

The conclusion remains, however, that preventive variations seem to have little effect on fear of crime as indicated by protective measures taken by commercial establishments.

Citizen Attitudes Toward Police

In addition to investigating citizen fear of crime and criminals, the preventive patrol experiment delved into citizen attitudes toward the police. Residents in the experimental area were asked, for instance, about the need for more police officers, about variations in patrol, police officer reputations, and effectiveness, police treatment of citizens, and about their satisfaction with police service.

The attitudes of businessmen toward police were studied in the course of the preventive patrol experiment for a variety of reasons. One was simply that businessmen's attitudes have seldom been studied in the past, although these people are often affected by crime in ways more crucial to their survival than are citizens in general. It is not only the businessman's personal comfort and safety that may be involved, but also the ability to remain in business that may be affected by crime. At the same time, businessmen are often influential in their communities. For these reasons, assessing their attitudes is often crucial to the development of new policing programs. Therefore, businessmen were asked similar questions about police effectiveness, treatment of citizens and so forth.

While the study of such attitudes is valuable in obtaining the impressions of a significant cross-section of the community, most of the citizens and businessmen interviewed were unlikely to have experienced recent actual contact with the police. Thus, another part of the preventive patrol experiment focused on determining citizens' responses to actual encounters with police officers. To determine such responses, citizens themselves, the police with whom they came in contact, and trained observers were all asked to complete reports on the encounter. Citizens were interviewed as soon as possible after the incident. Separate questionnaires were used, depending on whether the encounter was initiated by an officer or by a citizen.

Finally, a fourth measure was used to determine citizen attitudes. Here, in what has been given the title "Police-Citizen Transactions," the trained observers focused on the outcome of police-citizen interactions in terms of the patrol assignment of the officer involved, that is, reactive, control or proactive.

The next findings deal with citizen attitudes toward police, businessmen's attitudes toward police, police-citizen encounters initiated either by citizens (calls for service) or police (traffic arrests, suspect apprehension, etc.) and finally police-citizen transactions.

Finding 8: Citizen Attitudes Toward Police

Citizen attitudes toward police were not significantly affected by alterations in the level of preventive patrol.

A large number of questions in the Community Survey were designed to measure citizen attitudes toward the police. As a result, more comparisons were made here than in other cases and more instances of statistical significance were found. Altogether, 111 comparisons were made and statistical significance occurred 16 times. Items with significant differences included the need for more police officers in the city, the reputation of police officers, citizens' respect for police, police effectiveness, harassment, and change in the neighborhood police officers.

Of the 16 instances of significance, the change in reactive beats was greater five times, in control beats ten times, and in proactive beats once, demonstrating no consistent pattern of statistical significance. The indication is that there was little correlation between level of patrol and citizen attitudes.

Finding 9: Businessmen's Attitudes Toward Police

Businessmen's attitudes toward police were not significantly affected by changes in the level of routine preventive patrol.

Like citizens in the Community Survey, businessmen in the Commercial Survey were asked about their attitudes toward police. Some of the questions in the Commercial Survey were similar to those in the Community Survey and some specially selected with regard to businessmen's interests.

In all, 48 comparisons were made to measure differences in businessmen's attitudes, but not statistically significant differences were found or even approached. The clear indication here is that variations in the level of preventive patrol have no effect on businessmen's attitudes.

Finding 10: Police-Citizen Encounters

Citizen attitudes toward police officers encountered through the initiative of either the citizen or the officer were not significantly affected by changes in patrol level.

Citizen attitudes were measured by both questions asked of citizens themselves and observations of trained observers. Citizens and observers alike were asked about such items as response time, characteristics of the encounter, the attitude and demeanor of officers in the encounter, and citizen satisfaction. Observers in officer-initiated encounters also recorded things not likely to be noted by citizens, including the number of officers and police vehicles present.

Including both citizen-initiated and officer-initiated encounters, a total of 63 comparisons were made and no statistically significant differences were found.

* * *

Finding 11: Police-Citizen Transactions

The behavior of police officers toward citizens was not significantly affected by the officers' assignment to a reactive, control or proactive beat.

The finding is distinct from the previous finding in that the focus here is upon the police-citizen interaction in terms of the beat assignment of the officer rather than on the location of the contact. (Many police contacts with citizens take place outside of the officer's beat.) Data were recorded by participant observers riding with the officers.

In all, 18 comparisons were made between experimental areas, and no statistically significant differences were found.

Other Effects

Experimental Findings in Regard to Police Response Time

The time it takes for police officers to respond to a citizen call for assistance is usually considered an important measure of patrol effectiveness. The general principle is that the lower the response time, the more efficiently the police are doing their job.

But there are difficulties in determining how to measure response time given the numerous possible segments involved. For instance, is the response time cycle complete when the first officer arrives at the scene? Or when the last of several officers dispatched reaches the scene? Or when the first officer contacts the person making the call? For the purposes of the preventive patrol experiment, response time was defined as the time between receipt of a call from a dispatcher to the point when that unit contacted the citizen involved. In measuring citizen satisfaction with response time, the entire range of time required was considered, beginning with the citizen's contact with the police switchboard operator.

Response time was studied to see if experimental conditions would have any effect on the amount of time taken by police in answering citizen calls for service. Before the experiment began, the hypothesis was that experimental conditions would affect response time, particularly in proactive beats. It was believed that since more officers were assigned to proactive beats, response time would be significantly reduced in those beats.

Finding 12: Response Time

The amount of time taken by police in answering calls for service was not significantly affected by variations in the level of routine preventive patrol.

To obtain the finding, data were gathered on such matters as distance from the police car to the scene of incident, mean time from receipt of calls to start of call, mean time from receipt of call to arrival at scene, and observer's estimate of patrol car speed. Citizen estimates of time and satisfaction were also measured.

In the area of response time, a total of 42 comparisons were made between patrol conditions. Statistical significance occurred only once: in the number of officers present at the scene of incidents in the reactive beats. The reason for this is unclear, but it can be theorized that police officers were exhibiting their concern for the safety of fellow officers and citizens in reactive beats.

While variations in the level of patrol did not significantly affect police response time, the Kansas City findings suggest that more research is necessary. It appears that response time is not only the result of rate of speed and distance, but also reflects the attitude of the officers involved and possibly other variables not investigated in this study.

* * *

Experimental Findings in Regard to Traffic Accidents

Does the police visibility through routine preventive patrol have an effect upon traffic accidents? A common hypothesis is that it does, that reduction in patrol, for instance, will be followed by an increase in traffic accidents. Therefore the preventive patrol experiment involved some study of the presumed relationship.

The finding in this area is presented with considerable caution, however, since traffic patterns played no role in the selection of the experimental beats. It is possible (and in fact likely, given the area involved) that traffic patterns in the experimental area are not representative, and thus would not allow for reliable findings. In addition, the findings involved only accidents reported to the department by citizens and do not take into account accidents which occurred but were not reported.

Finding 13: Traffic Accidents

Variations in the level of routine preventive patrol had no significant effect upon traffic accidents.

A total of six comparisons were made in this area, with statistical significance not occurring in any.

Summary and Conclusion: Experimental Findings

Of the 648 comparisons used to produce the major findings of the preventive patrol experiment, statistical significance between pairs occurred 40 times representing approximately 6 percent of the total. Of these 40 findings, the change in the reactive beats was greater 15 times, in the control beats 19 times, and in the proactive beats 6 times. Given the large amount of data collected and the extremely diverse sources used, the overwhelming evidence is that decreasing or increasing routine preventive patrol within the range tested in this experiment had no effect on crime, citizen fear of crime, community attitudes toward the police on the delivery of police service, police response time or traffic accidents.

Jan. M. Chaiken, Peter W. Greenwood & Joan Petersilia

The Criminal Investigation Process: A Summary Report

Criminal investigation is one of the more important functions of municipal and county police departments. Yet many police administrators know little about the nature or effectiveness of their own department's investigative operations and even less about the situation in other departments.

At the request of the National Institute of Law Enforcement and Criminal Justice, the Rand Corporation undertook a nationwide study to fill some of these gaps in knowledge.[1] The objectives of the two-year study were—

- to describe, on a national scale, current investigative organization and practice;

- to assess the contribution of police investigation to the achievement of criminal justice goals;

- to ascertain the effectiveness of new technology and systems that are being adopted to enhance investigative performance;

- to determine how investigative effectiveness is related to difference in organizational form, staffing, procedures, and so forth.

While the objectives were broad, many questions of potential interest had to be excluded from consideration in order to have a study of

Source: Jan M. Chaiken, Peter W. Greenwood, and Joan Petersilia (1977). "The Criminal Investigation Process: A Summary Report." *Policy Analysis,* 3:187-217. Reprinted courtesy of Policy Analysis, University of California Press, Berkeley, California.

[1] This article summarizes the work of all the Rand researchers engaged in the study. In addition to the authors, they are: Robert Castro, Konrad Kellen, Eugene Poggio, Linda Prusoff, and Sorrel Wildhorn. The study was performed under Grant 73-NI-99-0037-G from the National Institute of Law Enforcement and Criminal Justice, Law Enforcement Assistance Administration, Department of Justice. The points of view or opinions stated here do not necessarily represent the official position or policies of the Department of Justice. The latest version of the complete study is Peter W. Greenwood et al., *The Criminal Investigation Process* (Lexington, Mass.: D. C. Heath, 1977).

manageable size. In particular, the study focused on Part I crimes,[2] thereby excluding analysis of how misdemeanors and vice, narcotics, and gambling offenses are investigated. Also, little attention was paid to personnel practices such as selection, promotion, and motivation of investigators.

Design of the Study

Several principles guided our study design. First, the research had to be conducted with the participation and oversight of experienced police officials from around the country. Second, information had to be collected from many police departments: single-city studies had already been conducted, and their lack of persuasiveness stemmed from the possibility that the host department was unique in some way. Third, in as many departments as possible, information had to be obtained through direct on-site interviews and observations.

We secured the participation of the law enforcement community by appointing a suitable advisory board,[3] retaining a prosecutor and retired federal and local investigators as consultants,[4] and assembling a panel of currently working investigators. The advisory board reviewed and vigorously criticized our research approach, data collection instruments, findings, and interpretations of the findings. The consultants assisted in designing data instruments and participated with Rand staff in on-site interviews in many locations. The panel of working investigators commented on the validity of our observations in other cities, by comparing them with their own daily experiences, and highlighted important issues that could not be captured by numerical data.

We collected data from a large number of departments by developing a comprehensive survey questionnaire and distributing it to all municipal or county law enforcement departments that had 150 or more full-time employees or that served a jurisdiction whose 1970 population exceeded 100,000. This survey produced extensive information from 153 jurisdictions (of the 300 solicited) on such topics as departmental characteristics, investigators' deployment, investigators' training and status, use of evidence technicians, nature of specialization, evaluation criteria, police-prosecutor interaction, case assignment, use of com-

---

[2] Part I crimes are criminal homicide, forcible rape, robbery, aggravated assault, burglary, larceny, and auto theft. Except in the case of homicide, the FBI definitions of these crimes include attempts.
[3] The advisory board consisted of Cornelius (Neil) J. Behan (New York City Police Department); James Fisk (member of the Los Angeles Police Commission); Thomas Hastings (Rochester, New York, Police Department); Jerry Wilson (former Chief of the Washington, D.C., Police Department); and Eugene Zoglio (professor, Prince George's Community College).
[4] Consultants were Sydney Cooper, Carmine Motto, Albert Seedman, Seymour Silver, and Raymond Sinetar.

puter files, and crime, clearance, and arrest rates.[5] For example, the number of officers assigned to investigative units was found to average 17.3 percent of the police force. Thus, the investigative function in the United States costs about $1 billion per year—about the same as the cost of the entire court system.[6]

On-site interviews were conducted in more than 25 of the 153 police agencies. Many of these were selected because they were known to have implemented novel investigative practices that were reportedly successful; others were selected on the basis of their survey responses indicating interesting programs or data resources and a desire to participate. Project staff and consultants visited each of these departments, observing and participating in the operations of the investigative units and discussing their procedures with personnel at various departmental levels. In some cities, Rand staff monitored individual investigators and their supervisors continuously over a period of several days to obtain realistic profiles of their activities.

Some departments gave us previously prepared written evaluations of their investigative programs. In addition, several departments cooperated closely with the Rand staff and provided access to data that were subsequently used in one of the component studies.

One useful data source, located and made available during the course of the survey, was the Kansas City (Missouri) Detective Case Assignment File, which had been maintained since 1971. This unique computer file contained daily information submitted by individual detectives, permitting us to determine, for each investigator and each investigative unit, the time spent on various activities, the number of cases handled, and the number of arrests and clearances produced. The file greatly facilitated our analyses of how detectives spend their time and to what purposes and effects.

Additional sources of information included a computer-readable file of 1972 Uniform Crime Reporting data provided by the FBI and a limited telephone survey of robbery and burglary victims.

Findings

Arrest and Clearance Rates

Several earlier studies, each conducted in a single city or in a small number of neighboring cities, had shown that *department-wide clear-*

---

[5] The complete results of the Rand survey are reported in Jan M. Chaiken, *The Criminal Investigation Process: Volume 11. Survey of Municipal and County Police Departments,* R-1777-DOl (Santa Monica, Calif.: The Rand Corporation, October 1975).

[6] See, for example, National Criminal Justice Information and Statistics Service, "Expenditure and Employment Data for the Criminal Justice system" (Washington, D.C.: U.S. Government Printing Office, updated annually).

ance[7] *and arrest statistics are not suitable measures of the effectiveness of investigative operations.* Our own study, using data from cities across the country, confirmed this observation in several different ways. The implication is that measures of effectiveness related to solving crimes must be defined carefully and can only be interpreted in conjunction with other information related to prosecution of arrestees, public satisfaction with the police, deterrence effects, and so forth. In a study in New York City, published in 1970, Greenwood found that the average number of clearances claimed for each burglary arrest varied from 1 to 20 across the city's precincts, depending primarily on how frequently clearances were credited on the basis of *modus operandi* only.[8] Similarly, Greenberg's 1972 study in six California departments found wide variation in clearance rates because of differences among departments in the strictness with which FBI "exceptional clearance" guidelines were applied.[9] Our own study[10] using 1972 data from all departments with 150 or more employees, showed that the average number of clearances claimed for each arrest for a Part I crime ranged from a low of 0.38 to a high of 4.04, a factor of over 10. The ratio from high to low was even larger for each individual crime type, such as robbery or auto theft. Some departments claim a clearance for an auto theft whenever the vehicle is recovered, while others will not claim a clearance unless the perpetrator is arrested and charged for the instant offense. Clearance statistics are also affected by the amount of effort devoted to classifying reported crimes as "unfounded" when the police find no evidence that a crime was actually committed. This practice both reduces reported crime rates and increases reported clearance rates.

With administrative discretion playing such a large role in determining a department's clearance rates, any attempt to compare effectiveness among departments using clearance rates is evidently meaningless. Even comparisons over time within a single department are unreliable unless steps are taken to assure that no change occurs in administrative practices concerning clearances and classification of crimes. Arrest rates, too, are unreliable measures of effectiveness, since arrests can be made

---

[7] A crime is *cleared* when a perpetrator is apprehended or is identified as unapprehendable. The latter possibility is intended to apply in "exceptional" circumstances, such as when the perpetrator is dead.

[8] Peter W. Greenwood, *An Analysis of the Apprehension Activities of the New York City Police Department*, R-529-NYC (New York: New York City-Rand Institute, September 1970). For the reader unfamiliar with this field, let us explain that more than one clearance can be claimed for a single arrest if the person arrested for a specific crime is then charged with, or admits to, crimes he committed elsewhere.

[9] Bernard Greenberg et al., *Enhancement of the Investigative Function, Volume I: Analysis and Conclusions; Volume III: Investigative Procedures— Selected Task Evaluation; Volume IV: Burglary Investigative Checklist and Handbook* (Menlo Park, Calif.: Stanford Research Institute, 1972). (Volume II is not available.)

[10] Chaiken, *Criminal Investigation Process: Volume 11*, pp. 36, 37.

without resulting in any clearance.[11] The frequency of such events can be judged from the fact that, in half of all departments, the number of arrests for Part I crimes exceeds the number of clearances.[12]

Quite apart from their unreliability is the fact that arrest and clearance rates reflect activities of patrol officers and members of the public more than they reflect activities of investigators. Isaacs,[13] Conklin,[14] and our own study showed that approximately 30 per cent of all clearances are the result of pickup arrests by patrol officers responding to the scene of the crime.[15] In roughly another 50 percent of cleared crimes (less for homicide and auto theft), the perpetrator is known when the crime report is first taken, and the main jobs for the investigator are to locate the perpetrator, take him or her into custody, and assemble the facts needed to present charges in court (see table 1). This means that around 20 percent of cleared crimes could possibly be attributed to investigative work, but our own study showed that most of these were also solved by patrol, officers, or by members of the public who spontaneously provided further information, or by routine investigative practices that could also have been followed by clerical personnel.[16]

In fact, we estimate that no more than 2.7 percent of all Part I crime clearances can be attributed to special techniques used by investigators. (These are called "special action cases" in table 2.) The remaining 97.3 percent of cleared crimes will be cleared no matter what the investigators do, so long as the obvious routine follow-up steps are taken. Of course, included in the 2.7 percent are the most interesting and publicly visible crimes reported to the department, especially homicides and commercial burglaries. But the thrust of our analysis is that all the time spent by investigators on difficult cases where the perpetrator is unknown results in only 2.7 percent of the clearances.

---

[11] In some jurisdictions, persons may be arrested "for investigation" without a crime being charged. In all jurisdictions, persons are occasionally arrested by error and are subsequently released by a prosecutor or magistrate without any clearance being claimed by the police.

[12] Instances in which several perpetrators are arrested for a single crime may also explain an arrest/clearance ratio of over 1.

[13] Herbert H. Isaacs, "A Study of Communications, Crimes, and Arrests in a Metropolitan Police Department," Appendix B of Institute of Defense Analyses, *Task Force Report: Science and Technology,* A Report to the President's Commission on Law Enforcement and Administration of Justice (Washington, D.C.: U.S. Government Printing Office, 1967).

[14] John Conklin, *Robbery and the Criminal Justice System* (Philadelphia, Pa.: J. B. Lippincott Co., 1972).

[15] After initial publication of the Rand study, this finding was further confirmed by a Police Foundation study, "Managing Investigations: the Rochester System," by Peter B. Bloch and James Bell (Washington, D.C., 1976). While that study was intended primarily to compare team policing with nonteam policing, the report presents data that make it possible to calculate the ratio of on-scene arrests to all clearances by arrest for three crimes. The data show that, in Rochester, 31.7 percent of burglary clearances by arrest, 31.1 percent of robbery clearances by arrest, and 28.7 percent of larceny clearances by arrest were the result of on-scene arrests.

[16] See Peter W. Greenwood, Jan M. Chaiken, Joan Petersilia, Linda Prusoff, Bob Castro, Konrad Kellen, Eugene Poggio, and Sorrel Wildhorn, *The Criminal Investigation Process: Volume III. Observations and Analysis* R-1778-DOI (Santa Monica, Calif.: The Rand Corporation, October 1975), chap. 6.

Table 1
Cleared Cases Having Initial Identification of Perpetrator
(As a Percentage of All Cleared Cases)

Crime Type	Arrest at Scene	Kansas City			Total Initial from Five Other Departments[c]
		Complete ID by Victim or Witness	Uniquely Linking Evidence[a]	Total Initial ID[b]	
Forgery/fraud	30.6	20.0	39.7	90.3	90.9
Auto theft	38.5	12.7	<7.8	>51.2[a]	47.4
Theft	48.4	8.6	17.2	74.2	70.0
Commercial burglary	24.4	16.9	16.9	58.2	80.0
Residential burglary	26.7	42.7	<6.2	>81.7[a]	80.0
Robbery	28.4	20.9	10.6	59.9	53.4
Felony morals	25.8	27.8	27.8	81.4	72.8
Aggravated assault	28.6	63.4	7.9	>91.1[a]	100.0
Homicide	28.3	34.8	10.9	74.0	42.9

NOTE: Numbers may not add to total because of rounding errors.

[a] If no cases of uniquely linking evidence were found in the sample, or if there were no cases other than those with initial identification, 95 percent confidence points are shown.

[b] I.e., the sum of the three preceding counties.

[c] Berkeley, Long Beach, and Los Angeles, California; Miami, Florida; and Washington, D.C.

Table 2
Special Action Cases (Percentage of All Cleared Cases)

Crime Type	Kansas City		Five Other Departments[a]	
	Sample Estimate	Maximum Estimate at 95% Confidence	Sample Estimate	Maximum Estimate at 95% Confidence
Forgery/fraud	0	5.7	0	12.7
Auto theft	0	6.9	0	14.6
Theft	0	3.2	0	25.9
Commercial burglary	4.9	12.4	10	39.4
Residential burglary	0	3.5	0	13.9
Robbery	7.1	16.6	9.5	15.6
Felony morals	0	14.5	9.1	36.4
Aggravated assault	0	5.9	0	25.9
Homicide	10.2	37.3	0	34.8
All types[b]	1.3	2.7		

[a] Berkeley, Long Beach and Los Angeles California; Miami, Florida; and Washington, D.C.

[b] This figure is shown for Kansas City only and reflects the relative numbers of cleared cases of each type in that city. The maximum estimate for the total is lower than the estimate for any single crime type, because the sample size is larger.

This finding has now been established for enough departments to leave little doubt of its general correctness, with some variation, for all departments. By establishing a restricted interpretation of what constitutes "routine processing," a department might find that investigative skill or "special action" contributes to as many as 10 percent of all its clearances. Even so, the basic conclusion remains the same. Only in cases of homicide, robbery, and commercial theft did we find that the quality of investigative effort could affect the clearance rate to any substantial extent. Conversely, the contribution of victims, witnesses, and patrol officers is most important to the identification and apprehension of criminal offenders.

Variations with Departmental Characteristics

Once the nature of investigators' contributions to arrest and clearance rates is understood, it must be anticipated that variations in these rates among departments will be explained primarily by characteristics that have nothing to do with the organization and deployment of investigators. This is in fact what we found from our survey data.[17] The three most important determinants of a department's arrest and clearance rates are the department's size, the region of the country it is located in, and its crime workload.

Large departments (measured by number of employees, budget, or population of the jurisdiction) claim more clearances per arrest in all crime categories than do smaller departments. However, the arrest rates of large and small departments do not differ.

Departments in the South Central states claim higher clearance rates than those in other regions, which follow in the order of North Central, South Atlantic, Northeast, and West. However, arrest rates vary in almost exactly the reverse order. Evidently, these differences reflect administrative practices or patterns of crime commission rather than differences in effectiveness.

In regard to crime workload, we found that departments having a large number of reported crimes per police officer have lower arrest rates than other departments. This relationship works in the following way: The annual number of arrests per police officer rises nearly (but not quite) in direct proportion to the number of reported crimes per police officer until a certain threshold is reached. Beyond this threshold, increasing workload is associated with very small increases in the number of arrests per police officer. The thresholds are at approximately 35 Part I crimes per police officer per year and 3.5 crimes against persons

---

[17] See Chaiken, *Criminal Investigation Process: Volume II*, pp. 38-47.

per police officer per year. These thresholds are fairly high, as only about 20 percent of departments have greater workload levels.[18]

These findings are consistent with the assumption that a city can increase its number of arrests or decrease the number of crimes (or both) by increasing the size of its police force, but the effect of added resources would be greatest for cities above the threshold.

In regard to clearance rates, the data showed that departments with high crime workloads tend to claim more clearances per arrest than cities with low crime workloads. As a result, clearance rates are less sensitive to workload than arrest rates are. Although clearance rates for every crime type were found to decrease with increasing workload, the decreases were not significant for some types of crimes.

These workload relationships apply to all police officers, not just investigators. Although investigators are known to make more arrests per year than patrol officers, and our data confirmed this, the effect is small: we could not find a significant variation in arrest or clearance rates according to the fraction of the force in investigative units. In other words, if the total number of officers in a department is kept fixed, switching some officers into or out of investigative units is not likely to have a substantial effect on arrest or clearance rates.

Aside from the effects of size, region of country, and workload on clearance and arrest rates, we did find a few smaller effects of possible interest. Departments that assign a major investigative role to patrolmen have lower clearance rates, but not lower arrest rates, than other departments. This appears to reflect the fact that patrolmen cannot carry files around with them and therefore do not clear old crimes with new arrests. Departments with specialized units (concentrating on a single crime, such as robbery) were found to have lower arrest rates, but not lower clearance rates, for the types of crimes in which they specialize, as compared with departments having generalist investigators. Departments in which investigators work in pairs had lower numbers of arrests per officer than those in which they work singly. Since we did not collect data permitting a comparison of the quality of arrests produced by solo and paired investigators, this finding must be interpreted with caution. Still, the practice of pairing investigators, which is common only in the Northeast, is brought into sufficient question to warrant further research.

Most other characteristics of investigators were found to be unrelated to arrest and clearance rates. These include the nature and extent of the investigators' training, their civil service rank or rate of pay, and the nature of their interactions with prosecutors. However, the lack of cor-

---

[18] The 1972 data revealed a linear relationship between arrests per officer and crime workload, up to the threshold, but the intercept of the straight line fit was at a positive value of arrests per officer. After 1972, crime rates in the United States generally increased. Since we did not perform any longitudinal analyses, we do not know whether the thresholds also increased or remained at the same levels.

relation probably indicates more about the inadequacies of arrest and clearance rates as measures of effectiveness than about the inherent value of training and other characteristics.

How the Investigator's Time Is Spent

From an analysis of the Kansas City (Missouri) computer-readable case assignment file, and from observations during site visits, we determined that, although a large proportion of reported crimes are assigned to an investigator, many of these receive no more attention than the reading of the initial crime incident report. That is, many cases are suspended at once. The data show that homicide, rape, and suicide invariably result in investigative activity, and that at least 60 percent of all other serious types of cases receive significant attention (at least half an hour of a detective's time). Overall, however, less than half of all reported crimes receive any serious consideration by an investigator, and the great majority of cases that are actively investigated receive less than one day's attention. Table 3 shows, for several crime types, the percentage of cases that detectives worked on during the study period (1 May 1973 to 30 April 1974).

Table 3
Percentage of Reported Cases that Detectives Worked On

Type of Incident	Percentage
Homicide	100.0
Rape	100.0
Suicide	100.0
Forgery/counterfeit	90.4
Kidnapping	73.3
Arson	70.4
Auto theft	65.5
Aggravated assault	64.4
Robbery	62.6
Fraud/embezzlement	59.6
Felony sex crimes	59.0
Common assault	41.8
Nonresidential burglary	36.3
Dead body	35.7
Residential burglary	30.0
Larceny	18.4
Vandalism	6.8
Lost property	0.9
All above types together	32.4

SOURCE: Kansas City Case Assignment File; cases reported from May through November 1973.

The net result is that the average detective does not actually work on a large number of cases each month, even though he may have a backlog of hundreds or thousands of cases that were assigned to him at some time in the past and are still theoretically his responsibility. Table 4 shows the number of worked-on cases per detective per month in the various units of the Kansas City Police Department.[19] Except in the case of the Missing Persons Unit, the number of worked-on cases per detective is generally under one per day. If we imagine that each case is assigned to a particular investigator as his responsibility, the table shows the average number of cases that an investigator would be responsible for and work on in a month.

Table 4
Average Number of Worked-On Cases per Detective per Month

Unit	No. of Cases
Crimes against persons	9.2
Homicide	11.2
Robbery	7.7
Sex Crimes	6.2
Crimes against property	16.9
Auto theft	19.5
Nonresidential burglary	9.4
Residential burglary/larceny	22.9
General assignment	18.6
Incendiary	7.8
Forgery/fraud/bunco	10.4
Shoplifting/pickpocket	20.9
Youth and women's	26.0
Missing persons	88.4

Source: Kansas City Assignment File.

Our data revealed that most of an investigator's casework time is consumed in reviewing reports, documenting files, and attempting to locate and interview victims. For cases that are solved (that is, where a suspect is identified), an investigator spends more time in postclearance processing than in identifying the perpetrator.

---

[19] "Worked-on" means that at least half an hour was spent on the case. The types of cases assigned to each unit are described in Greenwood et al., *Criminal Investigation Process: Volume III*, pp. 53-55. For example, the homicide unit handles not only homicides but also suicides and unattended deaths from natural causes.

For Kansas City, we found the following breakdown of investigators' time. About 45 percent is spent on activities not attributable to individual cases—doing administrative assignments, making speeches, traveling, reading teletypes, making general surveillances (of junkyards, pawnshops, gathering spots for juveniles, and the like), and occupying slack time (for example, in a unit that is on duty at night to respond to robberies and homicides). The remaining 55 percent of the time is spent on casework. Of this, 40 percent (or 22 percent of the total) is spent investigating crimes that are never solved; just over 12 percent (7 percent of the total) is spent investigating crimes that are eventually solved; and nearly 48 percent (26 percent of the total) is spent on cleared cases after they have been solved.[20] These figures, of course, apply only to Kansas City. But after reviewing them (and more detailed tabulations) with investigators from other cities, and after comparing them with our observational notes, we concluded that they are approximately correct for other cities, with variations primarily in the areas of slack time (if investigators are not on duty at night) and time spent in conference with prosecutors.

Thus, investigators spend about 93 percent of their time on activities that do not lead directly to solving previously reported crimes. How are they to be judged on the quality of these activities? The time they spend on cases after they have been cleared serves the important purpose of preparing cases for court: this activity will be discussed below. The time they spend on noncasework activities serves a general support function for casework and therefore may be useful in ways that are difficult to quantify. The time they spend on crimes that are never solved can only be judged in terms of its public relations value and possible deterrent value, because most of these crimes can be easily recognized at the start. (They are primarily the ones where no positive identification of the perpetrator is available at the scene of the crime.) Police administrators must ask themselves whether the efforts devoted to investigating crimes that are initially unsolved are justified by either the small number of solutions they produce or the associated public relations benefits.

Collecting and Processing Physical Evidence

A police agency's ability to collect and process physical evidence at the scene of a crime is thought to be an important component of the criminal investigation process. In our study, however, we analyzed only one aspect of the collection and processing of physical evidence—their role in contributing to the *solution* of crimes, as distinguished from their value in proving guilt once the crime is solved.

---

[20] Activities after the case is cleared can include processing the arrestees, vouchering property, meeting with prosecutors, appearing in court, contacting victims, and completing paper work.

Earlier studies have shown that evidence technicians are asked to process the crime scene in only a small number of felony offenses.[21] And, even when the crime scene is processed, a significant portion of the available evidence may not be retrieved.[22] Police administrators, aware of these deficiencies, have begun to experiment with a variety of organizational changes designed to increase the number of crime sites processed for physical evidence.

Our analysis of the collection and processing of physical evidence in six police departments that employ different procedures[23] confirmed that a department can achieve a relatively high rate of recovery of latent prints from crime scenes by investing sufficiently in evidence technicians and by routinely dispatching these technicians to the scene of felonies. The latent print recovery rate is also increased by processing the crime scene immediately after the incident has been reported, rather than at a later time. Some of our data supporting these conclusions are shown (for burglary cases) in the first three lines of table 5.

The last line of table 5, however, shows that the rate at which fingerprints are used to identify the perpetrator of a burglary is essentially unre-

Table 5

Productivity of Crime Scene Processing for Fingerprints, Residential Burglary Sample[a]

Item	Long Beach	Berkeley	Richmond
Percentage of cases where technicians were requested	58.0	76.6	87.6
Cases where prints were recovered, as percentage of cases where a technician was requested	50. 8	42.0	69.1
Cases where prints were recovered, as percentage of total cases	29.4	32.2	60.5
Cases where perpetrator was identified as a result of lifted prints, as percentage of total cases	1.5	1.1	1.2

[a] The sample comprises 200 randomly selected residential burglary cases (cleared and uncleared) from each of three departments.

[21] See Brian Parker and Joseph Peterson, "Physical Evidence Utilization in the Administration of Criminal Justice" (Berkeley, Calif.: School of Criminology, University of California, 1972).

[22] President's Commission on Crime in the District of Columbia, *Report of the President's Commission on Crime in the District of Columbia* (Washington, D.C.: U.S. Government Printing Office, 1966).

[23] The six departments are those in Berkeley, Long Beach, Los Angeles, and Richmond, California; in Miami, Florida; and in Washington, D.C. For further details, see Greenwood et al., *Criminal Investigation Process: Volume III*, chap. 7.

lated to the print recovery rate. From 1 to 2 percent of the burglary cases in each of three departments were cleared by identification from a latent print, despite substantial differences in operating procedures. In Richmond, evidence technicians are dispatched to nearly 90 percent of the reported burglaries and recover prints from 70 percent of the scenes they process, but the fraction of burglaries solved by fingerprints is about the same as in Long Beaeh or Berkeley, where evidence technicians are dispatched to the scene less frequently and lift prints less often.

Why does lifting more prints not result in a higher rate of identification? The most plausible explanation seems to be that police departments are severely limited in their capability for searching fingerprint files. If a suspect is known, there is little difficulty in comparing his prints with latent prints that have been collected. Thus, latent prints may help to confirm a suspect's identification obtained in other ways. But in the absence of an effective means of performing "cold searches" for matching prints (where the suspect is unknown), the availability of a latent print cannot help solve the crime.

From a comparison of the fingerprint identification sections in Washington, Los Angeles, Miami, and Richmond, we determined that, for all these departments, from 4 to 9 percent of all retrieved prints are eventually matched with those of a known suspect. However, the number of "cold-search" matches produced per man-year differed substantially among departments, according to the size of their inked print files and the attention devoted to this activity. In some departments, technicians performing cold searches produced far more case solutions per man-year than investigators.

We infer that an improved fingerprint *identification* capability will be more productive of identifications than a more intensive print *collection* effort. Although some techniques and equipment currently available to police departments were found to enhance identification capability, the technology needed to match single latent prints to inked prints is not fully developed and appears to us to be of high priority for research.

Preparing the Case for Prosecution

Police investigation, whether or not it can be regarded as contributing significantly to the *identification* of perpetrators, is a necessary police function because it is the principal means by which all relevant evidence is gathered and presented to the court so that a criminal prosecution can be made. Thus, police investigators can be viewed as serving a support function for prosecutors.

Prosecutors frequently contend that a high rate of case dismissals, excessive plea bargaining, and overly lenient sentences are common consequences of inadequate police investigation. The police, in response, often claim that even when they conduct thorough investigations, case dispositions are not significantly affected. We undertook a study to illuminate the issues surrounding this controversy about responsibility for prosecutorial failure.

On the basis of discussions with prosecutors, detectives, and police supervisors, we developed a data form containing 39 questions that a prosecutor might want the police to address in conducting a robbery investigation. When we used this form to analyze the completeness of robbery investigations in two California prosecutors' offices, chosen to reflect contrasting prosecutorial practices in felony case screening but similar workload and case characteristics,[24] we found that the department confronted by a stringent prosecutorial filing policy ("Jurisdiction A") was significantly more thorough in reporting follow-on investigative work than the department whose cases were more permissively filed ("Jurisdiction B"). Yet, even the former department fell short of supplying the prosecutor with all the information he desired: each of 39 evidentiary questions that prosecutors consider necessary for effective case presentation was, on the average, covered in 45 percent of the cases in Jurisdiction A. Twenty-six percent were addressed by the department in Jurisdiction B. (Table 6 lists the 39 questions. The summary entries indicate the percentage of cases where a question could be answered from information in the documents provided by the police to the prosecutor.)

We then determined whether the degree of thorough documentation of the police investigation was related to the disposition of cases, specifically to the rate of dismissals, the heaviness of plea bargaining, and the type of sentence imposed. Our analysis showed differences between the two jurisdictions. For example, none of the sampled cases was dismissed in Jurisdiction A; furthermore, 60 percent of the defendants pled guilty to the charges as filed. By comparison, in Jurisdiction B about one-quarter of the sampled cases were dismissed after filing, and only one-third of the defendants pled guilty to the charges as filed.

A comparison of the two offices' heaviness of plea bargaining is shown in table 7. Although plea bargaining appears to be lighter in Jurisdiction A, this may simply reflect that the gravity of criminal conduct was less in the A than the B cases; that is, special allegations were considerably more frequent to begin with in B. One cannot conclude that only the quality of documentation of the police investigation accounted for the difference.

A similar conclusion applies to the type of sentence imposed: while there were differences in sentencing, the variations in other case characteristics indicate that these differences might not necessarily be related to thoroughness of documentation. This analysis leads us to suggest

---

[24] Peter W. Greenwood et al., *Prosecution of Adult Felony Defendants in Los Angeles County: A Policy Perspective*, R-1127-DOJ (Santa Monica, Calif.: The Rand Corporation, March 1973) led us to expect significant differences in police investigative effort and prosecutorial posture between the two selected jurisdictions.

Table 6
Presence of Information in Police Reports (In Percentages)

Case Information Desirable for Prosecution	Jurisdiction A[a] Information from at Least One Source[b]	Jurisdiction B[a] Information from at Least One Source[b]
1. What INTERVIEWS were conducted?	100.0	100.0
Offense		
2. Is there a verbatim report of the instant OFFENSE?	90.4 ⎱	95.2 ⎱
3. Is there a verbatim report of the FORCE USED?	95.2	36.5
4. What was the PHYSICAL HARM to the victim?	47.6	18.5
5. Is there a detailed description of the PROPERTY taken?	90.4 57.5%	27.2 36.2%
6. What was the method of S(uspect)'s ESCAPE?	71.4	45.4
7. What type of VEHICLE was used by S?	38.0	45.4
8. What type of WEAPON was used by S?	85.7	63.6
9. If a gun was used, was it LOADED?	19.0	13.5
10. If a gun was used, when was it ACQUIRED?	28.4	.0
11. Where is the LOCATION of the weapon now?	9.5 ⎰	18.1 ⎰
Suspect		
12. Was S UNDER THE INFLUENCE of alcohol or drugs?	42.8 ⎱	22.7 ⎱
13. What are the details of S's DEFENSE?	18.9	.0
14. What is S's ECONOMIC STATUS?	14.2	4.5 14.0
15. Was S advised of his CONSTITUTIONAL RIGHTS?	100.0 39.3%	63.6
16. If multiple suspects, what is their RELATIONSHIP?	42.7	.0
17. Is there evidence of PRIOR OFFENSES by S?	66.6	9.0
18. Is there evidence of S's MOTIVES?	47.6	18.1
19. Is there evidence of past PSYCHIATRIC TREATMENT of S?	9.5	4.5
20. What is S's PAROLE OF PROBATION status?	37.8	18.1
21. Does S have an alcohol or drug ABUSE HISTORY?	23.8	9.0
22. Where is S EMPLOYED?	28.5 ⎰	4.5 ⎰
Victim/Witnesses		
23. What is the RELATIONSHIP between S and V(ictim)?	4.7 ⎱	9.0 ⎱
24. What is the CREDIBILITY of the W(itnesses)?	9.5	.0
25. Can the W make a CONTRIBUTION to the case prosecution?	23.8 31.1%	4.5 3.4%
26. Were MUG SHOTS shown to V or W?	51.7	4.5
27. If shown, are the PROCEDURES and RESULTS adequately described?	30.0	.0
28. Was a LINE-UP conducted?	53.0	.0
29. If conducted, are the PROCEDURES and RESULTS adequately described?	40.0	.0
30. Was an effort made to LIFT FINGERPRINTS at the scene?	41.0	4.5
31. If made, were USABLE FINGERPRINTS OBTAINED?	59.0	9.0
32. Were PHOTOS TAKEN at the crime scene?	35.0	4.5
33. Is the EXACT LOCATION from where the photos and prints were taken given?	29.0	.0
34. Did V VERIFY his statements in the crime report?	24.0	.0
35. Did V have IMPROPER MOTIVES in reporting the offense?	4.7 ⎰	.0 ⎰
Arrest		
36. What was the legal BASIS FOR SEARCH AND SEIZURE?	23.8 ⎱	36.3 ⎱
37. How was the LOCATION OF EVIDENCE learned?	33.3	32.0
38. How was the LOCATION OF S learned?	66.6 52.3%	68.1 52.2%
39. How was the ARREST OF S made?	85.7 ⎰	72.7 ⎰
Overall	45.0%	26.4%

NOTE: The percentages within the matrix refer only to the presence of information the police chose to record; they may not represent a complete picture of the information gathered by the police in the course of the investigation. It is possible that certain police officers record only "positive" information and assume that an omission of information automatically implies that the information is either not applicable or inappropriate in a specific case.

[a] Twenty-one robbery cases in each sample.

[b] Percentage of cases that presented this information from at least one source.

that the failure of police to document a case investigation thoroughly *may* contribute to a higher case dismissal rate and a weakening of the prosecutor's plea bargaining position.

Table 7
A Comparison Between A and B of Dispositions by Pleas of Guilty

Disposition	Percentage in Jurisdiction A	Percentage in Jurisdiction B
Plea of guilty to original charges	61.1	31.8
Plea of guilty to original charges but with special allegations stricken or not considered	27.7	22.7
Plea of guilty to 2d degree robbery reduced from 1st degree robbery	5.5	18.1
Plea of guilty to other lesser offense	5.5	4.5
Cases dismissed	—	22.7

NOTE: Because of rounding, columns do not add to 100 percent.

Relations between Victims and Police

Many investigators, as well as top-ranking police officials, have defended the investigative function, not because it contributes significantly to the identification of perpetrators, but because it is one of the principal contacts the police maintain with the victims of serious crimes. But, despite these verbal espousals of the public service function as an important part of the investigative role, our observations in departments across the country indicate that most police merely respond initially to the crime scene and file a cursory report; rarely do they subsequently contact the victims about the progress of the case. This is understandable, given the rising number of reported crimes and relatively constant police budgets.

While it seems reasonable to suggest that local police departments might win more public confidence by notifying the victim when the perpetrator has been identified, such a policy of routine feedback could be self-defeating. For example, if the police were to inform a victim that the perpetrator of his crime had been apprehended and was not being charged with his offense but being prosecuted on another, the victim, rather than feeling more confident in the police or the criminal justice system, might in fact become disillusioned. And a resentful victim could become highly vocal about his dissatisfactions and cause other citizens to be negative about police performance.

How much information to give the victim and when to give it were the questions behind a telephone survey we made of robbery and burglary victims. This study must be regarded as exploratory; the survey was conducted simply as an initial attempt to explore victims' feelings about receiving information feedback and about which types of information are most important.

Table 8
Kind of Information Wanted by Victims

Survey Question: As a Victim, Did You Want the Police to Inform You?	Yes	No	Indiff- erent	If Your Answer Was "Yes," How Important Was It to You to Be Informed?	
				Very	Somewhat
If your case was solved?	32 (89%)	1 (3%)	3 (8%)	26	6
If a suspect was arrested?	30 (83%)	5 (14%)	1 (3%)	22	8
If a defendant was tried?	27 (75%)	4 (11%)	5 (14%)	15	12
If a defendant was sentenced?	27 (75%)	4 (11%)	5 (14%)	16	11
What sentence was imposed?	27 (75%)	4 (11%)	5 (14%)	16	11
If the defendant was released from custody?	18 (50%)	11 (31%)	7 (19%)	11	7

The inquiry summarized by table 8 was accompanied by two pairs of questions, with the first question of each pair addressing the victim's desire to have feedback on a specific matter and the second eliciting his probable reaction if the feedback occurred. Table 9 displays the responses on whether or not the victim wanted to be told of a police decision to suspend or drop investigative effort on his case if such a decision were made: these responses suggest a consistent preference for knowledge about this police decision, but with an observable tendency to the contrary in cleared robbery cases (which involve a relatively small segment of the underlying population). Table 10 exhibits the victims' responses to the question of what their reactions would be if they were told that no further investigation was intended on their cases. We note that approximately one-third of our sample would react negatively to unfavorable feedback (and the proportion would be higher if the data were weighted to reflect the relative numbers of each crime type).

Table 9
Respondent's Desire to be Told of Police Decision to Suspend Investigation of His Case

Victim's Response	Burglary	Robbery	Total
Yes	16	10	26 (72%)
No	3	4	7 (19%)
Indifferent or no answer	1	2	3 (8%)
Total	20	16	36 (100%)

Table 10
Victim's Predicted Reaction to Information that Police
Will Suspend Investigation of His Case

Victim's Prediction of His Own Reaction	Burglary	Robbery	Total
Appreciative of being told and agreeable to police decision	3	1	4 (12%)
Understanding and resigned	11	7	18 (53%)
Disturbed and resistant	4	1	5 (15%)
Angry and resentful	2	5	7 (21%)
			34[a] (100%)

[a] Two victims were omitted: the response of one was not applicable, and the other declined to answer.

To the extent that our survey results may reach beyond the confines of our small sample, they broadly support the belief that there is a strong market for information feedback to victims from the police. But they also tend to confirm the view that some victims, if given unfavorable information, will develop undesirable attitudes toward the police. Finally, our results suggest that other repercussions from information feedback, of which the police are sometimes apprehensive, are of slight significance. Few victims, no matter how distressed by information coming from the police, indicated that they would act inimically to police interests.

Proactive Investigation Methods

In a departure from the typically reactive mode (so called, because the investigator does not focus on the case until after a crime has occurred) of most investigators assigned to Part I crimes, some police departments have shifted a small number of their investigators to more proactive investigation tactics. Proactive units usually deal with a particular type of offender, such as known burglars, robbery teams, or active fences. A number of such units have been supported on an experimental basis with funds from the Law Enforcement Assistance Administration.[25]

The proactive team members often work quite closely with other investigators, but, unlike regular investigators, they are not assigned a caseload of reported crimes. Instead, they are expected to generate other sources of information to identify serious offenders. These other sources may include informants they have cultivated, their own sur-

---

[25] For a description of five antirobbery units of this type, see Richard H. Ward et al., *Police Robbery Control Manual* (Washington, D.C.: National Institute of Law Enforcement and Criminal Justice, 1975).

veillance activities, or undercover fencing operations operated by the police themselves.

The primary objective in establishing these units is to reduce the incidence of the target crime. The reduction is supposed to result from the containment achieved by successfully arresting and prosecuting offenders and from the deterrent effect on others of the publicity given the proactive programs. Therefore, the arrest rates of these units are typically used as a measure of their primary effect; and changes in the rate of incidence of the target crime are also cited. The chief problem in using these two measures is the difficulty of isolating the unique effects of the proactive unit from other activities of the police department and from external factors affecting crime or arrest rates.

In the course of our study, we looked at several such units by either examining evaluation reports or making direct observations. In general, they all seemed to produce a much higher number of arrests for the officers assigned than did other types of patrol or investigative activities. Consistent effects on targeted crime rates could not be identified.

In order to determine which activities of these units actually resulted in arrests, we examined in considerable detail a sample of cases from two units, the Miami Stop Robbery unit and the Long Beach (California) Suppression of Burglary unit.

From the sample of robbery cases in Miami, we determined that, although the Stop officers averaged 4 arrests per man-month, half of which were for robbery, in 10 out of 11 of these arrests the Stop officer was simply executing a warrant obtained by some other unit or accompanying another officer to make the arrest. In Long Beach, the Suppression of Burglary officers averaged 2.4 arrests per man-month, half of which were for burglary or for receiving stolen property. An analysis of 27 of the arrests disclosed that just half (13) resulted from the unit's own work; the remaining arrests were by referral or were the result of routine investigation that could have been handled by any other unit.

Our general conclusion was that proactive techniques can be productive in making arrests, particularly for burglary and fencing. To be effective, however, the units must be staffed with highly motivated and innovative personnel. And the officers' efforts must be carefully monitored to preclude their diversion to making arrests for other units and to ensure that their tactics do not become so aggressive as to infringe on individual liberties.

Policy Implications

We have identified several distinguishable functions performed by investigators: preparing cases for prosecution after the suspects are in custody; apprehending known suspects; performing certain routine tasks that may lead to identifying unknown suspects; engaging in intensive investigations when there are no suspects or when it is not clear that a crime has been committed; and conducting proactive investigations. In addition, investigators engage in various administrative tasks and paperwork related to these functions.

We have enough information about the effectiveness of each function to begin asking whether the function should be performed at all and, if so, who should do it. The notion that all these functions must be performed by a single individual, or by officers having similar ranks or capabilities, does not stand up to scrutiny; in fact, many police departments have begun to assign distinguishable functions to separate units. Our own suggestions, to be presented below, support this development and extend it in certain ways. If a function now assigned to investigators can be performed as well or better, but at lower cost, by patrol officers, clerical personnel, or information systems, it should be removed from the investigators; if it serves the objectives of the prosecutor, then it should be responsive to the needs of the prosecutor; and, if especially competent investigators are required, the function should be assigned to a unit composed of such officers.

In this section we describe the implications of our findings for changes in the organization of the investigative function, the processing of physical evidence, and the role of the public.[26]

Preparing Cases for Prosecution

Postarrest investigative activity—not only important for prosecution but also one of the major activities now performed by investigators—can perhaps be done in a less costly or more effective manner.

Our observations indicate that the current coordination, or lack thereof, between the police and prosecutorial agencies does not support a healthy working relationship. It allows for a situation in which each can blame the other for outcomes in court that it views as unfavorable.

Most prosecutors do not have investigators on their staff. If they do, these investigators are usually occupied with "white-collar" offenses rather than street crimes. Generally, then, the prosecutor relies on police investigators to provide the evidence needed to prosecute and convict arrestees. But inherent in this situation is a conflict between prosecutor and police. An arrest is justified by *probable cause*—that is, by an articulable, reasonable belief that a crime was committed and that the arrestee was the offender. Often, the police are satisfied to document the justification for the arrest rather than expend further inves-

---

[26] For an expanded discussion of the policy implications, see Peter W. Greenwood and Joan Petersilia, *The Criminal Investigation Process: Volume I. Summary and Policy Implications*, R-177-DOJ (Santa Monica, Calif.: The Rand Corporation, October 1975).

tigative effort to strengthen the evidence in the case. The prosecutor, on the other hand, may be reluctant to file the charges preferred by the police, or to file at all, he believes the evidence would not suffice for a conviction, that is, as *proof beyond a reasonable doubt*. Many cases appear to be affected by the conflicting incentives of police and prosecutor, as reflected in failures to file and in lenient filing, early dismissals, or imbalanced bargaining.

One way of ameliorating this problem is to make explicit the types of information that the prosecutor and police agree are appropriate to collect and document, given the nature of the crime. The form we designed for robbery cases (summarized in table 6) gives an example of how such information can be made explicit. Each jurisdiction should develop appropriate forms for major categories of crimes. Such written documents would assist the police in becoming more knowledgeable about the type and amount of information that a prosecutor requires to establish guilt for each type of offense and in allocating their investigative efforts to provide this information.[27]

We observed that the prosecutor's strictness with respect to filing decisions can affect the thoroughness of case preparation. In turn, the thoroughness of documentation may affect the percentage of cases subsequently dismissed and the degree of plea bargaining. We suggest, therefore, that prosecutors be mindful of the level of investigative documentation in their jurisdictions, especially in offices where the officer presenting the case may not have participated in the investigation.

One rationale advanced in some police departments for minimizing the factual content of formal investigative reports is that these reports are subject to discovery by defense counsel and thereby facilitate the impeachment of prosecution witnesses, including policemen. Such departments believe that the results of detailed investigations are better communicated orally to the prosecutor's office. The results of our research, while not conclusive, tend to refute this argument. In the jurisdiction ("A") where detailed documentation is prepared, no such negative consequences were noted; but in the jurisdiction ("B") having less information in the documentation, oral communication failed in some instances to reach all the prosecutors involved in the case.

Above and beyond merely improving coordination between police and prosecutors, it is worthy of experimentation to assign the prosecutor responsibility for certain investigative efforts. We feel that a promising approach would be to place nearly all postarrest investigations under the authority of the prosecutor, either by assigning police officers to his office or by making investigators an integral part of his staff,

---

[27] Alternatives that might accomplish some similar aims include having the prosecutor provide the investigators with periodic evaluations of their case preparation efforts; training new investigators in case preparation; or having on-call attorneys assist in the preparation of serious cases.

depending on the local situation. A test of this arrangement would show whether it is an effective way of assuring that the evidentiary needs for a successful prosecution are met.

Apprehending Known Suspects

We have noted that, in a substantial fraction of the cases ultimately cleared, the perpetrator is known from information available at the scene of the crime. If he or she is already in custody, the case becomes a matter for postarrest processing, as discussed above. If the perpetrator is not in custody, it is important for the responding officer(s), whether from investigative or patrol units, to obtain and make a record of the evidence identifying the suspect. This requires that the responding officers be permitted adequate time to conduct an initial investigation, including the interviewing of possible witnesses, and that the crime-reporting form be designed in such a way that the presence of information identifying a suspect is unmistakably recorded.

Apprehending a known suspect may or may not be difficult. Assigning all such apprehension to investigators does not appear to be cost-effective, especially if the investigators are headquartered at some distance from the suspect's location and a patrol officer is nearby. We believe that certain patrol officers, whom we shall call generalist-investigators, could be trained to handle this function in such a way that the arrests are legally proper and a minimum number of innocent persons are brought in for questioning. Only when apprehension proves difficult should investigative units become involved.

Routine Investigative Actions

For crimes without initial identification of a suspect, we found that many of those eventually cleared are solved by routine investigative actions—for example, listing a stolen automobile in the "hot car" file, asking the victim to view a previously assembled collection of mug shots for the crime in question, checking pawnshop slips, awaiting phone calls from the public, and tracing ownership of a weapon.

One implication of this finding is that any steps a police department can take to convert investigative tasks into routine actions will increase the number of crimes solved. Technological improvements, especially in information systems, produced many of the clearances we identified as "routine." In the absence of good information systems, such clearances might never have occurred or might have been difficult to achieve. The ability of patrol officers to check rapidly whether a vehicle is stolen or, more important, whether the owner is wanted for questioning produced numerous case solutions in our samples. Well-organized and maintained mug-shot, *modus operandi,* or pawn-slip files also led to clearances.

A second implication is that it may not be necessary for *investigators,* who are usually paid more than patrol officers or clerks, to perform the functions that lead to routine clearances. We believe that an experiment should be conducted to determine the cost and effectiveness of having lower-paid personnel perform these tasks.

Once clerical processing is complete, some action by a police officer may still be needed; for example, the suspect may still have to be apprehended. Such action should be assigned to generalist investigators.

Investigating Crimes without Suspects

Two basic objectives are served by taking more than routine investigative action when the suspect is unknown. One objective is to solve the crime; the other is to demonstrate that the police care about the crime and the victim. The latter objective can be carried out by generalist-investigators who are responsible to a local commander concerned with all aspects of police-community relations. This type of investigative duty does not require specialized skills or centralized coordination. The officers performing it could readily shift between patrol and investigative duties. In departments with team policing, such investigations could be a task rotated among team members.

If the objective is actually to solve the crime, police departments must realize that the results will rarely be commensurate with the effort involved. An explicit decision must be made that the nature of the crime itself or public concern about the crime warrants a full follow-up investigation. A significant reduction in investigative efforts would be appropriate for all but the most serious offenses. If, in a less serious offense, a thorough preliminary investigation fails to establish a suspect's identity, then the victim should be notified that active investigation is being suspended until new leads appear (as a result, for example, of an arrest in another matter).

Serious crimes (homicide, rape, assault with great bodily injury, robbery, or first-degree burglary) warrant special investigative efforts. These efforts can best be provided by a Major Offenses Unit, manned by investigators who are well trained and experienced in examining crime scenes, interpreting physical evidence, and interrogating hostile suspects and fearful witnesses, and who are aided by modern information systems. One reason for establishing such a unit is to identify the investigative positions that require special skills and training and that demand knowledge of citywide crime patterns and developments. Our observations suggest, by way of contrast, that current staffing patterns rarely allow most investigators to see these highly serious cases. Therefore, when such cases arise, the investigators are frequently ill equipped to cope with them and unduly distracted by the burden of paper work on their routine cases.

A Major Offenses Unit would concentrate its efforts on a few *unsolved* serious felonies. The team would consist of a relatively small number of experienced investigators closely supervised by a team commander. From our observations, it appears that the most serious impediment to high-quality investigative work is the traditional method of case assignment and supervision. In nearly every department, a case is normally assigned to an individual investigator as his sole responsibility, whether he is a generalist, specialist, or engaged in team policing. Supervisors do not normally review the decisions he makes on how to pursue the investigation, and his decisions are largely unrecorded in the case file. Consequently, the relative priority an investigator gives to the tasks on a given case assigned to him depends largely on the number and nature of his other case assignments and on his personal predilections and biases. Caseload conflicts and personal predilections frequently lead an investigator to postpone unduly or perform improperly the critical tasks of a particular case assignment.

Assigning cases to investigative teams rather than to individuals could eliminate this problem. For effective operations, the team should include approximately six men and be led by a senior investigator knowledgeable about the local crime situation, criminal law, and police management. The leader's primary responsibility would be to keep informed of progress on the cases assigned to his team and to make the broad tactical decisions on the team's expenditure of effort. Each day the subordinate investigators would perform individually assigned tasks. A clerk delegated to the team would prepare progress reports to document the daily accomplishment on open cases and to assist the leader in making the allocation for the following day. These reports would also help the leader identify which of his men were most effective at which tasks. Such an approach should assure that significant steps in an investigation are objectively directed by an experienced senior investigator.

Proactive Investigations

Our research into proactive units let us call them "strike forces"—leads us to conclude that they can be relatively productive. In instances where such units were successful, they were manned by motivated and innovative personnel. The gain in employing them becomes illusory when mere quantity of arrests is emphasized, for then their efforts tend to be diverted into making arrests that are not the result of unique capabilities. We feel that departments should employ strike forces selectively and judiciously. The operation of strike forces necessitates careful procedural and legal planning to protect the officers involved and to ensure that the defendants they identify can be successfully prosecuted. These units also require close monitoring by senior officers to ensure that they do not become overly aggressive and infringe on individual privacy.

In all likelihood, the relative advantage of strike force operations in a particular department will not persist over a long period of time. The department must accustom itself to creating and then terminating strike forces, as circumstances dictate.

Processing Physical Evidence

Most police departments collect far more evidence (primarily fingerprints) than they can productively process. Our work shows that cold searches of inked fingerprint files could be far more effective than routine follow-up investigations in increasing the apprehension rate.

Fingerprint processing capabilities should be strengthened as follows. First, the reference print files should be organized by geographic area, with a fingerprint specialist assigned to each area; no area should have more than 5,000 sets of inked prints. Second, to assure a large number of "request searches," which imply a cooperative effort between investigator and fingerprint specialist, some communication links should be devised to help motivate and facilitate the reciprocal exchange of information between these two parties. Third, the fingerprint specialists should be highly trained, highly motivated, and not overloaded with other tasks that might detract from their primary function.

Several existing systems for storing and retrieving inked prints with specified characteristics (of the latent print or the offender) appear useful and were widely praised by departments that have them. However, further research might contribute a major technological improvement in the capability of police departments to match latent prints with inked prints.

Role of the Public

Our research persuaded us that actions by members of the public can strongly influence the outcome of cases. Sometimes private citizens hold the perpetrator at the scene of the crime. Sometimes they recognize the suspect or stolen property at a later time and call the investigator. Sometimes the victim or his relatives conduct a full-scale investigation on their own and eventually present the investigator with a solution. Collectively, these types of citizen involvement account for a sizable fraction of cleared cases.

Police departments should initiate programs designed to enhance the victim's desire to cooperate fully with the police. Such programs might both increase apprehension rates and improve the quality of prosecutions. Specifically, when major crimes are solved, police departments should announce the particular contribution of members of the public (respecting, of course, any person's desire for anonymity). A realistic picture of how crimes are solved will help eliminate the public's distorted image of detectives and will impress on them the importance of cooperating with police.

Reallocation of Investigative Resources

Ultimately, our suggestions imply a substantial shift of police resources from investigative to other units. However, such reallocations cannot be justified on the basis of current knowledge alone; they must await testing and evaluation of each of our recommendations. If we prove correct, most initial investigations would be assigned to patrol units under the direction of local commanders. To improve the quality of initial investigations, the patrol force would have to be augmented with a large number of generalist-investigators. These officers would also perform certain follow-up work, such as apprehending known suspects and improving communications with victims and witnesses of crimes. The resources needed to field generalist-investigators would be obtained by reducing the number of investigators.

Additional major reallocations of resources away from "traditional" reactive investigative units are implied by our suggestions to have clerical personnel and generalist-investigators perform routine processing of cases, to increase the use of information systems, to enhance capabilities for processing physical evidence, to increase the number of proactive investigative units, and to assign investigative personnel to the prosecutor for postarrest preparation of cases. If all these changes were made, the only remaining investigative units concerned with Part I crimes would be the Major Offenses Units. The number of investigators assigned to such units would ordinarily be well under half the current number of investigators in most departments.

In no way does our study suggest that total police resources be reduced. On the contrary, our analysis of FBI data suggests that such a reduction might lower arrest and clearance rates. Reallocating resources might lead to somewhat increased arrest and clearance rates, but our suggestions are intended primarily for the more successful prosecution of arrestees and for improved public relations.

We know that most of the changes we advocate are practical, because we observed them in operation in one or more departments. For example, a number of departments have recently introduced "case screening," whereby each crime report is examined to determine whether or not a follow-up investigation should be conducted. Our findings indicate that the decision rule for case screening can be quite simple. If a suspect is known, the case should be pursued; if no suspect is known after a thorough preliminary investigation, the case should be assigned for routine clerical processing unless it is serious enough to be assigned to the appropriate Major Offenses Unit. The definition of "serious" must be determined individually by each department, since it is essentially a political decision.

Another current innovation is "team policing," in which investigators are assigned to work with patrol officers who cover a specified geographical area. While there are many organizational variations of team policing,[28] most forms would permit the introduction of generalist-investigators having the functions we describe, and some already include such personnel.

We know of no jurisdiction in which the prosecutor currently administers postarrest investigations, although investigators have been assigned to several prosecutors' offices (for example, in Boston, New Orleans, and San Diego) to facilitate interactions with the police. Only a careful experiment will determine the feasibility and effectiveness of making the prosecutor responsible for postarrest investigations.

The National Institute of Law Enforcement and Criminal Justice has funded the introduction of revised investigative procedures in five jurisdictions. The experimental changes, which are based partly on the findings of our study, will be carefully evaluated to determine whether, to what extent, and under what circumstances they actually lead to improved effectiveness.

---

[28] See, for example, Peter B. Bloch and David Specht, *Neighborhood Team Policing* (Washington, D.C.: National Institute of Law Enforcement and Criminal Justice, December 1973).

Lawrence W. Sherman & Richard A. Berk

The Minneapolis
Domestic Violence Experiment*

Under a grant from the National Institute of Justice, the Minneapolis Police Department and the Police Foundation conducted an experiment from early 1981 to mid-1982 testing police responses to domestic violence. A technical report of the experiment can be found in the April 1984 issue of the *American Sociological Review*. This report summarizes the results and implications of the experiment. It also shows how the experiment was designed and conducted so the reader may understand and judge the findings.

Findings in Brief

The Minneapolis domestic violence experiment was the first scientifically controlled test for the effects of arrest for any crime. It found that arrest was the most effective of three standard methods police use to reduce domestic violence. The other police methods—attempting to counsel both parties or sending assailants away from home for several hours—were found to be considerably less effective in determining future violence in the cases examined. These were not life-threatening cases, but rather the minor assaults which make up the bulk of police calls to domestic violence.

The findings, standing alone as the result of one experiment, do not necessarily imply that all suspected assailants should be arrested. Other experiments in other settings are needed to learn more. But the preponderance of evidence in the Minneapolis study strongly suggests that the police should use arrest in most domestic violence cases.

Source: Lawrence W. Sherman and Richard A. Berk (1984). "The Minneapolis Domestic Violence Experiment." *Police Foundation Reports*, April, pp. 1-8. Reprinted by permission of The Police Foundation.

*The Minneapolis domestic violence experiment was conducted under Grant Number 80-IJ-CX-0042 from the Office of Research and Evaluation Methods, Crime Control Theory in Policing Program, National Institute of Justice, U.S. Department of Justice. Points of view or opinions stated in this report do not necessarily represent the official position of the U.S. Department of Justice, the Minneapolis Police Department, or the Police Foundation.

Why the Experiment Was Conducted

The purpose of the experiment was to address an intense debate about how police should respond to misdemeanors, cases of domestic violence. At least three viewpoints can be identified in this debate:

1. The traditional police approach of doing as little as possible, on the premise that offenders will not be punished by the courts even if they are arrested, and that the problems are basically not solvable.

2. The clinical psychologists' recommendations that police actively mediate or arbitrate disputes underlying the violence, restoring peace but not making any arrests.

3. The approach recommended by many women's groups and the Police Executive Research Forum (Loving, 1980) of treating the violence as a criminal offense subject to arrest.

If the purpose of police responses to domestic violence calls is to reduce the likelihood of that violence recurring, the question is which of these approaches is more effective than the others?

Policing Domestic Assaults

Police have been typically reluctant to make arrests for domestic violence (Berk and Loseke, 1981), as well as for a wide range of other kinds of offenses, unless a victim demands an arrest, a suspect insults an officer, or other factors are present (Sherman, 1980). Parnas' (1972) observation of the Chicago police found four categories of police action in these situations: negotiating or otherwise "talking out" the dispute; threatening the disputants and then leaving; asking one of the parties to leave the premises, or, very rarely, making an arrest.

Similar patterns are found in many other cities. Surveys of battered women who tried to have their domestic assailants arrested report that arrest occurred in only ten percent (Roy, 1977:35) or three percent (see Langley and Levy, 1977:219) of the cases. Surveys of police agencies in Illinois (Illinois Law Enforcement Commission, 1978) and New York (Office of the Minority Leader, 1978) found explicit policies against arrest in the majority of the agencies surveyed. Despite the fact that violence is reported to be present in one-third (Bard and Zacker, 1974) to two-thirds (Black, 1980) of all domestic disturbances police respond to, police department data show arrests in only five percent of those disturbances in Oakland (Hart, n.d., cited in Meyer and Lorimer,

1977:21), six percent of those disturbances in a Colorado city (Patrick, Ellis, and Hoffmeister, n.d., cited in Meyer and Lorimer, 1977:21), and six percent in Los Angeles County (Emerson, 1979).

The best available evidence on the frequency of arrest is the observations from the Black and Reiss study of Boston, Washington, and Chicago police in 1966 (Black, 1980:182). Police responding to disputes in those cities made arrests in 27 percent of violent felonies and 17 percent of the violent misdemeanors. Among married couples (Black, 1980:158), they made arrests in 26 percent of the cases, but tried to remove one of the parties in 38 percent of the cases.

The apparent preference of many police for separating the parties rather than arresting the offender has been attacked from two directions over the past 15 years. The original critique came from clinical psychologists who agreed that police should rarely make arrests (Potter, 1978:46; Fagin, 1978:123-124) in domestic assault cases and argued that police should mediate the disputes responsible for the violence. A highly publicized demonstration project teaching police special counseling skills for family crisis intervention (Bard, 1970) failed to show a reduction in violence, but was interpreted as a success nonetheless. By 1977, a national survey of police agencies with 100 or more officers found that over 70 percent reported a family crisis intervention training program in operation. Although it is not clear whether these programs reduced separation and increased mediation, a decline in arrests was noted for some (Wylie, *et. al.,* 1976). Indeed, many sought explicitly to *reduce* the number of arrests (University of Rochester, 1974; Ketterman and Kravitz, 1978).

By the mid-1970s, police practices were criticized from the opposite direction by feminist groups. Just as psychologists succeeded in having many police agencies respond to domestic violence as "half social work and half police work," feminists began to argue that police put "too much emphasis on the social work aspect and not enough on the criminal" (Langley and Levy, 1977:218). Widely publicized lawsuits in New York and Oakland sought to compel police to make arrests in every case of domestic assault, and state legislatures were lobbied successfully to reduce the evidentiary requirements needed for police to make arrests for misdemeanor domestic assaults. Some legislatures are now considering statutes requiring police to make arrests in these cases.

The feminist critique was bolstered by a study (Police Foundation, 1976) showing that for 85 percent of a sample of spouse killings, police had intervened at least once in the preceding two years. For 54 percent of these homicides, police had intervened five or more times. But it was impossible to determine from the data whether making more or fewer arrests would have reduced the homicide rate.

How the Experiment Was Designed

In order to find which police approach was most effective in deterring future domestic violence, the Police Foundation and the Minneapolis Police Department agreed to conduct a classic experiment. A classic experiment is a research design that allows scientists to discover the effects of one thing on another by holding constant all other possible causes of those effects. The design of the experiment called for a lottery selection, which ensured that there would be no difference among the three groups of suspects receiving the different police responses (Cook and Campbell, 1979). The lottery determined which of the three responses police officers would use on each suspect in a domestic assault case. According to the lottery, a suspect would be arrested, or sent from the scene of assault for eight hours, or given some form of advice, which could include mediation at an officer's discretion. In the language of the experiment, these responses were called the arrest, send, and advise treatments. The design called for a six-month follow-up period to measure the frequency and seriousness of any future domestic violence in all cases in which the police intervened.

The design applied only to simple (misdemeanor) domestic assaults, where both the suspect and the victim were present when the police arrived. Thus, the experiment included only those cases in which police were empowered, but not required, to make arrests under a recently liberalized Minnesota state law. The police officer must have a probable cause to believe that a cohabitant or spouse had assaulted the victim within the past four hours. Police need not have witnessed the assault. Cases of life-threatening or severe injury, usually labeled as a felony (aggravated assault), were excluded from the design.

The design called for each officer to carry a pad of report forms, color coded for the three different police responses. Each time the officers encountered a situation that fit the experiment's criteria, they were to take whatever action was indicated by the report form on the top of the pad. The forms were numbered and arranged for each officer in an order determined by the lottery. The consistency of the lottery assignment was to be monitored by research staff observers riding on patrol for a sample of evenings.

After a police action was taken at the scene of a domestic violence incident, the officer was to fill out a brief report and give it to the research staff for follow-up. As a further check on the lottery process, the staff logged in the reports and the order in which they were received and made sure that the sequence corresponded to the original assignment of responses.

Anticipating something of the background of victims in the experiment, a predominantly minority, female research staff was employed to contact the victims for a detailed, face-to-face interview, to be followed by telephone follow-up interviews every two weeks for 24 weeks. The interviews were designed primarily to measure the frequency and seriousness of victimizations caused by a suspect after police intervention. The research staff also collected criminal justice reports that mentioned suspect's names during the six-month follow-up period.

Conduct of the Experiment

As is common in field experiments, the actual research process in Minneapolis suffered some slippage from the original plan. This section recounts the difficulties encountered in conducting the experiment. None of these difficulties, however, proved finally detrimental to the experiment's validity.

In order to gather data as quickly as possible, the experiment was originally located in two of Minneapolis's four precincts, those with the highest density of domestic violence crime reports and arrests. The 34 officers assigned to those areas were invited to a three-day planning meeting and asked to participate in the study for one year. All but one agreed. The conference also produced a draft order for Chief Anthony Bouza's signature specifying the rules of the experiment. These rules created several new situations to be excluded from the experiment, including whether a suspect attempted to assault police officers, a victim persistently demanded an arrest, or both parties were injured. These additional exceptions allowed for the possibility that the lottery process would be violated more for the separation and mediation treatments than for the arrest treatment. However, a statistical analysis showed that these changes posed no threat to the validity of the experiment's findings.

The experiment began on March 17, 1981. The expectation was that it would take about one year to produce about 300 cases. In fact, the experiment ran until August 1, 1982, and produced 314 case reports. The officers agreed to meet monthly with Lawrence W. Sherman, the project director, and Nancy Wester, the project manager. By the third or fourth month, two facts became clear: Only about 15 to 20 officers either were coming to meetings or turning in cases and the rate at which the cases were turned in would make it difficult to complete the project in one year. By November, it was decided to recruit more officers in order to obtain cases more rapidly. Eighteen additional officers joined the project. But like the original group, most of these officers turned in only one or two cases. Indeed, three of the original officers produced almost 28 percent of the cases, in part because they worked a particularly violent beat and in part because they had a greater commitment to the study. A statistical analysis showed that the effects of police actions did not vary according to which officer was involved. Since the lottery was by officer, this condition created no validity problem for the cases in the study.

There is little doubt that many of the officers occasionally failed to follow fully the experimental design. Some of the failures were due to forgetfulness, such as leaving report pads at home or at the police station. Other failures derived from misunderstanding about whether the experiment applied in certain situations; application of experimental rules under complex circumstances was sometimes confusing. Finally, there were occasional situations that were simply not covered by experimental rules.

Whether any officer intentionally subverted the design is unclear. The plan to monitor the lottery process with ride-along observers broke down because of the unexpectedly low frequency of cases meeting the experimental criteria. Observers had to ride for many weeks before they observed an officer apply one of the treatments. An attempt was made to solve this with "chase alongs," in which observers rode in their own car with a portable police radio and drove to the scene of any domestic call dispatched to any officer in the precinct. Even this method failed.

Thus, the possibility existed that police officers, anticipating from the dispatch call a particular kind of incident and finding the upcoming experiment treatment inappropriate, may have occasionally decided to ignore the experiment. In effect, they may have chosen to exclude certain cases in violation of the experimental design. Such action would have biased the selection of the experiment's sample of cases, but there is little reason to believe it actually happened. On the other hand, had they, for example, not felt like filling out extra forms on a given day, this would not affect the validity of the experiment's results.

Table One shows the degree to which the three treatments were delivered as designed. Ninety-nine percent of the suspects targeted for arrest actually were arrested; 78 percent of those scheduled to receive advice did; and 73 percent of those to be sent out of the residence for eight hours actually were sent. One explanation for this pattern, consis-

Table 1
Designed and Delivered Police Treatments in Domestic Assault Cases

Designed Treatment	Delivered Treatment			
	Arrest	Advise	Separate	
ARREST	98.9% N=91	0.0% N=0	1.1% N=1	29.3% N=92
ADVISE	17.6% N=19	77.8% N=84	4.6% N=5	34.4% N=108
SEPARATE	22.8% N=26	4.4% N=5	72.8% N=83	36.3% N=114
TOTAL	43.3% N=136	28.3% N=89	28.3% N=89	100% N=314

tent with experimental guidelines, is that mediating and sending were more difficult ways for police to control a situation. There was a greater likelihood that officers might have to resort to arrest as a fall-back position. When the assigned treatment is arrest, there is no need for a fallback position. For example, some offenders may have refused to comply with an order to leave the premises.

This pattern could have biased estimates of the relative effectiveness of arrest by removing uncooperative and difficult offenders from mediation and separation treatments. Any deterrent effect of arrest could be underestimated and, in the extreme, arrest could be shown to increase the chance of repeat violence. In effect, the arrest group would have too many "bad guys" *relative* to the other treatments.

Fortunately, a statistical analysis of this process shows that the delivered treatments conformed very closely to the experimental design, with no problems of bias.

Things went less well with interviews of victims; only 205 (of 330, counting the few repeat victims twice) could be located and initial interviews obtained, a 62 percent completion rate. Many of the victims simply could not be found, either for the initial interview or for follow-ups. They had left town, moved somewhere else, or refused to answer the phone or doorbell. The research staff made up to 20 attempts to contact these victims and often employed investigative techniques (asking friends and neighbors) to find them. Sometimes these methods worked, only to have the victim give an outright refusal, or break one or more appointments to meet the interviewer at a "safe" location for the interview.

The response rate to the biweekly follow-up interviews was even lower than for the initial interview, as response rates have been in much research on women crime victims. After the first interview, for which the victims were paid $20, there was a gradual falloff in completed interviews with each successive wave; only 161 victims provided all 12 follow-up interviews over the six months, a completion rate of 49 percent. Whether paying for the follow-up interviews would have improved the response rate is unclear; it would have added over $40,000 to the cost of the research. When the telephone interviews yielded few reports of violence, every fourth interview was conducted in person.

Fortunately, there is absolutely no evidence that the experimental treatment assigned to the offender affected the victim's decision to grant initial interviews. Statistical tests showed there was *no* difference in victim's willingness to give interviews according to what police did, race of victim, or race of offender.

In sum, despite the practical difficulties of controlling an experiment and interviewing crime victims in an emotionally charged and violent social context, the experiment succeeded in producing a promising sample of 314 cases with complete official outcome measures and an apparent unbiased sample of responses from the victims in those cases.

Table 2
Victim and Suspect Characteristics Initial Interview Data and Police Sheets

A. Unemployment

Victims	61%
Suspects	60%

B. Relationship of Suspect to Victim

Divorced or separated husband	3%
Unmarried male lover	45%
Current husband	35%
Wife or girlfriend	2%
Son, brother, roommate, other	15%

C. Prior Assaults and Police Involvement

Victims assaulted by suspect, last six months	80%
Police intervention in domestic dispute, last six months	60%
Couple in counseling program	27%

D. Prior Arrests of Male Suspects

Ever arrested for any offense	59%
Ever arrested for crime against person	31%
Ever arrested on domestic violence statute	5%
Ever arrested on an alcohol offense	29%

E. Mean Age

Victims	30 years
Suspects	32 years

F. Education

	Victim	Suspect
< high school	43%	42%
high school only	33%	36%
> high school	24%	22%

G. Race

	Victim	Suspect
White	57%	45%
Black	23%	36%
Native-American	18%	16%
Other	2%	3%

N=205 (Those cases for which initial interviews were obtained)

Results

The 205 completed initial interviews provide some sense of who the subjects involved in domestic violence are, although the data may not properly represent the characteristics of the full sample of 314. They show the now familiar pattern that domestic violence cases coming to police attention disproportionately involve unmarried couples with lower than average educational levels, who are disproportionately minority and mixed race (black male, white female) and who are very likely to have had prior violent incidents with police intervention. The 60 percent unemployment rate for the experiment's suspects is strikingly high in a community with only about five percent of the workforce unemployed. The 59 percent prior arrest rate is also strikingly high, suggesting (with the 80 percent prior domestic assault rate) that the suspects generally are experienced law-breakers who are accustomed to police interventions. But with the exception of the heavy representation of Native-Americans due to Minneapolis' proximity to many Indian reservations, the characteristics in Table Two are probably close to those of domestic violence cases coming to police attention in other large U.S. cities.

Two kinds of measures of repeat violence were used in the experiment. One was a police record of an offender repeating domestic violence during the six-month follow-up period, either through an offense or an arrest report written by any officer in the department or through a subsequent report to the project research staff of an intervention by officers participating in the experiment. A second kind of measure came from the interviews in which the victims were asked if there had been a repeat incident with the same suspect, broadly defined to include an actual assault, threatened assault, or property damage.

The technical details of the analysis are reported in the April 1984 *American Sociological Review*. The bar graphs in Figures 1, 2 and 3 approximate equations presented in that article, which made statistical adjustments for such problems as the falloff in victim cooperation with the interviews. Figure 1 shows the results taken from the police records on subsequent violence. The arrest treatment is clearly an improvement over sending the suspect away, which produced two and a half times as many repeat incidents as arrest. The advise treatment was statistically not distinguishable from the other two police actions.

Figure 2 shows a somewhat different picture. According to the victims' reports of repeat violence, arrest is still the most effective police action. But the advise category, not sending the suspect away, produced the worst results, with almost twice as much violence as arrest. Sending the suspect away produced results that were not statistically distinguishable from the results of the other two actions. It is not clear why the order of the three levels of repeat violence is different for these two ways of measuring the violence. But it is clear that arrest works best by either measure.

Additional statistical analysis showed that these findings were basically the same for all categories of suspects. Regardless of the race, employment status, educational level, criminal history of the suspect, or how long the suspect was in jail when arrested, arrest still had the strongest violence reduction effect. There was one factor, however, that seemed to govern the effectiveness of arrest: whether the police showed interest in the victim's side of the story.

Figure 1
Percentage of Repeat Violence Over Six Months for Each Police Action

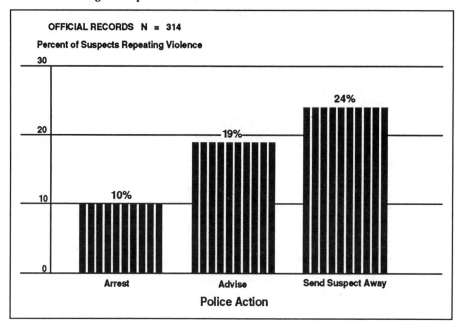

Figure 2
Percentage of Repeat Violence Over Six Months for Each Police Action

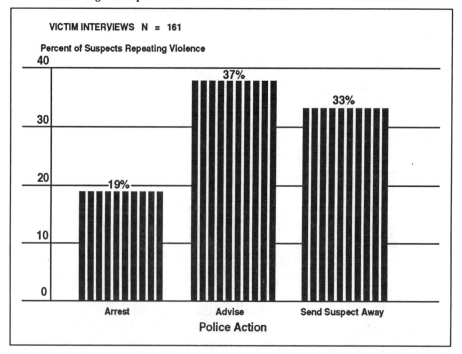

Figure 3 shows what happened to the effect of arrest on repeat violence incidents when the police do or do not take the time to listen to the victim, at least as the victim perceives it. If police do listen, that reduces the occurrence of repeat violence even more. But if the victims think the police did not take the time to listen, then the level of victim-reported violence is much higher. One interpretation of this finding is that by listening to the victim, the police "empower" her with their strength, letting the suspect know that she can influence their behavior. If police ignore the victim, the suspect may think he was arrested for arbitrary reasons unrelated to the victim and be less deterred from future violence.

Figure 3
Percentage of Repeat Violence Over Six Months for Each Police Action
and Listening to Victim

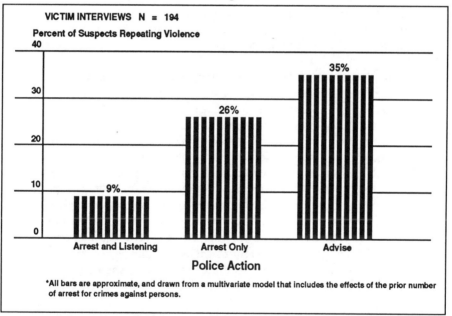

Conclusions and Policy Implications

It may be premature to conclude that arrest is always the best way for police to handle domestic violence, or that all suspects in such situations should be arrested. A number of factors suggest a cautious interpretation of the findings:

Sample Size. Because of the relatively small numbers of suspects in each subcategory (age, race, employment status, criminal history, etc.), it is possible that this experiment failed to discover that for some kinds of people, arrest may only make matters worse. Until subsequent research addresses that issue more thoroughly, it would be premature for state legislatures to pass laws requiring arrests in all misdemeanor domestic assaults.

Jail Time. Minneapolis may be unusual in keeping most suspects arrested for domestic assault in jail overnight. It is possible that arrest would not have as great a deterrent effect in other cities where suspects may be able to return home within an hour or so of arrest. On the other hand, Minneapolis seems to have the typical court response to domestic violence: only three out of 136 of the arrested suspects ever received a formal sanction from a judge.

Location. Minneapolis is unusual in other respects: a large Native-American population, a very low rate of violence, severe winters, and low unemployment rate. The cultural context of other cities may produce different effects of police actions in domestic violence cases.

Interviewer Effect. Strictly speaking, this experiment showed the effects of three police responses plus an intensive effort by middle class women to talk to victim's over a six-month follow-up. It is possible that the interviewers created a "surveillance" effect that deterred suspects. Whether the same effects would be found without the interviews is still an open question.

A replication of the experiment in a different city is necessary to address these questions. But police officers cannot wait for further research to decide how to handle the domestic violence they face each day. They must use the best information available. This experiment provides the only scientifically controlled comparison of different methods of reducing repeat violence. And on the basis of this study alone, police should probably employ arrest in most cases of minor domestic violence.

Legislative Implications. The findings clearly support the 1978 statutory reform in Minnesota that made the experiment possible. In many states the police are not able to make an arrest in domestic violence cases without the signed complaint of a victim. In at least one state (Maryland), police cannot make an arrest without a warrant issued by a magistrate. This experiment shows the vital importance of state legislatures empowering police to make probable cause arrests in cases of domestic simple assault.

Impact of the Experiment. As a result of the experiment's findings, the Minneapolis Police Department changed its policy on domestic assault in early March of 1984. The policy did not make arrest 100 percent mandatory. But it did require officers to file a written report explaining why they failed to make an arrest when it was legally possible to do so. The policy was explained to all patrol officers in a roll call videotape. The initial impact of the policy was to double the number of domestic assault arrests, from 13 the weekend before the policy took effect to 28 the first weekend after. On one day in mid-March there were 42 people in the Minneapolis jail on spouse assault charges, a record as far as local officials could remember.

The experiment apparently has done more than contributed to knowledge. It also has helped change police behavior in Minneapolis, and possibly in other cities as well. If the findings are truly generalizable, the experiment will help ultimately to reduce one of the most common forms of violent crime.

References

Bard, Morton (1970). "Training Police as Specialists in Family Crisis Intervention." U.S. Department of Justice.

Bard, Morton and Joseph Zacker (1974). "Assaultiveness and Alcohol Use in Family Disputes— Police Perceptions." Criminology 12:281-292.

Berk, Sarah Fenstermaker and Donileen R. Loseke (1981). "Handling Family Violence: Situational Determinants of Police Arrests in Domestic Disturbances." Law and Society Review 15:315-346.

Black, Donald (1980). The Manners and Customs of the Police. New York: Academic Press.

Cook, Thomas D. and Donald T. Campbell (1979). Quasi-Experimentation: Design and Analysis Issues for Field Settings. Chicago: Rand McNally.

Emerson, Charles D. (1979). "Family Violence: A Study by the Los Angeles County Sheriff's Department." Police Chief (June): 48-50.

Fagin, James A. (1978). "The Effects of Police Interpersonal Communications Skills on Conflict Resolution." Ph.D. Dissertation, Southern Illinois University. Ann Arbor: University Microfilms.

Illinois Law Enforcement Commission (1978). "Report on Technical Assistance Project—Domestic Violence Survey." (Abstract). Washington, D.C.: National Criminal Justice Reference Service.

Ketterman, Thomas and Marjorie Kravitz (1978). Police Crisis Intervention: A Selected Bibliography. Washington, D.C.: National Criminal Justice Reference Service.

Langley, Richard and Roger C. Levy (1977). Wife Beating: The Silent Crisis. New York: E.P. Dutton.

Loving, Nancy (1980). Responding to Spouse Abuse and Wife Beating: A Guide for Police. Washington, D.C.: Police Executive Research Forum.

Meyer, Jeanie Keeny and T.D. Lorimer (1977). Police Intervention Data and Domestic Violence: Exploratory Development and Validation of Prediction Models. Report prepared under grant #R01MH 27918 from National Institute of Mental Health. Kansas City, Mo., Police Department.

Office of the Minority Leader, State of New York (1978). Battered Women: Part I (Abstract). Washington, D.C.: National Criminal Justice Reference Service.

Parnas, Raymond I. (1972). "The Police Response to the Domestic Disturbance." pp. 206-236 in L. Radzinowics and M.E. Wolfgang, eds., The Criminal in the Arms of the Law. New York: Basic Books.

Police Foundation (1976). *Domestic Violence and the Police: Studies in Detroit and Kansas City.* Washington, D.C.: The Police Foundation.

Potter, Jane (1978). "The Police and the Battered Wife: The Search for Understanding." *Police Magazine* 1:40-50.

Roy, M. (ed.) (1977). *Battered Women.* New York: Van Nostrand Reinhold Co.

Sherman, Lawrence W. (1980). "Causes of Police Behavior: The Current State of Quantitative Research." *Journal of Research in Crime and Delinquency,* 17:69-100.

University of Rochester (1974). "FACIT—Family Conflict Intervention Experiment—Experimental Action Program." (Abstract). Washington, D.C.: National Criminal Justice Reference Service.

Wylie, P.B., L.F. Basinger, C.L. Heinecke and J.A. Reuckert (1976). "Approach to Evaluating a Police Program of Family Crisis Interventions in Six Demonstration Cities—Final Report." (Abstract). Washington, D.C.: National Criminal Justice Reference Service.

The success of the Minneapolis domestic violence experiment depended on the dedication and hard work of both the project staff and many police officers. The project staff: Nancy Wester, Project Manager, and Amy Curtis, Kay Gamble, Gayle Gubman, Donileen Loseke, Debra Morrow, Phyllis Newton, David Rauma, and Roy Roberts.

Minneapolis police officers taking part in the experiment:

Edward Belmore	Charles R. Howe	Stephen L. Persons
Dalyn R. Beske	James E. Howell	Thomas Peterson
Theodore J. Boran	Wayne E. Humphrey	Timothy K. Prill
Jeffrey A. Drew	George R. Jansen	Myron D. Rognlie
Perry Dunfee	Luther C. Koerner	David Rumpza
Dayton Dunn	Charles Lechelt	Michael R. Sauro
Michael J. Falkowski	David A. Lindman	Michael H. Schoeben
John T. Frazer	Carmelo Morcilio	Eugene A. Schreiber
Duane A. Frederickson	Marie Morse	Robert A. Thunder
Riley N. Gilchrist	William H. Nelson	Clinton Tucker
Manual J. Granroos	Craig Nordby	Matthew J. Vincent
Jack Hanson	Dennis Nordstrom	Thomas E. Wallick
Gregory S. Hestness	Keith L. Oldfather, Jr.	Martha Will
Philip Hogquist	James M. Palmborg	

Lawrence W. Sherman, Catherine H. Milton & Thomas V. Kelly

Team Policing

Foreword

The police administrator faces a dilemma. He is aware that corruption and the abuse of authority are constant dangers on his force, that rioting and collective violence have occurred before in his city and may occur again, and that people are frightened and want visible evidence of a massive police presence that will reduce crime. He also knows that, however much the city council may complain of rising crime rates, it is also concerned about rising tax rates and thus wants the police department run as economically as possible. For all these reasons, the police administrator is tempted to organize and operate his department along tight, quasi-military lines with strict supervision of patrol officers, a strong command structure that can deploy effectively large numbers of police in emergency situations, powerful and mobile tactical forces that can saturate areas experiencing high crime rates, and close controls over costs, scheduling, assignments, and discipline.

But he is also aware that his patrol officers exercise great discretion and thus can never be fully supervised, that much of their time is spent on noncriminal matters, that some parts of the community fear and distrust the police while other parts want closer contact with them, that massive displays of police power can sometimes exacerbate tense situations, and that quasi-military discipline can lower the morale and perhaps the effectiveness of many officers. For these reasons, he is tempted to organize his department along highly decentralized lines, with considerable discretionary authority to give patrol officers and their sergeants, great attention given to the resolution of community disputes and the provision of social services, and little use of tactical forces.

There are two reasons why the administrator regards this choice as posing a dilemma: First, he has very little evidence, other than his own hunches and the lore of his craft, which of these two models of policing

Source: Lawrence W. Sherman, Catherine H. Milton, and Thomas V. Kelly (1973). "Foreword," pp. ix-xii; "Introduction," pp. xiii-xvii; Chapter 1, "Elements of Team Policing," pp. 3-7; Chapter 5, "Obstacles to Team Policing," pp. 91-96; Chapter 7, "Summary and Conclusions," pp. 107-108. In *Team Policing: Seven Case Studies*. Washington, DC: The Police Foundation. Reprinted by permission of The Police Foundation.

is most likely to succeed, or even what "success" means. Second, being an experienced officer, he is aware that both theories of policing are correct in some measure, and thus gains from wholly adopting one will create costs from having foregone the other. For example, the military model may result in a prompt response to radio calls, but since answering all calls promptly means spending as little time as possible on any given call, an officer cannot learn much or be of much help to a citizen who calls. On the other hand, the service model will enable the officer to devote time and expertise to helping a citizen who calls but at the cost of postponing answering other calls or referring them to officers who are not as familiar with the area.

Even if the administrator could be clear in his own mind as to what he wants, he faces two important constraints on his freedom of action, one internal to the department and the other external to it. His officers, in all likelihood, will be accustomed to one way of doing things and they will see any effort to change that as a threat, not only to their habits and expectations, but to their promotion prospects, work schedules, and authority. Community groups, on the other hand, will be divided as to what they want: some neighborhoods may welcome tough, vigorous policing as a way of keeping the streets safe and the "kids in their place," while others may prefer a police force that is closely integrated with the community and perhaps even subject to its control. Indeed, it is likely that any given community will want both things at once—be tough and concerned, visible and invisible, enforcement-oriented and service-oriented.

Team policing should be seen as an effort, one of many possible, to test these competing views and form a realistic and objective assessment of what kinds of police deployment produce what results under which circumstances. This is not to say that it is merely an experiment, designed to satisfy curiosity or gather data. Rather, it is a police strategy—or more accurately, a collection of somewhat similar police strategies—which some police administrators believe may be a partial solution to the dilemma they face. In theory it combines the advantages of a substantial police presence in a neighborhood, deployed to put the maximum number of officers on the street during times of greatest need and supervised so as to encourage the maximum use of information about the area and its citizens, with the advantages of a police style devoted to servicing complaints, helping citizens, and establishing good relations.

But so far it is only a theory. It is still too early to tell whether this strategy will realize the expectations of its creators. In presenting the case studies and analysis that follows, the Police Foundation is not suggesting that team policing, in any of its many variants, is *the* answer to the police dilemma, or even that we are now in a position to know what an answer is. We believe that it is a promising approach but one that is still somewhat vague in conception, weak in execution, and uncertain in results. In time, we hope that by carefully designing and testing several different police strategies, various police departments will obtain information that can be widely disseminated as to circumstances under which one police strategy, or some combination of strategies, produces gains in crime control, citizen service, and community support. The Police Foundation is engaged in helping departments try approaches they have formulated to see what works and what does not.

It is this approach—testing and evaluating—rather than the substantive content of any given strategy that is important. Not every city, or every part of any city, may be well served by a single police strategy. Yet in the past, our police strategies were picked, or rather they emerged out of historical forces, without much systematic reflection as to how well they might help control crime, or help citizens. Indeed, until recently we did not think in terms of a police "strategy" or "style" that could be deliberately chosen. We tended instead to accept either what existed as historically foreordained or what was proposed by "leading authorities" as unquestionably correct. At one time our cities were policed by watchmen who not only walked a beat, but who managed it and the people on it with a minimum of supervision and relatively few arrests. Some cities still display the watchman style. In reaction to this, advocates of centralized control, close supervision, and maximum enforcement arose, whose textbooks and personal example created a new era of policing that was called "professionalism." Now some of the doctrines of that school are being questioned by those who believe that professionalism separated the police from the community and over-emphasized writing tickets and making arrests.

It is not the purpose of this publication to offer any new dogma to replace the dogmas of yesterday. It is rather to show how some cities went about the task of finding new solutions to the police dilemma and to offer some preliminary findings about what will happen as a result. In future publications, the Foundation will offer more systematic evidence on additional projects that are now underway.

JAMES Q. WILSON
Shattuck Professor of Government
Harvard University
Vice Chairman, Police Foundation

Introduction

The urban unrest of the 1960's made it clear that there was much dissatisfaction with government in general and the police in particular.

The kind of policing done in many communities was clearly not the kind of policing those communities wanted. Many police administrators ignored the basic issue of community differences, asking only for more money, men and equipment. But some police administrators met the crisis by reorganizing their departments to make them more responsive to the range of community needs in their cities.

Among the responses were a number of small pilot projects known by the general label of "team policing." Team policing meant something different in each city, but generally it has been an attempt to strike a new balance between the presumed efficiency needs of police centralization and community needs for police decentralization in order to be more responsive to citizens.

The term "team policing" originated in Aberdeen, Scotland immediately after World War II. The Aberdeen project began as an effort to counteract the low morale and boredom of single officers patrolling quiet streets. It allocated teams of five and ten men on foot and in cars to cover the city. The patrols were distributed according to concentration of crimes and calls for service, with the teams moved to different parts of the city as the workload demanded. The monotony and loneliness of the patrolmen were thus relieved.

A second form of team policing, called "Unit Beat Policing," appeared in the town of Accrington in the County of Coventry, England, in 1966. Its stated purpose was to overcome a shortage of manpower by effectively utilizing the existing limited resources. Under the Coventry Unit Beat Policing system, constables were organized into teams which remained in one specific area. Although the constables working in the same area did not patrol as a team, they all fed information about their area to a central collator who was responsible for the exchange of knowledge about that area. By maximizing coordination and the exchange of information through the collator, fewer men could cover a wider territory than they had previously been able to.

The Aberdeen system was abandoned in 1963 but had already been tried in Tucson, Arizona and a number of other small American cities. The Coventry form of policing is still in practice and has been expanded to other police forces in England; it is the form most prevalent in the United States and generally known as "neighborhood team policing." A third variant combines aspects of both the Aberdeen (manpower allocated according to workload) and Coventry (neighborhood-based) systems and was instituted in Richmond, California in 1968.

In 1967, the President's Commission on Law Enforcement and the Administration of Justice recommended the following:

> Police departments should commence experimentation with a team policing concept that envisions those officers with patrol and investigative duties combining under unified command with flexible assignments to deal with the crime problem in a defined sector.

By 1973 a number of American cities had experimented with team policing in one way or another. In theory, the patrol force is reorganized to include one or more quasi-autonomous teams, with a joint purpose of improving police services to the community and increasing job satisfaction of the patrol officers. Usually the team is based in a particular neighborhood. Each team has responsibility for police services in its neighborhood and is intended to work as a unit in close contact with the community to prevent crime and maintain order. In practice, team policing has not always been able to accomplish these goals, although it seems to have come very close in some cities. In others, team policing has become a label, a public relations device. In still others, there has been a measure of achievement, but it has been less than was anticipated by those who launched the project.

This study was undertaken to examine the team policing experience on a case-by-case basis and to get some preliminary indications of why team policing has worked well in some places and less well in others. Seven cities were chosen:

- two small cities—Holyoke, Massachusetts and Richmond, California

- two middle-sized cities—Dayton, Ohio and Syracuse, New York

- two large cities—Detroit, Michigan and Los Angeles, California

- one super-city—New York City.

Each case contains a brief background of the city and the department, as well as a description of that particular team program.

The case studies are not in-depth evaluations. They are reportorial accounts of the team policing experience in seven cities, with some subjective assessments made by persons on the scene. Efforts at more scientific evaluation were made in several of the cities, but since the team policing projects described were not planned and carried out under controlled experimental conditions, the opportunities for meaningful evaluation were limited. Recently in a number of cities, most notably Cincinnati, carefully planned and controlled team policing experiments have begun. By measuring pre-existing conditions and by collecting pertinent data during a period of controlled operations, these projects have the potential of producing reliable and useful evaluation results. Those experiments had not begun, however, when the authors were doing the field work for these case studies.

One of the goals of the Police Foundation is to provide better information about improvement programs developed in police departments around the country. Most police publications tell of new ideas and programs, but in a manner flattering to the creator of the programs. Discussion of the problems involved in implementing the innovation is usually avoided. Police administrators need to know the bad points as well as the good points of these programs in order to consider adopting them.

Team policing has clearly suffered from this problem of poor information exchange. Originally heralded with a great deal of favorable publicity, it has since become the subject of controversy in several parts of the country. The federal government's Law Enforcement Assistance Administration's 1970-71 Discretionary Grant Program specifically made funds available for team policing projects, and Model Cities funds have also been used to support such efforts in model city neighborhoods. Despite the favorable publicity, however, many police administrators have viewed team policing as a fad which has some merits in theory but is impossible to implement. Given the flow of both negative and positive reports, municipal government and police officials might understandably be confused as to just what team policing is all about. With objective and detailed information, however, more serious consideration of the idea could take place.

This book is intended to provide that information as a general introduction to team policing. We hope that police chiefs and planning directors, mayors, city managers, social scientists and others will use this as an aid to deciding whether team policing might be appropriate for their own communities. For those who do decide to implement neighborhood team policing, we recommend the prescriptive package published by the Law Enforcement Assistance Administration, *Neighborhood Team Policing* by Peter B. Bloch and David I. Specht. Their book is a practitioner's guide to the problems and processes of team policing. (It is available from the National Criminal Justice Reference Service, Washington, D.C. 20530.)

The first chapter of this book is an analysis of the elements of team policing. Chapter II presents descriptive case studies of team policing programs in seven different cities. The planning of team policing, the attempts to implement it, and the obstacles to its proper implementation are discussed in subsequent chapters. Chapter VI, on evaluations, suggests that well planned and controlled evaluations are difficult to achieve but that, whatever the quality of the evaluations and whatever difficulties in changing police organizations, team policing programs have had many benefits.

The data for this study was gathered over a two-year period. From February to June 1971, Lawrence Sherman (while serving as an Alfred P. Sloane Foundation New York City Urban Fellow) performed an informal monitoring of the Neighborhood Police Team program in New York City for Police Commissioner Patrick V. Murphy. During the summer of 1971, the Police Foundation sent Mr. Sherman to Detroit,

Michigan; Dayton, Ohio; Holyoke, Massachusetts; Syracuse, New York and Los Angeles, California, to review team programs. Each city was studied for two to six days, with at least 16 hours on patrol in each. Police officials at all levels were interviewed, as well as community leaders and residents, and relevant documents were reviewed.

Follow-up data was collected for the study in the fall of 1972 by Thomas Kelly, a free-lance journalist. In addition to the cities previously visited, Mr. Kelly also went to Richmond, California and studied the new Venice program in Los Angeles. Catherine Milton, Assistant Director of the Police Foundation, provided additional data on New York, Los Angeles, and Richmond.

Robert Wasserman, an administrative assistant to Chief Igleburger before the team program there was implemented and presently Director of Training and Education for the Boston Police Department, contributed additional data on the Dayton project and wrote that case study. Thomas McBride, former Police Foundation Staff Director, provided assistance throughout the research and writing and particularly contributed to the chapter on evaluations. Susan Michaelson, a consultant to the Police Foundation, provided research and editorial assistance throughout. The analysis and conceptualizations are primarily the contribution of Lawrence Sherman.

Elements of Team Policing

Police administrators in the 1960's confronted a dilemma in organizing their departments: the community wanted both more sensitive police and better crime control. Police administrators who attempted to professionalize their departments through more centralized control and motorized patrol were criticized by community leaders and riot commissions for having police who were insensitive to and isolated from the communities they were supposed to serve. Yet with rising crime rates, few police administrators could seriously consider a return to the inefficiencies of the traditional beat-cop. Team policing was one answer to this conflict of police goals and needs.

By the early 1970's team policing had become a popular idea among many police administrators. And yet, even now, no one really knows what it is, what it costs, or whether it is an improvement. This study cannot answer those questions; it can only describe what it looks like in a few cities.

Team policing is a term that has meant something different in every city in which it has been tried. But all of the team policing programs studied for this book—except Richmond—attempted to implement three basic operational elements which differ from conventional patrol concepts. These three elements are: geographic stability of patrol, maximum interaction among team members, and maximum communication among team members and the community.

1. *Geographic stability of patrol: i.e., permanent assignment of teams of police to small neighborhoods.* The geographic stability of patrol is the most basic element. The only city which did not assign its teams permanently to a neighborhood was Richmond, California. There, teams were assigned as units on staggered shifts. Each team remained on duty for eight hours, and a new team came on duty every four hours. We included Richmond in this study, however, because that city is small enough to function as a neighborhood and because the patrol officers function as team members in much the same way as those geographically-based teams, despite the assignment by time.

2. *Maximum interaction among team members, including close internal communication among all officers assigned to an area during a 24-hour period, seven days a week.* The element of encouraging interaction among team members was evident in all the team policing cities, but with considerable variation. Implicit in the concept of maximum interaction is exchange of information. One of the simplest means of accomplishing this exchange is through the scheduling of team conferences at regular intervals. Analogies may be found in the case conferences conducted by social workers or doctors, in which each professional describes several difficult cases of the previous week and opens them to discussion with his colleagues, soliciting criticism and advice. The police teams which followed a similar route with their conferences found that, in many instances, the cases were continuing problems covering more than one shift and required cooperation among several police officers. Those teams which did not have formal conferences had to rely on informal ways of communicating—a practice which was more successful when the team was stationed and thereby isolated in a separate building than when sharing a stationhouse with the regular patrol units. The other critical factor in communication was the team leader. When he encouraged sharing of information and was still able to instill a sense of teamsmanship, the members communicated more frequently and informally.

3. *Maximum communication among team members and the community.* The third element, maximum communication among team members and members of the community, seemed to be aided by regular meetings between teams and the community. These meetings were a means of emphasizing the cooperative aspects of the peacekeeping function, facilitating the flow of information, and assisting in the identification of community problems. Such conferences have been a vehicle for eliciting community involvement in the police function. Another technique, participation of community members in police work, has been

accomplished through auxiliary patrols, supply of information leading to arrests, and community voice in police policy-making. Such participation was designed to bring the police and community together in a spirit of cooperation. Finally, maximum communication among teams and the community has also been enhanced by an efficient system of referral of non-police problems (e.g., emotional problems, garbage collection, drug addiction) to appropriate service agencies. Teams that have developed their own neighborhood lists of social service units and names of social workers have made appropriate referrals far more quickly than through centralized traditional channels.

All of the cities in this study (except Richmond) attempted to achieve all three basic operational elements. The departments which were most successful in implementing these elements also had in common certain organizational supports: unity of supervision, lower-level flexibility in policy-making, unified delivery of services, and combined investigative and patrol functions.

1. *Unity of supervision.* Different supervisors controlling an area during the course of a day can create inconsistent police policies and approaches to community problems. It may be difficult, for example, for a group of young boys to understand why one police officer allows them to play baseball in the street between 8:00 a.m. and 4:00 p.m. while another forbids ball-playing from 4:00 p.m. to midnight. In order to maintain coherent and consistent police performance, then, it is preferable that one supervisor be responsible for a given area at all times and that his orders be obeyed. Unity of supervision is also useful for the effective performance of the officers as a team. If a team member has more than one supervisor giving him conflicting orders, he may determine that team policy-making is a myth and that the whole team concept is a hoax.

2. *Lower-level flexibility in policy-making.* Interaction among team members is most productive when the team has the flexibility to carry out its own operational decisions. Indeed, the very rationale for the sharing of information among team members is that they will use their increased knowledge to decide upon better strategies for the delivery of police services to their neighborhood. For example, decisions about mode of dress and duty schedules have been traditionally reserved for higher-ups, but several departments pushed those decisions down to the team level where information about neighborhood needs was most accurate.

The police administrators who advocated increased authority at lower levels of the hierarchy considered it a means of increasing responsibility and accountability of patrol officers. Former New York City Police Commissioner Patrick Murphy, for example, tried to loosen the strict rules governing behavior at all ranks in order to discourage "buck-passing" up the ranks. Supervisors at the precinct level were held accountable for the performance of patrol officers in their precincts, team leaders for their team members, team officers for themselves.

3. *Unified delivery of services.* Some departments extended the concept of team decision-making to complete control over the delivery of all police services in the team neighborhood. This included the team's power to decide when specialized police units were needed or when they would be disruptive. This concept was also designed to make the best use of local community knowledge developed by the officers who patrol an area every day. It does not deny the value of the local police generalist to decide when they are needed.

4. *Combined investigative and patrol functions.* In the absence of information supplied by the community, apprehension of a criminal is difficult. As a part of a larger unified delivery of services, team programs should seek to combine patrol and investigative functions, for the intuitive judgments required for effective investigations are enhanced by familiarity with the life of the community. As Egon Bittner has observed:

> To give circumstantial factors their correct weight in decision making it is necessary that they be intelligently appraised. That is, patrolmen must be able to draw on background information to be able to discern what particular constellations of facts and factors mean. In the case of the carefully deliberate policeman—by which is meant a man who organizes his activities with a view towards long-range peacekeeping and crime control objectives in the area of his patrol, knowing that what he does from case to case can create more or less calculable advantages or liabilities for himself in the future—the background information consists of an enormously detailed factual knowledge.[1]

When one considers that crimes of violence are usually committed by people known to the victim, it becomes clear that a knowledge of the human relationships in a community is of immeasurable value in solving crimes. It is instructive, though, that Bittner had to note the "case of the carefully deliberate policeman" as an exception to the rule. The cultivation of area knowledge has not been something for which the patrol officer has been rewarded in the United States. By contrast, an essential element in the English Unit Beat scheme is the "collator," the central receiver of daily area reports; each officer is evaluated partly according to how much quality information he feeds the collator.

The seven case studies that follow will describe the team policing programs in each city and the contexts in which they developed. Each will also discuss the three basic operational elements and four organizational supports of team policing in each city.

---

[1] Egon Bittner, *The Functions of the Police in Modern Society* (National Institute of Mental Health, November 1970), p. 90.

SUMMARY OF ELEMENTS
(The following summarizes the elements of team policing in each city.)

Operational Elements	Dayton	Detroit	New York	Syracuse	Holyoke	Los Angeles (Venice)	Richmond
Stable geographic assignment	+	+	−	+	+	+	•
Intra-team interaction	−	+	−	−	+	+	+
Formal team conferences	−	+	−	−	+	+	+
Police-community communication	+	+	−	−	+	+	•
Formal community conferences	+	•	•	−	+	+	•
Community participation in police work	+	+	+	•	+	+	•
Systematic referrals to social agencies	+	−	−	•	•	•	+
Organizational Supports							
Unity of Supervision	+	+	−	+	+	+	+
Lower-level flexibility	−	−	−	+	+	+	+
Unified delivery of services	+	−	−	+	+	+	•
Combined patrol and investigative functions	+	+	•	+	+	+	+

Key:
+   the element was planned and realized
−   the element was planned but not realized
•   the element was not planned

Obstacles to Team Policing

In addition to the inevitable influence of individual leaders, police department organization contributed three major obstacles to team policing: middle management, trial by peers, and dispatchers.

Middle Management

Team policing, as a method of decentralization, was designed to give more decision-making power to lower levels of the police organization. By fiat from the top, it gave powers to the bottom (patrol officers and sergeants) that had traditionally been reserved for the middle (lieutenants, captains, etc.). Thus team policing was a form of decentralization which gave less power to mid-management than it had under centralization. As a result, middle management often impeded their administrators' goals for team policing.

One way in which middle management limited the success of team policing was by failing, as precinct or division commanders, to deal with conflicts and problems arising out of team policing programs under their command. Conflicts frequently developed between team leaders and officers of the next higher rank—a problem apparently endemic to the team policing concept. It surfaced in England almost immediately, where despite the role definitions of inspectors as strategists and sergeants as tacticians, one Home Office study found that both ranks were confused and dissatisfied about their new roles. Detroit and New York had similar conflicts between lieutenants and sergeants that the precinct commanders simply ignored.

Another, more direct way in which middle management sometimes thwarted the goals of team policing was by simple bad-mouthing: sending out the word through informal channels of communication that this crazy team idea was a hoax. Precinct commanders were also able to undercut the operational freedom of the team leader. By limiting or discouraging the team leader's initiative on day-to-day issues, middle management could effectively defeat the program's goal of innovative team response to local conditions.

A third form of resistance by middle management was a frank expression to top management of disagreement about team policing issues. A Detroit precinct commander complained to the police commissioner that by implication the Beat Commander system criticized the precinct commander's performance, implying that his position was insufficient to insure adequate police service. In his frustration he exclaimed, "The people who wrote the guidelines for this thing didn't read the rules and regulations." The view that the rules and regulations are sacred and unchangeable subverts not only team policing, but any change at all.

Middle-management opposition is not unavoidable, however. If middle management is brought into the planning process for decentralization, it is entirely possible that its cooperation and support for the new system will be won. Although the commander of the first precinct in a city to try the team concept was usually involved in its planning (Detroit, New York, Los Angeles), most of the middle managers who would be affected by the program were not asked for their views, nor were they told about the program before its public announcement. But a participative and consensual form of planning with all middle management can cultivate their support for plans which might otherwise be resisted.

Most team programs have been perceived as giving more power to the bottom at the expense of the middle, a perception which has been the basis for middle management's opposition. It is possible, however, for the power of each level to be expanded simultaneously with benefits for the entire organization. A goal of team policing is to expand the effectiveness of the police in the community: talking to more people, establishing more positive and informal relationships, apprehending more criminals, and providing more and better service. This expanded role requires a new structure: the followers (patrol officers and sergeants) must do more leading of themselves, and the leaders (middle management) must lead in new and different ways. Mid-managers must analyze the new influx of information, plan for better manpower utilization in light of that information, and obtain more resources to support the expanded role of their officers—for example, arranging liaison with social service agencies, traffic and sanitation departments, and other city agencies. If their function is viewed more as support than as control, middle management can gain power under team policing rather than lose it.

Trial by Peers

Middle management was not the only obstacle to team policing. In most of the cities studied, the larger patrol force—those not involved in the team project—objected to team policing. The opposition was strongest when the project split a precinct or division. The first pilot teams formed new elites. The patrol officers had learned to accept the old elite forces (e.g., detectives), but they were not eager to accept new ones. The fact that the usefulness of the teams was necessarily unproven left them vulnerable to attack. Also, to outside patrol officers, the community aspects of team policing smacked of appeasement of hostile minorities.

There was also jealousy, in many instances stemming from the fact that the patrol officers first heard about the program through the news media—after the personnel had already been chosen. Not all patrol officers would have volunteered, but many would have liked to have had the chance to decide not to. When one is shut out of a newly-formed club, the natural response is to attack the club—and certain aspects of team programs were "clubby" and, superficially at least, elitist. The first Crime Control Teams in Syracuse wore white shirts while the rest of the patrol force wore blue, which prompted sarcastic remarks such as "the good guys wear white shirts." In New York, the Neighborhood Police Team in the 17th Precinct (midtown) was exempted from consulate guard duty, a detested detail. The apparent over-allocation of manpower to NPT areas (even though justified by workload figures) produced the charge from other precinct patrol officers that they had all the hard work. Detroit's Beat Command invited resentment by flaunting their accomplishment of reducing the average time required to complete radio runs from 40 minutes to 27. The freedom of team police officers in some cities produced irritation. In Syracuse, for example, the CCT was freed from roll calls. In New York, the orders establishing the Neighborhood Police Teams suspended portions of the Rules and Procedures manual—one that had been frequently violated in the field, anyway—to legitimize such things as chatting with neighborhood people and driving sick cases to the hospital. The overtime pay available to the Holyoke team was greatly resented by other patrol officers of the poorly paid department.

Given all of these irritations, one might except the outside patrol officers' field cooperation to be affected. With the exception of Holyoke (where the team had virtually seceded from the rest of the department), this did not happen. The team members were always backed up by non-team cars. None of the physical acts that too often characterize racial or religious animosity in police departments (vandalizing lockers, insulting graffiti, and even fights) occurred between team officers and the regular patrols. Instead, the opposition was evidenced by strong vocal criticism and political maneuvers to keep the team idea from spreading.

Dispatchers

Another non-team group, the radio dispatchers, greatly hampered team policing, often without intent. The dispatcher is under constant pressure, and he is not particularly concerned with neighborhood or team boundaries He must be converted to the primary assumption that the new neighborhood team should stay in its neighborhood. Teams frequently could not; New York teams often spent half their time outside their neighborhoods. When the team members found the neighborhood was a myth, many concluded that the team project was a hoax.

Sociologist Albert Reiss has made an observation on the Chicago Police Department's dispatching system, which should be applicable to other large cities:

> In Chicago in 1966, we observe that fewer than one-third of all criminal incidents were handled by beat cars in their own beat . . . . Many police administrators regard a patrolman's intelligence on a community to be of most importance in non-criminal matters, where an officer must exercise the greatest degree of discretion. However, despite this, officers in Chicago handled an even smaller proportion of all non-criminal incidents, arising from dispatches to their own beat, than criminal incidents . . . . Beat cars handled only one-third of all incidents, and one-fifth of all criminal incidents arising on their own beats.
>
> Based on these Chicago data, it appears conclusive that beat cars, whether dispatched or on routine preventive patrol, are more likely to handle incidents outside their own area than within it . . . . This problem may actually be due to the

fact that beat cars are dispatched to handle incidents outside their beat. Once a car is dispatched to handle a call outside its beat, the probability of its handling outside calls increases, since, while that car is in service, any call to its beat must be assigned to car from a neighboring beat. Calls to that beat in turn must be handled by a neighboring area. The problem of such chain effects is a familiar one in systems analysis.[22]

Today's radio systems give little latitude for the kind of screening which once occurred when calls came in at the precinct switchboard and the sergeant held the less important calls or threw out the ones from known neighborhood cranks. Computerized dispatch systems such as New York's SPRINT treat almost all calls as serious, and the widespread use of the "911" police telephone number has increased the volume enormously.

The Los Angeles Basic Car Plan attempted to cope with the dispatching problem. The "A" Basic Cars worked with "X" support cars on the heavy duty, 8:00 a.m. to 4:00 p.m. and 4:00 p.m. to midnight watches. The Basic Cars were to remain in their beats, while the X cars crossed boundaries. In practice, the distinction between A and X was often without substance. Dispatchers frequently assigned either, without regard for beats.

In Detroit, the Beat Command cars were out of their neighborhoods as much as a third of the time. Only after great pressure was placed on the dispatchers from the top did the percentage drop to 10-15%. The Detroit dispatchers were bitter about the pressure. They said the Beat Command car was often the closest car to the call, but they were forbidden to send it. In the end, the Detroit dispatchers gave the Beat Command cars no outside calls of any nature. They treated the two-sector area as an entirely separate precinct and sent cars from miles away to an emergency scene immediately adjoining the Beat Command boundaries even when the BC car was available. Obviously, city-wide application of this principle would be disastrous, turning the city into hundreds of non-cooperating police departments.

But the dispatchers are not the villains. Consider a huge roomful of clacking printers and blaring loudspeakers on a hot summer night with calls backlogged for two hours. Each dispatcher has 30 to 70 sector cars to dispatch. If an available car happens to be labelled team, he will assign that car to the necessary job regardless. Indeed, the pressure grows so intense that in one city on an especially busy evening, a captain tried to prod a dispatcher into faster clearing of calls; the dispatcher, in response, stood up, vomited, threw his shield to the floor, gave his captain an obscene gesture, announced that he was reporting sick, and walked away.

---

[22] Albert Reiss, *The Police and the Public* (New Haven: Yale University Press, 1971), pp. 98-99.

There were reasons why team cars were often the most frequently available. The size of a team may be determined by computation of precinct manpower to area workload. The logic of the method, however, had only one weakness: it was never used for the other sectors of the precinct. The result of making workload calculations for one area but not the others could result (and did) in the assignment of more officers to the team area and a decrease in the number in other areas. It was difficult to persuade others that team policing would make better use of available manpower when the apparent result was to double the manpower assigned to the team area while reducing it everywhere else. The second reason that the team cars in Detroit and New York were frequently available was that the number of team men on duty was (sometimes) related to time workload while the number of non-team men on duty was not. Teams which assigned the most officers during peak hours were unrushed while the rest of the precinct was backlogged with calls. Non-team officers concluded erroneously that the teams were not doing their share of the work.

The dispatching difficulty is not insurmountable, and it is not universal. There is relatively little boundary difficulty in Holyoke or Venice (LA). In the dispatching issue, small cities or self-contained units like Venice have a clear advantage—the pressure is less and the boundaries are easier to maintain.

Summary and Conclusions

On the basis of the team programs discussed in this report, it would be tempting to conclude that team policing had certain consequences for crime, community relations, and police morale and productivity. The data are far too scant, however, to make such conclusions final. More important is the question many readers will have: should we try team policing in our police department? Most important is the question: how can we decide whether team policing makes sense?

Team policing was conceived as a means to an end—a decentralized professional patrol style. In none of the cities studied has that end yet been achieved. The many problems and obstacles experienced by team policing projects merely demonstrate the depth of the change they attempt, which cannot realistically succeed overnight. In all the team policing cities, there were three major reasons that team policing either failed or reached only partial success. These were:

1. Mid-management of the departments, seeing team policing as a threat to their power, subverted and, in some cases, actively sabotaged the plans.

2. The dispatching technology did not permit the patrols to remain in their neighborhoods, despite the stated intentions of adjusting that technology to the pilot projects.

3. The patrols never received a sufficiently clear definition of how their behavior and role should differ from that of a regular patrol; at the same time, they were considered an elite group by their peers who often resented not having been chosen for the project.

Even if team policing can be implemented as conceived, it is still unclear what effects it may have. To the extent that team policing makes police more responsive to community demands, it might put the police in a crossfire of conflicting goals. On one hand, a decentralized professional model of policing is conceived by many police administrators as a means of making the police "nice guys": polite, observant of citizen's constitutional rights, sensitive to the management of conflict, and honest. On the other hand, the community may make strong demands for the police to be "tough guys" in order to clean up crime, in ways that, if not illegal, are in contradiction to the model conceived by police administrators. For example, data from the evaluation of the New York City program shows that some teams increased the use of aggressive tactics, specifically illegal stop-and-frisks.[26] Early data from the Cincinnati evaluation tentatively suggests the same trend.[27]

There is at present a great concern among police forces and in American cities at large to consider change, to make police officers more responsive to the community. This concern has surfaced in many projects in addition to those labelled "team policing."[28] Whether a specific community should adopt team policing, however, depends first on that community's goals, and second on that community's judgment of team policing's effectiveness within its own situation. Most of all, it depends on both the commitment and the available resources to manage a complex process of institutional and community change.

---

[26] Peter B. Bloch and David I. Specht, *Evaluation Report on Operation Neighborhood* (Washington, D.C.: The Urban Institute, 1972).

[27] Joseph H. Lewis, Director of Evaluation, Police Foundation, personal communication, August 3, 1973.

[28] Efforts to reestablish foot patrol (the pinpoint patrol program in Kansas City) or bicycle patrol (in Baltimore, New York City, and Isla Vista, California) reflect the need on the part of both community and police for more personal contact between the two groups. The Urban Group in the New Orleans Police Department, the Beat Committees in Dallas, and the Pilot District Project in Washington all attempt to improve community relations.

Herman Goldstein

Improving Policing:
A Problem-Oriented Approach*

The police have been particularly susceptible to the "means over ends" syndrome, placing more emphasis in their improvement efforts on organization and operating methods than on the substantive outcome of their work. This condition has been fed by the professional movement within the police field, with its concentration on the staffing, management, and organization of police agencies. More and more persons are questioning the widely held assumption that improvements in the internal management of police departments will enable the police to deal more effectively with the problems they are called upon to handle. If the police are to realize a greater return on the investment made in improving their operations, and if they are to mature as a profession, they must concern themselves more directly with the end product of their efforts.

Meeting this need requires that the police develop a more systematic process for examining and addressing the problems that the public expects them to handle. It requires identifying these problems in more precise terms, researching each problem, documenting the nature of the current police response, assessing its adequacy and the adequacy of existing authority and resources, engaging in a broad exploration of alternatives to present responses, weighing the merits of these alternatives, and choosing from among them.

Improvements in staffing, organization, and management remain important, but they should be achieved—and may, in fact, be more achievable—within the context of a more direct concern with the outcome of policing.

Source: Herman Goldstein (1979). "Improving Policing: A Problem-Oriented Approach," *Crime and Delinquency,* 25:236-258. Reprinted by permission of Sage Publications, Inc.

*The author is indebted to the University of Wisconsin Extension Department of Law for making the time available to produce this article as part of a larger effort to reexamine the university's role in research and training for the police.

> Complaints from passengers wishing to use the Bagnall to
> Greenfields bus service that "the drivers were speeding past
> queues of up to 30 people with a smile and a wave of a hand"
> have been met by a statement pointing out that it is impossible
> for the drivers to keep their timetable if they have to stop for
> passengers."[1]

All bureaucracies risk becoming so preoccupied with running their
organization and getting so involved in their methods of operating that
they lose sight of the primary purposes for which they were created.
The police seem unusually susceptible to this phenomenon.

One of the most popular new developments in policing is the use of
officers as decoys to apprehend offenders in high-crime areas. A speaker at a recent conference for police administrators, when asked to summarize new developments in the field, reported on a sixteen-week
experiment in his agency with the use of decoys, aimed at reducing
street robberies.

One major value of the project, the speaker claimed, was its contribution to the police department's public image. Apparently, the public
was intrigued by the clever, seductive character of the project, especially
by the widely publicized demonstrations of the makeup artists' ability
to disguise burly officers. The speaker also claimed that the project
greatly increased the morale of the personnel working in the unit. The
officers found the assignment exciting and challenging, a welcome
change from the tedious routine that characterizes so much of regular
police work, and they developed a high esprit de corps.

The effect on robberies, however, was much less clear. The methodology used and the problems in measuring crime apparently prevented
the project staff from reaching any firm conclusions. But it was reported that, of the 216 persons arrested by the unit for robbery during the
experiment, more than half would not have committed a robbery, in the
judgment of the unit members, if they had not been tempted by the situation presented by the police decoys. Thus, while the total impact of the
project remains unclear, it can be said with certainty that the experiment actually increased the number of robberies by over 100 in the six-
teen weeks of the experiment.

The account of this particular decoy project (others have claimed
greater success) is an especially poignant reminder of just how serious
an imbalance there is within the police field between the interest in
organizational and procedural matters and the concern for the substance of policing. The assumption, of course, is that the two are related, that improvements in internal management will eventually increase
the capacity of the police to meet the objectives for which police agen-

---

[1] Newspaper report from the Midlands of England, cited in Patrick Ryan, "Get Rid of the People,
and the System Runs Fine," *Smithsonian*, September 1977, p. 140.

cies are created. But the relationship is not that clear and direct and is increasingly being questioned.

Perhaps the best example of such questioning relates to response time. Tremendous resources were invested during the past decade in personnel, vehicles, communications equipment, and new procedures in order to increase the speed with which the police respond to calls for assistance. Much less attention was given in this same period to what the officer does in handling the variety of problems he confronts on arriving, albeit fast, where he is summoned. Now, ironically, even the value of a quick response is being questioned.[2]

This article summarizes the nature of the "means over ends" syndrome in policing and explores ways of focusing greater attention on the results of policing—on the effect that police efforts have on the problems that the police are expected to handle.

The "Means Over Ends" Syndrome

Until the late 1960s, efforts to improve policing in this country concentrated almost exclusively on internal management: streamlining the organization, upgrading personnel, modernizing equipment, and establishing more businesslike operating procedures. All of the major commentators on the police since the beginning of the century—Leonhard F. Fuld (1909), Raymond B. Fosdick (1915), August Vollmer (1936), Bruce Smith (1940), and O.W. Wilson (1950)—stressed the need to improve the organization and management of police agencies. Indeed, the emphasis on internal management was so strong that professional policing was defined primarily as the application of modern management concepts to the running of a police department.

The sharp increase in the demands made on the police in the late 1960s (increased crime, civil rights demonstrations, and political protest) led to several national assessments of the state of policing.[3] The published findings contained some criticism of the professional model of police organization, primarily because of its impersonal character

---

[2] The recent study in Kansas City found that the effect of response time on the capacity of the police to deal with crime was negligible, primarily because delays by citizens in reporting crimes make the minutes saved by the police insignificant. See Kansas City, Missouri, Police Department, *Response Time Analysis,* Executive Summary (Kansas City, 1977).

[3] See President's Commission on Law Enforcement and Administration of Justice, *The Challenge of Crime in a Free Society* (Washington, D.C.: Govt. Printing Office, 1967); National Advisory Commission on Civil Disorders, *Report of the National Advisory Commission on Civil Disorders* (Washington, D.C.: Govt. Printing Office, 1968); National Commission on the Causes and Prevention of Violence, *To Establish Justice, to Insure Domestic Tranquility,* Final Report (Washington, D.C.: Govt. Printing Office, 1969); President's Commission on Campus Unrest, *Report of the President's Commission on Campus Unrest* (Washington, D.C.: Govt. Printing Office, 1970); and National Advisory Commission on Criminal Justice Standards and Goals, *Police* (Washington, D.C.: Govt. Printing Office, 1973).

and failure to respond to legitimate pressures from within the community.[4] Many recommendations were made for introducing a greater concern for the human factors in policing, but the vast majority of the recommendations that emerged from the reassessments demonstrated a continuing belief that the way to improve the police was to improve the organization. Higher recruitment standards, college education for police personnel, reassignment and reallocation of personnel, additional training, and greater mobility were proposed. Thus the management-dominated concept of police reform spread and gained greater stature.

The emphasis on secondary goals—on improving the organization—continues to this day, reflected in the prevailing interests of police administrators, in the factors considered in the selection of police chiefs and the promotion of subordinates, in the subject matter of police periodicals and texts, in the content of recently developed educational programs for the police, and even in the focus of major research projects.

At one time this emphasis was appropriate. When Vollmer, Smith, and Wilson formulated their prescriptions for improved policing, the state of the vast majority of police agencies was chaotic: Personnel were disorganized, poorly equipped, poorly trained, inefficient, lacking accountability, and often corrupt. The first priority was putting the police house in order. Otherwise, the endless crises that are produced by an organization out of control would be totally consuming. Without a minimum level of order and accountability, an agency cannot be redirected—however committed its administrators may be to addressing more substantive matters.

What is troubling is that administrators of those agencies that have succeeded in developing a high level of operating efficiency have not gone on to concern themselves with the end results of their efforts—with the actual impact that their streamlined organizations have on the problems the police are called upon to handle.

The police seem to have reached a plateau at which the highest objective to which they aspire is administrative competence. And, with some scattered exceptions, they seem reluctant to move beyond this plateau—toward creating a more systematic concern for the end product of their efforts. But strong pressures generated by several new developments may now force them to do so.

1. The Financial Crisis

The growing cost of police services and the financial plight of most city governments, especially those under threat of Proposition 13 movements, are making municipal officials increasingly reluctant to appro-

---

[4] *See,* for example, National Advisory Commission on Civil Disorders, *Report,* p. 155.

priate still more money for police service without greater assurance that their investment will have an impact on the problems that the police are expected to handle. Those cities that are already reducing their budgets are being forced to make some of the hard choices that must be made in weighing the impact of such cuts on the nature of the service rendered to the public.

2. Research Findings

Recently completed research questions the value of two major aspects of police operations—preventive patrol and investigations conducted by detectives.[5] Some police administrators have challenged the findings;[6] others are awaiting the results of replication.[7] But those who concur with the results have begun to search for alternatives, aware of the need to measure the effectiveness of a new response before making a substantial investment in it.

3. Growth of a Consumer Orientation

Policing has not yet felt the full impact of consumer advocacy. As citizens press for improvement in police service, improvement will increasingly be measured in terms of results. Those concerned about battered wives, for example, could not care less whether the police who respond to such calls operate with one or two officers in a car, whether the officers are short or tall, or whether they have a college education. Their attention is on what the police do for the battered wife.

---

[5] George L. Kelling et al., *The Kansas City Preventive Patrol Experiment: A Summary Report* (Washington, D.C.: Police Foundation, 1974); and Peter W. Greenwood et al., *The Criminal Investigation Process*, 3 vols. (Santa Monica, Calif.: Rand Corporation, 1976).

[6] For questioning by a police administrator of the findings of the Kansas City Preventive Patrol Project, see Edward M. Davis and Lyle Knowles, "A Critique of the Report: An Evaluation of the Kansas City Preventive Patrol Experiment," *Police Chief*, June 1975, pp. 22-27. For a review of the Rand study on detectives, see Daryl F. Gates and Lyle Knowles, "An Evaluation of the Rand Corporation's Analysis of the Criminal Investigation Process," *Police Chief*, July 1976, p. 20. Each of the two papers is followed by a response from the authors of the original studies. In addition, for the position of the International Association of Chiefs of Police on the results of the Kansas City project, see "IACP Position Paper on the Kansas City Preventive Patrol Experiment," *Police Chief*, September 1975. p. 16.

[7] The National Institute of Law Enforcement and Criminal Justice is sponsoring a replication of the Kansas City Preventive Patrol Experiment and is supporting further explorations of the criminal investigation process. See National Institute of Law Enforcement and Criminal Justice, *Program Plan, Fiscal Year 1978* (Washington, D.C.: Govt. Printing Office, 1977), p. 12.

4. Questioning the Effectiveness of the Best-Managed Agencies

A number of police departments have carried out most, if not all, of the numerous recommendations for strengthening a police organization and enjoy a national reputation for their efficiency, their high standards of personnel selection and training, and their application of modern technology to their operations. Nevertheless, their communities apparently continue to have the same problems as do others with less advanced police agencies.[8]

5. Increased Resistance to Organizational Change

Intended improvements that are primarily in the form of organizational change, such as team policing, almost invariably run into resistance from rank-and-file personnel. Stronger and more militant unions have engaged some police administrators in bitter and prolonged fights over such changes.[9] Because the costs in terms of disruption and discontent are so great, police administrators initiating change will be under increasing pressure to demonstrate in advance that the results of their efforts will make the struggle worthwhile.

Against this background, the exceptions to the dominant concern with the police organization and its personnel take on greater significance. Although scattered and quite modest, a number of projects and training programs carried out in recent years have focused on a single problem that the public expects the police to handle, such as child abuse, sexual assault, arson, or the drunk driver.[10] These projects and programs, by their very nature, subordinate the customary priorities of police reform, such as staffing, management, and equipment, to a concern about a specific problem and the police response to it.

Some of the earliest support for this type of effort was reflected in the crime-specific projects funded by the Law Enforcement Assistance Administration.[11] Communities—not just the police—were encouraged

---

[8] Admittedly precise appraisals and comparisons are difficult. For a recent example of an examination by the press of one department that has enjoyed a reputation for good management, see "The LAPD: How Good Is It?" *Los Angeles Times*, Dec. 15, 1977.

[9] Examples of cities in which police unions recently have fought vigorously to oppose innovations introduced by police administrators are Boston, Massachusetts, and Troy, New York.

[10] These programs are reflected in the training opportunities routinely listed in such publications as *Police Chief, Criminal Law Reporter, Law Enforcement News,* and *Crime Control Digest,* and by the abstracting service of the National Criminal Justice Reference Center.

[11] See, for example, National Institute of Law Enforcement and Criminal Justice, Law Enforcement Assistance Administration, "Planning Guidelines and Program to Reduce Crime," mimeographed (Washington, D.C., 1972), pp. vi-xiii. For a discussion of the concept, see Paul K. Wormeli and Steve E. Kolodney, "The Crime-Specific Model: A New Criminal Justice Perspective," *Journal of Research in Crime and Delinquency,* January 1972, pp. 54-65.

to direct their attention to a specific type of crime and to make those changes in existing operations that were deemed necessary to reduce its incidence. The widespread move to fashion a more effective police response to domestic disturbances is probably the best example of a major reform that has, as its principal objective, improvement in the quality of service delivered, and that calls for changes in organization, staffing, and training only as these are necessary to achieve the primary goal.

Are these scattered efforts a harbinger of things to come? Are they a natural development in the steadily evolving search for ways to improve police operations? Or are they, like the programs dealing with sexual assault and child abuse, simply the result of the sudden availability of funds because of intensified citizen concern about a specific problem? Whatever their origin, those projects that do subordinate administrative considerations to the task of improving police effectiveness in dealing with a specific problem have a refreshing quality to them.

What is the End Product of Policing?

To urge a more direct focus on the primary objectives of a police agency requires spelling out these objectives more clearly. But this is no easy task, given the conglomeration of unrelated, ill-defined, and often inseparable jobs that the police are expected to handle.

The task is complicated further because so many people believe that the job of the police is, first and foremost, to enforce the law: to regulate conduct by applying the criminal law of the jurisdiction. One commentator on the police recently claimed: "We do not say to the police: 'Here is the problem. Deal with it.' We say: 'Here is a detailed code. Enforce it.'"[12] In reality, the police job is perhaps most accurately described as dealing with problems.[13] Moreover, enforcing the criminal code is itself only a means to an end—one of several that the police employ in getting their job done.[14] The emphasis on law enforcement, therefore, is nothing more than a continuing preoccupation with means.

Considerable effort has been invested in recent years in attempting to define the police function: inventorying the wide range of police

---

[12] Ronald J. Allen, "The Police and Substantive Rulemaking: Reconciling Principle and Expediency," *University of Pennsylvania Law Review,* November 1976, p. 97.

[13] Egon Bittner comes close to this point of view when he describes police functioning as applying immediate solutions to an endless array of problems. See Egon Bittner, "Florence Nightingale in Pursuit of Willie Sutton," in *The Potential for Reform of Criminal Justice,* Herbert Jacob, ed. (Beverly Hills, Calif.: Sage, 1974), p. 30. James Q. Wilson does also when he describes policing as handling situations. See James Q. Wilson, *Varieties of Police Behavior: The Management of Law and Order in Eight Communities* (Cambridge, Mass.: Harvard University Press, 1968), p. 31.

[14] I develop this point in an earlier work. See Herman Goldstein, *Policing a Free Society* (Cambridge, Mass.: Ballinger, 1977), pp. 30, 34-35.

responsibilities, categorizing various aspects of policing, and identify-ing some of the characteristics common to all police tasks.[15] This work will be of great value in refocusing attention on the end product of policing, but the fact that it is still going on is not cause to delay giving greater attention to substantive matters. It is sufficient, for our purposes here, simply to acknowledge that the police job requires that they deal with a wide range of behavioral and social problems that arise in a community—that the end product of policing consists of dealing with these *problems*.

By problems, I mean the incredibly broad range of troublesome sit-uations that prompt citizens to turn to the police, such as street rob-beries, residential burglaries, battered wives, vandalism, speeding cars, runaway children, accidents, acts of terrorism, even fear. These and other similar problems are the essence of police work. They are the rea-son for having a police agency.

Problems of this nature are to be distinguished from those that fre-quently occupy police administrators, such as lack of manpower, inade-quate supervision, inadequate training, or strained relations with police unions. They differ from those most often identified by operating per-sonnel, such as lack of adequate equipment, frustrations in the prosecu-tion of criminal cases, or inequities in working conditions. And they dif-fer, too, from the problems that have occupied those advocating police reform, such as the multiplicity of police agencies, the lack of lateral entry, and the absence of effective controls over police conduct.

Many of the problems coming to the attention of the police become their responsibility because no other means has been found to solve them. They are the residual problems of society. It follows that expecting the police to solve or eliminate them is expecting too much. It is more realistic to aim at reducing their volume, preventing repetition, alleviat-ing suffering, and minimizing the other adverse effects they produce.

Developing the Overall Process

To address the substantive problems of the police requires develop-ing a commitment to a more systematic process for inquiring into these problems. Initially, this calls for identifying in precise terms the prob-lems that citizens look to the police to handle. Once identified, each problem must be explored in great detail. What do we know about the problem? Has it been researched? If so, with what results? What more should we know? Is it a proper concern of government? What authority and resources are available for dealing with it? What is the current police response? In the broadest-ranging search for solutions, what

---

[15] In the 1977 book I presented a brief summary of these studies. Ibid., pp. 26-28.

would constitute the most intelligent response? What factors should be considered in choosing from among alternatives? If a new response is adopted, how does one go about evaluating its effectiveness? And finally, what changes, if any, does implementation of a more effective response require in the police organization?

This type of inquiry is not foreign to the police. Many departments conduct rigorous studies of administrative and operational problems. A police agency may undertake a detailed study of the relative merits of adopting one of several different types of uniforms. And it may regularly develop military-like plans for handling special events that require the assignment of large numbers of personnel.[16] However, systematic analysis and planning have rarely been applied to the specific behavioral and social problems that constitute the agency's routine business. The situation is somewhat like that of a private industry that studies the speed of its assembly line, the productivity of its employees, and the nature of its public relations program, but does not examine the quality of its product.

Perhaps the closest police agencies have come to developing a system for addressing substantive problems has been their work in crime analysis. Police routinely analyze information on reported crimes to identify patterns of criminal conduct, with the goal of enabling operating personnel to apprehend specific offenders or develop strategies to prevent similar offenses from occurring. Some police departments have, through the use of computers, developed sophisticated programs to analyze reported crimes.[17] Unfortunately, these analyses are almost always put to very limited use—to apprehend a professional car thief or to deter a well-known cat burglar—rather than serving as a basis for rethinking the overall police response to the problem of car theft or cat burglaries. Nevertheless, the practice of planning operational responses based on an analysis of hard data, now a familiar concept to the police, is a helpful point of reference in advocating development of more broadly based research and planning.

The most significant effort to use a problem orientation for improving police responses was embodied in the crime-specific concept initiated in California in 1971[18] and later promoted with LEAA funds throughout the country. The concept was made an integral part of the anticrime program launched in eight cities in January 1972, aimed at bringing about reductions in five crime categories: murder, rape,

---

[16] For an up-to-date description of the concept of planning and research as it has evolved in police agencies, see O.W. Wilson and Roy C. McLaren, *Police Administration,* 4th ed. (New York: McGraw-Hill, 1977), pp. 157-181.

[17] For examples, see National Institute of Law Enforcement and Criminal Justice, *Police Crime Analysis Unit Handbook* (Washington, D.C.: Govt. Printing Office, 1973), pp. 90-92, 113-121.

[18] For a brief description, see Joanne W. Rockwell, "Crime Specific . . . An Answer?" *Police Chief,* September 1972, p. 38.

assault, robbery, and burglary.[19] This would have provided an excellent opportunity to develop and test the concept, were it not for the commitment that this politically motivated program carried to achieving fast and dramatic results: a 5 percent reduction in each category in two years and a 20 percent reduction in five years. These rather naive, unrealistic goals and the emphasis on quantifying the results placed a heavy shadow over the program from the outset. With the eventual abandonment of the projects, the crime-specific concept seems to have lost ground as well. However, the national evaluation of the program makes it clear that progress was made, despite the various pressures, in planning a community's approach to the five general crime categories. The "crime-oriented planning, implementation and evaluation" process employed in all eight cities had many of the elements one would want to include in a problem-oriented approach to improving police service. [20]

Defining Problems with Greater Specificity

The importance of defining problems more precisely becomes apparent when one reflects on the long-standing practice of using overly broad categories to describe police business. Attacking police problems under a categorical heading—"crime" or "disorder," "delinquency," or even "violence"—is bound to be futile. While police business is often further subdivided by means of the labels tied to the criminal code, such as robbery, burglary, and theft, these are not adequate, for several reasons.

First, they frequently mask diverse forms of behavior. Thus, for example, incidents classified under "arson" might include fires set by teenagers as a form of vandalism, fires set by persons suffering severe psychological problems, fires set for the purpose of destroying evidence of a crime, fires set by persons (or their hired agents) to collect insurance, and fires set by organized criminal interests to intimidate. Each type of incident poses a radically different problem for the police.

Second, if police depend heavily on categories of criminal offenses to define problems of concern to them, others may be misled to believe that, if a given form of behavior is not criminal, it is of no concern to the police. This is perhaps best reflected in the proposals for decriminalizing prostitution, gambling, narcotic use, vagrancy, and public intoxication. The argument, made over and over again, is that removing the criminal label will reduce the magnitude and complexity of the police function, freeing personnel to work on more serious matters and ridding the police of some of the negative side effects, such as corruption,

---

[19] The program is described in Eleanor Chelimsky, *High Impact Anti-Crime Program, Final Report,* vol. 2 (Washington, D.C.: Govt. Printing Office, 1976), pp. 19-38.
[20] Ibid., pp. 145-50, 418-21.

that these problems produce. But decriminalization does not relieve the police of responsibility. The public expects drunks to be picked up if only because they find their presence on the street annoying or because they feel that the government has an obligation to care for persons who cannot care for themselves. The public expects prostitutes who solicit openly on the streets to be stopped, because such conduct is offensive to innocent passersby, blocks pedestrian or motor traffic, and contributes to the deterioration of a neighborhood. The problem is a problem for the police whether or not it is defined as a criminal offense.

Finally, use of offense categories as descriptive of police problems implies that the police role is restricted to arresting and prosecuting offenders. In fact, the police job is much broader, extending, in the case of burglary, to encouraging citizens to lock their premises more securely, to eliminating some of the conditions that might attract potential burglars, to counseling burglary victims on ways they can avoid similar attacks in the future, and to recovering and returning burglarized property.

Until recently, the police role in regard to the crime of rape was perceived primarily as responding quickly when a report of a rape was received, determining whether a rape had really occurred (given current legal definitions), and then attempting to identify and apprehend the perpetrator. Today, the police role has been radically redefined to include teaching women how to avoid attack, organizing transit programs to provide safe movement in areas where there is a high risk of attack, dealing with the full range of sexual assault not previously covered by the narrowly drawn rape statutes, and—perhaps most important—providing needed care and support to the rape victim to minimize the physical and mental damage resulting from such an attack. Police are now concerned with sexual assault not simply because they have a direct role in the arrest and prosecution of violators, but also because sexual assault is a community problem which the police and others can affect in a variety of ways.

It seems desirable, at least initially in the development of a problem-solving approach to improved policing, to press for as detailed a breakdown of problems as possible. In addition to distinguishing different forms of behavior and the apparent motivation, as in the case of incidents commonly grouped under the heading of "arson," it is helpful to be much more precise regarding locale and time of day, the type of people involved, and the type of people victimized. Different combinations of these variables may present different problems, posing different policy questions and calling for radically different solutions.[21]

---

[21] For an excellent example of what is needed, see the typology of vandalism developed by the British sociologist, Stanley Cohen, quoted in Albert M. Williams, Jr., "Vandalism," *Management Information Service Report* (Washington, D.C.: International City Management Association, May 1976), pp 1-2. Another excellent example of an effort to break down a problem of concern to the police—in this case, heroin—is found in Mark Harrison Moore, *Buy and Bust: The Effective Regulation of an Illicit Market in Heroin* (Lexington, Mass.: Lexington Books, 1977), p. 8.3.

For example, most police agencies already separate the problem of purse snatching in which force is used from the various other forms of conduct commonly grouped under robbery. But an agency is likely to find it much more helpful to go further—to pinpoint, for example, the problem of teenagers snatching the purses of elderly women waiting for buses in the downtown section of the city during the hours of early darkness. Likewise, a police agency might find it helpful to isolate the robberies of grocery stores that are open all night and are typically staffed by a lone attendant; or the theft of vehicles by a highly organized group engaged in the business of transporting them for sale in another jurisdiction; or the problem posed by teenagers who gather around hamburger stands each evening to the annoyance of neighbors, customers, and management. Eventually, similar problems calling for similar responses may be grouped together, but one cannot be certain that they are similar until they have been analyzed.

In the analysis of a given problem, one may find, for example, that the concern of the citizenry is primarily fear of attack, but the fear is not warranted, given the pattern of actual offenses. Where this situation becomes apparent, the police have two quite different problems: to deal more effectively with the actual incidents where they occur, and to respond to the groundless fears. Each calls for a different response.

The importance of subdividing problems was dramatically illustrated by the recent experience of the New York City Police Department in its effort to deal more constructively with domestic disturbances. An experimental program, in which police were trained to use mediation techniques, was undertaken with obvious public support. But, in applying the mediation techniques, the department apparently failed to distinguish sufficiently those cases in which wives were repeatedly subject to physical abuse. The aggravated nature of the latter cases resulted in a suit against the department in which the plaintiffs argued that the police are mandated to enforce the law when *any* violation comes to their attention. In the settlement, the department agreed that its personnel would not attempt to reconcile the parties or to mediate when a felony was committed.[22] However, the net effect of the suit is likely to be more far reaching. The vulnerability of the department to criticism for not having dealt more aggressively with the aggravated cases has

---

[22] See Bruno v. Codd, 90 Misc. 2d 1047, 396 N.Y.5.2d 974 (1977), finding a cause of action against the New York City Police Department for failing to protect battered wives. On June 26, 1978, the city agreed to a settlement with the plaintiffs in which it committed the police to arrest in all cases in which "there is reasonable cause to believe that a husband has committed a felony against his wife and/or has violated an Order of Protection or Temporary Order of Protection." See Consent Decree. Bruno against McGuire, New York State Supreme Court, index #21946/76. (Recognizing the consent decree, the New York Appellate Court, First Department, in July of 1978 [#3020] dismissed an appeal in the case as moot in so far as it involved the police department. From a reading of the court's reversal as to the other parts of the case, however, it appears that it would also have reversed the decision of the lower court in sustaining the action against the police department if there had not been a consent decree.)

dampened support—in New York and elsewhere—for the use of alternatives to arrest in less serious cases, even though alternatives still appear to represent the more intelligent response.

One of the major values in subdividing police business is that it gives visibility to some problems which have traditionally been given short shrift, but which warrant more careful attention. The seemingly minor problem of noise, for example, is typically buried in the mass of police business lumped together under such headings as "complaints," "miscellaneous," "noncriminal incidents," or "disturbances." Both police officers and unaffected citizens would most likely be inclined to rank it at the bottom in any list of problems. Yet the number of complaints about noise is high in many communities—in fact, noise is probably among the most common problems brought by the public to the police.[23] While some of those complaining may be petty or unreasonable, many are seriously aggrieved and justified in their appeal for relief: Sleep is lost, schedules are disrupted, mental and emotional problems are aggravated. Apartments may become uninhabitable. The elderly woman living alone, whose life has been made miserable by inconsiderate neighbors, is not easily convinced that the daily intrusion into her life of their noise is any less serious than other forms of intrusion. For this person, and for many like her, improved policing would mean a more effective response to the problem of the noise created by her neighbors.

Researching the Problem

Without a tradition for viewing in sufficiently discrete terms the various problems making up the police job, gathering even the most basic information about a specific problem—such as complaints about noise—can be extremely difficult.

First, the magnitude of the problem and the various forms in which it surfaces must be established. One is inclined to turn initially to police reports for such information. But overgeneralization in categorizing incidents, the impossibility of separating some problems, variations in the reporting practices of the community, and inadequacies in report writing seriously limit their value for purposes of obtaining a full picture of the problem. However, if used cautiously, some of the information in police files may be helpful. Police agencies routinely collect and store large amounts of data, even though they may not use them to evaluate the effectiveness of their responses. Moreover, if needed information is not available, often it can be collected expeditiously in a well-

---

[23] It was reported that, on a recent three-day holiday weekend in Madison, Wisconsin, police handled slightly more than 1,000 calls, of which 118 were for loud parties and other types of noise disturbances. See "Over 1,000 Calls Made to Police on Weekend," *Wisconsin State Journal* (Madison, Wisc.: June 1, 1978).

managed department, owing to the high degree of centralized control of field operations.

How does one discover the nature of the current police response? Administrators and their immediate subordinates are not a good source. Quite naturally, they have a desire to provide an answer that reflects well on the agency, is consistent with legal requirements, and meets the formal expectations of both the public and other agencies that might have a responsibility relating to the problem. But even if these concerns did not color their answers, top administrators are often so far removed from street operations, in both distance and time, that they would have great difficulty describing current responses accurately.

Inquiry, then, must focus on the operating level. But mere questioning of line officers is not likely to be any more productive. We know from the various efforts to document police activity in the field that there is often tremendous variation in the way in which different officers respond to the same type of incident.[24] Yet the high value placed on uniformity and on adhering to formal requirements and the pressures from peers inhibit officers from candidly discussing the manner in which they respond to the multitude of problems they handle—especially if the inquiry comes from outside the agency. But one cannot afford to give up at this point, for the individualized practices of police officers and the vast amount of knowledge they acquire about the situations they handle, taken together, are an extremely rich resource that is too often overlooked by those concerned about improving the quality of police services. Serious research into the problems police handle requires observing police officers over a period of time. This means accompanying them as they perform their regular assignments and cultivating the kind of relationship that enables them to talk candidly about the way in which they handle specific aspects of their job.

The differences in the way in which police respond, even in dealing with relatively simple matters, may be significant. When a runaway child is reported, one officer may limit himself to obtaining the basic facts. Another officer, sensing as much of a responsibility for dealing with the parents' fears as for finding the child and looking out for the child's interests, may endeavor to relieve the parents' anxiety by providing information about the runaway problem and about what they might expect. From the standpoint of the consumers—in this case, the parents—the response of the second officer is vastly superior to that of the first.

---

[24] See, for example, the detailed accounts of police functioning in Minneapolis, in Joseph M. Livermore, "Policing," *Minnesota Law Review*, March 1971, pp. 649-729. Among the works describing the police officers' varying styles in responding to similar situations are Wilson, *Varieties of Police Behavior*; Albert J. Reiss, Jr., *The Police and the Public* (New Haven, Conn.: Yale University Press, 1971); Jerome H. Skolnick, *Justice without Trial: Law Enforcement in Democratic Society* (New York: John Wiley, 1966); and Egon Bittner, *The Functions of the Police in Modern Society: A Review of Background Factors, Current Practices, and Possible Role Models* (Washington, D.C.: Govt. Printing Office, 1970).

In handling more complicated matters, the need to improvise has prompted some officers to develop what appear to be unusually effective ways of dealing with specific problems. Many officers develop a unique understanding of problems that frequently come to their attention, learning to make important distinctions among different forms of the same problem and becoming familiar with the many complicating factors that are often present. And they develop a feel for what, under the circumstances, constitute the most effective responses. After careful evaluation, these types of responses might profitably be adopted as standard for an entire police agency. If the knowledge of officers at the operating level were more readily available, it might be useful to those responsible for drafting crime-related legislation. Many of the difficulties in implementing recent changes in statutes relating to sexual assault, public drunkenness, drunk driving, and child abuse could have been avoided had police expertise been tapped.

By way of example, if a police agency were to decide to explore the problem of noise, the following questions might be asked. What is the magnitude of the problem as reflected by the number of complaints received? What is the source of the complaints: industry, traffic, groups of people gathered outdoors, or neighbors? How do noise complaints from residents break down between private dwellings and apartment houses? How often are the police summoned to the same location? How often are other forms of misconduct, such as fights, attributable to conflicts over noise? What is the responsibility of a landlord or an apartment house manager regarding noise complaints? What do the police now do in responding to such complaints? How much of the police procedure has been thought through and formalized? What is the authority of the police in such situations? Is it directly applicable or must they lean on somewhat nebulous authority, such as threatening to arrest for disorderly conduct or for failure to obey a lawful order, if the parties fail to quiet down? What works in police practice and what does not work? Are specific officers recognized as more capable of handling such complaints? If so, what makes them more effective? Do factors outside the control of a police agency influence the frequency with which complaints are received? Are noise complaints from apartment dwellers related to the manner in which the buildings are constructed? And what influence, if any, does the relative effectiveness of the police in handling noise complaints have on the complaining citizen's willingness to cooperate with the police in dealing with other problems, including criminal conduct traditionally defined as much more serious?

Considerable knowledge about some of the problems with which the police struggle has been generated outside police agencies by criminologists, sociologists, psychologists, and psychiatrists. But as has been pointed out frequently, relatively few of these findings have influenced the formal policies and operating decisions of practitioners.[25] Admittedly, the quality of many such studies is poor. Often the practitioner finds it difficult to draw out from the research its significance for his operations. But most important, the police have not needed to employ these studies because they have not been expected to address specific problems in a systematic manner. If the police were pressured to examine in great detail the problems they are expected to handle, a review of the literature would become routine. If convinced that research findings had practical value, police administrators would develop into more sophisticated users of such research; their responsible criticism could, in turn, contribute to upgrading the quality and usefulness of future research efforts.

Exploring Alternatives

After the information assembled about a specific problem is analyzed, a fresh, uninhibited search should be made for alternative responses that might be an improvement over what is currently being done. The nature of such a search will differ from past efforts in that, presumably, the problem itself will be better defined and understood, the commitment to past approaches (such as focusing primarily on the identification and prosecution of offenders) will be shelved temporarily, and the search will be much broader, extending well beyond the present or future potential of just the police.

But caution is in order. Those intent on improving the operations of the criminal justice system (by divesting it of some of its current burdens) and those who are principally occupied with improving the operating efficiency of police agencies frequently recommend that the problem simply be shifted to some other agency of government or to the private sector. Such recommendations often glibly imply that a health department or a social work agency, for example, is better equipped to handle the problem. Experience over the past decade, however, shows that this is rarely the case.[26] Merely shifting responsibility for the problem, without some assurance that more adequate provisions have been made for dealing with it, achieves nothing.

Police in many jurisdictions, in a commendable effort to employ alternatives to the criminal justice system, have arranged to make refer-

---

[25] See, for example, the comments of Marvin Wolfgang in a Congressionally sponsored discussion of federal support for criminal justice research, reported in the U.S. House, Committee on the Judiciary, Subcommittee on Crime, *New Directions for Federal Involvement in Crime Control* (Washington, D.C.: Govt. Printing Office, 1977). Wolfgang claims that research in criminology and criminal justice has had little impact on the administration of justice or on major decision makers.

[26] For further discussion of this point, see American Bar Association, *The Urban Police Function*, Approved Draft (Chicago: American Bar Association, 1978), pp. 41-42.

rals to various social, health, and legal agencies. By tying into the services provided by the whole range of other helping agencies in the community, the police in these cities have taken a giant step toward improving the quality of their response. But there is a great danger that referral will come to be an end in itself, that the police and others advocating the use of such a system will not concern themselves adequately with the consequences of referral. If referral does not lead to reducing the citizens' problem, nothing will have been gained by this change. It may even cause harm: Expectations that are raised and not fulfilled may lead to further frustration; the original problem may, as a consequence, be compounded; and the resulting bitterness about government services may feed the tensions that develop in urban areas.

The search for alternatives obviously need not start from scratch. There is much to build on. Crime prevention efforts of some police agencies and experiments with developing alternatives to the criminal justice system and with diverting cases from the system should be reassessed for their impact on specific problems; those that appear to have the greatest potential should be developed and promoted.[27] Several alternatives should be explored for each problem.

1. Physical and Technical Changes

Can the problem be reduced or eliminated through physical or technical changes? Some refer to this as part of a program of "reducing opportunities" or "target hardening." Extensive effort has already gone into reducing, through urban design, factors that contribute to behavior requiring police attention.[28] Improved locks on homes and cars, the requirement of exact fares on buses,[29] and the provision for mailing social security checks directly to the recipients' banks exemplify recent efforts to control crime through this alternative.

What additional physical or technical changes might be made that would have an effect on the problem? Should such changes be mandatory, or can they be voluntary? What incentives might be offered to encourage their implementation?

---

[27] Many of these programs are summarized in David E. Aaronson et al., *The New Justice: Alternatives to Conventional Criminal Adjudication* (Washington, D.C.: Govt. Printing Office, 1977); and David E. Aaronson et al., *Alternatives to Conventional Criminal Adjudication: Guidebook for Planners and Practitioners,* Caroline S. Cooper, ed. (Washington, D.C.: Govt. Printing Office, 1977).

[28] The leading work on the subject is Oscar Newman, *Defensible Space: Crime Prevention through Urban Design* (New York: Macmillan, 1972). See also Westinghouse National Issues Center, *Crime Prevention through Environmental Design—A Special Report* (Washington, D.C.: National League of Cities, 1977),

[29] For a summary of a survey designed to assess the effect of this change, see Russell Grindle and Thomas Aceituno, "Innovations in Robbery Control," in *The Prevention and Control of Robbery,* vol. 1, Floyd Feeney and Adrianne Weir, eds. (Davis, Calif.: University of California. 1973), pp. 315-20.

2. Changes in the Provision of Government Services

Can the problem be alleviated by changes in other government services? Some of the most petty but annoying problems the police must handle originate in the policies, operating practices, and inadequacies of other public agencies: the scattering of garbage because of delays in collection, poor housing conditions because of lax code enforcement, the interference with traffic by children playing because they have not been provided with adequate playground facilities, the uncapping of hydrants on hot summer nights because available pools are closed. Most police agencies long ago developed procedures for relaying reports on such conditions to the appropriate government service. But relatively few police agencies see their role as pressing for changes in policies and operations that would eliminate the recurrence of the same problems. Yet the police are the only people who see and who must become responsible for the collective negative consequences of current policies.

3. Conveying Reliable Information

What many people want, when they turn to the police with their problems, is simply reliable information.[30] The tenant who is locked out by his landlord for failure to pay the rent wants to know his rights to his property. The car owner whose license plates are lost or stolen wants to know what reporting obligations he has, how he goes about replacing the plates, and whether he can drive his car in the meantime. The person who suspects his neighbors of abusing their child wants to know whether he is warranted in reporting the matter to the police. And the person who receives a series of obscene telephone calls wants to know what can be done about them. Even if citizens do not ask specific questions, the best response the police can make to many requests for help is to provide accurate, concise information.

4. Developing New Skills among Police Officers

The greatest potential for improvement in the handling of some problems is in providing police officers with new forms of specialized training. This is illustrated by several recent developments. For example, the major component in the family-crisis intervention projects

---

[30] In one of the most recent of a growing number of studies of how police spend their time, it was reported that, of the 18,012 calls made to the police serving a community of 24,000 people in a four-month period; 59.98 percent were requests for information. Police responded to 65 percent of the calls they received by providing information by telephone. See 1. Robert Lilly, "What Are the Police Now Doing?" *Journal of Police Science and Administration*, January 1978, p. 56.

launched all over the country is instruction of police officers in the peculiar skills required to de-escalate highly emotional family quarrels. First aid training for police is being expanded, consistent with the current trend toward greater use of paramedics. One unpleasant task faced by the police, seldom noted by outsiders, is notifying families of the death of a family member. Often, this problem is handled poorly. In 1976, a film was made specifically to demonstrate how police should carry out this responsibility.[31] Against this background of recent developments, one should ask whether specialized training can bring about needed improvement in the handling of each specific problem.

5. New Forms of Authority

Do the police need a specific, limited form of authority which they do not now have? If the most intelligent response to a problem, such as a person causing a disturbance in a bar, is to order the person to leave, should the police be authorized to issue such an order, or should they be compelled to arrest the individual in order to stop the disturbance? The same question can be asked about the estranged husband who has returned to his wife's apartment or about the group of teenagers annoying passersby at a street corner. Police are called upon to resolve these common problems, but their authority is questionable unless the behavior constitutes a criminal offense. And even then, it may not be desirable to prosecute the offender. Another type of problem is presented by the intoxicated person who is not sufficiently incapacitated to warrant being taken into protective custody, but who apparently intends to drive his car. Should a police officer have the authority to prevent the person from driving by temporarily confiscating the car keys or, as a last resort, by taking him into protective custody? Or must the officer wait for the individual to get behind the wheel and actually attempt to drive and then make an arrest? Limited specific authority may enable the police to deal more directly and intelligently with a number of comparable situations.

6. Developing New Community Resources

Analysis of a problem may lead to the conclusion that assistance is needed from another government agency. But often the problem is not clearly within the province of an existing agency, or the agency may be unaware of the problem or, if aware, without the resources to do anything about it. In such cases, since the problem is likely to be of little

---

[31] *Death Notification* (New York: Harper & Row, 1976).

concern to the community as a whole, it will probably remain the responsibility of the police, unless they themselves take the initiative, as a sort of community ombudsman, in getting others to address it.

A substantial percentage of all police business involves dealing with persons suffering from mental illness. In the most acute cases, where the individual may cause immediate harm to himself or others, the police are usually authorized to initiate an emergency commitment. Many other cases that do not warrant hospitalization nevertheless require some form of attention: The number of these situations has increased dramatically as the mental health system has begun treating more and more of its patients in the community. If the conduct of these persons, who are being taught to cope with the world around them, creates problems for others or exceeds community tolerance, should they be referred back to a mental health agency? Or, because they are being encouraged to adjust to the reality of the community, should they be arrested if their behavior constitutes a criminal offense? How are the police to distinguish between those who have never received any assistance, and who should therefore be referred to a mental health agency, and those who are in community treatment? Should a community agency establish services for these persons comparable to the crisis-intervention services now offered by specially organized units operating in some communities?

Such crisis-intervention units are among a number of new resources that have been established in the past few years for dealing with several long-neglected problems: detoxification centers for those incapacitated by alcohol, shelters and counseling for runaways, shelters for battered wives, and support services for the victims of sexual assault. Programs are now being designed to provide a better response to citizen disputes and grievances, another long neglected problem. Variously labeled, these programs set up quasi-judicial forums that are intended to be inexpensive, easily accessible, and geared to the specific needs of their neighborhoods. LEAA has recently funded three such experimental programs, which they call Neighborhood Justice Centers.[32] These centers will receive many of their cases from the police.

Thus, the pattern of creating new services that bear a relationship with police operations is now well established, and one would expect that problem-oriented policing will lead to more services in greater variety.

---

[32] The concept is described in Daniel McGillis and Joan Mullen, *Neighborhood Justice Centers: An Analysis of Potential Models* (Washington, D.C.: Govt. Printing Office, 1977). See also R. F. Conner and R. Suretta, *The Citizen Dispute Settlement Program: Resolving Disputes outside the Courts—Orlando, Florida* (Washington, D.C.: American Bar Association, 1977).

7. Increased Regulation

Can the problem be handled through a tightening of regulatory codes? Where easy access to private premises is a factor, should city building codes be amended to require improved lock systems? To reduce the noise problem, should more soundproofing be required in construction? The incidence of shoplifting is determined, in part, by the number of salespeople employed, the manner in which merchandise is displayed, and the use made of various anti-shoplifting devices. Should the police be expected to combat shoplifting without regard to the merchandising practices by a given merchant, or should merchants be required by a "merchandising code" to meet some minimum standards before they can turn to the police for assistance?

8. Increased Use of City Ordinances

Does the problem call for some community sanction less drastic than a criminal sanction? Many small communities process through their local courts, as ordinance violations, as many cases of minor misconduct as possible. Of course, this requires that the community have written ordinances, usually patterned after the state statutes, that define such misconduct. Several factors make this form of processing desirable for certain offenses: It is less formal than criminal action; physical detention is not necessary; cases may be disposed of without a court appearance; the judge may select from a wide range of alternative penalties; and the offender is spared the burden of a criminal record. Some jurisdictions now use a system of civil forfeitures in proceeding against persons found to be in possession of marijuana, though the legal status of the procedure is unclear in those states whose statutes define possession as criminal and call for a more severe fine or for imprisonment.

9. Use of Zoning

Much policing involves resolving disputes between those who have competing interests in the use made of a given sidewalk, street, park, or neighborhood. Bigger and more basic conflicts in land use were resolved long ago by zoning, a concept that is now firmly established. Recently, zoning has been used by a number of cities to limit the pornography stores and adult movie houses in a given area. And at least one city has experimented with the opposite approach, creating an adult entertainment zone with the hope of curtailing the spread of such establishments and simplifying the management of attendant problems. Much more experimentation is needed before any judgment can be made as to the value of zoning in such situations.

Implementing the Process

A fully developed process for systematically addressing the problems that make up police business would call for more than the three steps just explored—defining the problem, researching it, and exploring alternatives. I have focused on these three because describing them may be the most effective way of communicating the nature of a problem-oriented approach to improving police service. A number of intervening steps are required to fill out the processes: methods for evaluating the effectiveness of current responses, procedures for choosing from among available alternatives, means of involving the community in the decision making, procedures for obtaining the approval of the municipal officials to whom the police are formally accountable, methods for obtaining any additional funding that may be necessary, adjustments in the organization and staffing of the agency that may be required to implement an agreed-upon change, and methods for evaluating the effectiveness of the change.

How does a police agency make the shift to problem-oriented policing? Ideally, the initiative will come from police administrators. What is needed is not a single decision implementing a specific program or a single memorandum announcing a unique way of running the organization. The concept represents a new way of looking at the process of improving police functioning. It is a way of thinking about the police and their function that, carried out over an extended period, would be reflected in all that the administrator does: in the relationship with personnel, in the priorities he sets in his own work schedule, in what he focuses on in addressing community groups, in the choice of training curriculums, and in the questions raised with local and state legislators. Once introduced, this orientation would affect subordinates, gradually filter through the rest of the organization, and reach other administrators and agencies as well.

An administrator's success will depend heavily, in particular, on the use made of planning staff, for systematic analysis of substantive problems requires developing a capacity within the organization to collect and analyze data and to conduct evaluations of the effectiveness of police operations. Police planners (now employed in significant numbers) will have to move beyond their traditional concern with operating procedures into what might best be characterized as "product research."

The police administrator who focuses on the substance of policing should be able to count on support from others in key positions in the police field. Colleges with programs especially designed for police personnel may exert considerable leadership through their choice of offerings and through the subject matter of individual courses. In an occupation in which so much deference is paid to the value of a college education, if college instructors reinforce the impression that purely administrative matters are the most important issues in policing, police personnel understandably will not develop their interests beyond this concern.

Likewise, the LEAA, its state and local offspring, and other grant-making organizations have a unique opportunity to draw the attention of operating personnel to the importance of addressing substantive problems. The manner in which these organizations invest their funds sends a strong message to the police about what is thought to be worthwhile.

Effect on the Organization

In the context of this reordering of police priorities, efforts to improve the staffing, management, and procedures of police agencies must continue.

Those who have been strongly committed to improving policing through better administration and organization may be disturbed by any move to subordinate their interests to a broader concern with the end product of policing. However, a problem-oriented approach to police improvement may actually contribute in several important ways to achieving their objectives.

The approach calls for the police to take greater initiative in attempting to deal with problems rather than resign themselves to living with them. It calls for tapping police expertise. It calls for the police to be more aggressive partners with other public agencies. These changes, which would place the police in a much more positive light in the community, would also contribute significantly to improving the working environment within a police agency—an environment that suffers much from the tendency of the police to assume responsibility for problems which are unsolvable or ignored by others. And an improved working environment increases, in turn, the potential for recruiting and keeping qualified personnel and for bringing about needed organizational change.

Focusing on problems, because it is a practical and concrete approach, is attractive to both citizens and the police. By contrast, some of the most frequent proposals for improving police operations, because they do not produce immediate and specifically identifiable results, have no such attraction. A problem-oriented approach, with its greater appeal, has the potential for becoming a vehicle through which long-sought organizational change might be more effectively and more rapidly achieved.

Administrative rule making, for example, has gained considerable support from policy makers and some police administrators as a way of structuring police discretion, with the expectation that applying the concept would improve the quality of the decisions made by the police in the field. Yet many police administrators regard administrative rule making as an idea without practical significance. By contrast, police administrators are usually enthusiastic if invited to explore the problem of car theft or vandalism. And within such exploration, there is the opportunity to demonstrate the value of structuring police discretion in responding to reports of vandalism and car theft. Approached from this practical point of view, the concept of administrative rule making is more likely to be implemented.

Long-advocated changes in the structure and operations of police agencies have been achieved because of a concentrated concern with a given problem: The focus on the domestic disturbance, originally in New York and now elsewhere, introduced the generalist-specialist concept that has enabled many police agencies to make more effective use of their personnel; the problem in controlling narcotics and the high mobility of drug sellers motivated police agencies in many metropolitan areas to pool their resources in special investigative units, thereby achieving in a limited way one of the objectives of those who have urged consolidation of police agencies; and the recent interest in the crime of rape has resulted in widespread backing for the establishment of victim-support programs. Probably the support for any of these changes could not have been generated without the problem-oriented context in which they have been advocated.

An important factor contributing to these successes is that a problem-oriented approach to improvement is less likely to be seen as a direct challenge to the police establishment and the prevailing police value system. As a consequence, rank-and-file personnel do not resist and subvert the resulting changes. Traditional programs to improve the police—labeled as efforts to "change," "upgrade," or "reform" the police or to "achieve minimum standards"—require that police officers openly acknowledge their own deficiencies. Rank-and-file officers are much more likely to support an innovation that is cast in the form of a new response to an old problem—a problem with which they have struggled for many years and which they would like to see handled more effectively. It may be that addressing the quality of the police product will turn out to be the most effective way of achieving the objectives that have for so long been the goal of police reform.

Robert Trojanowicz & Bonnie Bucqueroux

The Ten Principles
of Community Policing

The following is a basic definition of Community Policing:

Community Policing is a new philosophy of policing, based on the concept that police officers and private citizens working together in creative ways can help solve contemporary community problems related to crime, fear of crime, social and physical disorder, and neighborhood decay. The philosophy is predicated on the belief that achieving these goals requires that police departments develop a new relationship with the law-abiding people in the community, allowing them a greater voice in setting local police priorities and involving them in efforts to improve the overall quality of life in their neighborhoods. It shifts the focus of police work from handling random calls to solving community problems.

The Community Policing philosophy is expressed in a new organizational strategy that allows police departments to put theory into practice. This requires freeing some patrol officers from the isolation of the patrol car and the incessant demands of the police radio, so that these officers can maintain direct, face-to-face contact with people in the same defined geographic (beat) area every day. This new Community Policing Officer (CPO) serves as a generalist, an officer whose mission includes developing imaginative, new ways to address the broad spectrum of community concerns embraced by the Community Policing philosophy. The goal is to allow CPOs to *own* their beat areas, so that they can develop the rapport and trust that is vital in encouraging people to become involved in efforts to address the problems in their neighborhoods. The CPO acts as the police department's outreach to the community, serving as the people's link to other public and private agencies that can help. The CPO not only enforces the law, but supports and supervises community-based efforts aimed at local concerns. The CPO allows people

Source: Robert Trojanowicz and Bonnie Bucqueroux (1990). "The Ten Principles of Community Policing," pp. xiii-xv, "What It Is," pp. 5-6. In *Community Policing: A Contemporary Perspective.* Cincinnati, OH: Anderson Publishing Co. Reprinted by permission of the publisher.

direct input in setting day-to-day, local police priorities, in exchange for their cooperation and participation in efforts to police themselves.

Community Policing requires both a philosophical shift in the way that police departments think about their mission, as well as a commitment to the structural changes this new form of policing demands. Community Policing provides a new way for the police to provide decentralized and personalized police service that offers every law-abiding citizen an opportunity to become active in the police process.

The Ten Principles of Community Policing

1. Community Policing is both a philosophy and an organizational strategy that allows the police and community residents to work closely together in new ways to solve the problems of crime, fear of crime, physical and social disorder, and neighborhood decay. The philosophy rests on the belief that law-abiding people in the community deserve input into the police process, in exchange for their participation and support. It also rests on the belief that solutions to contemporary community problems demand freeing both people and the police to explore creative, new ways to address neighborhood concerns beyond a narrow focus on individual crime incidents.

2. Community Policing's organizational strategy first demands that everyone in the department, including both civilian and sworn personnel, must investigate ways to translate the philosophy into practice. This demands making the subtle but sophisticated shift so that everyone in the department understands the need to focus on solving community problems in creative, new ways that can include challenging and enlisting people in the process of policing themselves. Community Policing also implies a shift within the department that grants greater autonomy to line officers, which implies enhanced respect for their judgment as police professionals.

3. To implement true Community Policing, police departments must also create and develop a new breed of line officer, the Community Policing Officer (CPO), who acts as the direct link between the police and people in the community. As the department's community outreach specialists, CPOs must be freed from the isolation of the patrol car and the demands of the police radio, so that they can maintain daily, direct, face-to-face contact with the people they serve in a clearly defined beat area.

4. The CPO's broad role demands continuous, sustained contact with the law-abiding people in the community, so that together they can explore creative new solutions to local concerns involving crime, fear of crime, disorder, and decay, with private citizens serving as unpaid volunteers. As full-fledged law enforcement officers, CPOs respond to calls

for service and make arrests, but they also go beyond this narrow focus to develop and monitor broad-based, long-term initiatives that can involve community residents in efforts to improve the overall quality of life in the area over time. As the community's ombudsman, CPOs also link individuals and groups in the community to the public and private agencies that offer help.

5. Community Policing implies a new contract between the police and the citizens it serves, one that offers the hope of overcoming widespread apathy, at the same time it restrains any impulse to vigilantism. This new relationship, based on mutual trust, also suggests that the police serve as a catalyst, challenging people to accept their share of the responsibility for solving their own individual problems, as well as their share of the responsibility for the overall quality of life in the community. The shift to Community Policing also means a slower response time for non-emergency calls and that citizens themselves will be asked to handle more of their minor concerns, but in exchange this will free the department to work with people on developing long-term solutions for pressing community concerns.

6. Community Policing adds a vital proactive element to the traditional reactive role of the police, resulting in full-spectrum police service. As the only agency of social control open 24 hours a day, seven days a week, the police must maintain the ability to respond to immediate crises and crime incidents, but Community Policing broadens the police role so that they can make a greater impact on making changes today that hold the promise of making communities safer and more attractive places to live tomorrow.

7. Community Policing stresses exploring new ways to protect and enhance the lives of those who are most vulnerable—juveniles, the elderly, minorities, the poor, the disabled, the homeless. It both assimilates and broadens the scope of previous outreach efforts, such as Crime Prevention and Police/Community Relations units, by involving the entire department in efforts to prevent and control crime in ways that encourage the police and law-abiding people to work together with mutual respect and accountability.

8. Community Policing promotes the judicious use of technology, but it also rests on the belief that nothing surpasses what dedicated human beings, talking and working together, can achieve. It invests trust in those who are on the front lines together on the street, relying on their combined judgment, wisdom, and expertise to fashion creative new approaches to contemporary community concerns.

9. Community Policing must be a fully integrated approach that involves everyone in the department, with the CPOs as specialists in bridging the gap between the police and the people they serve. The Community Policing approach plays a crucial role internally, within the police department, by providing information and assistance about the

community and its problems, and by enlisting broadbased community support for the department's overall objectives.

10. Community Policing provides decentralized, personalized police service to the community. It recognizes that the police cannot impose order on the community from outside, but that people must be encouraged to think of the police as a resource they can use in helping to solve contemporary community concerns. It is not a tactic to be applied, then abandoned, but an entirely new way of thinking about the police role in society, a philosophy that also offers a coherent and cohesive organizational plan that police departments can modify to suit their specific needs.

James Q. Wilson & George L. Kelling

Broken Windows:
The Police and Neighborhood Safety

In the mid-1970s, the state of New Jersey announced a "Safe and Clean Neighborhoods Program," designed to improve the quality of community life in twenty-eight cities. As part of that program, the state provided money to help cities take police officers out of their patrol cars and assign them to walking beats. The governor and other state officials were enthusiastic about using foot patrol as a way of cutting crime, but many police chiefs were skeptical. Foot patrol, in their eyes, had been pretty much discredited. It reduced the mobility of the police, who thus had difficulty responding to citizen calls for service, and it weakened headquarters control over patrol officers.

Many police officers also disliked foot patrol, but for different reasons: it was hard work, it kept them outside on cold, rainy nights, and it reduced their chances for making a "good pinch." In some departments, assigning officers to foot patrol had been used as a form of punishment. And academic experts on policing doubted that foot patrol would have any impact on crime rates; it was, in the opinion of most, little more than a sop to public opinion. But since the state was paying for it, the local authorities were willing to go along.

Five years after the program started, The Police Foundation, in Washington, D.C., published an evaluation of the foot-patrol project. Based on its analysis of a carefully controlled experiment carried out chiefly in Newark, the foundation concluded, to the surprise of hardly anyone, that foot patrol had not reduced crime rates. But residents of the foot-patrolled neighborhoods seemed to feel more secure than persons in other areas, tended to believe that crime had been reduced, and seemed to take fewer steps to protect themselves from crime (staying home with the doors locked, for example). Moreover, citizens in the foot-patrol areas had a more favorable opinion of the police than did those living elsewhere. And officers walking beats had higher morale, greater job satisfaction, and a more favorable attitude toward citizens in their neighborhoods than did officers assigned to patrol cars.

These findings may be taken as evidence that the skeptics were right—foot patrol has no effect on crime; it merely fools the citizens into thinking that they are safer. But in our view, and in the view of the authors of the Police Foundation study (of whom Kelling was one), the citizens of Newark were not fooled at all. They knew what the foot-patrol officers were doing, they knew it was different from what motorized officers do, and they knew that having officers walk beats did in fact make their neighborhoods safer.

But how can a neighborhood be "safer" when the crime rate has not gone down—in fact, may have gone up? Finding the answer requires first that we understand what most often frightens people in public places. Many citizens, of course, are primarily frightened by crime, especially crime involving a sudden, violent attack by a stranger. This risk is very real, in Newark as in many large cities. But we tend to overlook or forget another source of fear—the fear of being bothered by disorderly people. Not violent people, nor, necessarily, criminals, but disreputable or obstreperous or unpredictable people: panhandlers, drunks, addicts, rowdy teenagers, prostitutes, loiterers, the mentally disturbed.

What foot-patrol officers did was to elevate, to the extent they could, the level of public order in these neighborhoods. Though the neighborhoods were predominantly black and the foot patrolmen were mostly white, this "order-maintenance" function of the police was performed to the general satisfaction of both parties.

One of us (Kelling) spent many hours walking with Newark foot-patrol officers to see how they defined "order" and what they did to maintain it. One beat was typical: a busy but dilapidated area in the heart of Newark, with many abandoned buildings, marginal shops (several of which prominently displayed knives and straight-edged razors in their windows), one large department store, and, most important, a train station and several major bus stops. Though the area was run-down, its streets were filled with people, because it was a major transportation center. The good order of this area was important not only to those who lived and worked there but also to many others, who had to move through it on their way home, to supermarkets, or to factories.

The people on the street were primarily black; the officer who walked the street was white. The people were made of "regulars" and "strangers." Regulars included both "decent folk" and some drunks and derelicts who were always there but who "knew their place." Strangers were, well, strangers, and viewed suspiciously, sometimes apprehensively. The officer—call him Kelly—knew who the regulars were, and they knew him. As he saw his job, he was to keep an eye on strangers, and make certain that the disreputable regulars observed some informal but widely understood rules. Drunks and addicts could sit on the stoops, but could not lie down. People could drink on side streets, but not at the main intersection. Bottles had to be in paper bags.

Talking to, bothering, or begging from people waiting at the bus stop was strictly forbidden. If a dispute erupted between a businessman and a customer, the businessman was assumed to be right, especially if the customer was a stranger. If a stranger loitered, Kelly would ask him if he had any means of support and what his business was; if he gave unsatisfactory answers, he was sent on his way. Persons who broke the informal rules, especially those who bothered people at bus stops, were arrested for vagrancy. Noisy teenagers were told to keep quiet.

These rules were defined and enforced in collaboration with the "regulars" on the street. Another neighborhood might have different rules, but these, everybody understood, were the rules for *this* neighborhood. If someone violated them, the regulars not only turned to Kelly for help but also ridiculed the violator. Sometimes what Kelly did could be described as "enforcing the law," but just as often it involved taking informal or extralegal steps to help protect what the neighborhood had decided was the appropriate level of public order. Some of the things he did probably would not withstand a legal challenge.

A determined skeptic might acknowledge that a skilled foot-patrol officer can maintain order but still insist that this sort of "order" has little to do with the real sources of community fear—that is, violent crime. To a degree, that is true. But two things must be borne in mind. First, outside observers should not assume that they know how much of the anxiety now endemic in many big-city neighborhoods stems from a fear of "real" crime and how much from a sense that the street is disorderly, a source of distasteful, worrisome encounters. The people of Newark, to judge from their behavior and their remarks to interviewers, apparently assign a high value to public order, and feel relieved and reassured when the police help them maintain that order.

Second, at the community level, disorder and crime are usually inextricably linked, in a kind of developmental sequence. Social psychologists and police officers tend to agree that if a window in a building is broken *and is left unrepaired*, all the rest of the windows will soon be broken. This is as true in nice neighborhoods as in run-down ones. Window-breaking does not necessarily occur on a large scale because some areas are inhabited by determined window-breakers whereas others are populated by window-lovers; rather, one unrepaired broken window is a signal that no one cares, and so breaking more windows costs nothing. (It has always been fun.)

Philip Zombardo, a Stanford psychologist, reported in 1969 on some experiments testing the broken-window theory. He arranged to have an automobile without license plates parked with its hood up on a street in the Bronx and a comparable automobile on a street in Palo Alto, California. The car in the Bronx was attacked by "vandals" within ten minutes of its "abandonment." The first to arrive were a family—father, mother, and young son—who removed the radiator and battery. Within twenty-four hours, virtually everything of value had been removed. Then random destruction began—windows were smashed, parts torn off, upholstery ripped. Children began to use the car as a playground. Most of the adult "vandals" were well-dressed, apparently clean-cut whites. The car in Palo Alto sat untouched for more than a week. Then Zimbardo smashed part of it with a sledgehammer. Soon, passersby were joining in. Within a few hours, the car had been turned upside down and utterly destroyed. Again, the "vandals" appeared to be primarily respectable whites.

Untended property becomes fair game for people out for fun or plunder, and even for people who ordinarily would not dream of doing such things and who probably consider themselves law-abiding. Because of the nature of community life in the Bronx—its anonymity, the frequency with which cars are abandoned and things are stolen or broken, the past experience of "no one caring"—vandalism begins much more quickly than it does in staid Palo Alto, where people have come to believe that private possessions are cared for, and that mischievous behavior is costly. But vandalism can occur anywhere once communal barriers—the sense of mutual regard and the obligations of civility—are lowered by actions that seem to signal that "no one cares."

We suggest that "untended" behavior also leads to the breakdown of community controls. A stable neighborhood of families who care for their homes, mind each other's children, and confidently frown on unwanted intruders can change, in a few years or even a few months, to an inhospitable and frightening jungle. A piece of property is abandoned, weeds grow up, a window is smashed. Adults stop scolding rowdy children; the children, emboldened, become more rowdy. Families move out, unattached adults move in. Teenagers gather in front of the corner store. The merchant asks them to move; they refuse. Fights occur. Litter accumulates. People start drinking in front of the grocery; in time, an inebriate slumps to the sidewalk and is allowed to sleep it off. Pedestrians are approached by panhandlers.

At this point it is not inevitable that serious crime will flourish or violent attacks on strangers will occur. But many residents will think that crime, especially violent crime, is on the rise, and they will modify their behavior accordingly. They will use the streets less often, and when on the streets will stay apart from their fellows, moving with averted eyes, silent lips, and hurried steps. "Don't get involved." For some residents, this growing atomization will matter little, because the neighborhood is not their "home" but "the place where they live." Their interests are elsewhere; they are cosmopolitans. But it will matter greatly to other people, whose lives derive meaning and satisfaction from local attachments rather than worldly involvement; for them, the neighborhood will cease to exist except for a few reliable friends whom they arrange to meet.

Such an area is vulnerable to criminal invasion. Though it is not inevitable, it is more likely that here, rather than in places where people are confident they can regulate public behavior by informal controls, drugs will change hands, prostitutes will solicit, and cars will be stripped. That the drunks will be robbed by boys who do it as a lark, and the prostitute's customers will be robbed by men who do it purposefully and perhaps violently. That muggings will occur.

Among those who find it difficult to move away from this are the elderly. Surveys of citizens suggest that the elderly are much less likely to be the victims of crime than younger persons, and some have inferred from this that the well-known fear of crime voiced by the elderly is an exaggeration; perhaps we ought not to design special programs to protect older persons; perhaps we should even try to talk them out of their mistaken fears. This argument misses the point. The prospect of a confrontation with an obstreperous teenager or a drunken panhandler can be as fear-inducing for defenseless persons as the prospect of meeting an actual robber; indeed, to a defenseless person, the two kinds of confrontation are often indistinguishable. Moreover, the lower rate at which the elderly are victimized is a measure of the steps they have already taken—chiefly, staying behind locked doors—to minimize the risks they face. Young men are more frequently attacked than older women, not because they are easier or more lucrative targets but because they are on the streets more.

Nor is the connection between disorderliness and fear made only by the elderly. Susan Estrich, of the Harvard Law School, has recently gathered together a number of surveys on the sources of public fear. One, done in Portland, Oregon, indicated that three fourths of the adults interviewed cross to the other side of a street when they see a gang of teenagers; another survey, in Baltimore, discovered that nearly half would cross the street to avoid even a single strange youth. When an interviewer asked people in a housing project where the most dangerous spot was, they mentioned a place where young persons gathered to drink and play music, despite the fact that not a single crime had occurred there. In Boston public housing projects, the greatest fear was expressed by persons living in the buildings where disorderliness and incivility, not crime, were the greatest. Knowing this helps one understand the significance of such otherwise harmless displays as subway graffiti. As Nathan Glazer has written, the proliferation of graffiti, even when not obscene, confronts the subway rider with the "inescapable knowledge that the environment he must endure for an hour or more a day is uncontrolled and uncontrollable, and that anyone can invade it to do whatever damage and mischief the mind suggests."

In response to fear, people avoid one another, weakening controls. Sometimes they call the police. Patrol cars arrive, an occasional arrest occurs, but crime continues and disorder is not abated. Citizens complain to the police chief, but he explains that his department is low on personnel and that the courts do not punish petty or first-time offenders. To the residents, the police who arrive in squad cars are either ineffective or uncaring; to the police, the residents are animals who deserve each other. The citizens may soon stop calling the police, because "they can't do anything."

The process we call urban decay has occurred for centuries in every city. But what is happening today is different in at least two important respects. First, in the period before, say, World War II, city dwellers—because of money costs, transportation difficulties, familial and church connections—could rarely move away from the neighborhood problems. When movement did occur, it tended to be along public-transit routes. Now mobility has become exceptionally easy for all but the poorest or those who are blocked by racial prejudice. Earlier crime waves had a kind of built-in self-correcting mechanism: the determination of a neighborhood or community to reassert control over its turf. Areas in Chicago, New York, and Boston would experience crime and gang wars, and then normalcy would return, as the families for whom no alternative residences were possible reclaimed their authority over the streets.

Second, the police in this earlier period assisted in that reassertion of authority by acting, sometimes violently, on behalf of the community. Young toughs were roughed up, people were arrested "on suspicion" or for vagrancy, and prostitutes and petty thieves were routed. "Rights" were something enjoyed by decent folk, and perhaps also by the serious professional criminal, who avoided violence and could afford a lawyer.

This pattern of policing was not an aberration or the result of occasional excess. From the earliest days of the nation, the police function was seen primarily as that of a night watchman: to maintain order against the chief threats to order—fire, wild animals, and disreputable behavior. Solving crimes was viewed not as a police responsibility but as a private one. In the March, 1969, *Atlantic,* one of us (Wilson) wrote a brief account of how the police role had slowly changed from maintaining order to fighting crimes. The change began with the creation of private detectives (often ex-criminals), who worked on a contingency-fee basis for individuals who had suffered losses. In time, the detectives were absorbed into municipal agencies and paid a regular salary; simultaneously, the responsibility for prosecuting thieves was shifted from the aggrieved private citizen to the professional prosecutor. This process was not complete in most places until the twentieth century.

In the 1960s, when urban riots were a major problem, social scientists began to explore carefully the order-maintenance function of the police, and to suggest ways of improving it—not to make streets safer (its original function) but to reduce the incidence of mass violence. Order-maintenance became, to a degree, coterminous with "community relations." But, as the crime wave that began in the early 1960s continued without abatement throughout the decade and into the 1970s, attention shifted to the role of the police as crime-fighters. Studies of police behavior ceased, by and large, to be accounts of the order-maintenance function and became, instead, efforts to propose and test ways whereby the police could solve more crimes, make more arrests, and gather better evidence. If these things could be done, social scientists assumed, citizens would be less fearful.

A great deal was accomplished during this transition, as both police chiefs and outside experts emphasized the crime-fighting function in their plans, in the allocation of resources, and in deployment of personnel. The police may well have become better crime-fighters as a result. And doubtless they remained aware of their responsibility for order. But the link between order-maintenance and crime-prevention, so obvious to earlier generations, was forgotten.

That link is similar to the process whereby one broken window becomes many. The citizen who fears the ill-smelling drunk, the rowdy teenager, or the importuning beggar is not merely expressing his distaste for unseemly behavior; he is also giving voice to a bit of folk wisdom that happens to be a correct generalization—namely, that serious street crime flourishes in areas in which disorderly behavior goes unchecked. The unchecked panhandler is, in effect, the first broken window. Muggers and robbers, whether opportunistic or professional, believe they reduce their chances of being caught or even identified if they operate on streets where potential victims are already intimidated by prevailing conditions. If the neighborhood cannot keep a bothersome panhandler from annoying passersby, the thief may reason, it is even less likely to call the police to identify a potential mugger or to interfere if the mugging actually takes place.

Some police administrators concede that this process occurs, but argue that motorized-patrol officers can deal with it as effectively as foot-patrol officers. We are not so sure. In theory, an officer in a squad car can observe as much as an officer on foot; in theory, the former can talk to as many people as the latter. But the reality of police-citizen encounters is powerfully altered by the automobile. An officer on foot cannot separate himself from the street people; if he is approached, only his uniform and his personality can help him manage whatever is about to happen. And he can never be certain what that will be—a request for directions, a plea for help, an angry denunciation, a teasing remark, a confused babble, a threatening gesture.

In a car, an officer is more likely to deal with street people by rolling down the window and looking at them. The door and the window exclude the approaching citizen; they are a barrier. Some officers take advantage of this barrier, perhaps unconsciously, by acting differently if in the car than they would on foot. We have seen this countless times. The police car pulls up to a corner where teenagers are gathered. The window is rolled down. The officer stares at the youths. They stare back. The officer says to one, "C'mere." He saunters over, conveying to his friends by his elaborately casual style the idea he is not intimidated by authority. "What's your name?" "Chuck." "Chuck who?" "Chuck Jones." "What'ya doing, Chuck?" "Nothin'." "Got a P.O. [parole officer]?" "Nah." "Sure?" "Yeah." "Stay out of trouble, Chuckie." Meanwhile the other boys laugh and exchange comments among themselves, probably at the officer's expense. The officer stares harder. He cannot be certain what is being said, nor can he join in and, by displaying his own skill at street banter, prove that he cannot be "put down." In the process, the officer has learned almost nothing, and the boys have decided the officer is an alien force who can be safely disregarded, even mocked.

Our experience is that most citizens like to talk to a police officer. Such exchanges give them a sense of importance, provide them with the basis for gossip, and allow them to explain to the authorities what is worrying them (whereby they gain a modest but significant sense of having "done something" about the problem). You approach a person on foot more easily, and talk to him more readily, than you do a person in a car. Moreover, you can more easily retain some anonymity if you draw an officer aside for a private chat. Suppose you want to pass on a tip about who is stealing handbags, or who offered to sell you a stolen TV. In the inner city, the culprit, in all likelihood, lives nearby. To walk up to a marked patrol car and lean in the window is to convey a visible signal that you are a "fink."

The essence of the police role in maintaining order is to reinforce the informal control mechanisms of the community itself. The police cannot, without committing extraordinary resources, provide a substitute for that informal control. On the other hand, to reinforce those natural forces the police must accommodate them. And therein lies the problem.

Should police activity on the street be shaped, in important ways, by the standards of the neighborhood rather than by the rules of the state? Over the past two decades, the shift of police from order-maintenance to law-enforcement has brought them increasingly under the influence of legal restrictions, provoked by media complaints and enforced by court decisions and departmental orders. As a consequence, the order-maintenance functions of the police are now governed by rules developed to control police relations with suspected criminals. This is, we think, an entirely new development. For centuries, the role of the police as watchmen was judged primarily not in terms of its compliance with appropriate procedures but rather in terms of its attaining a desired objective. The objective was order, an inherently ambiguous term but a condition that people in a given community recognized when they saw it. The means were the same as those the community itself would employ, if its members were sufficiently determined, courageous, and authoritative. Detecting and apprehending criminals, by contrast, was a means to an end, not an end in itself; a judicial determination of guilt or innocence was the hoped-for result of the law-enforcement mode. From the first, the police were expected to follow rules defining that process, though states differed in how stringent the rules should be. The criminal-apprehension process was always understood to involve individual rights, the violation of which was unacceptable because it meant that the violating officers would be acting as a judge and jury—and that was not his job. Guilt or innocence was to be determined by universal standards under special procedures.

Ordinarily, no judge or jury ever sees the persons caught up in a dispute over the appropriate level of neighborhood order. That is true not only because most cases are handled informally on the street but also because no universal standards are available to settle arguments over disorder, and thus a judge may be any wiser or more effective than a police officer. Until quite recently in many states, and even today in some places, the police make arrests on such charges as "suspicious person" or "vagrancy" or "public drunkenness"—charges with scarcely any legal meaning. These charges exist not because society wants judges to punish vagrants or drunks but because it wants an officer to have the legal tools to remove undesirable persons from a neighborhood when informal efforts to preserve order in the streets have failed.

Once we begin to think of all aspects of police work as involving the application of universal rules under special procedures, we inevitably ask what constitutes an "undesirable person" and why we should "criminalize" vagrancy or drunkenness. A strong and commendable desire to see that people are treated fairly makes us worry about allowing the police to rout persons who are undesirable by some vague or parochial standard. A growing and not-so-commendable utilitarianism leads us to doubt that any behavior that does not "hurt" another person should be made illegal. And thus many of us who watch over the police are reluctant to allow them to perform, in the only way they can, a function that every neighborhood desperately wants them to perform.

This wish to "decriminalize" disreputable behavior that "harms no one"—and thus remove the ultimate sanction the police can employ to maintain neighborhood order—is, we think, a mistake. Arresting a single drunk or a single vagrant who has harmed no identifiable person seems unjust, and in a sense it is. But failing to do anything about a score of drunks or a hundred vagrants may destroy an entire community. A particular rule that seems to make sense in the individual case makes no sense when it is made a universal rule and applied to all cases. It makes no sense because it fails to take into account the connection between one broken window left untended and a thousand broken windows. Of course, agencies other than the police could attend to the problems posed by drunks or the mentally ill, but in most communities—especially where the "deinstitutionalization" movement has been strong—they do not.

The concern about equity is more serious. We might agree that certain behavior makes one person more undesirable than another, but how do we ensure that age or skin color or national origin or harmless mannerism will not also become the basis for distinguishing the undesirable from the desirable? How do we ensure, in short, that the police do not become the agents of neighborhood bigotry?

We can offer no wholly satisfactory answer to this important question. We are not confident that there *is* a satisfactory answer, except to hope that by their selection, training, and supervision, the police will be inculcated with a clear sense of the outer limit of their discretionary authority. That limit, roughly, is this—the police exist to help regulate behavior, not to maintain the racial or ethnic purity of a neighborhood.

Consider the case of the Robert Taylor Homes in Chicago, one of the largest public-housing projects in the country. It is home for nearly 20,000 people, all black, and extends over ninety-two acres along South State Street. It was named after a distinguished black who had been, during the 1940s, chairman of the Chicago Housing Authority. Not long after it opened, in 1962, relations between project residents and the police deteriorated badly. The citizens felt that the police were insensitive or brutal; the police, in turn, complained of unprovoked attacks on them. Some Chicago officers tell of times they were afraid to enter the Homes. Crime rates soared.

Today, the atmosphere has changed. Police-citizen relations have improved—apparently, both sides learned something from the earlier experience. Recently, a boy stole a purse and ran off. Several young persons who saw the theft voluntarily passed along to the police information on the identity and residence of the thief, and they did this publicly, with friends and neighbors looking on. But problems persist, chief among them the presence of youth gangs that terrorize residents and recruit members in the project. The people expect the police to "do something" about this, and the police are determined to do just that.

But do what? Though the police can obviously make arrests whenever a gang member breaks the law, a gang can form, recruit, and congregate without breaking the law. And only a tiny fraction of gang-related crimes can be solved by an arrest; thus if an arrest is the only recourse for the police, the residents' fears will go unassuaged. The police will soon feel helpless, and the residents will again believe that the police "do nothing." What the police in fact do is to chase known gang members out of the project. In the words of one officer, "We kick ass." Project residents both know and approve of this. The tacit police-citizen alliance in the project is reinforced by the police view that the cops and the gangs are the two rival sources of power in the area, and that the gangs are not going to win.

None of this is easily reconciled with any conception of due process or fair treatment. Since both residents and gang members are black, race is not a factor. But it could be. Suppose a white project confronted a black gang, or vice versa. We would be apprehensive about the police taking sides. But the substantive problem remains the same: how can the police strengthen the informal social-control mechanisms of natural communities in order to minimize fear in public places? Law enforcement, per se, is no answer. A gang can weaken or destroy a community by standing about in a menacing fashion and speaking rudely to passersby without breaking the law.

We have difficulty thinking about such matters, not simply because the ethical and legal issues are so complex but because we have become accustomed to thinking of the law in essentially individualistic terms. The law defines *my* rights, punishes *his* behavior, and is applied by *that* officer because of *this* harm. We assume, in thinking this way, that what is good for the individual is good for the community, and what doesn't matter when it happens to one person won't matter if it happens to many. Ordinarily, those are plausible assumptions. But in cases where behavior that is tolerable to one person is intolerable to many others, the reaction of others—fear, withdrawal, flight—may ultimately make matters worse for everyone, including the individual who first professed his indifference.

It may be their greater sensitivity to communal as opposed to individual needs that helps explain why the residents of small communities are more satisfied with their police than are the residents of similar neighborhoods in big cities. Elinor Ostrom and her co-workers at Indiana University compared the perception of police services in two poor, all-black Illinois towns—Phoenix and East Chicago Heights—with those of three comparable all-black neighborhoods in Chicago. The level of criminal victimization and the quality of police-community relations appeared to be about the same in the towns and the Chicago neighborhoods. But the citizens living in their own villages were much more likely than those in Chicago neighborhoods to say that they do not stay at home for fear of crime, to agree that the local police have "the right to take any action necessary" to deal with problems, and to agree that the police "look out for the needs of the average citizen." It is possible that the residents of the small towns saw themselves as engaged in a collaborative effort to maintain a certain standard of communal life, whereas those of the big city felt themselves to be simply requesting and supplying particular services on an individual basis.

If this is true, how should a wise police chief deploy his meager forces? The first answer is that nobody knows for certain, and the most prudent course of action would be to try further variations on the Newark experiment, to see more precisely what works in what kinds of neighborhoods. The second answer is also a hedge—many aspects of order-maintenance in neighborhoods can probably best be handled in ways that involve the police minimally, if at all. A busy, bustling shopping center and a quiet, well-tended suburb may need almost no visible police presence. In both cases, the ratio of respectable to disreputable people is ordinarily so high as to make informal social control effective.

Even in areas that are in jeopardy from disorderly elements, citizen action without substantial police involvement may be sufficient. Meetings between teenagers who like to hang out on a particular corner and adults who want to use that corner might well lead to an amicable agreement on a set of rules about how many people can be allowed to congregate, where, and when.

Where no understanding is possible—or if possible, not observed— citizen patrols may be a sufficient response. There are two traditions of communal involvement in maintaining order. One, that of the "community watchmen," is as old as the first settlement of the New World. Until well into the nineteenth century, volunteer watchmen, not policemen, patrolled their communities to keep order. They did so, by and large, without taking the law into their own hands—without, that is, punishing persons or using force. Their presence deterred disorder or alerted the community to disorder that could not be deterred. There are hundreds of such efforts today in communities all across the nation. Perhaps the best known is that of the Guardian Angels, a group of unarmed young persons who first came to public attention when they began patrolling New York City subways but who claim now to have chapters in more than thirty American cities. Unfortunately, we have little information about the effect of these groups on crime. It is possible, however, that whatever their effect on crime, citizens find their presence reassuring, and that they thus contribute to maintaining a sense of order and civility.

The second tradition is that of the "vigilante." Rarely a feature of the settled communities of the East, it was primarily to be found in those frontier towns that grew up in advance of the reach of government. More than 350 vigilante groups are known to have existed; their distinctive feature was that their members did take the law into their own hands, by acting as judge, jury, and often executioner as well as policeman. Today, the vigilante movement is conspicuous by its rarity, despite the great fear expressed by citizens that the older cities are becoming "urban frontiers." But some community-watchmen groups have skirted the line, and others may cross it in the future. An ambiguous case, reported in *The Wall Street Journal*, involved a citizens' patrol in the Silver Lake area of Belleville, New Jersey. A leader told the reporter, "We look for outsiders." If a few teenagers from outside the neighborhood enter it, "we ask them their business," he said. "If they say they're going down the street to see Mrs. Jones, fine, we let them pass. But then we follow them down the block to make sure they're really going to see Mrs. Jones."

Though citizens can do a great deal, the police are plainly the key to order-maintenance. For one thing, many communities, such as the Robert Taylor Homes, cannot do the job by themselves. For another, no citizen in a neighborhood, even an organized one, is likely to feel the sense of responsibility that wearing a badge confers. Psychologists have done many studies on why people fail to go to the aid of persons being attacked or seeking help, and they have learned that the cause is not "apathy" or "selfishness" but the absence of some plausible grounds for feeling that one must personally accept responsibility. Ironically, avoiding responsibility is easier when a lot of people are standing about. On streets and in public places, where order is so important, many people are likely to be "around," a fact that reduces the chance of any one person acting as the agent of the community. The police officer's uniform singles him out as a person who must accept responsibility if asked. In addition, officers, more easily than their fellow citizens, can be expected to distinguish between what is necessary to protect the safety of the street and what merely protects its ethnic purity.

But the police forces of America are losing, not gaining, members. Some cities have suffered substantial cuts in the number of officers available for duty. These cuts are not likely to be reversed in the near future. Therefore, each department must assign its existing officers with great care. Some neighborhoods are so demoralized and crime-ridden as to make foot patrol useless; the best the police can do with limited resources is respond to the enormous number of calls for service. Other neighborhoods are so stable and serene as to make foot patrol unnecessary. The key is to identify neighborhoods at the tipping point—where the public order is deteriorating but not unreclaimable, where the streets are used frequently but by apprehensive people, where a window is likely to be broken at any time, and must quickly be fixed if all are not to be shattered.

Most police departments do not have ways of systematically identifying such areas and assigning officers to them. Officers are assigned on the basis of crime rates (meaning that marginally threatened areas are often stripped so that police can investigate crimes in areas where the situation is hopeless) or on the basis of calls for service (despite the fact that most citizens do not call the police when they are merely frightened or annoyed). To allocate patrol wisely, the department must look at the neighborhoods and decide, from first-hand evidence, where an additional officer will make the greatest difference in promoting a sense of safety.

One way to stretch limited police resources is being tried in some public-housing projects. Tenant organizations hire off-duty police officers for patrol work in their buildings. The costs are not high (at least not per resident), the officer likes the additional income, and the residents feel safer. Such arrangements are probably more successful than hiring night watchmen, and the Newark experiment helps us understand why. A private security guard may deter crime or misconduct by his presence, and he may go to the aid of persons needing help, but he may well not intervene—that is, control or drive away—someone challenging community standards. Being a sworn officer—a "real cop"— seems to give one the confidence, the sense of duty, and the aura of authority necessary to perform this difficult task.

Patrol officers might be encouraged to go to and from duty stations on public transportation and, while on the bus or subway car, enforce rules about smoking, drinking, disorderly conduct, and the like. The enforcement need involve nothing more than ejecting the offender (the offense, after all, is not one with which a booking officer or a judge wishes to be bothered). Perhaps the random but relentless maintenance of standards on buses would lead to conditions on buses that approximate the level of civility we now take for granted on airplanes.

But the most important requirement is to think that to maintain order in precarious situations is a vital job. The police know this is one of their functions, and they also believe, correctly, that it cannot be done to the exclusion of criminal investigation and responding to calls. We may have encouraged them to suppose, however, on the basis of our oft-repeated concerns about serious, violent crime, that they will be judged exclusively on their capacity as crime-fighters. To the extent that this is the case, police administrators will continue to concentrate police personnel in the highest-crime areas (though not necessarily in the areas most vulnerable to criminal invasion), emphasize their training in the law and criminal apprehension (and not their training in managing street life), and join too quickly in campaigns to decriminalize "harmless" behavior (though public drunkenness, street prostitution, and pornographic displays can destroy a community more quickly than any team of professional burglars).

Above all, we must return to our long-abandoned view that the police ought to protect communities as well as individuals. Our crime statistics and victimization surveys measure individual losses, but they do not measure communal losses. Just as physicians now recognize the importance of fostering health rather than simply treating illness, so the police—and the rest of us—ought to recognize the importance of maintaining, intact, communities without broken windows.

Subject Index

Name Index